THE 2014 – 2015 COMPENSATION HANDBOOK FOR CHURCH STAFF

Richard R. Hammar, J.D., LL.M., CPA

CHRISTIANITY TODAY
a global media ministry

The 2014–2015 Compensation Handbook for Church Staff
Copyright ©2013 by Christianity Today International

ISBN-10: 1614079013
ISBN-13: 978-1-61407-901-9

Christianity Today International
465 Gundersen Drive
Carol Stream, IL 60188
(630) 260-6200
ChristianityToday.com
YourChurchResources.com

CREDITS
Data compiled and analyzed by: Cynia Solver, Solver Solutions (solversolutions.net)
Edited by: Dawn M. Brandon
Executive Editor: Marian V. Liautaud
Cover design: Phil Marcelo
Interior design: Dawn M. Brandon

10   9   8   7   6   5   4   3   2   1   15   14   13

Printed in the United States of America

CONTENTS

1

BEFORE YOU BEGIN

If you've ever had questions

or needed guidance when it comes to compensation planning for your church staff, you've picked up the right resource. Welcome to the 2014–2015 Compensation Handbook for Church Staff. As you read through this introductory chapter, you'll learn about the many ways you can use this book to meet your compensation planning needs.

The *Compensation Handbook* was developed to provide church leaders and employees with a current and reliable picture of compensation practices across a broad spectrum of U.S. churches. It presents survey data from more than 3,500 churches, representing over 7,500 staff members. The survey data was obtained from January through March 2013 from subscribers of one or more of the following publications: *Church Law & Tax Report*, *Church Finance Today*, *Leadership Journal*, and various Christianity Today e-newsletters and Web channels.

The information included can play an important role in determining equitable compensation packages for church staff members. The *Compensation Handbook* can help you:

* **Determine appropriate compensation levels** for 14 key pastoral, professional, and support staff positions, both full-time and part-time. (Note: Ten of these positions have information for both full-time and part-time individuals. Four positions are unique: Senior Pastors and Executive/Administrative Pastors have information for full-time individuals only, while Child Care Providers (which is new this year)

and Musicians/Vocalists have information for part-time individuals only.)

* **Develop effective compensation packages** with guidelines given in the Special Section to help you maximize net income while remaining in compliance with federal tax laws.

* **Provide church workers with a statistical framework** for evaluating their present compensation packages. Comparisons can be made regarding church size, budget, setting, and other important variables.

* **Establish an objective standard** for evaluating requests for raises and changes in benefits.

* **Promote equitable and fair compensation practices** by assisting denominational offices and other ecclesiastical organizations in understanding and guiding churches' financial practices.

* **Better understand** the nature of church compensation planning.

How to Make the Best Use of This Book

Compensation planning is a multifaceted process. This book is one tool you can use to measure appropriate levels of compensation, but it is not a complete guide. Many factors go into determining compensation planning, and this book attempts to help you explore those aspects knowledgeably.

Informative charts are featured throughout the book. You can find the background information you need to use the data in these tables with ease and accuracy in chapter 2, Using the Compensation Tables. Included in this chapter is an example that illustrates how to determine the compensation range for a Senior Pastor. You can use the same process to examine all staff positions.

Chapter 3 provides comparisons among the overall averages for each of the 14 staff positions included in this study. Table 3-1 gives a comparative listing of each position.

Chapters 4 through 17 provide detailed information on each individual staff position. Each chapter begins by providing an employment profile for each staff position. Natural curiosity will pull most church staff members immediately to the chapter on their position. Remember, though, that understanding chapters 2 and 3 is critical to using this book effectively.

Also, at the end of each of these chapters, you will find worksheets that serve as a handy tool to help you extract the correct data for each aspect of compensation surveyed to determine the appropriate range for your particular church and staff. These worksheets are also available online at **YourChurchResources. com\Employment\The 2014-2015 Compensation Handbook for Church Staff**.

Chapter 18 provides a statistical abstract of the churches participating in this study. This data is useful for learning more about the churches that contributed information. The participating church profile includes the percentage of church budgets devoted to salaries, the percentage of churches that contribute to their Senior Pastor's or Solo Pastor's Social Security, the percentage that reimburse professional expenses, and more. It also includes church attendance and financial condition over the past year by worship attendance and region.

The Special Section: Tax Law & Compensation Planning by Richard Hammar provides critical information for completing the compensation planning process. Anyone engaged in this type of planning for church staff members must become familiar with some basic federal tax laws, since the structure of a compensation package can either help or hurt a church staff member. This special section explores in detail the major (and often hard-to-understand) laws that affect compensation planning. It also provides tax saving tips that can benefit everyone. Additional resources are also listed in this section.

Background Information

The results in the charts that follow represent positions that were reported among those participating in the survey. The sampling population used represents the positions reported from subscribers to *Church Law & Tax Report, Church Finance Today,*

Leadership Journal, and various Christianity Today e-newsletters and Web channels. Therefore, certain church sizes, budget sizes, and denominations have a stronger representation than others. To the extent possible, we have attempted to organize the data in ways that avoid small samples. At times, however, a small sample simply reflects a reality, such as fewer rural churches with attendance over 1,000 or churches smaller than 100 with a full-time bookkeeper. Nevertheless, sample size should be taken into account when considering the value of any particular finding.

Here are a few additional facts to help clarify the data analyses that follow.

* **Averages, medians, and quartiles** (lowest 25% and highest 25%) are based on individuals receiving the item in the compensation and/or benefits packages. Zeros are not included in the calculations.

* **Wide gaps** between averages and medians are due to a wider range of data reported.

* **A footnote that says** "Not enough responses to provide meaningful data" means either one or both of the following are true:

  • There are less than eight people responding.
  • There are relatively few responses (maybe more than eight), with a wide gap between the lowest and highest values.

* **Blanks** (no response) and zeros are treated similarly and are not part of the compensation median, quartile, and average calculations.

* **Figures** that appeared unrealistic or fell outside the normal distribution were eliminated to avoid skewing the results.

* **Total Compensation** includes base salary, housing allowance, and parsonage amounts. Given that many individuals do not receive both a housing allowance and a parsonage, Total Compensation as presented is not calculated by adding base salary, housing, and parsonage amounts. Rather, the Total

Compensation figures are calculated for each individual and reported in aggregate. As a result, in some instances, the Total Compensation figure is less than individual entries of base salary, housing, and parsonage amounts added together.

* **This is also true in regard to Total Benefits.** Given that many individuals do not receive all or some of certain benefits (health, life, and disability insurance; retirement; and continuing education), Total Benefits figures are not calculated by adding each benefit together. Rather, the Total Benefits figures are calculated for each individual and reported in aggregate.

* **Please note:** In some instances, a total insurance premium was reported without the breakdown of individual premiums for health, life, and disability insurance. In these situations, the total insurance premium was included in the Total Benefits figure, as it is unknown how to distribute the total premiums across each category.

* **Hourly Rate** is provided for part-time positions. Hourly Rate is calculated by taking the base salary divided by (the number of hours per week compensated for multiplied by 52 weeks). In other words: base salary divided by (# weekly hours x 52) = hourly rate. Housing, parsonage, and benefits are not included in this calculation.

* **Some percentages** may not always add up to 100% due to rounding. This particularly refers to the data found at the beginning of each section titled Employment Profile.

* **For reporting purposes**, Adult Ministry and Christian Education Pastor/Director positions were combined due to the overlap in job descriptions and similarities in the findings.

Explanation of Data Distribution

In the charts that follow, averages, medians, and quartiles (noted as Lowest 25% and Highest 25%) are used to represent survey findings.

The **average**, also called the mean, is a value that depends equally on all of the data. It is calculated by taking the sum of all the data values and dividing by the total number of data values. Please keep in mind that the averages, as presented, are not the averages of the highest and lowest quartiles but an average of the overall data.

The **median** is a value that divides the higher half of the data set from the lower half of the data set. When sorting the data set from lowest to highest, the median is the middle value.

A **quartile** is one of three values that divide sorted data from a particular table into quarters. The first quartile, called **Lowest 25%** in this handbook, is the value that separates the lowest 25% of the sorted data from the highest 75%. The third

quartile, called **Highest 25%** in this handbook, is the value that separates the highest 25% of the sorted data from the lowest 75%. The second quartile, called **median** in this handbook, is the middle value among the data; i.e., 50% of the data is higher than the median, and 50% of the data is lower.

For example, in tables showing compensation ranges for a specific position, the Lowest 25% value (first quartile) means that 25% of respondents reported lower compensation amounts than this first quartile value, while 75% of respondents reported higher compensation amounts.

The same is true with the third quartile, or the upper quartile, which cuts off the highest 25% of the data. This actually means that the number shown represents a number that exceeds 1–75% of the people in the population represented in the report. The upper quartile is reported as Highest 25% by church income for each position.

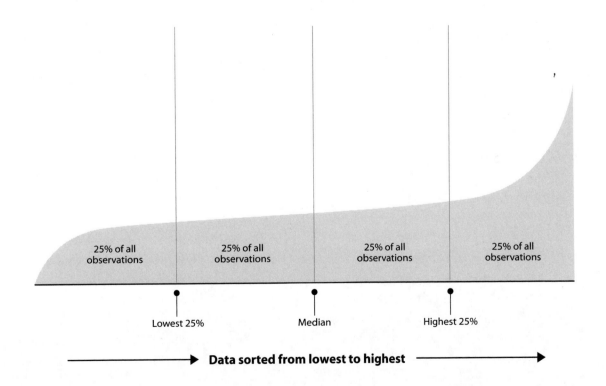

25% of all observations | 25% of all observations | 25% of all observations | 25% of all observations

Lowest 25%   Median   Highest 25%

Data sorted from lowest to highest

2

USING THE COMPENSATION TABLES

The following chapters present compensation patterns for 14 major positions within the local church. These profiles are the statistical heart of the Compensation Handbook. This chapter is designed to help you interpret the tables and maximize your use of the information in this book.

Each staff position has its own chapter, including compensation tables, an overview of the findings, and a worksheet to help you apply the data. The tables are for full-time staff members, except for the last tables in each chapter, which provide data for part-time staff members. Note, however, that data for part-time Senior Pastors and Executive/Administrative Pastors are not provided because few churches hire for these positions on a part-time basis. On the other hand, Musicians/Accompanists/Vocalists and Child Care Providers tables are for part-time positions only, since these roles are rarely filled as full-time positions.

A comparative summary of all the positions is presented in chapter 3.

Interpreting the Tables

Each chapter contains tables that portray compensation averages according to several key identifiers, grouped according to the most meaningful breaks. They include the following:

* **Church income (from all sources).** Question asked: "Approximately what is your total annual church budget this past year?"

* **Worship attendance (weekend).** Question asked: "Approximately how many people, including children, attend all weekend worship services?"

* **Church setting.** Question asked: "Which of the following best describes the setting in which your church is located?"

* **Region.** Question asked: "In what state is your church located?" (Regional breakout by state is included in the appendix.)

* **Education.** Question asked: "What is this person's highest level of education?"

* **Years employed (in current position).** Question asked: "How long has this person been in this position?"

* **Denomination.** Question asked: "What is your church's denomination or fellowship?"

* **Gender.** Question asked: "What is this person's gender?"

Each table provides key characteristics that include:

* **Average weekend worship attendance.** Question asked: "Approximately how many people, including children, attend all weekend worship services?"

* **Average church income.** Question asked: "Approximately what was your total annual church budget this past year?"

* **Average number of years employed.** Question asked: "How long has this person been in this position?"

* **Average number of paid vacation days.** Question asked: "How many paid vacation days does this person receive?"

* **Percentage who are college graduates or higher.** Question asked: "What is this person's highest level of education?"

* **Percentage who receive automobile reimbursement.** Question asked: "Does the church help with this person's automobile expenses?"

* **Percentage who are ordained.** Question asked: "Is this person ordained, licensed, or commissioned?"

* **Percentage who supervise one or more people.** Question asked: "Does this person supervise one or more people?"

* **Average percentage salary increase this year.** Question asked: "What was this person's salary increase in the past year?"

NOTE: Data is based on responses of those who reported a salary increase. In a few instances, some respondents indicated that they

did not receive an increase, and some even experienced a salary decrease.

In addition, each table provides several columns of data for these compensation and benefit items (Compensation and Benefits are listed separately):

COMPENSATION
* **Base Salary:** annual base salary
* **Housing:** allowance for housing expenses*
* **Parsonage:** rental value of parsonage plus allowance*

BENEFITS
* **Retirement:** pension/retirement contribution
* **Continuing Education**
* **Insurance:** amount of premiums paid to insurance companies for:

  * Health Insurance
  * Life Insurance
  * Disability Insurance

The data shown in the first table for each full-time position is Annual Compensation by Church Income. Since Church Income is an important variable in compensation, we've provided expanded data for your reference by including the Highest 25% and Lowest 25% data in addition to the Median and Average as presented in the rest of the tables.

The number listed after Lowest 25% represents a number that exceeds the base salary of 1–25% of the people in the population represented in the report. Similarly, the number following Highest 25% represents a number that exceeds the base salary of 1–75% of the people in the population represented in the report. For more information, please see section titled "Explanation of Data Distribution" in chapter 1.

Consider the example in Illustration 2-1 for a Senior Pastor position.

In gathering data, we allowed respondents to use their own judgment in determining the definition of housing and parsonage.

Illustration 2-1: Sample Figures for Senior Pastor Position

	Data Distribution*	CHURCH INCOME				
		$250K & Under	$251–$500K	$501–$750K	$751K–$1M	Over $1 Million
COMPENSATION						
Base Salary	Highest 25%	$42,000	$53,250	$64,400	$64,000	$90,633
	Median	$30,000	$40,000	$50,780	$53,000	$68,008
	Lowest 25%	$22,512	$31,975	$41,500	$44,244	$52,241
	Average	$31,367	$44,044	$53,696	$54,981	$77,205
Housing	Highest 25%	$24,000	$30,000	$31,750	$39,250	$45,600
	Median	$19,586	$24,000	$25,000	$30,000	$34,080
	Lowest 25%	$12,000	$18,000	$20,000	$24,000	$26,400
	Average	$18,692	$24,922	$26,648	$30,748	$36,466
Parsonage	Highest 25%	$14,520	$18,000	$24,000	$20,000	$40,000
	Median	$9,840	$12,000	$16,136	$18,000	$24,000
	Lowest 25%	$7,200	$9,000	$9,700	$8,282	$4,000
	Average	$11,478	$13,196	$19,966	$22,936	$26,400
Total Compensation	**Highest 25%**	**$59,350**	**$75,921**	**$91,000**	**$91,500**	**$125,000**
	Median	**$49,050**	**$64,000**	**$75,000**	**$80,000**	**$103,368**
	Lowest 25%	**$37,570**	**$55,343**	**$66,400**	**$72,000**	**$86,300**
	Average	**$47,212**	**$67,073**	**$79,845**	**$84,651**	**$108,063**

Notice that in the first column for Base Salary, figures are shown in four categories: Highest 25%, Median, Lowest 25%, and Average. After Highest 25%, the number $42,000 appears. This means that 25% of all Senior Pastors serving a church with an income of $250,000 and under make $42,000 or more in Base Salary. Another way to say this is that 75% of Senior Pastors in a church with an income of $250,000 and under make less than $42,000 in Base Salary.

Next is the Median, where the number $30,000 appears. This number is the value that divides the higher half of the data set from the lower half of the data set. This means that 50% of all Senior Pastors serving a church with an income of $250,000 and under make $30,000 or more in Base Salary. Another way to say this is that 50% of Senior Pastors in a church with an income of $250,000 and under make less than $30,000 in Base Salary.

For the category Lowest 25%, the number $22,512 appears, which indicates that 25% of all Senior

Pastors in a church with an income of $250,000 and under make $22,512 or less. Again, another way to say this is that 75% of Senior Pastors in a church with an income of $250,000 and under make more than $22,512.

In the Average category, the number $31,367 is listed. This number represents the average amount of the salaries for all Senior Pastors in a church with an income of $250,000 and under.

All calculated figures, including those for the categories Highest 25%, Median, Lowest 25%, and Average, are based on individuals receiving the specific items in the Compensation chart (the same is true of the Benefits chart).

Medians and averages are provided for each full-time position by the following data breaks in addition to Church Income for your reference.

＊ **Worship attendance**
＊ **Church setting**

* **Region**
* **Education**
* **Years employed (in current position)**

* **Denomination**
* **Gender**

Total Compensation plus Benefits Comparisons

At the bottom of each compensation chart is a category that lists Total Compensation. These numbers include base salary, housing allowance, and parsonage allowance. Likewise, at the bottom of each Benefits chart is a category that lists Total Benefits. These numbers include health insurance, life insurance, disability insurance, retirement, and continuing education benefits. A separate box in the table, Total Compensation plus Benefits, includes all of the Compensation and Benefits items. Note: Totals are the key figures for compensation analysis.

Rounding errors may exist in some of the data in this study. They do not, however, impact the final results in any significant way.

In general, church income, attendance, education, geographical setting, and years of service play

some role in almost every church—as they increase, compensation increases. Yet the correlation between these variables and employee compensation accounts for only part of the variation in compensation figures by position. These factors, while important, must be viewed in the context of other factors, the combination of which ultimately determines compensation and benefits.

As an example, theology may play a significant role in some churches in the determination of compensation. In churches that promote financial prosperity as a sign of God's blessing, the pastor may receive a disproportionate amount of the church's total income. A building program may be the controlling factor somewhere else. In general, education, geographical setting, and years of service play some role in almost every church.

Using the Tables to Plan Compensation

The most important use of this handbook is for compensation planning. The following example, which has been illustrated using a sample worksheet, shows one approach of how this book can be used.

EXAMPLE: PLANNING THE COMPENSATION OF A SENIOR PASTOR

Pastor Miller has served as First Bible Church's Senior Pastor for the past five years. First Bible Church is a suburban congregation in the South Atlantic region with an average worship attendance of 275 and an annual budget of $378,000. Pastor Miller has a Master of Divinity degree.

This example provides relevant data that can be used in coordination with the tables in this book. Variables we will look at include the church's income ($378,000), worship attendance (275), the pastor's length of service (eight years) and educational background (Master's degree), and the geographical setting (in this case, a suburb of a large city) and region (South Atlantic) of the church.

KEY POINT

The goal is not to come up with a single compensation number but rather to identify a compensation range. Once that range is determined, a variety of factors will affect the final choice of a specific level of compensation.

STEP 1

Since church income is one of the most important variables, the first step is to use Table 4-1: Annual Compensation of Full-Time Senior Pastors by Church Income, found in chapter 4, to provide some working boundaries on both the upper and lower limits. We can examine the range of the middle 50% of respondents by looking at the Lowest 25% and the Highest 25% numbers across church income levels. The main data we are interested in is found at the bottom of each table in the box labeled Total Compensation plus Benefits. Since Pastor Miller's church income is $378,000, we will look at the second level ($251–$500K). The following is the range of the middle 50% (Lowest 25%–Highest 25%) of Senior Pastors' compensation plus benefits at the ($251–$500K) level from Table 4-1.

$65,000 on the low end to
$90,000 on the high end

The median for this distribution is $76,400.

These figures serve as a broad range of average compensation plus benefits for Senior Pastors in churches with incomes between $251K and $500K. This means that 25% of Senior Pastors at this church income level make less than $65,000, while 25% of them make more than $90,000.

STEP 2

For a narrower, more relevant range, we will identify median compensation plus benefits in other comparable settings. We will examine each of the following variables: church income (Table 4-1), worship attendance (Table 4-2), church setting (Table 4-3), region (Table 4-4), education (Table 4-5), and years employed (Table 4-6). The main data we are interested in is found at the bottom of each table in the box labeled Total Compensation plus Benefits.

The worksheet in Illustration 2-2 enables us to establish a median compensation plus benefits range. This is based on the data provided above. The following is the range of median compensation plus benefits:

$73,400 on the low end to
$94,275 on the high end

STEP 3

After establishing a relevant base compensation plus benefits range in Step 2, the next step is to determine whether Pastor Miller's final compensation plus benefits should fit within that range, and if so, where, or whether the compensation plus benefits should be above or below that range based on key variables, and if so, how much above or below.

Since church income and worship attendance are two important factors in determining compensation, we will start by looking at these factors across each of the variables in the tables listed above. If church income or attendance skews higher compared to the averages across the key variables, it might suggest moving toward or above the higher end of the range determined in Step 2. On the other hand, if church income or attendance skews lower compared to the averages, it might suggest moving toward or below the lower end of the range.

The sample worksheet in Illustration 2-3 shows that the average church income across Pastor Miller's key data ranges from $367,155 to $1,002,500. The average worship attendance ranges from 198 to 533. Pastor Miller's church income ($378,000) and worship attendance (275) are closer to the lower end of the range of the averages of other church income levels. Based on this pastor's specific characteristics, it would be a variable that might suggest moving slightly toward the lower end of the range.

STEP 4

The next step is to examine additional variables that might impact compensation plus benefits, such as years of service, education, and church setting. They

Illustration 2-2: Senior Pastor Worksheet

Looking at the table and page number as indicated on the "Reference" columns, locate the range that defines your church. Refer to instructions below for step-by-step help.

	Enter your church data below	The 2014–2015 Compensation Handbook for Church Staff		Enter *Compensation Handbook* data below			
				Highest 25%	Median	Lowest 25%	Average
Church Income	$378,000	Table 4-1	page 27	$90,000	$76,400	$65,000	$78,409
Worship Attendance	275	Table 4-2	page 28	n/a	$73,400	n/a	$77,486
Church Setting (metro, suburb, small town, or farming area)	Suburb of a large city	Table 4-3	page 29	n/a	$94,275	n/a	$97,740
Region	South Atalantic	Table 4-4	page 30	n/a	$86,738	n/a	$89,344
Person's Education	Master's	Table 4-5	page 31	n/a	$83,100	n/a	$87,728
Years Employed	5 years	Table 4-6	page 32	n/a	$76,532	n/a	$81,182
Denomination (if applicable)	n/a	Table 4-7	page 33	n/a	$	n/a	$

are helpful in deciding whether an individual is in the upper or lower part of the range identified in Step 2.

In general, as years of service and education increase, compensation plus benefits will also increase. Also, Senior Pastors serving at churches located in metropolitan and suburban settings tend to earn more than those located in small towns or rural settings.

STEP 5

The fifth step is to take into account the unique circumstances that define each individual situation. One factor is the cost of living in your area. Is it higher or lower than the national average? Your local Chamber of Commerce or a real estate agency can help you obtain that information. Other factors such as denominational affiliation (see Table 4-7), theological beliefs, pastoral performance, financial

needs, goodwill, the local economy, personal motivation, congregational goals, internal church politics, and many other considerations will also contribute to the final decision. For some churches, that may mean a final compensation package much lower or much higher than the projected range listed in Step 2.

How that compensation will be divided up will vary greatly from one church to another, and even from one individual staff member to another. Care should be taken, however, to avoid gender discrimination. This is a widespread problem involving many churches (see Table 4-8). In addition, a large disparity between the pastor's compensation and that of other staff members can have an impact on the rate of increase the pastor may experience in future years. Often, once a staff member has reached the upper limits of his or her compensation range,

Illustration 2-3: Key Data Comparison

Data for example	Median compensation plus benefits from this study	Average church income	Average worship attendance
Pastor Miller at First Bible Church	To be determined	$378,000	275
Table 4-1 Church Income: $251K–$500K	$76,400	**$367,155**	224
Table 4-2 Worship Attendance: 101–300	73,400	$407,836	**198**
Table 4-3 Church Setting: Suburb of large city	94,275	**$1,002,050**	**533**
Table 4-4 Region: South Atlantic	$86,738	$843,320	389
Table 4-5 Education: Master	$83,100	$723,580	404

future raises may be somewhat smaller in order to better compensate other staff members.

The final determination of compensation plus benefits is unique to every congregation. It would not be surprising to see a range of compensation for Pastor Miller somewhere between the broader range of $73,400–$94,275. Higher compensation levels are possible and could be argued to be reasonable. It would be unlikely, however, for Pastor Miller to exceed $125,000, which would fall outside the limits of the Highest 25% range

for churches similar to First Bible Church. Such a compensation level would require independent justification to avoid the possibility of intermediate sanctions (see the Special Section for a discussion of intermediate sanctions). Also, remember that a crucial step in this decision-making process must involve an awareness of tax law, which is covered in the Special Section.

The detailed process above can be used for each of the 12 full-time staff positions found in this handbook.

3

COMPENSATION PROFILES: GENERAL COMPARISONS

This chapter provides comparisons of the average compensations for the 12 full-time and part-time staff positions included in this study. A summary table exists for each of the variables examined. More detailed analysis can be found in the individual chapter for each staff position.

Note: Ten positions have information for both full-time and part-time staff. Four positions are unique: Senior Pastors and Executive/Administrative Pastors have information for full-timers only, while Child Care Providers (new this year) and Musicians/Vocalists have information only for part-timers.

Senior Pastors and Executive/Administrative Pastors rank at the top in total compensation plus benefits.

Music/Choir/Worship Pastors/Directors and Associate Pastors receive the next highest compensation amounts, followed generally by Solo Pastors and Adult Ministry/Christian Education Pastors/Directors. Youth Pastors and Administrators come next, with an almost equal average compensation. The tables presented later in this chapter provide compensation comparisons according to the averages for each position.

General Trends

As stated earlier, in general, church income, attendance, education, geographical setting, and years of service play some role in almost every church's compensation plans. Church income proved the biggest factor affecting compensation and benefits in this study.

Please note this about gender differences: female staff members consistently receive significantly lower compensation, in all, than their male counterparts. On average, women earned approximately 80% of the compensation of men. In other words, males earned about 29% more than females. Some of the difference can be explained on the basis of demographic factors, such as education.

Benefits vary significantly from one position to the next. This is especially true for health insurance and retirement programs. The numbers of church staff receiving health insurance varied from 42% to 71%, depending on the position. A similar gap is seen among those reported receiving retirement benefits (41% to 67%). Part-time staff members receive fewer fringe benefits.

This study examined the rate of increase with respect to compensation plus benefits and church income, and compensation plus benefits and church attendance. In this context, *rate of increase* refers to the percent change in compensation with respect to size of church budget or church attendance.

In general, most staff positions' compensation plus benefits increased at every budget level. The greatest increases across positions are seen at the highest levels (from $751,000–$1,000,000 to Over $1,000,000). For those that had an increase at each budget level, the average is 19% and ranges from 2% to 48%. Similar trends could be seen based on church attendance.

The following tables provide comparisons of compensation and benefits packages.

Table 3-1: Percentages of Full-Time Staff Receiving and Reporting Compensation Plus Benefits

	Senior Pastors	Solo Pastors	Executive or Administrative Pastors	Associate Pastors	Adult Ministry/ Christian Education Pastors/ Directors	Youth Pastors/ Directors
TOTAL REPORTING	1119	624	291	535	196	418
Base Salary	98%	96%	100%	99%	97%	99%
Housing	87%	73%	77%	81%	55%	67%
Parsonage	11%	23%	2%	6%	3%	7%
Health Insurance*	64%	51%	71%	68%	56%	68%
Life Insurance*	26%	11%	34%	27%	31%	25%
Disability Insurance*	22%	14%	30%	27%	31%	24%
Retirement	67%	60%	59%	60%	57%	55%
Continuing Education	31%	40%	32%	29%	30%	33%
Received salary increase	51%	38%	60%	55%	56%	61%
Received paid vacation	96%	94%	99%	95%	97%	94%
Received auto reimbursement/allowance	61%	63%	44%	53%	45%	51%

	Children's/ Preschool Pastors/ Directors	Music/Choir/ Worship Pastors/ Directors	Admin- istrators	Bookkeepers/ Accountants	Secretaries/ Administrative Assistants	Custodians
TOTAL REPORTING	276	295	351	202	385	188
Base Salary	99%	99%	100%	100%	100%	100%
Housing	39%	60%	13%	2%	2%	1%
Parsonage	1%	1%	0%	0%	0%	1%
Health Insurance*	58%	71%	57%	52%	42%	62%
Life Insurance*	29%	35%	32%	33%	21%	34%
Disability Insurance*	23%	32%	26%	25%	16%	26%
Retirement	54%	67%	53%	49%	41%	46%
Continuing Education	29%	31%	24%	9%	8%	4%
Received salary increase	58%	59%	54%	56%	57%	59%
Received paid vacation	94%	96%	98%	98%	95%	95%
Received auto reimbursement/allowance	37%	47%	27%	23%	19%	25%

Only those reporting individual insurance premiums for Health, Life, or Disability (not total insurance premiums) are included.

Table 3-2: Percentages of Part-Time Staff Receiving and Reporting Compensation Plus Benefits

	Solo Pastors	Associate Pastors	Adult Ministry/ Christian Education Pastors/Directors	Youth Pastors/ Directors	Children's/ Preschool Pastors/ Directors	Music/Choir/ Worship Pastors/ Directors
TOTAL REPORTING	116	153	71	124	188	213
Base Salary	81%	86%	89%	90%	96%	98%
Housing	57%	42%	21%	26%	6%	5%
Parsonage	9%	3%	1%	2%	1%	0%
Health Insurance*	16%	17%	7%	5%	5%	2%
Life Insurance*	3%	5%	3%	1%	1%	2%
Disability Insurance*	3%	4%	4%	0%	3%	2%
Retirement	20%	15%	8%	2%	7%	5%
Continuing Education	19%	20%	15%	8%	10%	8%
Received salary increase	26%	29%	46%	31%	46%	45%
Received paid vacation	69%	52%	48%	46%	48%	44%
Received auto reimbursement/allowance	35%	45%	31%	28%	22%	13%

	Admin- istrators	Bookkeepers/ Accountants	Secretaries/ Administrative Assistants	Bookkeepers/ Accountants	Musicians/ Vocalists	Child Care Providers
TOTAL REPORTING	110	304	535	314	116	128
Base Salary	97%	99%	100%	100%	100%	100%
Housing	5%	2%	1%	0%	0%	0%
Parsonage	0%	1%	0%	0%	0%	0%
Health Insurance*	10%	5%	4%	3%	1%	0%
Life Insurance*	1%	2%	1%	2%	1%	0%
Disability Insurance*	3%	3%	2%	4%	0%	1%
Retirement	9%	11%	6%	4%	5%	4%
Continuing Education	6%	5%	3%	1%	3%	0%
Received salary increase	51%	47%	50%	41%	36%	22%
Received paid vacation	53%	42%	58%	34%	36%	12%
Received auto reimbursement/allowance	15%	10%	11%	7%	4%	4%

Only those reporting individual insurance premiums for Health, Life, or Disability (not total insurance premiums) are included.

Table 3-3: Annual Compensation Plus Benefits Averages for Full-Time Church Staff

	Average Compensation	Range as determined by Lowest 25% quartile - Highest 25% quartile (50%)
Senior Pastors	$88,814	$62,711 - $107,812
Solo Pastors	$62,634	$42,708 - $75,650
Executive or Administrative Pastors	$86,999	$65,351 - $105,200
Associate Pastors	$68,040	$50,499 - $80,393
Adult Ministry/Christian Education Pastors/Directors	$63,320	$47,800 - $74,635
Youth Pastors/Directors	$57,254	$43,320 - $67,014
Children's/Preschool Pastors/Directors	$54,246	$40,475 - $64,990
Music/Choir/Worship Pastors/Directors	$68,597	$52,000 - $82,987
Administrators	$57,145	$40,735 - $69,371
Bookkeepers/Accountants	$43,214	$33,960 - $50,416
Secretaries/Administrative Assistants	$33,404	$26,885 - $39,238
Custodians	$40,176	$30,311 - $49,332

Table 3-4: Annual Compensation Plus Benefits Averages for Full-Time Church Staff by Church Income

	CHURCH INCOME				
	$250K & Under	$251-$500K	$501-$750K	$751K-$1M	Over $1 Million
Senior Pastors	$53,274	$78,409	$94,873	$100,676	$127,927
Solo Pastors	$53,354	$79,179	$84,213	$97,714	$118,579
Executive or Administrative Pastors	$55,808	$54,441	$67,842	$74,953	$97,472
Associate Pastors	$50,464	$54,868	$66,571	$69,052	$76,589
Adult Ministry/Christian Education Pastors/Directors	-	$37,999	$55,771	$62,789	$66,449
Youth Pastors/Directors	$41,076	$48,970	$53,958	$52,471	$63,971
Children's/Preschool Pastors/Directors	$36,750	$36,305	$49,040	$48,450	$58,668
Music/Choir/Worship Pastors/Directors	-	$51,481	$57,935	$61,111	$75,464
Administrators	$37,603	$41,242	$46,091	$50,313	$69,296
Bookkeepers/Accountants	-	$32,933	$36,082	$38,370	$48,915
Secretaries/Administrative Assistants	$23,863	$29,348	$33,622	$34,424	$36,926
Custodians	-	-	$31,841	$34,863	$44,019

- Not enough response to provide meaningful data.

Table 3-5: Annual Compensation Plus Benefits Averages for Full-Time Church Staff by Worship Attendance

	WORSHIP ATTENDANCE					
	100 or less	101-300	301-500	501-750	751-1,000	Over 1,000
Senior Pastors	$48,123	$77,486	$97,275	$106,978	$115,923	$144,304
Solo Pastors	$50,898	$71,071	$85,797	$115,092	-	-
Executive or Administrative Pastors	-	$57,612	$73,253	$76,531	$83,244	$105,571
Associate Pastors	$44,695	$58,209	$66,861	$74,762	$74,498	$76,451
Adult Ministry/Christian Education Pastors/Directors	-	$45,531	$60,533	$62,541	$55,128	$70,597
Youth Pastors/Directors	-	$48,467	$52,250	$58,582	$63,377	$68,557
Children's/Preschool Pastors/Directors	-	$43,215	$47,943	$50,384	$61,312	$61,805
Music/Choir/Worship Pastors/Directors	-	$60,448	$61,110	$72,310	$70,895	$78,587
Administrators	$39,264	$46,983	$52,900	$57,994	$58,765	$74,655
Bookkeepers/Accountants	-	$34,550	$39,110	$42,397	$42,849	$54,034
Secretaries/Administrative Assistants	$23,963	$30,528	$34,692	$35,233	$36,050	$34,722
Custodians	-	$33,096	$35,393	$42,995	$43,696	$44,926

- Not enough response to provide meaningful data.

Table 3-6: Annual Compensation Plus Benefits Averages for Full-Time Church Staff by Church Setting

	CHURCH SETTING			
	Metro-politan city	Suburb of large city	Small town or rural city	Farming area
Senior Pastors	$91,116	$97,740	$78,187	$67,629
Solo Pastors	$65,235	$65,430	$59,350	$49,589
Executive or Administrative Pastors	$85,073	$94,410	$77,912	-
Associate Pastors	$69,217	$72,712	$62,891	$58,471
Adult Ministry/Christian Education Pastors/Directors	$60,391	$61,950	$61,001	-
Youth Pastors/Directors	$58,902	$60,970	$52,882	$46,481
Children's/Preschool Pastors/Directors	$56,979	$53,963	$51,895	-
Music/Choir/Worship Pastors/Directors	$73,689	$70,117	$64,158	-
Administrators	$58,838	$59,834	$53,305	-
Bookkeepers/Accountants	$44,329	$46,799	$39,160	-
Secretaries/Administrative Assistants	$33,390	$35,697	$30,896	$28,339
Custodians	$43,748	$42,271	$35,997	-

- Not enough response to provide meaningful data.

Table 3-7: Annual Compensation Plus Benefits Averages for Full-Time Church Staff by Region

	REGION								
	New England	Middle Atlantic	South Atlantic	E-N Central	E-S Central	W-N Central	W-S Central	Mountain	Pacific
Senior Pastors	$96,782	$84,535	$89,344	$82,516	$87,167	$86,971	$96,710	$81,523	$87,075
Solo Pastors	$67,660	$64,297	$63,628	$58,286	$56,002	$54,501	$57,656	$60,979	$62,490
Executive or Administrative Pastors	-	$83,122	$86,199	$85,072	$86,742	$86,211	$93,805	$76,315	$91,763
Associate Pastors	$78,589	$72,570	$70,842	$64,822	$62,623	$63,553	$70,500	$59,868	$69,820
Adult Ministry/Christian Education Pastors/Directors	-	$60,737	$62,628	$61,388	$58,622	$60,259	$57,107	$65,378	$64,616
Youth Pastors/Directors	$53,255	$56,369	$59,222	$55,309	$57,291	$51,494	$63,253	$55,136	$58,669
Children's/Preschool Pastors/Directors	-	$48,851	$55,772	$57,910	$58,484	$52,842	$51,957	$49,641	$54,748
Music/Choir/Worship Pastors/Directors	-	$69,017	$75,804	$65,369	$68,806	$66,086	$71,380	$62,128	$63,205
Administrators	$63,297	$57,242	$59,924	$53,582	$56,975	$52,585	$57,547	$53,186	$58,316
Bookkeepers/Accountants	-	$43,279	$45,394	$45,852	$37,732	$39,926	$41,194	$44,955	$44,516
Secretaries/Administrative Assistants	$39,122	$34,142	$35,855	$30,768	$32,621	$32,236	$30,922	$28,743	$36,604
Custodians	-	$44,249	$42,987	$37,966	$33,168	$43,730	$31,125	$38,249	$45,907

- Not enough response to provide meaningful data.

Table 3-8: Annual Compensation Plus Benefits Averages for Full-Time Church Staff by Education

	EDUCATION			
	Less than Bachelor	Bachelor	Master	Doctorate
Senior Pastors	$69,519	$78,515	$87,728	$101,819
Solo Pastors	$49,942	$51,122	$63,246	$68,672
Executive or Administrative Pastors	$75,698	$88,193	$85,735	$101,244
Associate Pastors	$59,373	$63,201	$71,534	$83,143
Adult Ministry/Christian Education Pastors/Directors	$40,024	$63,791	$67,335	$64,106
Youth Pastors/Directors	$51,458	$55,892	$62,790	-
Children's/Preschool Pastors/Directors	$44,723	$53,268	$60,093	-
Music/Choir/Worship Pastors/Directors	$53,344	$67,448	$73,861	$80,900
Administrators	$48,695	$58,483	$66,220	$66,250
Bookkeepers/Accountants	$39,962	$46,342	$52,591	-
Secretaries/Administrative Assistants	$32,269	$34,630	$33,723	-
Custodians	$37,983	$46,197	-	-

- Not enough response to provide meaningful data.

Table 3-9: Annual Compensation Plus Benefits Averages for Full-Time Church Staff by Years Employed

	YEARS EMPLOYED			
	Less than 6 years	6-10 years	11-15 years	Over 15 years
Senior Pastors	$81,182	$86,908	$89,812	$94,019
Solo Pastors	$58,164	$59,498	$66,638	$61,572
Executive or Administrative Pastors	$84,130	$89,518	$85,221	$104,212
Associate Pastors	$63,578	$70,479	$72,145	$80,595
Adult Ministry/Christian Education Pastors/Directors	$61,256	$58,703	$62,508	$68,557
Youth Pastors/Directors	$52,688	$64,493	$69,624	$85,344
Children's/Preschool Pastors/Directors	$49,888	$55,775	$56,862	$61,857
Music/Choir/Worship Pastors/Directors	$63,330	$70,213	$74,332	$77,238
Administrators	$55,832	$57,153	$59,605	$56,512
Bookkeepers/Accountants	$41,490	$43,489	$46,006	$42,846
Secretaries/Administrative Assistants	$30,320	$31,674	$36,471	$36,945
Custodians	$37,598	$41,070	$41,032	$49,749

Table 3-10: Annual Compensation Plus Benefits Averages for Full-Time Church Staff by Denomination

	DENOMINATION					
	Assemblies of God	Baptist	Independent/ Nondenom.	Lutheran	Methodist	Presby-terian
Senior Pastors	$79,411	$86,733	$84,641	$99,992	$108,996	$109,866
Solo Pastors	$60,240	$56,289	$56,732	$67,511	$70,035	$68,205
Executive or Administrative Pastors	$85,101	$83,189	$90,197	-	$96,213	$92,099
Associate Pastors	$57,202	$65,056	$69,019	$81,393	$69,157	$83,906
Adult Ministry/Christian Education Pastors/Directors	$51,012	$69,708	$65,668	$53,424	$43,465	$58,750
Youth Pastors/Directors	$49,602	$59,464	$61,860	$51,610	$49,461	$57,418
Children's/Preschool Pastors/Directors	$51,410	$57,628	$57,256	-	$42,249	$45,811
Music/Choir/Worship Pastors/Directors	$62,498	$73,612	$67,493	-	$56,647	$75,069
Administrators	$43,220	$61,385	$62,183	$60,474	$46,837	$61,706
Bookkeepers/Accountants	$36,862	$40,099	$46,348	-	$43,687	$48,100
Secretaries/Administrative Assistants	$28,812	$33,472	$33,507	$31,705	$32,543	$36,426
Custodians	$40,887	$37,715	$40,473	-	$37,762	$47,197

- Not enough response to provide meaningful data.

Table 3-11: Annual Compensation Plus Benefits Averages for Full-Time Church Staff by Gender

	GENERAL — GENDER	
	Male	Female
Senior Pastors	$88,059	$62,737
Solo Pastors	$60,911	$55,952
Executive or Administrative Pastors	$90,377	$61,864
Associate Pastors	$69,091	$62,905
Adult Ministry/Christian Education Pastors/Directors	$71,632	$48,064
Youth Pastors/Directors	$58,206	$47,396
Children's/Preschool Pastors/Directors	$63,119	$50,007
Music/Choir/Worship Pastors/Directors	$71,152	$54,353
Administrators	$68,456	$49,373
Bookkeepers/Accountants	$49,394	$42,568
Secretaries/Administrative Assistants	$39,426	$32,971
Custodians	$41,300	$30,944

Table 3-12: Annual Compensation Plus Benefits Averages for Part-Time Church Staff by Church Income

	CHURCH INCOME				
	$250K & Under	$251-$500K	$501-$750K	$751K-$1M	Over $1 Million
Solo Pastors	$21,301	-	-	-	-
Associate Pastors	$23,414	$15,144	$30,159	$26,950	$29,357
Adult Ministry/Christian Education Pastors/Directors	$15,840	$21,677	$15,269	$17,655	$22,772
Youth Pastors/Directors	$10,109	$15,313	$18,380	$16,174	$21,440
Children's/Preschool Pastors/Directors	$11,221	$14,232	$17,761	$18,256	$19,582
Music/Choir/Worship Pastors/Directors	$8,921	$12,516	$17,563	$19,785	$17,711
Administrators	$11,304	$21,111	$24,389	$28,615	$35,876
Bookkeepers/Accountants	$7,917	$12,091	$14,967	$17,045	$24,392
Secretaries/Administrative Assistants	$11,850	$15,322	$15,271	$17,299	$17,537
Custodians	$6,211	$10,267	$13,805	$13,515	$15,097
Musicians/Vocalists	$6,527	$8,262	$9,638	$12,712	$16,227
Child Care Providers	$4,006	$2,432	$3,786	$6,462	$5,580

- Not enough response to provide meaningful data.

4

SENIOR PASTORS

Employment Profile

Senior Pastors provided a significant number of responses to this survey, with 1,119 full-time positions reported. Senior Pastors are defined as the lead pastor in a church where there are multiple paid pastoral ministry positions. As expected, this group is quite diverse.

All Senior Pastors responding to this survey are ordained, and nearly all are male (97%). More than two-thirds (68%) have a graduate degree, and about nine in 10 (89%) Senior Pastors are employed by the church rather than self-employed.

This profile is similar to those from the previous two surveys (2011 and 2009) except for education. The percentage of those who have graduate degrees dropped four percentage points, from 72% to 68%.

The chart below provides a demographic profile of this sample.

	Full-Time	Part-Time
Number of respondents	1,119	49
Ordained	100%	-
Average years employed	11	-
Male	97%	-
Female	3%	-
Self-employed (receives 1099)	11%	-
Church employee (receives W-2)	89%	-
High school diploma	4%	-
Associate degree	5%	-
Bachelor's degree	23%	-
Master's degree	46%	-
Doctoral degree	22%	-

Total Compensation plus Benefits Package Analysis

The following analyses are based on data in the tables you will find later in this chapter. The tables show compensation plus benefits data for Senior Pastors who serve full-time and are presented according to church income, church attendance, church setting, region, education, years employed, denomination, and gender. In this way, the Senior Pastor's compensation plus benefits can be analyzed and compared from a variety of useful perspectives.

The total compensation plus benefits amount includes the base salary; housing allowance and/or parsonage amount; health, life, and disability insurance payments; retirement contribution; and educational funds.

A worksheet at the end of this chapter is provided to help you apply the data to your church's situation.

The Senior Pastor is one of the most highly paid positions in the local church and receives the most comprehensive benefits package. Nearly nine in 10 Senior Pastors receive a housing allowance, but only a slim percentage, a little more than one in 10, live in church-provided parsonages. More than six in 10 (64%) full-time Senior Pastors receive health insurance benefits and retirement benefits (67%).

About one-fourth of Senior Pastors receive life insurance benefits (26%) and disability insurance benefits (22%).

The majority of respondents (51%) received salary increases "in the past year." This is an increase of 11 percentage points compared to the previous study.

Compensation Plus Benefits	Full-Time	Part-Time
Base Salary	98%	-
Housing	87%	-
Parsonage	11%	-
Health Insurance*	64%	-
Life Insurance*	26%	-
Disability Insurance*	22%	-
Retirement	67%	-
Continuing Education	31%	-
Received salary increase	51%	-
Received paid vacation	96%	-
Received auto reimbursement/allowance	61%	-

* Only those reporting individual premiums for Health, Life, or Disability (not total insurance premiums) are included.

KEY POINTS

✳ More than half of full-time Senior Pastors who responded serve churches with an annual church budget of $500,000 or less and a worship attendance of 300 or less.

✳ In general, as church income, worship attendance, the minister's education level, and years employed increase, the average compensation plus benefits package for Senior Pastors also increases.

✳ About four in 10 Senior Pastors surveyed serve churches in a small town/rural city setting (41%) or suburb of a large city (37%). The church budget in metropolitan and suburban settings is higher than that in small towns or farming areas.

✳ Senior Pastors serving churches in suburban or metropolitan settings have the highest compensation and benefits packages.

✳ Regionally, the lowest average compensation and benefits packages are in East-North Central and Mountain regions.

✳ Full-time male Senior Pastors receive 40% more in compensation plus benefits than female Senior Pastors.

Compensation & Benefits: National Averages for Full-Time Senior Pastors*		
	Full-Time	**Part-Time**
	Senior Pastor data only	**Combined Solo and Senior Pastor data***
2000		$66,096
2001		$69,543
2002		$71,232
2003		$73,230
2004		$74,969
2005		$77,096
2006	$87,284	$78,339
2007	$81,067	$70,789
2008	$81,113	$72,519
2009	$80,745	$70,806
2011	$82,938	$73,098
2013	$88,814**	$79,520**

*National averages for Senior Pastors from 1998 to 2005 include data for both Senior and Solo Pastors. Detailed data for each position are available beginning in 2006. Refer to chapter 5 for Solo Pastor's data.

**The above trend is made available for your reference only. In addition to reviewing this overall data, please refer to the detailed tables using your church's income, attendance, setting, region, and denomination as well as the person's education, gender, and years employed for guidance in compensating this position.

Table 4-1: Annual Compensation of Full-Time Senior Pastors by Church Income

CHARACTERISTICS	Data Distribution*	CHURCH INCOME				
		$250K & Under	$251-$500K	$501-$750K	$751K-$1M	Over $1 Million
Average weekend worship attendance		126	224	336	480	1,061
Average church income		$151,772	$367,155	$617,710	$894,823	$2,867,332
Average # of years employed		9	11	11	11	13
Average # of paid vacation days		21	22	23	24	22
% College graduate or higher		87%	91%	96%	97%	95%
% Who receive auto reimbursement/allowance		53%	65%	64%	64%	64%
% Ordained		100%	100%	100%	99%	100%
% Supervise one or more people		91%	99%	100%	98%	98%
Average % salary increase (for those who had an increase) this year		5.9%	3.9%	3.3%	3.4%	3.8%
COMPENSATION						
Base Salary	Highest 25%	$42,000	$53,250	$64,400	$64,000	$90,633
	Median	$30,000	$40,000	$50,780	$53,000	$68,008
	Lowest 25%	$22,512	$31,975	$41,500	$44,244	$52,241
	Average	$31,367	$44,044	$53,696	$54,981	$77,205
Housing	Highest 25%	$24,000	$30,000	$31,750	$39,250	$45,600
	Median	$19,586	$24,000	$25,000	$30,000	$34,080
	Lowest 25%	$12,000	$18,000	$20,000	$24,000	$26,400
	Average	$18,692	$24,922	$26,648	$30,748	$36,466
Parsonage	Highest 25%	$14,520	$18,000	$24,000	$20,000	$40,000
	Median	$9,840	$12,000	$16,136	$18,000	$24,000
	Lowest 25%	$7,200	$9,000	$9,700	$8,282	$4,000
	Average	$11,478	$13,196	$19,966	$22,936	$26,400
Total Compensation	**Highest 25%**	**$59,350**	**$75,921**	**$91,000**	**$91,500**	**$125,000**
	Median	**$49,050**	**$64,000**	**$75,000**	**$80,000**	**$103,368**
	Lowest 25%	**$37,570**	**$55,343**	**$66,400**	**$72,000**	**$86,300**
	Average	**$47,212**	**$67,073**	**$79,845**	**$84,651**	**$108,063**
BENEFITS						
Health Insurance	Highest 25%	$12,000	$14,400	$14,962	$17,000	$16,892
	Median	$8,875	$10,800	$11,422	$12,681	$13,016
	Lowest 25%	$5,000	$6,200	$7,200	$9,426	$10,000
	Average	$9,466	$10,703	$11,741	$13,292	$13,679
Life Insurance	Highest 25%	$1,016	$1,090	$800	$1,000	$1,000
	Median	$500	$580	$318	$600	$325
	Lowest 25%	$300	$300	$192	$360	$134
	Average	$1,146	$811	$711	$774	$842
Disability Insurance	Highest 25%	$759	$1,000	$1,159	$1,000	$932
	Median	$370	$640	$600	$759	$649
	Lowest 25%	$300	$458	$300	$650	$373
	Average	$536	$834	$924	$1,184	$807
Retirement	Highest 25%	$5,400	$8,000	$9,000	$10,000	$12,210
	Median	$3,300	$5,000	$6,000	$6,700	$8,000
	Lowest 25%	$2,000	$3,000	$3,000	$3,500	$4,457
	Average	$4,131	$5,789	$6,580	$7,688	$9,374
Continuing Education	Highest 25%	$1,500	$1,513	$2,000	$2,000	$3,000
	Median	$1,000	$1,000	$1,500	$1,500	$2,000
	Lowest 25%	$550	$500	$1,000	$1,000	$1,000
	Average	$1,370	$1,250	$1,795	$1,556	$2,110
Total Benefits	**Highest 25%**	**$14,350**	**$18,500**	**$21,900**	**$24,609**	**$27,828**
	Median	**$7,960**	**$12,243**	**$16,500**	**$16,500**	**$20,925**
	Lowest 25%	**$3,000**	**$6,825**	**$9,668**	**$8,350**	**$12,949**
	Average	**$9,409**	**$13,077**	**$16,348**	**$17,218**	**$21,103**
TOTAL COMPENSATION PLUS BENEFITS	**Highest 25%**	**$68,253**	**$90,000**	**$109,000**	**$112,147**	**$146,736**
	Median	**$53,600**	**$76,400**	**$92,595**	**$100,000**	**$123,608**
	Lowest 25%	**$42,460**	**$65,000**	**$80,328**	**$85,300**	**$102,537**
	Average	**$53,274**	**$78,409**	**$94,873**	**$100,676**	**$127,927**
Number of Respondents		300	279	161	101	257

- Not enough response to provide meaningful data.

* For detailed description and definitions of Data Distribution (Highest 25%, Median, Lowest 25%, and Average), see chapter 1, Explanation of Data Distribution.

Table 4-2: Annual Compensation of Full-Time Senior Pastors by Worship Attendance

	Data Distribution*	WORSHIP ATTENDANCE					
		100 or less	101-300	301-500	501-750	751-1,000	Over 1,000
CHARACTERISTICS							
Average weekend worship attendance		68	198	403	629	881	1,865
Average church income		$170,680	$407,836	$830,935	$1,125,631	$1,498,173	$3,127,280
Average # of years employed		9	11	12	12	15	14
Average # of paid vacation days		20	22	23	23	23	22
% College graduate or higher		81%	92%	96%	93%	98%	92%
% Who receive auto reimbursement/allowance		49%	64%	63%	66%	62%	53%
% Ordained		99%	100%	100%	99%	100%	100%
% Supervise one or more people		86%	98%	99%	98%	97%	99%
Average % salary increase (for those who had an increase) this year		7.2%	3.9%	3.3%	3.5%	3.9%	4.4%
COMPENSATION							
Base Salary	Median	$29,000	$40,325	$50,000	$59,957	$63,000	$84,375
	Average	$29,055	$43,457	$53,128	$72,916	$64,396	$86,538
Housing	Median	$18,000	$24,000	$29,026	$27,500	$33,000	$40,000
	Average	$17,299	$24,460	$30,009	$28,721	$33,638	$42,118
Parsonage	Median	$8,063	$14,400	$16,136	-	-	-
	Average	$10,829	$14,703	$19,345	-	-	-
Total Compensation	**Median**	**$44,200**	**$63,000**	**$79,800**	**$85,000**	**$98,300**	**$120,000**
	Average	**$42,907**	**$66,087**	**$82,264**	**$89,398**	**$98,070**	**$125,078**
BENEFITS							
Health Insurance	Median	$7,700	$10,333	$12,144	$13,607	$12,000	$12,432
	Average	$8,922	$11,036	$12,531	$13,604	$12,398	$12,454
Life Insurance	Median	$513	$600	$409	$450	$400	$300
	Average	$998	$805	$729	$678	$786	$940
Disability	Median	$500	$600	$760	$625	$675	$300
	Average	$706	$772	$894	$1,159	$710	$940
Retirement	Median	$3,000	$5,000	$6,150	$6,027	$7,801	$8,093
	Average	$4,283	$5,916	$7,657	$7,351	$8,488	$9,830
Continuing Education	Median	$1,000	$1,000	$1,500	$1,500	$1,750	$1,500
	Average	$1,341	$1,393	$1,767	$1,902	$1,897	$2,048
Total Benefits	**Median**	**$7,000**	**$12,426**	**$16,600**	**$17,406**	**$17,958**	**$20,838**
	Average	**$8,907**	**$13,466**	**$16,928**	**$18,270**	**$19,523**	**$21,043**
TOTAL COMPENSATION PLUS BENEFITS	**Median**	**$48,609**	**$73,400**	**$93,475**	**$103,810**	**$112,800**	**$139,535**
	Average	**$48,123**	**$77,486**	**$97,275**	**$106,978**	**$115,923**	**$144,304**
Number of Respondents		170	478	204	103	65	92

- Not enough response to provide meaningful data.

* For detailed description and definitions of Data Distribution (Median and Average), see chapter 1, Explanation of Data Distribution.

Table 4-3: Annual Compensation of Full-Time Senior Pastors by Church Setting

	Data Distribution*	CHURCH SETTING			
		Metro-politan city	Suburb of large city	Small town or rural city	Farming area
CHARACTERISTICS					
Average weekend worship attendance		491	533	342	223
Average church income		$984,880	$1,002,050	$584,692	$407,818
Average # of years employed		13	11	11	11
Average # of paid vacation days		22	22	22	22
% College graduate or higher		90%	95%	89%	88%
% Who receive auto reimbursement/allowance		55%	58%	64%	80%
% Ordained		100%	100%	100%	100%
% Supervise one or more people		96%	97%	96%	96%
Average % salary increase (for those who had an increase) this year		4.3%	3.8%	4.2%	3.2%
COMPENSATION					
Base Salary	Median	$50,000	$50,000	$42,000	$41,337
	Average	$53,602	$54,314	$46,527	$50,970
Housing	Median	$28,000	$30,000	$22,500	$20,000
	Average	$28,651	$31,154	$23,410	$20,491
Parsonage	Median	$13,500	$18,000	$10,000	$8,520
	Average	$14,320	$20,616	$13,629	$10,341
Total Compensation	**Median**	**$75,000**	**$79,500**	**$64,550**	**$55,804**
	Average	**$78,154**	**$83,288**	**$66,997**	**$57,894**
BENEFITS					
Health Insurance	Median	$11,642	$12,000	$10,633	$8,954
	Average	$11,831	$12,422	$11,044	$9,635
Life Insurance	Median	$500	$438	$450	-
	Average	$892	$856	$822	-
Disability Insurance	Median	$620	$650	$649	-
	Average	$772	$826	$900	-
Retirement	Median	$6,000	$6,000	$5,000	$3,782
	Average	$8,299	$7,301	$5,984	$4,808
Continuing Education	Median	$2,000	$1,200	$1,000	$1,000
	Average	$2,195	$1,650	$1,408	$1,455
Total Benefits	**Median**	**$14,507**	**$16,698**	**$12,050**	**$10,218**
	Average	**$16,004**	**$16,944**	**$13,589**	**$11,594**
TOTAL COMPENSATION PLUS BENEFITS	**Median**	**$88,122**	**$94,275**	**$76,466**	**$68,150**
	Average	**$91,116**	**$97,740**	**$78,187**	**$67,629**
Number of Respondents		195	409	459	51

- Not enough response to provide meaningful data.

* For detailed description and definitions of Data Distribution (Median and Average), see chapter 1, Explanation of Data Distribution.

Table 4-4: Annual Compensation of Full-Time Senior Pastors by Region

	Data Distribution*	REGION								
		New England	Middle Atlantic	South Atlantic	E-N Central	E-S Central	W-N Central	W-S Central	Mountain	Pacific
CHARACTERISTICS										
Average weekend worship attendance		337	381	389	388	480	437	568	467	466
Average church income		$649,523	$677,734	$843,320	$648,795	$931,912	$731,146	$1,148,164	$710,753	$815,168
Average # of years employed		15	12	10	11	10	11	10	14	12
Average # of paid vacation days		25	24	21	23	19	23	20	22	22
% College graduate or higher		96%	92%	92%	93%	93%	90%	88%	92%	91%
% Who receive auto reimbursement/allowance		65%	70%	63%	67%	54%	55%	58%	59%	52%
% Ordained		100%	99%	100%	100%	100%	100%	99%	100%	99%
% Supervise one or more people		100%	95%	98%	96%	100%	98%	93%	98%	96%
Average % salary increase (for those who had an increase) this year		4.1%	3.0%	4.0%	3.5%	5.6%	4.2%	5.0%	3.1%	4.8%
COMPENSATION										
Base Salary	Median	$50,000	$44,000	$48,603	$46,000	$45,106	$45,800	$53,177	$40,175	$45,000
	Average	$50,313	$46,171	$54,008	$48,213	$50,788	$48,192	$58,544	$44,480	$53,073
Housing	Median	$33,000	$22,250	$25,000	$24,000	$24,500	$24,532	$27,000	$24,000	$30,000
	Average	$33,127	$24,879	$27,132	$24,655	$25,964	$26,705	$28,951	$26,420	$31,324
Parsonage	Median	-	$10,559	$12,000	$12,000	$14,000	$15,500	$7,500	-	$12,600
	Average	-	$15,807	$14,418	$12,255	$23,640	$20,883	$11,425	-	$17,305
Total Compensation	**Median**	**$80,000**	**$66,911**	**$70,456**	**$67,066**	**$66,054**	**$71,000**	**$77,057**	**$67,914**	**$72,000**
	Average	**$80,483**	**$70,469**	**$76,301**	**$70,325**	**$75,744**	**$73,701**	**$84,811**	**$69,364**	**$74,955**
BENEFITS										
Health Insurance	Median	$14,537	$12,000	$11,016	$12,000	$11,867	$12,000	$10,330	$10,000	$11,856
	Average	$13,529	$11,501	$11,864	$12,313	$11,822	$11,697	$10,442	$10,695	$11,598
Life Insurance	Median	-	$408	$500	$325	$500	$434	$600	$749	$300
	Average	-	$1,061	$717	$560	$646	$792	$1,468	$1,130	$745
Disability Insurance	Median	-	$524	$648	$672	$648	$450	$600	$842	$600
	Average	-	$725	$800	$834	$856	$859	$923	$791	$804
Retirement	Median	$6,000	$5,600	$5,600	$5,241	$6,100	$4,800	$6,069	$5,698	$5,109
	Average	$7,954	$7,011	$7,237	$6,150	$7,876	$5,916	$8,324	$6,193	$6,071
Continuing Education	Median	$1,000	$1,350	$1,000	$1,300	$1,900	$1,200	$1,200	$1,000	$1,500
	Average	$1,367	$1,624	$1,407	$1,668	$1,907	$1,617	$1,680	$1,320	$2,028
Total Benefits	**Median**	**$18,305**	**$14,674**	**$15,000**	**$14,000**	**$17,916**	**$13,340**	**$11,300**	**$11,918**	**$14,071**
	Average	**$19,262**	**$15,398**	**$15,713**	**$15,031**	**$17,032**	**$14,596**	**$14,608**	**$13,760**	**$14,757**
TOTAL COMPENSATION PLUS BENEFITS	**Median**	**$98,275**	**$79,301**	**$86,738**	**$82,110**	**$81,965**	**$83,200**	**$84,121**	**$77,366**	**$84,684**
	Average	**$96,782**	**$84,535**	**$89,344**	**$82,516**	**$87,167**	**$86,971**	**$96,710**	**$81,523**	**$87,075**
Number of Respondents		26	105	227	218	71	121	125	86	139

- Not enough response to provide meaningful data.

* For detailed description and definitions of Data Distribution (Median and Average), see chapter 1, Explanation of Data Distribution.

Table 4-5: Annual Compensation of Full-Time Senior Pastors by Education

	Data Distribution*	EDUCATION			
		Less than Bachelor	Bachelor	Master	Doctorate
CHARACTERISTICS					
Average weekend worship attendance		343	403	404	563
Average church income		$567,901	$670,398	$723,580	$1,166,121
Average # of years employed		14	12	10	12
Average # of paid vacation days		19	21	23	23
% College graduate or higher		0%	100%	100%	100%
% Who receive auto reimbursement/allowance		47%	51%	64%	67%
% Ordained		99%	100%	100%	100%
% Supervise one or more people		96%	94%	98%	97%
Average % salary increase (for those who had an increase) this year		4.1%	4.8%	3.8%	3.9%
COMPENSATION					
Base Salary	Median	$36,000	$42,000	$46,000	$52,121
	Average	$47,830	$48,217	$49,871	$56,976
Housing	Median	$23,000	$24,000	$24,582	$30,000
	Average	$23,056	$24,975	$26,666	$31,760
Parsonage	Median	$14,400	$9,000	$12,000	$14,400
	Average	$13,502	$13,688	$15,711	$18,242
Total Compensation	**Median**	**$58,500**	**$64,128**	**$69,980**	**$81,000**
	Average	**$62,027**	**$68,119**	**$74,496**	**$86,251**
BENEFITS					
Health Insurance	Median	$9,426	$10,044	$12,000	$12,000
	Average	$9,204	$11,032	$12,245	$11,946
Life Insurance	Median	$450	$312	$500	$500
	Average	$1,660	$693	$789	$868
Disability Insurance	Median	$600	$665	$600	$700
	Average	$613	$755	$828	$942
Retirement	Median	$3,796	$3,600	$5,771	$7,595
	Average	$4,968	$4,713	$6,811	$8,779
Continuing Education	Median	$700	$1,070	$1,150	$1,500
	Average	$950	$1,498	$1,549	$1,933
Total Benefits	**Median**	**$8,652**	**$11,560**	**$15,144**	**$16,500**
	Average	**$10,539**	**$12,615**	**$15,796**	**$17,831**
TOTAL COMPENSATION PLUS BENEFITS	**Median**	**$66,350**	**$75,515**	**$83,100**	**$97,975**
	Average	**$69,519**	**$78,515**	**$87,728**	**$101,819**
Number of Respondents		94	256	511	249

- *Not enough response to provide meaningful data.*

* *For detailed description and definitions of Data Distribution (Median and Average), see chapter 1, Explanation of Data Distribution.*

Table 4-6: Annual Compensation of Full-Time Senior Pastors by Years Employed

	Data Distribution*	Less than 6 years	6-10 years	11-15 years	Over 15 years
CHARACTERISTICS					
Average weekend worship attendance		326	423	456	560
Average church income		$649,995	$818,766	$785,746	$985,224
Average # of years employed		3	8	13	24
Average # of paid vacation days		20	22	23	24
% College graduate or higher		94%	92%	91%	88%
% Who receive auto reimbursement/allowance		59%	59%	62%	65%
% Ordained		99%	100%	100%	100%
% Supervise one or more people		96%	96%	98%	97%
Average % salary increase (for those who had an increase) this year		4.6%	4.5%	3.3%	3.5%
COMPENSATION					
Base Salary	Median	$45,000	$43,000	$46,364	$50,000
	Average	$48,918	$47,283	$49,324	$56,624
Housing	Median	$24,000	$25,000	$25,614	$26,000
	Average	$25,765	$27,401	$27,052	$28,685
Parsonage	Median	$11,500	$15,216	$17,150	$11,800
	Average	$14,149	$15,300	$22,689	$11,469
Total Compensation	**Median**	**$65,874**	**$67,277**	**$72,228**	**$74,782**
	Average	**$70,259**	**$72,994**	**$75,722**	**$80,769**
BENEFITS					
Health Insurance	Median	$11,000	$11,812	$11,713	$12,000
	Average	$11,324	$12,107	$11,881	$11,666
Life Insurance	Median	$418	$330	$500	$575
	Average	$754	$641	$954	$1,033
Disability Insurance	Median	$650	$603	$700	$625
	Average	$881	$772	$896	$831
Retirement	Median	$5,523	$5,000	$5,700	$6,000
	Average	$6,354	$6,332	$6,701	$7,845
Continuing Education	Median	$1,200	$1,450	$1,000	$1,500
	Average	$1,538	$1,646	$1,523	$1,820
Total Benefits	**Median**	**$12,000**	**$14,500**	**$15,200**	**$14,700**
	Average	**$13,993**	**$15,620**	**$16,287**	**$15,826**
TOTAL COMPENSATION PLUS BENEFITS	**Median**	**$76,532**	**$82,400**	**$87,100**	**$90,310**
	Average	**$81,182**	**$86,908**	**$89,812**	**$94,019**
Number of Respondents		389	242	173	304

- Not enough response to provide meaningful data.

* For detailed description and definitions of Data Distribution (Median and Average), see chapter 1, Explanation of Data Distribution.

Table 4-7: Annual Compensation of Full-Time Senior Pastors by Denomination

	Data Distribution*	Assemblies of God	Baptist	Independent/ Nondenom.	Lutheran	Methodist	Presby-terian
CHARACTERISTICS							
Average weekend worship attendance		417	414	522	466	486	392
Average church income		$688,630	$859,003	$855,766	$921,263	$895,045	$1,028,495
Average # of years employed		11	11	13	13	6	10
Average # of paid vacation days		20	21	21	28	25	25
% College graduate or higher		77%	96%	85%	100%	100%	100%
% Who receive auto reimbursement/allowance		55%	69%	42%	83%	68%	74%
% Ordained		99%	100%	100%	100%	100%	100%
% Supervise one or more people		95%	97%	96%	100%	100%	98%
Average % salary increase (for those who had an increase) this year		4.6%	4.0%	4.7%	2.8%	3.1%	3.1%
COMPENSATION							
Base Salary	Median	$40,325	$43,000	$47,526	$53,871	$67,000	$50,000
	Average	$45,565	$47,905	$52,531	$58,489	$71,011	$54,887
Housing	Median	$24,000	$25,000	$25,000	$23,540	$17,630	$34,540
	Average	$26,428	$27,349	$27,718	$24,106	$20,192	$35,253
Parsonage	Median	-	$15,000	$14,760	-	$12,000	-
	Average	-	$17,858	$18,701	-	$12,817	-
Total Compensation	**Median**	**$62,896**	**$68,472**	**$70,000**	**$78,000**	**$82,499**	**$81,228**
	Average	**$68,200**	**$73,631**	**$75,466**	**$82,312**	**$89,138**	**$87,507**
BENEFITS							
Health Insurance	Median	$10,322	$11,020	$10,528	$12,000	$12,000	$16,390
	Average	$10,510	$11,681	$10,538	$14,333	$12,000	$16,603
Life Insurance	Median	$286	$600	$463	-	$225	$387
	Average	$1,192	$935	$969	-	$302	$647
Disability Insurance	Median	-	$600	$658	$1,326	-	$650
	Average	-	$856	$858	$1,456	-	$662
Retirement	Median	$4,595	$5,974	$4,000	$8,000	$10,500	$10,000
	Average	$6,218	$6,467	$5,013	$8,374	$10,506	$10,498
Continuing Education	Median	$1,750	$1,500	$1,000	$1,000	$1,000	$1,843
	Average	$2,177	$1,775	$1,646	$1,503	$1,622	$1,880
Total Benefits	**Median**	**$12,487**	**$15,600**	**$12,000**	**$18,000**	**$21,800**	**$23,475**
	Average	**$13,719**	**$15,630**	**$12,546**	**$18,990**	**$20,555**	**$23,516**
TOTAL COMPENSATION PLUS BENEFITS	**Median**	**$75,160**	**$82,322**	**$83,056**	**$83,200**	**$103,910**	**$105,512**
	Average	**$79,411**	**$86,733**	**$84,641**	**$99,992**	**$108,996**	**$109,866**
Number of Respondents		93	292	250	29	59	61

- Not enough response to provide meaningful data.

* For detailed description and definitions of Data Distribution (Median and Average), see chapter 1, Explanation of Data Distribution.

Table 4-8: Annual Compensation of Full-Time Senior Pastors by Gender

	Data Distribution*	GENDER	
		Male	Female
CHARACTERISTICS			
Average weekend worship attendance		442	160
Average church income		$812,737	$377,162
Average # of years employed		11	8
Average # of paid vacation days		22	21
% College graduate or higher		92%	81%
% Who receive auto reimbursement/allowance		61%	45%
% Ordained		100%	97%
% Supervise one or more people		97%	94%
Average % salary increase (for those who had an increase) this year		4.0%	4.5%
COMPENSATION			
Base Salary	Median	$47,000	$33,000
	Average	$51,379	$35,186
Housing	Median	$25,000	$21,399
	Average	$27,262	$23,700
Parsonage	Median	$12,000	-
	Average	$15,457	-
Total Compensation	**Median**	**$70,000**	**$48,500**
	Average	**$75,174**	**$56,456**
BENEFITS			
Health Insurance	Median	$11,912	$7,020
	Average	$11,740	$8,406
Life Insurance	Median	$475	-
	Average	$823	-
Disability Insurance	Median	$648	-
	Average	$835	-
Retirement	Median	$5,400	$9,090
	Average	$6,765	$8,695
Continuing Education	Median	$1,200	$750
	Average	$1,644	$988
Total Benefits	**Median**	**$14,400**	**$9,600**
	Average	**$15,293**	**$12,033**
TOTAL COMPENSATION PLUS BENEFITS	**Median**	**$83,787**	**$52,983**
	Average	**$88,059**	**$62,737**
Number of Respondents		1085	31

- Not enough response to provide meaningful data.

* For detailed description and definitions of Data Distribution (Median and Average), see chapter 1, Explanation of Data Distribution.

Senior Pastor Worksheet

	Enter your church data below	The 2014–2015 Compensation Handbook for Church Staff		Enter *Compensation Handbook* data below			
				Highest 25%	Median	Lowest 25%	Average
Church Income	$ 1,000,000	Table 4-1	page 27	$ 112	$ 100	$ 85	$ 101
Worship Attendance		Table 4-2	page 28	n/a	$ 93	n/a	$ 97
Church Setting (metro, suburb, small town, or farming area)		Table 4-3	page 29	n/a	$ 94	n/a	$ 98
Region		Table 4-4	page 30	n/a	$ 98	n/a	$ 96
Person's Education		Table 4-5	page 31	n/a	$ 83	n/a	$ 87
Years Employed		Table 4-6	page 32	n/a	$ 90	n/a	$ 94
Denomination (if applicable)		Table 4-7	page 33	n/a	$ 82	n/a	$ 86

Looking at the table and page number references indicated in the *2014–2015 Compensation Handbook for Church Staff* columns above, locate the appropriate range for your church. Refer to the instructions below for step-by-step help.

FILLING OUT THE WORKSHEET

1. Fill in the gray boxes under *Enter your church data* with your church demographic information as follows:

   ▶ **Income** (Total annual church budget in past year)
   ▶ **Worship attendance** (Number of people, including children, who attend all weekend services)
   ▶ **Church setting** (Metropolitan city, suburb of large city, small town or rural city, or farming area)

   ▶ **Region** (Locate your state's region in the appendix on page 346.)
   ▶ **Education** (Highest level of education: less than bachelor, bachelor, master, or doctorate)

2. Use Table 4-1 (page 27) in your *2014–2015 Compensation Handbook for Church Staff* to enter data pertinent to your church. In the heading (top row), locate your church **income** from the five available ranges. Follow that column to the bottom rows, and copy the *Highest 25%*, *Median*, *Lowest 25%*, and *Average* amounts onto your worksheet.

3. Use Table 4-2 (page 28) on your *2014–2015 Compensation Handbook for Church Staff* to enter data pertinent to your church. In the heading (top row), locate your church's

worship attendance from the six available ranges. Follow that column to the bottom rows, and copy the *Median* and *Average* amounts onto your worksheet.

4. Use Table 4-3 (page 29) on your *2014–2015 Compensation Handbook for Church Staff* to enter data pertinent to your church. In the heading (top row), choose the **church setting** that best describes your church. Follow that column to the bottom rows, and copy the *Median* and *Average* amounts onto your worksheet.

5. Use Table 4-4 (page 30) on your *2014–2015 Compensation Handbook for Church Staff* to enter data pertinent to your church. In the heading (top row), look for the **region** where your church is located. Follow that column to the bottom rows, and copy the *Median* and *Average* amounts onto your worksheet.

6. Use Table 4-5 (page 31) on your *2014–2015 Compensation Handbook for Church Staff* to enter data pertinent to your Senior Pastor. In the heading (top row), look for **your Senior Pastor's highest level of education**. Follow that column to the bottom rows, and copy the *Median* and *Average* amounts onto your worksheet.

7. Use Table 4-6 (page 32) on your *2014–2015 Compensation Handbook for Church Staff* to enter data pertinent to your Senior Pastor. In the heading (top row), locate the **number of years your Senior Pastor has been employed**. Follow that column to the bottom rows, and copy the *Median* and *Average* amounts onto your worksheet.

8. Use Table 4-7 (page 33) on your *2014–2015 Compensation Handbook for Church Staff* to enter data pertinent to your church. In the heading (top row), look for **your church's denominational affiliation**. Follow that column to the bottom rows, and copy the *Median* and *Average* amounts onto your worksheet. If your church is not affiliated with a denomination, leave this section blank.

DETERMINING COMPENSATION

This tool will not provide you with a single compensation amount but rather with a range of values to help you determine the compensation appropriate to your situation.

1. Look at the values in the shaded *Median* column. Circle the **lowest** and the **highest** values. **This is the range of the median compensation plus benefits for churches similar to yours.**

2. For a variety of reasons, compensation plus benefits may be higher or lower than the range established in this table. Income and attendance are two significant factors affecting church compensation packages. If church income or attendance skews higher, you might want to consider moving toward or above the higher end of the range. Likewise, if church income or attendance skews lower, you may consider moving the package toward or below the lower end of the range.

3. Examine additional variables that might impact the compensation package you offer, such as years of service, education, and church setting.

4. Determine other circumstances unique to your situation, such as cost of living in your area, theological beliefs, pastoral performance, financial needs, the local economy, personal motivation, congregational goals, and others.

5. You now have a compensation package range based on the *2014–2015 Compensation Handbook*. Since each church and position are unique, your final compensation package will be based on additional factors unique to your situation.

5

SOLO PASTORS

Employment Profile

Solo Pastors are a unique group of church staff members. Solo Pastors are set apart from the previous group of Senior Pastors in that they are the only ministerial staff serving their congregation. The church may employ nonpastoral staff, such as a Church Secretary or Custodian. With 624 full-time positions reported in this survey, participants provided significant information for study.

Nearly all Solo Pastors are ordained; about nine in 10 are male. On average, full-time Solo Pastors have been in their current positions for nine years, while part-time Solo Pastors have been in their positions for five years. Most of those working full-time are church employees rather than self-employed. About seven in 10 of them have graduate degrees.

While the overall percentage of part-time Solo Pastors with a graduate degree dropped from 61% to 55%, the percentage of those with a doctoral degree doubled since the last study was conducted.

The chart below provides a demographic profile of this sample.

	Full-Time	Part-Time
Number of respondents	624	116
Ordained	99%	100%
Average years employed	9	5
Male	92%	86%
Female	8%	14%
Self-employed (receives 1099)	19%	40%
Church employee (receives W-2)	81%	60%
High school diploma	5%	6%
Associate degree	5%	11%
Bachelor's degree	20%	28%
Master's degree	54%	39%
Doctoral degree	15%	16%

Total Compensation plus Benefits Package Analysis

The following analyses are based on data in the tables you will find later in this chapter. The tables show compensation plus benefits data for full-time and part-time Solo Pastors and are presented according to church income, church attendance, church setting, region, education, years employed, denomination, and gender. In this way, the Solo Pastor's compensation plus benefits can be analyzed and compared from a variety of useful perspectives.

The total compensation plus benefits amount includes the base salary; housing allowance and/or parsonage amount; health, life, and disability insurance payments; retirement contribution; and educational funds.

A worksheet at the end of this chapter is provided to help you apply the data to your church's situation.

The average compensation for a full-time Solo Pastor is 29% lower than that of a full-time Senior Pastor who has additional pastoral staff. The compensation difference is most likely related to the fact that Solo Pastors serve in smaller churches.

Nearly three-fourths of full-time Solo Pastors receive housing benefits. This represents a six-percentage-point increase from the previous study. In contrast, the percentage of those who count the parsonage as part of their benefits package saw a six-percentage-point decline, from 29% to 23%, referring to the same study. More than half receive health insurance, and six in 10 receive retirement benefits.

Thirty-eight percent received salary increases, representing an eight-percentage-point increase over respondents who reported receiving a salary increase in the last study.

Compensation Plus Benefits	Full-Time	Part-Time
Base Salary	96%	81%
Housing	73%	57%
Parsonage	23%	9%
Health Insurance*	51%	16%
Life Insurance*	11%	3%
Disability Insurance*	14%	3%
Retirement	60%	20%
Continuing Education	40%	19%
Received salary increase	38%	26%
Received paid vacation	94%	69%
Received auto reimbursement/allowance	63%	35%

*Only those reporting individual premiums for Health, Life, or Disability (not total insurance premiums) are included.

KEY POINTS

* Nearly all full-time Solo Pastors serve in churches with an income of $500,000 or less and a worship attendance of 300 or less.

* In general, as church income, worship attendance, and the minister's education level increase, compensation and benefits for full-time Solo Pastors also increase.

* Compensation and benefits packages of full-time Solo Pastors seem to increase as their years of service increase, peaking between 11 and 15 years.

* Generally, full-time Solo Pastors serving churches in a metropolitan city or a suburban setting have the highest compensation and benefits packages compared to those who serve in small towns or farming areas. Church income in these settings is also higher, which greatly impacts overall compensation.

* Some regional differences emerge across average compensation and benefits packages for full-time Solo Pastors. The lowest packages are found in the West-North Central region, while the highest are found in the New England region.

Compensation & Benefits: National Averages for Full-Time Solo Pastors*	
2000	
2001	
2002	
2003	
2004	
2005	
2006	$59,852
2007	$56,797
2008	$60,162
2009	$56,189
2011	$57,181
2013	$62,634**

* National averages for Senior Pastors from 1998-2005 include data for both Senior and Solo Pastors. Beginning in 2006, we are able to provide detailed data for each position. Refer to Chapter 5 for Solo Pastors' data.

** The above trend is made available for your reference only. In addition to looking at this overall data, please refer to the detailed tables using your church's income, attendance, setting, region, and denomination as well as the person's education, gender, and years employed for guidance in compensating this position.

Table 5-1: Annual Compensation of Full-Time Solo Pastors by Church Income

CHARACTERISTICS	Data Distribution*	CHURCH INCOME				
		$250K & Under	$251-$500K	$501-$750K	$751K-$1M	Over $1 Million
Average weekend worship attendance		85	164	281	853	895
Average church income		$126,884	$336,144	$608,126	$918,564	$1,715,933
Average # of years employed		9	9	10	12	14
Average # of paid vacation days		21	22	22	19	22
% College graduate or higher		89%	94%	100%	75%	93%
% Who receive auto reimbursement/allowance		62%	76%	42%	63%	63%
% Ordained		99%	100%	100%	100%	100%
% Supervise one or more people		67%	93%	100%	100%	100%
Average % salary increase this year (for those who had an increase this year)		4.8%	3.3%	4.0%	-	3.9%
COMPENSATION						
Base Salary	Highest 25%	$40,000	$48,250	$66,904	$73,250	$85,000
	Median	$30,800	$42,947	$52,116	$60,544	$62,000
	Lowest 25%	$20,800	$32,581	$43,369	$38,900	$37,214
	Average	$31,193	$43,837	$53,242	$56,298	$66,107
Housing	Highest 25%	$24,000	$30,000	$29,000	-	$43,500
	Median	$16,800	$25,000	$24,000	-	$33,000
	Lowest 25%	$9,800	$19,875	$21,600	-	$24,600
	Average	$17,077	$24,472	$25,313	-	$36,723
Parsonage	Highest 25%	$12,000	$17,820	-	-	-
	Median	$9,000	$12,664	-	-	-
	Lowest 25%	$6,000	$11,280	-	-	-
	Average	$11,081	$13,844	-	-	-
Total Compensation	**Highest 25%**	**$55,000**	**$73,000**	**$85,000**	**$99,413**	**$123,516**
	Median	**$45,000**	**$65,973**	**$74,600**	**$83,500**	**$101,170**
	Lowest 25%	**$34,562**	**$55,000**	**$65,096**	**$74,900**	**$67,050**
	Average	**$45,576**	**$64,988**	**$71,232**	**$81,891**	**$99,214**
BENEFITS						
Health Insurance	Highest 25%	$13,100	$15,800	$17,569	$10,630	$15,508
	Median	$8,480	$12,000	$11,374	$9,800	$13,236
	Lowest 25%	$4,912	$8,000	$4,000	$5,979	$5,703
	Average	$9,276	$12,234	$10,823	$8,626	$11,823
Life Insurance	Highest 25%	$850	$800	-	-	-
	Median	$560	$600	-	-	-
	Lowest 25%	$425	$203	-	-	-
	Average	$712	$758	-	-	-
Disability Insurance	Highest 25%	$608	$775	-	-	-
	Median	$400	$500	-	-	-
	Lowest 25%	$245	$275	-	-	-
	Average	$657	$641	-	-	-
Retirement	Highest 25%	$6,105	$10,330	$8,976	-	$13,009
	Median	$4,108	$6,890	$7,432	-	$10,287
	Lowest 25%	$2,137	$4,000	$4,250	-	$5,900
	Average	$4,966	$8,159	$7,802	-	$11,250
Continuing Education	Highest 25%	$1,400	$1,500	-	-	-
	Median	$1,000	$1,000	-	-	-
	Lowest 25%	$500	$600	-	-	-
	Average	$1,235	$1,560	-	-	-
Total Benefits	**Highest 25%**	**$15,500**	**$21,600**	**$25,205**	**$19,250**	**$21,480**
	Median	**$7,775**	**$14,400**	**$18,529**	**$14,379**	**$18,612**
	Lowest 25%	**$4,450**	**$7,100**	**$5,500**	**$11,050**	**$13,955**
	Average	**$10,348**	**$15,242**	**$16,443**	**$15,823**	**$19,263**
TOTAL COMPENSATION PLUS BENEFITS	**Highest 25%**	**$67,525**	**$92,375**	**$102,169**	**$117,574**	**$137,414**
	Median	**$52,225**	**$77,760**	**$85,512**	**$98,332**	**$115,300**
	Lowest 25%	**$39,450**	**$63,518**	**$66,110**	**$89,150**	**$96,608**
	Average	**$53,354**	**$79,179**	**$84,213**	**$97,714**	**$118,579**
Number of Respondents		482	90	19	8	6

- Not enough response to provide meaningful data.

* For detailed description and definitions of Data Distribution (Highest 25%, Median, Lowest 25%, and Average), see chapter 1, Explanation of Data Distribution.

Table 5-2: Annual Compensation of Full-Time Solo Pastors by Worship Attendance

	Data Distribution*	WORSHIP ATTENDANCE					
		100 or less	101-300	301-500	501-750	751-1,000	Over 1,000
CHARACTERISTICS							
Average weekend worship attendance		66	159	389	663	-	-
Average church income		$122,004	$260,073	$726,508	$1,354,500	-	-
Average # of years employed		9	9	15	16	-	-
Average # of paid vacation days		21	21	18	22	-	-
% College graduate or higher		89%	91%	91%	100%	-	-
% Who receive auto reimbursement/allowance		62%	69%	42%	38%	-	-
% Ordained		99%	100%	100%	100%	-	-
% Supervise one or more people		63%	87%	100%	100%	-	-
Average % salary increase this year (for those who had an increase this year)		5.1%	4.0%	-	-	-	-
COMPENSATION							
Base Salary	Median	$30,000	$41,070	$46,198	$61,000	-	-
	Average	$29,536	$41,332	$49,540	$60,502	-	-
Housing	Median	$16,827	$20,800	$24,000	$31,500	-	-
	Average	$16,884	$21,256	$25,804	$39,225	-	-
Parsonage	Median	$9,000	$11,490	$0	-	-	-
	Average	$10,955	$11,837	-	-	-	-
Total Compensation	**Median**	**$44,000**	**$58,000**	**$63,548**	**$99,000**	**-**	**-**
	Average	**$45,594**	**$59,176**	**$73,194**	**$114,729**	**-**	**-**
BENEFITS							
Health Insurance	Median	$8,050	$10,680	$10,630	-	-	-
	Average	$9,083	$11,128	$8,298	-	-	-
Life Insurance	Median	$600	$500	-	-	-	-
	Average	$834	$602	-	-	-	-
Disability	Median	$400	$465	-	-	-	-
	Average	$663	$672	-	-	-	-
Retirement	Median	$4,450	$5,285	$4,175	-	-	-
	Average	$5,165	$6,568	$7,163	-	-	-
Continuing Education	Median	$800	$1,000	-	-	-	-
	Average	$1,051	$1,594	-	-	-	-
Total Benefits	**Median**	**$7,204**	**$12,000**	**$14,582**	**$16,711**	**-**	**-**
	Average	**$9,941**	**$14,005**	**$12,604**	**$15,365**	**-**	**-**
TOTAL COMPENSATION PLUS BENEFITS	**Median**	**$51,000**	**$69,190**	**$79,667**	**$117,800**	**-**	**-**
	Average	**$50,898**	**$71,071**	**$85,797**	**$115,092**	**-**	**-**
Number of Respondents		380	206	12	8	5	6

- Not enough response to provide meaningful data.

* For detailed description and definitions of Data Distribution (Median and Average), see chapter 1, Explanation of Data Distribution.

Table 5-3: Annual Compensation of Full-Time Solo Pastors by Church Setting

	Data Distribution*	CHURCH SETTING			
		Metro-politan city	Suburb of large city	Small town or rural city	Farming area
CHARACTERISTICS					
Average weekend worship attendance		139	142	136	84
Average church income		$276,081	$261,597	$202,333	$128,220
Average # of years employed		10	10	9	9
Average # of paid vacation days		20	21	21	21
% College graduate or higher		93%	88%	90%	86%
% Who receive auto reimbursement/allowance		49%	59%	68%	72%
% Ordained		99%	99%	100%	99%
% Supervise one or more people		79%	75%	74%	58%
Average % salary increase this year (for those who had an increase this year)		8.0%	4.1%	4.2%	4.3%
COMPENSATION					
Base Salary	Median	$36,200	$33,164	$33,000	$31,729
	Average	$39,625	$35,604	$34,832	$30,565
Housing	Median	$20,000	$22,000	$18,000	$11,000
	Average	$22,239	$22,153	$18,854	$10,603
Parsonage	Median	$9,000	$20,800	$9,600	$6,950
	Average	$11,554	$22,800	$9,811	$8,794
Total Compensation	**Median**	**$52,646**	**$54,850**	**$48,600**	**$42,700**
	Average	**$55,179**	**$55,997**	**$49,879**	**$41,964**
BENEFITS					
Health Insurance	Median	$9,100	$9,450	$10,000	$7,400
	Average	$10,863	$9,575	$9,986	$9,111
Life Insurance	Median	$500	$650	$558	-
	Average	$829	$713	$721	-
Disability Insurance	Median	$414	$433	$400	$350
	Average	$1,015	$652	$719	$606
Retirement	Median	$5,741	$5,300	$4,800	$4,516
	Average	$7,559	$5,805	$5,764	$4,922
Continuing Education	Median	$1,000	$1,000	$1,000	$950
	Average	$1,781	$1,453	$1,330	$1,223
Total Benefits	**Median**	**$10,750**	**$10,033**	**$9,964**	**$7,270**
	Average	**$13,445**	**$11,810**	**$11,600**	**$10,309**
TOTAL COMPENSATION PLUS BENEFITS	**Median**	**$62,330**	**$64,400**	**$57,213**	**$47,100**
	Average	**$65,235**	**$65,430**	**$59,350**	**$49,589**
Number of Respondents		89	147	313	75

- Not enough response to provide meaningful data.

* For detailed description and definitions of Data Distribution (Median and Average), see chapter 1, Explanation of Data Distribution.

Table 5-4: Annual Compensation of Full-Time Solo Pastors by Region

	Data Distribution*	REGION								
		New England	Middle Atlantic	South Atlantic	E-N Central	E-S Central	W-N Central	W-S Central	Mountain	Pacific
CHARACTERISTICS										
Average weekend worship attendance		82	123	162	114	143	106	155	220	121
Average church income		$164,348	$230,714	$310,587	$167,222	$241,043	$183,542	$217,821	-	$195,799
Average # of years employed		11	10	9	9	7	8	10	12	10
Average # of paid vacation days		26	23	19	21	18	22	19	21	22
% College graduate or higher		100%	89%	88%	89%	90%	94%	82%	89%	89%
% Who receive auto reimbursement/allowance		75%	69%	68%	63%	51%	79%	49%	54%	53%
% Ordained		100%	100%	100%	100%	98%	99%	100%	96%	99%
% Supervise one or more people		65%	77%	78%	69%	73%	67%	71%	79%	75%
Average % salary increase this year (for those who had an increase this year)		3.5%	4.1%	3.1%	5.3%	5.1%	4.2%	5.6%	4.5%	7.0%
COMPENSATION										
Base Salary	Median	$30,600	$36,000	$32,853	$32,000	$32,500	$34,000	$34,500	$37,100	$32,000
	Average	$35,117	$36,830	$36,293	$34,983	$35,276	$33,623	$33,623	$35,935	$30,480
Housing	Median	$24,660	$17,613	$19,750	$19,000	$13,000	$18,000	$18,000	$19,875	$24,000
	Average	$23,439	$18,076	$20,668	$18,608	$14,083	$16,572	$17,562	$20,461	$24,756
Parsonage	Median	$15,600	$11,200	$10,080	$7,000	-	$6,250	$10,560	-	$11,500
	Average	$16,688	$16,170	$11,677	$9,698	-	$6,504	$11,835	-	$11,213
Total Compensation	**Median**	**$53,600**	**$50,000**	**$52,573**	**$47,000**	**$42,000**	**$47,100**	**$48,000**	**$49,200**	**$55,000**
	Average	**$57,542**	**$53,574**	**$52,716**	**$49,319**	**$48,716**	**$46,898**	**$64,450**	**$50,807**	**$53,833**
BENEFITS										
Health Insurance	Median	$8,050	$11,127	$9,600	$9,109	$6,500	$8,460	$11,000	$10,870	$10,800
	Average	$10,447	$10,931	$9,687	$9,252	$7,194	$9,135	$10,555	$10,760	$10,752
Life Insurance	Median	-	$515	$530	$650	-	$900	$900	-	$600
	Average	-	$524	$756	$886	-	$1,364	$1,364	-	$643
Disability Insurance	Median	-	$300	$428	$340	-	$550	-	-	-
	Average	-	$574	$942	$575	-	$694	-	-	-
Retirement	Median	$6,000	$5,000	$5,650	$4,000	$4,050	$4,230	$4,740	$4,996	$6,000
	Average	$6,960	$5,587	$7,464	$5,348	$5,116	$4,788	$6,147	$5,386	$6,283
Continuing Education	Median	$600	$900	$1,000	$1,000	$1,000	$1,000	$1,200	-	$1,500
	Average	$967	$1,463	$1,572	$1,126	$1,416	$975	$2,207	-	$1,783
Total Benefits	**Median**	**$10,830**	**$12,000**	**$10,200**	**$8,450**	**$5,538**	**$8,050**	**$10,418**	**$11,000**	**$10,744**
	Average	**$12,624**	**$12,660**	**$12,574**	**$11,017**	**$8,900**	**$9,992**	**$12,651**	**$12,383**	**$12,494**
TOTAL COMPENSATION PLUS BENEFITS	**Median**	**$68,988**	**$62,750**	**$62,660**	**$55,700**	**$49,303**	**$54,781**	**$52,645**	**$57,985**	**$63,829**
	Average	**$67,660**	**$64,297**	**$63,628**	**$58,286**	**$56,002**	**$54,501**	**$57,656**	**$60,979**	**$62,490**
Number of Respondents		28	94	102	131	41	71	57	28	72

- Not enough response to provide meaningful data.

* For detailed description and definitions of Data Distribution (Median and Average), see chapter 1, Explanation of Data Distribution.

Table 5-5: Annual Compensation of Full-Time Solo Pastors by Education

	Data Distribution*	EDUCATION			
		Less than Bachelor	Bachelor	Master	Doctorate
CHARACTERISTICS					
Average weekend worship attendance		121	107	126	189
Average church income		$181,494	$173,521	$216,908	$315,640
Average # of years employed		12	10	9	10
Average # of paid vacation days		18	19	22	22
% College graduate or higher		0%	100%	100%	100%
% Who receive auto reimbursement/allowance		40%	52%	71%	68%
% Ordained		100%	99%	99%	100%
% Supervise one or more people		73%	62%	75%	82%
Average % salary increase this year (for those who had an increase this year)		8.4%	5.3%	4.1%	4.0%
COMPENSATION					
Base Salary	Median	$30,040	$29,500	$33,455	$34,125
	Average	$30,433	$31,901	$35,710	$39,402
Housing	Median	$15,000	$17,000	$19,550	$21,000
	Average	$16,508	$18,610	$19,277	$21,929
Parsonage	Median	$12,000	$8,250	$9,291	$10,000
	Average	$15,700	$9,000	$10,865	$14,133
Total Compensation	**Median**	**$40,010**	**$43,100**	**$51,398**	**$51,000**
	Average	**$44,444**	**$44,358**	**$52,887**	**$57,238**
BENEFITS					
Health Insurance	Median	$7,250	$7,500	$10,000	$10,200
	Average	$9,985	$8,533	$10,023	$10,968
Life Insurance	Median	-	-	$500	$646
	Average	-	-	$517	$1,080
Disability Insurance	Median	-	$428	$400	$440
	Average	-	$714	$688	$607
Retirement	Median	$2,900	$3,800	$5,000	$6,000
	Average	$4,094	$5,022	$5,956	$7,377
Continuing Education	Median	$1,000	$900	$1,000	$1,000
	Average	$1,117	$1,310	$1,379	$1,582
Total Benefits	**Median**	**$5,349**	**$7,750**	**$10,500**	**$13,873**
	Average	**$8,522**	**$9,829**	**$12,150**	**$13,914**
TOTAL COMPENSATION PLUS BENEFITS	**Median**	**$46,600**	**$50,193**	**$61,618**	**$61,734**
	Average	**$49,942**	**$51,122**	**$63,246**	**$68,672**
Number of Respondents		65	126	333	95

- Not enough response to provide meaningful data.

* For detailed description and definitions of Data Distribution (Median and Average), see chapter 1, Explanation of Data Distribution.

Table 5-6: Annual Compensation of Full-Time Solo Pastors by Years Employed

	Data Distribution*	YEARS EMPLOYED			
		Less than 6 years	6-10 years	11-15 years	Over 15 years
CHARACTERISTICS					
Average weekend worship attendance		118	107	187	144
Average church income		$204,842	$181,445	$270,402	$257,144
Average # of years employed		3	8	13	24
Average # of paid vacation days		20	20	21	24
% College graduate or higher		91%	89%	92%	85%
% Who receive auto reimbursement/allowance		65%	59%	65%	63%
% Ordained		100%	99%	99%	99%
% Supervise one or more people		75%	72%	72%	72%
Average % salary increase this year (for those who had an increase this year)		5.3%	3.7%	4.6%	3.9%
COMPENSATION					
Base Salary	Median	$34,000	$30,900	$33,000	$30,000
	Average	$35,486	$33,100	$37,495	$35,008
Housing	Median	$19,400	$18,000	$21,400	$18,450
	Average	$19,400	$17,290	$20,872	$19,904
Parsonage	Median	$9,581	$10,000	$6,500	$10,000
	Average	$11,123	$11,376	$9,791	$13,714
Total Compensation	**Median**	**$49,200**	**$48,150**	**$50,590**	**$47,750**
	Average	**$49,806**	**$49,619**	**$55,068**	**$52,413**
BENEFITS					
Health Insurance	Median	$9,950	$8,780	$10,170	$9,000
	Average	$9,839	$9,922	$10,594	$9,307
Life Insurance	Median	$556	$560	$550	$660
	Average	$703	$513	$908	$954
Disability Insurance	Median	$465	$350	$514	$354
	Average	$646	$508	$651	$1,060
Retirement	Median	$4,900	$4,800	$5,100	$4,850
	Average	$5,294	$6,141	$6,405	$6,518
Continuing Education	Median	$1,000	$600	$1,500	$1,000
	Average	$1,405	$1,234	$1,913	$999
Total Benefits	**Median**	**$9,944**	**$9,600**	**$10,493**	**$9,093**
	Average	**$11,097**	**$12,484**	**$12,760**	**$11,388**
TOTAL COMPENSATION PLUS BENEFITS	**Median**	**$56,427**	**$58,849**	**$62,795**	**$55,000**
	Average	**$58,164**	**$59,498**	**$66,638**	**$61,572**
Number of Respondents		269	136	89	126

- Not enough response to provide meaningful data.

* For detailed description and definitions of Data Distribution (Median and Average), see chapter 1, Explanation of Data Distribution.

Table 5-7: Annual Compensation of Full-Time Solo Pastors by Denomination

	Data Distribution*	DENOMINATION					
		Assemblies of God	Baptist	Independent/ Nondenom.	Lutheran	Methodist	Presby-terian
CHARACTERISTICS							
Average weekend worship attendance		167	128	159	111	127	110
Average church income		$302,369	$215,731	$199,721	$213,924	$244,796	$259,947
Average # of years employed		10	10	12	10	5	8
Average # of paid vacation days		17	19	19	26	23	24
% College graduate or higher		72%	91%	81%	100%	93%	100%
% Who receive auto reimbursement/allowance		45%	65%	38%	95%	75%	91%
% Ordained		100%	100%	99%	100%	100%	100%
% Supervise one or more people		79%	75%	63%	74%	91%	89%
Average % salary increase this year (for those who had an increase this year)		8.4%	5.3%	5.6%	3.6%	3.3%	3.8%
COMPENSATION							
Base Salary	Median	$31,000	$30,000	$29,000	$38,680	$44,000	$32,750
	Average	$33,036	$31,094	$33,596	$39,958	$45,012	$34,329
Housing	Median	$24,000	$18,000	$19,700	$20,000	$9,000	$22,500
	Average	$24,195	$17,886	$19,758	$20,732	$10,957	$23,140
Parsonage	Median	-	$8,000	$7,800	$11,724	$9,553	$9,800
	Average	-	$12,266	$9,630	$12,256	$11,059	$11,919
Total Compensation	**Median**	**$45,120**	**$46,910**	**$46,000**	**$58,620**	**$50,000**	**$50,500**
	Average	**$53,290**	**$51,216**	**$50,451**	**$56,646**	**$54,532**	**$54,392**
BENEFITS							
Health Insurance	Median	$7,250	$8,100	$7,650	$9,600	$12,000	$11,813
	Average	$9,817	$10,404	$8,146	$10,256	$11,745	$12,140
Life Insurance	Median	-	$538	$770	-	-	-
	Average	-	$803	$1,221	-	-	-
Disability Insurance	Median	-	$473	-	-	-	$428
	Average	-	$758	-	-	-	$437
Retirement	Median	$1,800	$4,000	$2,400	$6,000	$5,425	$6,103
	Average	$4,287	$4,748	$4,249	$7,195	$6,560	$7,788
Continuing Education	Median	-	$1,000	$1,100	$1,000	$750	$1,000
	Average	-	$1,403	$2,133	$1,205	$1,376	$1,513
Total Benefits	**Median**	**$7,700**	**$8,600**	**$7,375**	**$9,800**	**$17,400**	**$15,500**
	Average	**$10,607**	**$11,023**	**$8,859**	**$12,315**	**$16,047**	**$14,134**
TOTAL COMPENSATION PLUS BENEFITS	**Median**	**$53,700**	**$52,250**	**$50,700**	**$67,800**	**$70,000**	**$65,103**
	Average	**$60,240**	**$56,289**	**$56,732**	**$67,511**	**$70,035**	**$68,205**
Number of Respondents		29	150	97	39	59	44

- Not enough response to provide meaningful data.

* For detailed description and definitions of Data Distribution (Median and Average), see chapter 1, Explanation of Data Distribution.

Table 5-8: Annual Compensation of Full-Time Solo Pastors by Gender

	Data Distribution*	GENERENDER	
		Male	Female
CHARACTERISTICS			
Average weekend worship attendance		137	75
Average church income		$227,211	$161,897
Average # of years employed		10	6
Average # of paid vacation days		21	25
% College graduate or higher		90%	88%
% Who receive auto reimbursement/allowance		63%	68%
% Ordained		99%	100%
% Supervise one or more people		72%	80%
Average % salary increase this year (for those who had an increase this year)		4.6%	3.5%
COMPENSATION			
Base Salary	Median	$32,852	$34,500
	Average	$35,315	$33,868
Housing	Median	$19,800	$14,000
	Average	$19,666	$14,796
Parsonage	Median	$9,000	$12,000
	Average	$11,224	$12,866
Total Compensation	**Median**	**$50,000**	**$46,000**
	Average	**$51,575**	**$46,476**
BENEFITS			
Health Insurance	Median	$9,600	$9,600
	Average	$9,946	$9,446
Life Insurance	Median	$556	-
	Average	$736	-
Disability Insurance	Median	$400	$669
	Average	$701	$949
Retirement	Median	$4,800	$5,700
	Average	$5,927	$5,734
Continuing Education	Median	$1,000	$900
	Average	$1,469	$866
Total Benefits	**Median**	**$10,000**	**$8,100**
	Average	**$11,779**	**$11,324**
TOTAL COMPENSATION PLUS BENEFITS	**Median**	**$57,940**	**$56,434**
	Average	**$60,911**	**$55,952**
Number of Respondents		572	50

- Not enough response to provide meaningful data.

* For detailed description and definitions of Data Distribution (Median and Average), see chapter 1, Explanation of Data Distribution.

Table 5-9: Annual Compensation of Part-Time Solo Pastors by Church Income

	Data Distribution*	CHURCH INCOME				
		$250K & Under	$251-$500K	$501-$750K	$751K-$1M	Over 1 Million
CHARACTERISTICS						
Average weekend worship attendance		52	-	-	-	-
Average church income		$67,255	-	-	-	-
Average # of years employed		6	-	-	-	-
Average # of paid vacation days		14	-	-	-	-
% College graduate or higher		84%	-	-	-	-
% Who receive auto reimbursement/allowance		35%	-	-	-	-
% Ordained		100%	-	-	-	-
% Supervise one or more people		49%	-	-	-	-
Average % salary increase (for those who had an increase) this year		7.2%	-	-	-	-
HOURLY RATE						
Base Rate	Average	$15	-	-	-	-
COMPENSATION						
Base Salary	Median	$12,904	-	-	-	-
	Average	$14,643	-	-	-	-
Housing	Median	$10,000	-	-	-	-
	Average	$11,051	-	-	-	-
Parsonage	Median	$6,500	-	-	-	-
	Average	$8,745	-	-	-	-
Total Compensation	**Median**	**$15,730**	**-**	**-**	**-**	**-**
	Average	**$19,670**	**-**	**-**	**-**	**-**
BENEFITS						
Health Insurance	Median	$5,796	-	-	-	-
	Average	$5,938	-	-	-	-
Life Insurance	Median	-	-	-	-	-
	Average	-	-	-	-	-
Disability Insurance	Median	-	-	-	-	-
	Average	-	-	-	-	-
Retirement	Median	$2,450	-	-	-	-
	Average	$2,905	-	-	-	-
Continuing Education	Median	$700	-	-	-	-
	Average	$977	-	-	-	-
Total Benefits	**Median**	**$2,800**	**-**	**-**	**-**	**-**
	Average	**$4,602**	**-**	**-**	**-**	**-**
TOTAL COMPENSATION PLUS BENEFITS	**Median**	**$16,870**	**-**	**-**	**-**	**-**
	Average	**$21,301**	**-**	**-**	**-**	**-**
Number of Respondents		110	2	0	0	0

- Not enough response to provide meaningful data.

* For detailed description and definitions of Data Distribution (Median and Average), see chapter 1, Explanation of Data Distribution.

Table 5-10: Annual Compensation of Part-Time Solo Pastors by Worship Attendance

	Data Distribution*	WORSHIP ATTENDANCE					
		100 or less	101-300	301-500	501-750	751-1,000	Over 1,000
CHARACTERISTICS							
Average weekend worship attendance		42	186	-	-	-	-
Average church income		$58,108	$217,100	-	-	-	-
Average # of years employed		5	11	-	-	-	-
Average # of paid vacation days		14	11	-	-	-	-
% College graduate or higher		81%	100%	-	-	-	-
% Who receive auto reimbursement/allowance		35%	30%	-	-	-	-
% Ordained		100%	100%	-	-	-	-
% Supervise one or more people		47%	80%	-	-	-	-
Average % salary increase (for those who had an increase) this year		7.1%	-	-	-	-	-
HOURLY RATE							
Base Rate	Average	$15	$17	-	-	-	-
COMPENSATION							
Base Salary	Median	$12,000	$27,200	-	-	-	-
	Average	$13,067	$24,560	-	-	-	-
Housing	Median	$10,000	-	-	-	-	-
	Average	$10,655	-	-	-	-	-
Parsonage	Median	$5,500	-	-	-	-	-
	Average	$8,223	-	-	-	-	-
Total Compensation	**Median**	**$14,400**	**$46,000**	-	-	-	-
	Average	**$17,734**	**$38,740**	-	-	-	-
BENEFITS							
Health Insurance	Median	$5,796	-	-	-	-	-
	Average	$5,938	-	-	-	-	-
Life Insurance	Median	-	-	-	-	-	-
	Average	-	-	-	-	-	-
Disability	Median	-	-	-	-	-	-
	Average	-	-	-	-	-	-
Retirement	Median	$2,400	-	-	-	-	-
	Average	$2,734	-	-	-	-	-
Continuing Education	Median	$700	-	-	-	-	-
	Average	$977	-	-	-	-	-
Total Benefits	**Median**	**$2,600**	-	-	-	-	-
	Average	**$4,555**	-	-	-	-	-
TOTAL COMPENSATION PLUS BENEFITS	**Median**	**$15,550**	**$46,000**	-	-	-	-
	Average	**$19,400**	**$39,390**	-	-	-	-
Number of Respondents		105	10	1	0	0	0

- Not enough response to provide meaningful data.

* For detailed description and definitions of Data Distribution (Median and Average), see chapter 1, Explanation of Data Distribution.

Table 5-11: Annual Compensation of Part-Time Solo Pastors by Church Setting

	Data Distribution*	CHURCH SETTING			
		Metro-politan city	Suburb of large city	Small town or rural city	Farming area
CHARACTERISTICS					
Average weekend worship attendance		65	73	53	44
Average church income		$90,912	$90,795	$65,060	$44,495
Average # of years employed		7	7	5	5
Average # of paid vacation days		13	17	14	12
% College graduate or higher		72%	95%	88%	67%
% Who receive auto reimbursement/allowance		24%	29%	39%	44%
% Ordained		100%	100%	100%	100%
% Supervise one or more people		67%	57%	45%	33%
Average % salary increase (for those who had an increase) this year		-	-	6.6%	-
HOURLY RATE					
Base Rate	Average	$15	$14	$16	$16
COMPENSATION					
Base Salary	Median	$13,250	$15,860	$12,000	$9,600
	Average	$16,060	$16,171	$14,586	$8,841
Housing	Median	$11,000	$14,400	$8,000	$10,000
	Average	$12,080	$17,508	$9,784	$7,958
Parsonage	Median	-	-	-	-
	Average	-	-	-	-
Total Compensation	**Median**	**$12,000**	**$21,000**	**$19,150**	**$12,000**
	Average	**$20,393**	**$23,872**	**$19,481**	**$13,499**
BENEFITS					
Health Insurance	Median	-	$7,200	$6,000	-
	Average	-	$7,466	$6,016	-
Life Insurance	Median	-	-	-	-
	Average	-	-	-	-
Disability Insurance	Median	-	-	-	-
	Average	-	-	-	-
Retirement	Median	-	-	$2,500	-
	Average	-	-	$3,034	-
Continuing Education	Median	-	-	$1,000	-
	Average	-	-	$1,182	-
Total Benefits	**Median**	-	**$7,200**	**$2,800**	-
	Average	-	**$7,303**	**$4,939**	-
TOTAL COMPENSATION PLUS BENEFITS	**Median**	**$13,700**	**$24,000**	**$20,633**	**$12,000**
	Average	**$21,209**	**$27,524**	**$21,084**	**$14,078**
Number of Respondents		25	22	51	18

- Not enough response to provide meaningful data.

* For detailed description and definitions of Data Distribution (Median and Average), see chapter 1, Explanation of Data Distribution.

Table 5-12: Annual Compensation of Part-Time Solo Pastors by Region

	Data Distribution*	REGION								
		New England	Middle Atlantic	South Atlantic	E-N Central	E-S Central	W-N Central	W-S Central	Mountain	Pacific
CHARACTERISTICS										
Average weekend worship attendance		41	104	38	44	84	50	48	-	49
Average church income		$60,460	$88,500	$52,745	$63,065	$99,735	$61,110	$66,333	-	$70,715
Average # of years employed		6	4	5	4	8	4	6	-	7
Average # of paid vacation days		14	19	14	18	10	10	8	-	13
% College graduate or higher		70%	92%	85%	88%	93%	-	78%	-	86%
% Who receive auto reimbursement/allowance		20%	46%	40%	38%	53%	38%	0%	-	23%
% Ordained		100%	100%	100%	100%	100%	100%	100%	-	100%
% Supervise one or more people		33%	54%	55%	46%	73%	-	56%	-	43%
Average % salary increase (for those who had an increase) this year		3.5%	5.2%	-	-	4.0%	-	-	-	-
HOURLY RATE										
Base Rate	Average	$14	$14	$20	$16	$15	-	-	-	-
COMPENSATION										
Base Salary	Median	$16,870	$15,600	$9,540	$13,125	$13,680	-	-	-	$9,480
	Average	$16,163	$16,067	$10,593	$14,704	$17,959	-	-	-	$8,551
Housing	Median	-	$14,064	$7,000	$12,000	$10,000	-	-	-	$12,000
	Average	-	$13,663	$7,875	$11,361	$11,640	-	-	-	$13,305
Parsonage	Median	-	-	-	$10,250	-	-	-	-	-
	Average	-	-	-	$10,169	-	-	-	-	-
Total Compensation	**Median**	**$22,500**	**$23,904**	**$9,540**	**$19,150**	**$21,350**	**$13,500**	**$14,400**	**-**	**$12,000**
	Average	**$22,747**	**$23,523**	**$12,482**	**$23,707**	**$25,442**	**$18,270**	**$14,389**	**-**	**$14,939**
BENEFITS										
Health Insurance	Median	-	-	-	-	-	-	-	-	-
	Average	-	-	-	-	-	-	-	-	-
Life Insurance	Median	-	-	-	-	-	-	-	-	-
	Average	-	-	-	-	-	-	-	-	-
Disability Insurance	Median	-	-	-	-	-	-	-	-	-
	Average	-	-	-	-	-	-	-	-	-
Retirement	Median	-	-	-	-	-	-	-	-	-
	Average	-	-	-	-	-	-	-	-	-
Continuing Education	Median	-	-	-	-	-	-	-	-	-
	Average	-	-	-	-	-	-	-	-	-
Total Benefits	**Median**	**-**	**-**	**-**	**$1,750**	**-**	**-**	**-**	**-**	**-**
	Average	**-**	**-**	**-**	**$4,357**	**-**	**-**	**-**	**-**	**-**
TOTAL COMPENSATION PLUS BENEFITS	**Median**	**$24,900**	**$31,747**	**$10,800**	**$20,425**	**$24,097**	**$13,835**	**$15,600**	**-**	**$12,110**
	Average	**$24,377**	**$28,247**	**$14,069**	**$25,104**	**$26,720**	**$18,954**	**$15,189**	**-**	**$16,013**
Number of Respondents		10	13	20	24	15	8	9	3	14

- Not enough response to provide meaningful data.

* For detailed description and definitions of Data Distribution (Median and Average), see chapter 1, Explanation of Data Distribution.

Table 5-13: Annual Compensation of Part-Time Solo Pastors by Education

	Data Distribution*	EDUCATION			
		Less than Bachelor	Bachelor	Master	Doctorate
CHARACTERISTICS					
Average weekend worship attendance		37	61	58	75
Average church income		$47,069	$72,762	$73,066	$94,878
Average # of years employed		5	6	4	9
Average # of paid vacation days		9	13	16	15
% College graduate or higher		0%	100%	100%	100%
% Who receive auto reimbursement/allowance		30%	24%	42%	41%
% Ordained		100%	100%	100%	100%
% Supervise one or more people		29%	52%	48%	72%
Average % salary increase (for those who had an increase) this year		-	-	6.1%	-
HOURLY RATE					
Base Rate	Average	$17	$15	$15	$15
COMPENSATION					
Base Salary	Median	$9,000	$15,300	$12,000	$15,476
	Average	$11,265	$13,538	$13,691	$19,489
Housing	Median	$8,275	$10,500	$13,000	$10,000
	Average	$8,975	$11,307	$12,876	$11,973
Parsonage	Median	-	-	-	-
	Average	-	-	-	-
Total Compensation	**Median**	**$12,000**	**$15,600**	**$18,825**	**$20,500**
	Average	**$12,823**	**$18,757**	**$21,124**	**$25,056**
BENEFITS					
Health Insurance	Median	-	-	-	-
	Average	-	-	-	-
Life Insurance	Median	-	-	-	-
	Average	-	-	-	-
Disability Insurance	Median	-	-	-	-
	Average	-	-	-	-
Retirement	Median	-	-	$2,500	-
	Average	-	-	$3,288	-
Continuing Education	Median	-	-	$700	-
	Average	-	-	$873	-
Total Benefits	**Median**	-	**$1,450**	**$3,184**	-
	Average	-	**$2,800**	**$5,688**	-
TOTAL COMPENSATION PLUS BENEFITS	**Median**	**$12,000**	**$15,600**	**$21,650**	**$26,400**
	Average	**$13,303**	**$19,064**	**$23,970**	**$27,650**
Number of Respondents		20	33	45	18

- Not enough response to provide meaningful data.

* For detailed description and definitions of Data Distribution (Median and Average), see chapter 1, Explanation of Data Distribution.

Table 5-14: Annual Compensation of Part-Time Solo Pastors by Years Employed

	Data Distribution*	YEARS EMPLOYED			
		Less than 6 years	6-10 years	11-15 years	Over 15 years
CHARACTERISTICS					
Average weekend worship attendance		55	54	66	-
Average church income		$66,015	$62,872	$91,666	-
Average # of years employed		3	8	12	-
Average # of paid vacation days		15	12	-	-
% College graduate or higher		80%	81%	90%	-
% Who receive auto reimbursement/allowance		41%	33%	0%	-
% Ordained		100%	100%	100%	-
% Supervise one or more people		44%	60%	70%	-
Average % salary increase (for those who had an increase) this year		7.0%	-	-	-
HOURLY RATE					
Base Rate	Average	$15	$17	-	-
COMPENSATION					
Base Salary	Median	$12,000	$15,300	$15,000	-
	Average	$13,054	$15,656	$13,171	-
Housing	Median	$9,000	$12,000	-	-
	Average	$10,950	$13,197	-	-
Parsonage	Median	$4,500	-	-	-
	Average	$7,217	-	-	-
Total Compensation	**Median**	**$14,232**	**$17,613**	**$24,250**	**-**
	Average	**$18,331**	**$20,379**	**$23,682**	**-**
BENEFITS					
Health Insurance	Median	$6,725	-	-	-
	Average	$5,494	-	-	-
Life Insurance	Median	-	-	-	-
	Average	-	-	-	-
Disability Insurance	Median	-	-	-	-
	Average	-	-	-	-
Retirement	Median	$2,450	-	-	-
	Average	$2,807	-	-	-
Continuing Education	Median	$850	-	-	-
	Average	$1,040	-	-	-
Total Benefits	**Median**	**$3,000**	**-**	**-**	**-**
	Average	**$4,347**	**-**	**-**	**-**
TOTAL COMPENSATION PLUS BENEFITS	**Median**	**$15,264**	**$18,813**	**$24,250**	**-**
	Average	**$19,997**	**$22,992**	**$24,402**	**-**
Number of Respondents		75	21	10	6

- Not enough response to provide meaningful data.

* For detailed description and definitions of Data Distribution (Median and Average), see chapter 1, Explanation of Data Distribution.

Table 5-15: Annual Compensation of Part-Time Solo Pastors by Denomination

	Data Distribution*	DENOMINATION					
		Assemblies of God	Baptist	Independent/ Nondenom.	Lutheran	Methodist	Presby- terian
CHARACTERISTICS							
Average weekend worship attendance		-	67	38	-	47	36
Average church income		-	$78,400	$54,835	-	$71,633	$62,875
Average # of years employed		-	5	7	-	3	4
Average # of paid vacation days		-	12	13	-	21	14
% College graduate or higher		-	87%	75%	-	87%	100%
% Who receive auto reimbursement/allowance		-	35%	15%	-	53%	57%
% Ordained		-	100%	100%	-	100%	100%
% Supervise one or more people		-	63%	37%	-	50%	50%
Average % salary increase (for those who had an increase) this year		-	6.3%	-	-	-	-
HOURLY RATE							
Base Rate	Average	-	$14	$17	-	$16	-
COMPENSATION							
Base Salary	Median	-	$11,000	$12,500	-	$20,000	$10,250
	Average	-	$11,788	$13,529	-	$17,872	$10,107
Housing	Median	-	$14,000	$14,400	-	$4,750	-
	Average	-	$14,386	$14,986	-	$4,702	-
Parsonage	Median	-	-	-	-	-	-
	Average	-	-	-	-	-	-
Total Compensation	**Median**	-	**$17,483**	**$14,700**	-	**$23,904**	**$11,750**
	Average	-	**$17,974**	**$21,532**	-	**$23,273**	**$12,563**
BENEFITS							
Health Insurance	Median	-	-	-	-	-	-
	Average	-	-	-	-	-	-
Life Insurance	Median	-	-	-	-	-	-
	Average	-	-	-	-	-	-
Disability Insurance	Median	-	-	-	-	-	-
	Average	-	-	-	-	-	-
Retirement	Median	-	-	-	-	$1,455	-
	Average	-	-	-	-	$1,876	-
Continuing Education	Median	-	-	-	-	$1,000	-
	Average	-	-	-	-	$1,339	-
Total Benefits	**Median**	-	**$4,800**	-	-	**$2,000**	-
	Average	-	**$4,863**	-	-	**$3,383**	-
TOTAL COMPENSATION PLUS BENEFITS	**Median**	-	**$20,250**	**$14,400**	-	**$28,000**	**$12,250**
	Average	-	**$19,432**	**$20,923**	-	**$26,206**	**$16,844**
Number of Respondents		5	31	20	4	15	8

- Not enough response to provide meaningful data.

* For detailed description and definitions of Data Distribution (Median and Average), see chapter 1, Explanation of Data Distribution.

Table 5-16: Annual Compensation of Part-Time Solo Pastors by Gender

	Data Distribution*	GENDER	
		Male	Female
CHARACTERISTICS			
Average weekend worship attendance		63	35
Average church income		$76,947	$45,807
Average # of years employed		6	4
Average # of paid vacation days		13	15
% College graduate or higher		84%	75%
% Who receive auto reimbursement/allowance		33%	38%
% Ordained		100%	100%
% Supervise one or more people		51%	53%
Average % salary increase (for those who had an increase) this year		7.1%	-
HOURLY RATE			
Base Rate	Average	$16	$14
COMPENSATION			
Base Salary	Median	$13,000	$8,400
	Average	$14,750	$10,652
Housing	Median	$13,000	$3,600
	Average	$13,197	$4,217
Parsonage	Median	$5,250	-
	Average	$7,556	-
Total Compensation	**Median**	**$17,180**	**$9,600**
	Average	**$20,433**	**$14,072**
BENEFITS			
Health Insurance	Median	$5,396	-
	Average	$5,820	-
Life Insurance	Median	-	-
	Average	-	-
Disability Insurance	Median	-	-
	Average	-	-
Retirement	Median	$2,500	-
	Average	$3,110	-
Continuing Education	Median	$650	-
	Average	$898	-
Total Benefits	**Median**	**$3,084**	**$2,000**
	Average	**$5,082**	**$2,406**
TOTAL COMPENSATION PLUS BENEFITS	**Median**	**$19,500**	**$11,600**
	Average	**$21,939**	**$15,515**
Number of Respondents		97	16

- Not enough response to provide meaningful data.

* For detailed description and definitions of Data Distribution (Median and Average), see chapter 1, Explanation of Data Distribution.

Full-Time Solo Pastor Worksheet

	Enter your church data below	The 2014–2015 Compensation Handbook for Church Staff		Enter *Compensation Handbook* data below			
				Highest 25%	Median	Lowest 25%	Average
Church Income	$	Table 5-1	page 41	$	$	$	$
Worship Attendance		Table 5-2	page 42	n/a	$	n/a	$
Church Setting (metro, suburb, small town, or farming area)		Table 5-3	page 43	n/a	$	n/a	$
Region		Table 5-4	page 44	n/a	$	n/a	$
Person's Education		Table 5-5	page 45	n/a	$	n/a	$
Years Employed		Table 5-6	page 46	n/a	$	n/a	$
Denomination (if applicable)		Table 5-7	page 47	n/a	$	n/a	$

Looking at the table and page number references indicated in the *2014–2015 Compensation Handbook for Church Staff* columns above, locate the appropriate range for your church. Refer to the instructions below for step-by-step help.

FILLING OUT THE WORKSHEET

1. Fill in the gray boxes under *Enter your church data* with your church demographic information as follows:

   ▶ **Income** (Total annual church budget in past year)
   ▶ **Worship attendance** (Number of people, including children, who attend all weekend services)
   ▶ **Church setting** (Metropolitan city, suburb of large city, small town or rural city, or farming area)

▶ **Region** (Locate your state's region in the appendix on page 346.)
▶ **Education** (Highest level of education: less than bachelor, bachelor, master, or doctorate)

2. Use Table 5-1 (page 41) in your *2014–2015 Compensation Handbook for Church Staff* to enter data pertinent to your church. In the heading (top row), locate your church **income** from the five available ranges. Follow that column to the bottom rows, and copy the *Highest 25%*, *Median*, *Lowest 25%*, and *Average* amounts onto your worksheet.

3. Use Table 5-2 (page 42) on your *2014–2015 Compensation Handbook for Church Staff* to enter data pertinent to your church. In the heading (top row), locate your church's

worship attendance from the six available ranges. Follow that column to the bottom rows, and copy the *Median* and *Average* amounts onto your worksheet.

4. Use Table 5-3 (page 43) on your *2014–2015 Compensation Handbook for Church Staff* to enter data pertinent to your church. In the heading (top row), choose the **church setting** that best describes your church. Follow that column to the bottom rows, and copy the *Median* and *Average* amounts onto your worksheet.

5. Use Table 5-4 (page 44) on your *2014–2015 Compensation Handbook for Church Staff* to enter data pertinent to your church. In the heading (top row), look for the **region** where your church is located. Follow that column to the bottom rows, and copy the *Median* and *Average* amounts onto your worksheet.

6. Use Table 5-5 (page 45) on your *2014–2015 Compensation Handbook for Church Staff* to enter data pertinent to your Solo Pastor. In the heading (top row), look for **your Solo Pastor's highest level of education**. Follow that column to the bottom rows, and copy the *Median* and *Average* amounts onto your worksheet.

7. Use Table 5-6 (page 46) on your *2014–2015 Compensation Handbook for Church Staff* to enter data pertinent to your Solo Pastor. In the heading (top row), locate the **number of years your Solo Pastor has been employed**. Follow that column to the bottom rows, and copy the *Median* and *Average* amounts onto your worksheet.

8. Use Table 5-7 (page 47) on your *2014–2015 Compensation Handbook for Church Staff* to enter data pertinent to your church. In the heading (top row), look for **your church's denominational affiliation**. Follow that column to the bottom rows, and copy the *Median* and *Average* amounts onto your worksheet. If your church is not affiliated with a denomination, leave this section blank.

DETERMINING COMPENSATION

This tool will not provide you with a single compensation amount but rather with a range of values to help you determine the compensation appropriate to your situation.

1. Look at the values in the shaded *Median* column. Circle the **lowest** and the **highest** values. **This is the range of the median compensation plus benefits for churches similar to yours.**

2. For a variety of reasons, compensation plus benefits may be higher or lower than the range established in this table. Income and attendance are two significant factors affecting church compensation packages. If church income or attendance skews higher, you might want to consider moving toward or above the higher end of the range. Likewise, if church income or attendance skews lower, you may consider moving the package toward or below the lower end of the range.

3. Examine additional variables that might impact the compensation package you offer, such as years of service, education, and church setting.

4. Determine other circumstances unique to your situation, such as cost of living in your area, theological beliefs, pastoral performance, financial needs, the local economy, personal motivation, congregational goals, and others.

5. You now have a compensation package range based on the *2014–2015 Compensation Handbook*. Since each church and position are unique, your final compensation package will be based on additional factors unique to your situation.

Part-Time Solo Pastor Worksheet

	Enter your church data below	The 2014–2015 Compensation Handbook for Church Staff		Enter *Compensation Handbook* data below			
				Highest 25%	Median	Lowest 25%	Average
Church Income	$	Table 5-9	page 49	$	$	$	$
Worship Attendance		Table 5-10	page 50	n/a	$	n/a	$
Church Setting (metro, suburb, small town, or farming area)		Table 5-11	page 51	n/a	$	n/a	$
Region		Table 5-12	page 52	n/a	$	n/a	$
Person's Education		Table 5-13	page 53	n/a	$	n/a	$
Years Employed		Table 5-14	page 54	n/a	$	n/a	$
Denomination (if applicable)		Table 5-15	page 55	n/a	$	n/a	$

Looking at the table and page number references indicated in the ***2014–2015 Compensation Handbook for Church Staff*** columns above, locate the appropriate range for your church. Refer to the instructions below for step-by-step help.

FILLING OUT THE WORKSHEET

1. Fill in the gray boxes under ***Enter your church data*** with your church demographic information as follows:

    ▶ **Income** (Total annual church budget in past year)
    ▶ **Worship attendance** (Number of people, including children, who attend all weekend services)
    ▶ **Church setting** (Metropolitan city, suburb of large city, small town or rural city, or farming area)

    ▶ **Region** (Locate your state's region in the appendix on page 346.)
    ▶ **Education** (Highest level of education: less than bachelor, bachelor, master, or doctorate)

2. Use Table 5-9 (page 49) in your *2014–2015 Compensation Handbook for Church Staff* to enter data pertinent to your church. In the heading (top row), locate your church **income** from the five available ranges. Follow that column to the bottom rows, and copy the ***Highest 25%***, ***Median***, ***Lowest 25%***, and ***Average*** amounts onto your worksheet.

3. Use Table 5-10 (page 50) on your *2014–2015 Compensation Handbook for Church Staff* to enter data pertinent to your church. In the heading (top row), locate your church's

worship attendance from the six available ranges. Follow that column to the bottom rows, and copy the *Median* and *Average* amounts onto your worksheet.

4. Use Table 5-11 (page 51) on your *2014–2015 Compensation Handbook for Church Staff* to enter data pertinent to your church. In the heading (top row), choose the **church setting** that best describes your church. Follow that column to the bottom rows, and copy the *Median* and *Average* amounts onto your worksheet.

5. Use Table 5-12 (page 52) on your *2014–2015 Compensation Handbook for Church Staff* to enter data pertinent to your church. In the heading (top row), look for the **region** where your church is located. Follow that column to the bottom rows, and copy the *Median* and *Average* amounts onto your worksheet.

6. Use Table 5-13 (page 53) on your *2014–2015 Compensation Handbook for Church Staff* to enter data pertinent to your Solo Pastor. In the heading (top row), look for **your Solo Pastor's highest level of education**. Follow that column to the bottom rows, and copy the *Median* and *Average* amounts onto your worksheet.

7. Use Table 5-14 (page 54) on your *2014–2015 Compensation Handbook for Church Staff* to enter data pertinent to your Solo Pastor. In the heading (top row), locate the **number of years your Solo Pastor has been employed**. Follow that column to the bottom rows, and copy the *Median* and *Average* amounts onto your worksheet.

8. Use Table 5-15 (page 55) on your *2014–2015 Compensation Handbook for Church Staff* to enter data pertinent to your church. In the heading (top row), look for **your church's denominational affiliation**. Follow that column

to the bottom rows, and copy the *Median* and *Average* amounts onto your worksheet. If your church is not affiliated with a denomination, leave this section blank.

DETERMINING COMPENSATION

This tool will not provide you with a single compensation amount but rather with a range of values to help you determine the compensation appropriate to your situation.

1. Look at the values in the shaded *Median* column. Circle the **lowest** and the **highest** values. **This is the range of the median compensation plus benefits for churches similar to yours.**

2. For a variety of reasons, compensation plus benefits may be higher or lower than the range established in this table. Income and attendance are two significant factors affecting church compensation packages. If church income or attendance skews higher, you might want to consider moving toward or above the higher end of the range. Likewise, if church income or attendance skews lower, you may consider moving the package toward or below the lower end of the range.

3. Examine additional variables that might impact the compensation package you offer, such as years of service, education, and church setting.

4. Determine other circumstances unique to your situation, such as cost of living in your area, theological beliefs, pastoral performance, financial needs, the local economy, personal motivation, congregational goals, and others.

5. You now have a compensation package range based on the *2014–2015 Compensation Handbook*. Since each church and position are unique, your final compensation package will be based on additional factors unique to your situation.

6

EXECUTIVE/ ADMINISTRATIVE PASTORS

Employment Profile

Executive/Administrative Pastors are those who handle ministry staff supervision, management, and development. More than nine in 10 Executive/Administrative Pastors who responded to our survey serve full-time. For this reason, we do not provide part-time data for this position.

Nearly nine in 10 Executive/Administrative Pastors are ordained and male, and 96% are employed by the church. On average, they've been in their current positions for seven years. More than five in 10 have graduate degrees.

The chart below provides a demographic profile of this sample.

	Full-Time	Part-Time
Number of respondents	**291**	**27**
Ordained	87%	-
Average years employed	7	-
Male	88%	-
Female	12%	-
Self-employed (receives 1099)	4%	-
Church employee (receives W-2)	96%	-
High school diploma	5%	-
Associate degree	6%	-
Bachelor's degree	34%	-
Master's degree	44%	-
Doctoral degree	10%	-

Total Compensation plus Benefits Package Analysis

The following analyses are based on data in the tables you will find later in this chapter. The tables show compensation plus benefits data for Executive/Administrative Pastors who serve full-time and are presented according to church income, church attendance, church setting, region, education, years employed, denomination, and gender. In this way, Executive or Administrative Pastors' compensation plus benefits can be analyzed and compared from a variety of useful perspectives.

The total compensation plus benefits amount includes the base salary; housing allowance and/or parsonage amount; health, life, and disability insurance payments; retirement contribution; and educational funds.

A worksheet at the end of this chapter is provided to help you apply the data to your church's situation.

Similar to full-time Senior Pastors, the full-time Executive/Administrative Pastor is one of the highest paid positions with comprehensive benefits packages in the local church. More than three-fourths of Executive/Administrative Pastors receive housing allowances. Seven in 10 also receive health insurance, and six in 10 receive retirement benefits.

Six in 10 received salary increases, representing a 16-percentage-point increase over respondents who reported receiving salary increase in the last study.

Compensation Plus Benefits	Full-Time	Part-Time
Base Salary	100%	-
Housing	77%	-
Parsonage	2%	-
Health Insurance*	71%	-
Life Insurance*	34%	-
Disability Insurance*	30%	-
Retirement	59%	-
Continuing Education	32%	-
Received salary increase	60%	-
Received paid vacation	99%	-
Received auto reimbursement/allowance	44%	-

Only those reporting individual premiums for Health, Life, or Disability (not total insurance premiums) are included.

KEY POINTS

* Two-thirds of full-time Executive/ Administrative Pastors serve in churches with an income of over $1,000,000. Forty-two percent serve in churches with a worship attendance of over 1,000.

* In general, as worship attendance increases, compensation and benefits for full-time Executive/Administrative Pastors also increase.

* Nearly half of full-time Executive/Administrative Pastors serve in churches set in a suburb of a large city. They generally receive higher compensation and benefits packages compared to those in other settings.

* Full-time male Executive/Administrative Pastors receive 46% more in compensation plus benefits than female Executive/Administrative Pastors.

Compensation & Benefits: National Averages for Full-Time Executive/Administrative Pastors*	
2000	
2001	
2002	
2003	
2004	
2005	
2006	
2007	$81,279
2008	$79,625
2009	$77,972
2011	$78,938
2013	$86,999**

No historical data available before 2007.

** *The above trend is made available for your reference only. In addition to looking at this overall data, please refer to the detailed tables using your church's income, attendance, setting, region, and denomination as well as the person's education, gender, and years employed for guidance in compensating this position.*

Table 6-1: Annual Compensation of Full-Time Executive/Administrative Pastors by Church Income

CHARACTERISTICS	Data Distribution*	CHURCH INCOME				
		$250K & Under	$251-$500K	$501-$750K	$751K-$1M	Over $1 Million
Average weekend worship attendance		355	217	430	568	1,677
Average church income		$170,214	$381,719	$673,403	$892,547	$2,944,988
Average # of years employed		4	8	6	7	8
Average # of paid vacation days		18	18	18	19	20
% College graduate or higher		93%	73%	88%	91%	89%
% Who receive auto reimbursement/allowance		29%	27%	42%	39%	48%
% Ordained		86%	80%	94%	86%	86%
% Supervise one or more people		100%	93%	94%	94%	97%
Average % salary increase (for those who had an increase) this year		-	4.7%	4.1%	4.5%	4.1%
COMPENSATION						
Base Salary	Highest 25%	$46,145	$48,000	$51,000	$53,000	$72,000
	Median	$38,500	$35,000	$43,000	$39,303	$53,900
	Lowest 25%	$13,500	$20,000	$36,500	$31,500	$41,366
	Average	$33,507	$31,612	$41,894	$43,535	$58,217
Housing	Highest 25%	-	$24,000	$28,000	$28,800	$40,000
	Median	-	$20,000	$19,000	$25,000	$30,000
	Lowest 25%	-	$3,600	$13,000	$20,000	$24,770
	Average	-	$16,293	$19,826	$26,238	$32,297
Parsonage	Highest 25%	-	-	-	-	-
	Median	-	-	-	-	-
	Lowest 25%	-	-	-	-	-
	Average	-	-	-	-	-
Total Compensation	**Highest 25%**	**$60,057**	**$53,780**	**$73,000**	**$74,333**	**$98,000**
	Median	**$44,645**	**$44,700**	**$62,000**	**$64,450**	**$80,000**
	Lowest 25%	**$38,500**	**$35,950**	**$49,400**	**$56,076**	**$65,000**
	Average	**$49,128**	**$46,522**	**$61,112**	**$66,128**	**$85,532**
BENEFITS						
Health Insurance	Highest 25%	$11,532	$13,000	$14,000	$12,000	$14,000
	Median	$5,500	$4,416	$10,600	$9,885	$11,082
	Lowest 25%	$3,500	$2,400	$7,000	$4,900	$6,341
	Average	$6,914	$6,944	$10,271	$8,828	$11,101
Life Insurance	Highest 25%	-	-	-	$654	$500
	Median	-	-	-	$250	$300
	Lowest 25%	-	-	-	$125	$132
	Average	-	-	-	$408	$549
Disability Insurance	Highest 25%	-	-	$800	-	$636
	Median	-	-	$490	-	$409
	Lowest 25%	-	-	$350	-	$197
	Average	-	-	$833	-	$482
Retirement	Highest 25%	-	$5,360	$4,050	$3,817	$7,200
	Median	-	$3,939	$2,882	$2,475	$4,250
	Lowest 25%	-	$2,168	$1,525	$1,914	$2,723
	Average	-	$3,754	$3,021	$3,368	$5,446
Continuing Education	Highest 25%	-	-	$1,500	$1,500	$2,700
	Median	-	-	$750	$1,000	$1,800
	Lowest 25%	-	-	$375	$750	$1,000
	Average	-	-	$1,160	$1,447	$2,095
Total Benefits	**Highest 25%**	**$14,300**	**$14,325**	**$16,000**	**$13,351**	**$20,100**
	Median	**$6,500**	**$7,289**	**$9,600**	**$9,519**	**$13,035**
	Lowest 25%	**$2,060**	**$4,698**	**$5,150**	**$3,600**	**$6,525**
	Average	**$7,288**	**$9,569**	**$11,230**	**$9,077**	**$14,056**
TOTAL COMPENSATION PLUS BENEFITS	**Highest 25%**	**$68,607**	**$61,500**	**$80,783**	**$82,500**	**$114,200**
	Median	**$52,950**	**$52,008**	**$69,344**	**$74,290**	**$91,470**
	Lowest 25%	**$43,926**	**$39,322**	**$58,642**	**$66,892**	**$73,799**
	Average	**$55,808**	**$54,441**	**$67,842**	**$74,953**	**$97,472**
Number of Respondents		14	15	33	36	187

- Not enough response to provide meaningful data.

* For detailed description and definitions of Data Distribution (Highest 25%, Median, Lowest 25%, and Average), see chapter 1, Explanation of Data Distribution.

Table 6-2: Annual Compensation of Full-Time Executive/Administrative Pastors by Worship Attendance

	Data Distribution*	WORSHIP ATTENDANCE					
		100 or less	101-300	301-500	501-750	751-1,000	Over 1,000
CHARACTERISTICS							
Average weekend worship attendance		-	227	430	654	886	2,227
Average church income		-	$495,154	$1,054,786	$1,478,765	$1,414,993	$3,631,676
Average # of years employed		-	8	7	5	7	8
Average # of paid vacation days		-	18	20	17	19	21
% College graduate or higher		-	89%	90%	89%	81%	91%
% Who receive auto reimbursement/allowance		-	43%	50%	43%	28%	49%
% Ordained		-	83%	90%	82%	91%	88%
% Supervise one or more people		-	85%	100%	94%	95%	99%
Average % salary increase (for those who had an increase) this year		-	5.7%	3.1%	4.1%	3.8%	4.6%
COMPENSATION							
Base Salary	Median	-	$35,000	$42,794	$45,200	$48,000	$60,872
	Average	-	$32,604	$42,581	$49,419	$48,127	$64,192
Housing	Median	-	$22,080	$25,000	$25,000	$26,000	$31,215
	Average	-	$19,368	$26,436	$24,300	$27,627	$34,104
Parsonage	Median	-	-	-	-	-	-
	Average	-	-	-	-	-	-
Total Compensation	**Median**	-	**$47,000**	**$64,400**	**$63,000**	**$69,500**	**$89,108**
	Average	-	**$50,169**	**$64,605**	**$66,777**	**$71,899**	**$93,851**
BENEFITS							
Health Insurance	Median	-	$7,000	$10,000	$11,934	$9,600	$11,023
	Average	-	$7,697	$10,384	$9,998	$9,980	$11,226
Life Insurance	Median	-	$305	$268	-	$450	$300
	Average	-	$370	$422	-	$506	$598
Disability	Median	-	-	-	-	$631	$400
	Average	-	-	-	-	$709	$434
Retirement	Median	-	$3,518	$3,120	$2,397	$3,372	$4,500
	Average	-	$3,409	$4,245	$3,144	$4,409	$5,945
Continuing Education	Median	-	$500	$1,000	$1,000	$1,800	$2,000
	Average	-	$906	$1,264	$2,020	$2,300	$2,074
Total Benefits	**Median**	-	**$6,542**	**$10,000**	**$11,283**	**$10,050**	**$13,250**
	Average	-	**$8,215**	**$11,700**	**$10,669**	**$12,197**	**$14,570**
TOTAL COMPENSATION PLUS BENEFITS	**Median**	-	**$53,218**	**$72,050**	**$75,300**	**$80,135**	**$100,555**
	Average	-	**$57,612**	**$73,253**	**$76,531**	**$83,244**	**$105,571**
Number of Respondents		5	35	48	35	43	122

- Not enough response to provide meaningful data.

* For detailed description and definitions of Data Distribution (Median and Average), see chapter 1, Explanation of Data Distribution.

Table 6-3: Annual Compensation of Full-Time Executive/Administrative Pastors by Church Setting

	Data Distribution*	CHURCH SETTING			
		Metro-politan city	Suburb of large city	Small town or rural city	Farming area
CHARACTERISTICS					
Average weekend worship attendance		1,568	1,391	896	-
Average church income		$2,781,655	$2,396,145	$1,457,323	-
Average # of years employed		8	7	7	-
Average # of paid vacation days		19	20	20	-
% College graduate or higher		83%	90%	89%	-
% Who receive auto reimbursement/allowance		32%	45%	48%	-
% Ordained		90%	86%	87%	-
% Supervise one or more people		93%	96%	99%	-
Average % salary increase (for those who had an increase) this year		4.5%	4.2%	4.7%	-
COMPENSATION					
Base Salary	Median	$56,182	$49,200	$43,000	-
	Average	$56,780	$54,534	$45,463	-
Housing	Median	$25,000	$30,000	$25,000	-
	Average	$25,450	$32,760	$26,059	-
Parsonage	Median	-	-	-	-
	Average	-	-	-	-
Total Compensation	**Median**	**$75,000**	**$75,000**	**$63,508**	-
	Average	**$76,517**	**$82,747**	**$68,126**	-
BENEFITS					
Health Insurance	Median	$9,300	$10,778	$10,950	-
	Average	$8,716	$10,769	$10,606	-
Life Insurance	Median	$260	$284	$480	-
	Average	$369	$596	$550	-
Disability Insurance	Median	$380	$500	$450	-
	Average	$385	$616	$537	-
Retirement	Median	$3,725	$3,732	$4,000	-
	Average	$5,358	$4,773	$4,519	-
Continuing Education	Median	$1,500	$1,500	$1,200	-
	Average	$1,912	$2,003	$1,510	-
Total Benefits	**Median**	**$9,859**	**$13,000**	**$9,876**	-
	Average	**$11,013**	**$13,472**	**$11,809**	-
TOTAL COMPENSATION PLUS BENEFITS	**Median**	**$83,000**	**$87,106**	**$75,150**	**-**
	Average	**$85,073**	**$94,410**	**$77,912**	**-**
Number of Respondents		59	132	95	3

- Not enough response to provide meaningful data.

* For detailed description and definitions of Data Distribution (Median and Average), see chapter 1, Explanation of Data Distribution.

Table 6-4: Annual Compensation of Full-Time Executive/Administrative Pastors by Region

	Data Distribution*	REGION								
		New England	Middle Atlantic	South Atlantic	E-N Central	E-S Central	W-N Central	W-S Central	Mountain	Pacific
CHARACTERISTICS										
Average weekend worship attendance	-	784	1,209	1,224	1,844	1,412	1,181	932	1,551
Average church income	-	$1,712,320	$2,279,051	$1,785,097	$3,101,155	$2,163,998	$2,267,861	$1,368,357	$2,526,865
Average # of years employed	-	7	7	7	7	6	7	6	10
Average # of paid vacation days	-	21	18	21	18	19	19	19	20
% College graduate or higher	-	89%	90%	94%	89%	100%	94%	80%	71%
% Who receive auto reimbursement/allowance	-	33%	41%	48%	39%	36%	50%	33%	51%
% Ordained	-	78%	80%	87%	89%	95%	94%	81%	97%
% Supervise one or more people	-	96%	89%	98%	100%	100%	100%	100%	95%
Average % salary increase (for those who had an increase) this year	-	3.3%	4.5%	3.8%	3.2%	4.7%	4.5%	6.7%	5.1%
COMPENSATION										
Base Salary	Median	-	$49,210	$52,700	$42,852	$54,087	$49,750	$52,430	$45,800	$45,000
	Average	-	$54,453	$55,145	$50,312	$54,657	$49,554	$56,152	$44,451	$46,342
Housing	Median	-	$26,200	$25,000	$25,500	$20,000	$25,000	$27,250	$26,000	$30,000
	Average	-	$30,092	$27,341	$29,971	$24,420	$27,622	$28,584	$25,735	$33,421
Parsonage	Median	-	-	-	-	-	-	-	-	-
	Average	-	-	-	-	-	-	-	-	-
Total Compensation	**Median**	-	**$70,000**	**$73,500**	**$67,433**	**$76,000**	**$72,500**	**$81,047**	**$61,920**	**$78,862**
	Average	-	**$70,269**	**$76,119**	**$73,367**	**$81,939**	**$78,217**	**$83,493**	**$64,058**	**$81,014**
BENEFITS										
Health Insurance	Median	-	$11,305	$11,900	$12,000	$7,000	$9,300	$8,000	$10,201	$9,924
	Average	-	$11,679	$11,880	$10,799	$7,643	$8,634	$9,471	$9,729	$9,797
Life Insurance	Median	-	-	$400	$295	-	$250	$300	-	$212
	Average	-	-	$588	$663	-	$474	$372	-	$374
Disability Insurance	Median	-	-	$490	$450	-	-	$600	-	$197
	Average	-	-	$510	$628	-	-	$678	-	$373
Retirement	Median	-	$2,638	$4,589	$3,242	$4,500	$2,250	$5,159	$3,136	$4,000
	Average	-	$4,640	$5,272	$4,295	$7,620	$3,820	$5,299	$4,256	$4,419
Continuing Education	Median	-	$2,500	$750	$1,500	-	$1,000	$1,750	-	$1,500
	Average	-	$2,078	$1,117	$1,977	-	$1,605	$1,950	-	$1,544
Total Benefits	**Median**	-	**$14,287**	**$13,200**	**$12,150**	**$10,000**	**$12,181**	**$8,000**	**$13,215**	**$9,855**
	Average	-	**$13,881**	**$12,658**	**$13,526**	**$12,941**	**$11,546**	**$11,347**	**$12,256**	**$11,476**
TOTAL COMPENSATION PLUS BENEFITS	**Median**	-	**$82,100**	**$78,565**	**$79,127**	**$74,250**	**$81,112**	**$92,436**	**$74,753**	**$88,783**
	Average	-	**$83,122**	**$86,199**	**$85,072**	**$86,742**	**$86,211**	**$93,805**	**$76,315**	**$91,763**
Number of Respondents		3	27	59	52	18	22	50	21	39

- Not enough response to provide meaningful data.

* For detailed description and definitions of Data Distribution (Median and Average), see chapter 1, Explanation of Data Distribution.

Table 6-5: Annual Compensation of Full-Time Executive/Administrative Pastors by Education

	Data Distribution*	EDUCATION			
		Less than Bachelor	Bachelor	Master	Doctorate
CHARACTERISTICS					
Average weekend worship attendance		1,148	1,328	1,123	1,709
Average church income		$2,032,872	$2,340,489	$1,959,177	$2,491,303
Average # of years employed		7	8	7	8
Average # of paid vacation days		18	20	20	21
% College graduate or higher		0%	100%	100%	100%
% Who receive auto reimbursement/allowance		36%	41%	46%	48%
% Ordained		85%	81%	92%	89%
% Supervise one or more people		94%	96%	98%	96%
Average % salary increase (for those who had an increase) this year		4.9%	4.7%	4.4%	3.1%
COMPENSATION					
Base Salary	Median	$45,200	$49,000	$45,500	$60,617
	Average	$43,903	$53,541	$50,363	$65,144
Housing	Median	$26,500	$30,000	$26,000	$30,000
	Average	$25,805	$30,522	$27,758	$32,307
Parsonage	Median	-	-	-	-
	Average	-	-	-	-
Total Compensation	**Median**	**$65,000**	**$72,250**	**$73,000**	**$87,210**
	Average	**$68,846**	**$79,168**	**$74,023**	**$88,234**
BENEFITS					
Health Insurance	Median	$8,000	$9,885	$10,782	$14,028
	Average	$8,525	$9,866	$10,374	$13,102
Life Insurance	Median	$270	$388	$300	$348
	Average	$444	$685	$411	$588
Disability Insurance	Median	$350	$360	$500	$490
	Average	$478	$394	$603	$630
Retirement	Median	$3,450	$3,673	$3,810	$5,188
	Average	$4,660	$4,318	$4,991	$6,005
Continuing Education	Median	-	$1,500	$1,500	$1,500
	Average	-	$1,538	$1,895	$2,022
Total Benefits	**Median**	**$9,100**	**$10,250**	**$11,823**	**$14,287**
	Average	**$10,969**	**$11,149**	**$13,232**	**$13,973**
TOTAL COMPENSATION PLUS BENEFITS	**Median**	**$74,600**	**$81,000**	**$80,981**	**$97,250**
	Average	**$75,698**	**$88,193**	**$85,735**	**$101,244**
Number of Respondents		33	99	127	29

- Not enough response to provide meaningful data.

* For detailed description and definitions of Data Distribution (Median and Average), see chapter 1, Explanation of Data Distribution.

Table 6-6: Annual Compensation of Full-Time Executive/Administrative Pastors by Years Employed

	Data Distribution*	YEARS EMPLOYED			
		Less than 6 years	6-10 years	11-15 years	Over 15 years
CHARACTERISTICS					
Average weekend worship attendance		1,173	1,267	1,427	1,480
Average church income		$1,907,594	$2,332,317	$2,146,827	$3,250,386
Average # of years employed		3	8	13	23
Average # of paid vacation days		18	20	23	24
% College graduate or higher		88%	89%	89%	91%
% Who receive auto reimbursement/allowance		39%	38%	51%	73%
% Ordained		85%	87%	93%	91%
% Supervise one or more people		97%	93%	100%	100%
Average % salary increase (for those who had an increase) this year		5.2%	3.4%	4.1%	3.2%
COMPENSATION					
Base Salary	Median	$48,000	$45,000	$49,400	$61,714
	Average	$52,343	$49,495	$48,484	$64,926
Housing	Median	$25,000	$30,000	$26,000	$27,588
	Average	$27,191	$30,103	$30,004	$34,396
Parsonage	Median	-	-	-	-
	Average	-	-	-	-
Total Compensation	**Median**	**$70,000**	**$70,000**	**$77,094**	**$79,431**
	Average	**$74,841**	**$77,262**	**$75,349**	**$89,942**
BENEFITS					
Health Insurance	Median	$10,816	$10,300	$8,144	$9,924
	Average	$10,235	$10,357	$9,041	$10,767
Life Insurance	Median	$238	$379	$500	$280
	Average	$518	$554	$520	$377
Disability Insurance	Median	$380	$470	$300	$500
	Average	$509	$514	$441	$684
Retirement	Median	$3,250	$3,950	$5,129	$4,500
	Average	$4,137	$4,539	$6,429	$6,259
Continuing Education	Median	$1,500	$2,300	$500	-
	Average	$1,844	$2,155	$854	-
Total Benefits	**Median**	**$10,965**	**$10,610**	**$9,176**	**$15,450**
	Average	**$11,823**	**$12,745**	**$11,431**	**$14,950**
TOTAL COMPENSATION PLUS BENEFITS	**Median**	**$79,654**	**$80,981**	**$84,470**	**$94,006**
	Average	**$84,130**	**$89,518**	**$85,221**	**$104,212**
Number of Respondents		144	71	45	22

- Not enough response to provide meaningful data.

* For detailed description and definitions of Data Distribution (Median and Average), see chapter 1, Explanation of Data Distribution.

Table 6-7: Annual Compensation of Full-Time Executive/Administrative Pastors by Denomination

	Data Distribution*	DENOMINATION					
		Assemblies of God	Baptist	Independent/ Nondenom.	Lutheran	Methodist	Presby- terian
CHARACTERISTICS							
Average weekend worship attendance		1,547	942	1,515	-	1,125	1,456
Average church income		$2,187,474	$2,031,469	$2,312,369	-	$3,097,386	$2,994,153
Average # of years employed		7	7	8	-	6	8
Average # of paid vacation days		20	18	20	-	23	25
% College graduate or higher		74%	92%	86%	-	100%	100%
% Who receive auto reimbursement/allowance		53%	51%	31%	-	25%	69%
% Ordained		91%	95%	86%	-	50%	69%
% Supervise one or more people		94%	97%	96%	-	100%	100%
Average % salary increase (for those who had an increase) this year		4.4%	4.2%	4.8%	-	-	3.3%
COMPENSATION							
Base Salary	Median	$45,039	$42,409	$51,182	-	$69,587	$49,210
	Average	$51,861	$47,019	$53,551	-	$81,791	$52,613
Housing	Median	$28,000	$25,000	$29,500	-	-	$28,000
	Average	$28,721	$26,997	$30,892	-	-	$32,000
Parsonage	Median	-	-	-	-	-	-
	Average	-	-	-	-	-	-
Total Compensation	**Median**	**$74,469**	**$65,750**	**$75,000**	**-**	**$75,500**	**$79,062**
	Average	**$78,640**	**$72,095**	**$79,410**	**-**	**$85,319**	**$80,983**
BENEFITS							
Health Insurance	Median	$12,000	$10,000	$10,000	-	-	$13,000
	Average	$9,614	$10,163	$10,298	-	-	$13,100
Life Insurance	Median	$250	$300	$360	-	-	$400
	Average	$373	$404	$685	-	-	$778
Disability Insurance	Median	-	$261	$473	-	-	-
	Average	-	$428	$548	-	-	-
Retirement	Median	$2,375	$5,159	$3,190	-	-	$5,200
	Average	$3,756	$5,373	$4,510	-	-	$7,738
Continuing Education	Median	-	$1,500	$1,200	-	-	$1,500
	Average	-	$1,747	$1,797	-	-	$1,800
Total Benefits	**Median**	**$4,350**	**$10,170**	**$11,750**	**-**	**$10,763**	**$17,954**
	Average	**$7,658**	**$12,840**	**$12,553**	**-**	**$10,895**	**$18,777**
TOTAL COMPENSATION PLUS BENEFITS	**Median**	**$76,925**	**$73,500**	**$85,284**	**-**	**$90,350**	**$91,701**
	Average	**$85,101**	**$83,189**	**$90,197**	**-**	**$96,213**	**$92,099**
Number of Respondents		32	78	99	5	8	13

- Not enough response to provide meaningful data.

* For detailed description and definitions of Data Distribution (Median and Average), see chapter 1, Explanation of Data Distribution.

Table 6-8: Annual Compensation of Full-Time Executive/Administrative Pastors by Gender

	Data Distribution*	GENDER	
		Male	Female
CHARACTERISTICS			
Average weekend worship attendance		1,294	989
Average church income		$2,188,291	$1,879,839
Average # of years employed		7	9
Average # of paid vacation days		20	19
% College graduate or higher		90%	78%
% Who receive auto reimbursement/allowance		45%	33%
% Ordained		91%	58%
% Supervise one or more people		99%	80%
Average % salary increase (for those who had an increase) this year		4.4%	4.5%
COMPENSATION			
Base Salary	Median	$49,210	$41,247
	Average	$53,135	$43,403
Housing	Median	$26,700	$30,000
	Average	$29,027	$28,031
Parsonage	Median	-	-
	Average	-	-
Total Compensation	**Median**	**$75,000**	**$49,400**
	Average	**$79,206**	**$56,609**
BENEFITS			
Health Insurance	Median	$10,778	$5,298
	Average	$10,814	$5,895
Life Insurance	Median	$300	$362
	Average	$552	$370
Disability Insurance	Median	$400	$495
	Average	$529	$512
Retirement	Median	$4,000	$3,000
	Average	$4,994	$3,601
Continuing Education	Median	$1,500	$1,500
	Average	$1,799	$1,609
Total Benefits	**Median**	**$12,256**	**$6,039**
	Average	**$13,108**	**$7,475**
TOTAL COMPENSATION PLUS BENEFITS	**Median**	**$85,000**	**$54,193**
	Average	**$90,377**	**$61,864**
Number of Respondents		255	36

- Not enough response to provide meaningful data.

* For detailed description and definitions of Data Distribution (Median and Average), see chapter 1, Explanation of Data Distribution.

Executive/Administrative Pastor Worksheet

	Enter your church data below	The 2014–2015 Compensation Handbook for Church Staff		Enter *Compensation Handbook* data below			
				Highest 25%	Median	Lowest 25%	Average
Church Income	$	Table 6-1	page 65	$	$	$	$
Worship Attendance		Table 6-2	page 66	n/a	$	n/a	$
Church Setting (metro, suburb, small town, or farming area)		Table 6-3	page 67	n/a	$	n/a	$
Region		Table 6-4	page 68	n/a	$	n/a	$
Person's Education		Table 6-5	page 69	n/a	$	n/a	$
Years Employed		Table 6-6	page 70	n/a	$	n/a	$
Denomination (if applicable)		Table 6-7	page 71	n/a	$	n/a	$

Looking at the table and page number references indicated in the *2014–2015 Compensation Handbook for Church Staff* columns above, locate the appropriate range for your church. Refer to the instructions below for step-by-step help.

FILLING OUT THE WORKSHEET

1. Fill in the gray boxes under *Enter your church data* with your church demographic information as follows:

   ▶ **Income** (Total annual church budget in past year)
   ▶ **Worship attendance** (Number of people, including children, who attend all weekend services)
   ▶ **Church setting** (Metropolitan city, suburb of large city, small town or rural city, or farming area)

   ▶ **Region** (Locate your state's region in the appendix on page 346.)
   ▶ **Education** (Highest level of education: less than bachelor, bachelor, master, or doctorate)

2. Use Table 6-1 (page 65) in your *2014–2015 Compensation Handbook for Church Staff* to enter data pertinent to your church. In the heading (top row), locate your church **income** from the five available ranges. Follow that column to the bottom rows, and copy the *Highest 25%*, *Median*, *Lowest 25%*, and *Average* amounts onto your worksheet.

3. Use Table 6-2 (page 66) on your *2014–2015 Compensation Handbook for Church Staff* to enter data pertinent to your church. In the heading (top row), locate your church's

worship attendance from the six available ranges. Follow that column to the bottom rows, and copy the *Median* and *Average* amounts onto your worksheet.

4. Use Table 6-3 (page 67) on your *2014–2015 Compensation Handbook for Church Staff* to enter data pertinent to your church. In the heading (top row), choose the **church setting** that best describes your church. Follow that column to the bottom rows, and copy the *Median* and *Average* amounts onto your worksheet.

5. Use Table 6-4 (page 68) on your *2014–2015 Compensation Handbook for Church Staff* to enter data pertinent to your church. In the heading (top row), look for the **region** where your church is located. Follow that column to the bottom rows, and copy the *Median* and *Average* amounts onto your worksheet.

6. Use Table 6-5 (page 69) on your *2014–2015 Compensation Handbook for Church Staff* to enter data pertinent to your Executive/Administrative Pastor. In the heading (top row), look for **your Executive/Administrative Pastor's highest level of education**. Follow that column to the bottom rows, and copy the *Median* and *Average* amounts onto your worksheet.

7. Use Table 6-6 (page 70) on your *2014–2015 Compensation Handbook for Church Staff* to enter data pertinent to your Executive/Administrative Pastor. In the heading (top row), locate the **number of years your Executive/Administrative Pastor has been employed**. Follow that column to the bottom rows, and copy the *Median* and *Average* amounts onto your worksheet.

8. Use Table 6-7 (page 71) on your *2014–2015 Compensation Handbook for Church Staff* to enter data pertinent to your church. In the heading (top row), look for **your**

church's denominational affiliation. Follow that column to the bottom rows, and copy the *Median* and *Average* amounts onto your worksheet. If your church is not affiliated with a denomination, leave this section blank.

DETERMINING COMPENSATION

This tool will not provide you with a single compensation amount but rather with a range of values to help you determine the compensation appropriate to your situation.

1. Look at the values in the shaded *Median* column. Circle the **lowest** and the **highest** values. **This is the range of the median compensation plus benefits for churches similar to yours.**

2. For a variety of reasons, compensation plus benefits may be higher or lower than the range established in this table. Income and attendance are two significant factors affecting church compensation packages. If church income or attendance skews higher, you might want to consider moving toward or above the higher end of the range. Likewise, if church income or attendance skews lower, you may consider moving the package toward or below the lower end of the range.

3. Examine additional variables that might impact the compensation package you offer, such as years of service, education, and church setting.

4. Determine other circumstances unique to your situation, such as cost of living in your area, theological beliefs, pastoral performance, financial needs, the local economy, personal motivation, congregational goals, and others.

5. You now have a compensation package range based on the *2014–2015 Compensation Handbook*. Since each church and position are unique, your final compensation package will be based on additional factors unique to your situation.

7

ASSOCIATE PASTORS

Employment Profile

The roles and duties of the Associate Pastor are quite diverse, depending upon the church. For this survey, an Associate or Assistant Pastor is any paid pastor who assists the Senior Pastor in general or specific ministries other than those specifically listed in the survey. (This excludes Executive, Education, Music, Youth, and Children's Pastors, who were surveyed and reported separately.)

The role of an Associate Pastor may include positions or responsibilities such as Assimilation Pastor, Congregational Care Pastor, Counseling Pastor, Disabilities Ministry Pastor, Ethnic Ministries Pastor, Evangelism Pastor, Family Life Pastor, Lay Pastor, Membership Pastor, Missions Pastor, Outreach Pastor, Prayer Pastor, Teaching/Preaching Pastor, Visitation Pastor, etc.

More than nine in 10 full-time Associate Pastors are ordained; 85% are males. More than nine in 10 are employed by the church rather than self-employed. The majority have a graduate degree.

Almost one-quarter of the Associate Pastors in this survey serve on a part-time basis. More than eight in 10 part-time Associate Pastors are ordained; more than six in 10 are males.

The chart below provides a demographic profile of this sample.

	Full-Time	Part-Time
Number of respondents	**535**	**153**
Ordained	91%	82%
Average years employed	7	6
Male	85%	63%
Female	15%	37%
Self-employed (receives 1099)	7%	13%
Church employee (receives W-2)	93%	87%
High school diploma	6%	11%
Associate degree	6%	8%
Bachelor's degree	33%	34%
Master's degree	50%	42%
Doctoral degree	6%	5%

Total Compensation plus Benefits Package Analysis

The following analyses are based on data in the tables you will find later in this chapter. The tables show compensation plus benefits data for full-time and part-time Associate Pastors and are presented according to church income, church attendance, church setting, region, education, years employed, denomination, and gender. In this way, the Associate Pastor's compensation plus benefits can be analyzed and compared from a variety of useful perspectives.

The total compensation plus benefits amount includes the base salary; housing allowance and/or parsonage amount; health, life, and disability insurance payments; retirement contribution; and educational funds.

A worksheet at the end of this chapter is provided to help you apply the data to your church's situation.

Full-time Associate Pastors receive approximately the same benefits as Senior or Executive Pastors. Just like Executive Pastors, Associate Pastors are less likely than a Senior Pastor to live in a church-owned parsonage. On average, Associate Pastors tend to receive overall compensation that is about 75% of what Senior Pastors receive but about 10% more than that of Solo Pastors. About six in 10 full-time Associate Pastors receive health insurance and retirement benefits.

Fifty-five percent of full-time Associate Pastors received salary increases, representing a 13-percentage-point increase over respondents who reported receiving a salary increase in the last study.

The percentage of full-time Associate Pastors who receive benefits (listed below) increased since last measured in 2011 except for continuing education.

Compensation Plus Benefits	Full-Time	Part-Time
Base Salary	99%	86%
Housing	81%	42%
Parsonage	6%	3%
Health Insurance*	68%	17%
Life Insurance*	27%	5%
Disability Insurance*	27%	4%
Retirement	60%	15%
Continuing Education	29%	20%
Received salary increase	55%	29%
Received paid vacation	95%	52%
Received auto reimbursement/allowance	53%	45%

Only those reporting individual premiums for Health, Life, or Disability (not total insurance premiums) are included.

KEY POINTS

* Nearly half of full-time Associate Pastors serve in churches with an income higher than $1,000,000 and a worship attendance of more than 500.

* In general, as church income, the minister's education, and years employed increase, average compensation and benefits for full-time Associate Pastors also increase.

* Full-time Associate Pastors serving churches in a suburban setting or metropolitan city have higher compensation and benefits packages compared to those serving churches in a small town/rural city or a farming area.

* About half of part-time Associate Pastors serve in churches with an income of $500,000 or less.

Compensation & Benefits: National Averages for Full-Time Associate Pastors	
2000	$51,973
2001	$54,729
2002	$58,072
2003	$59,742
2004	$61,263
2005	$64,034
2006	$66,310
2007	$64,842
2008	$64,775
2009	$62,024
2011	$62,918
2013	$68,040*

The above trend is made available for your reference only. In addition to looking at this overall data, please refer to the detailed tables using your church's income, attendance, setting, region, and denomination as well as the person's education, gender, and years employed for guidance in compensating this position.

Table 7-1: Annual Compensation of Full-Time Associate Pastors by Church Income

CHARACTERISTICS	Data Distribution*	CHURCH INCOME				
		$250K & Under	$251-$500K	$501-$750K	$751K-$1M	Over $1 Million
Average weekend worship attendance		292	242	332	548	1,388
Average church income		$176,316	$379,569	$626,617	$924,643	$2,430,465
Average # of years employed		5	6	7	6	8
Average # of paid vacation days		18	18	18	19	19
% College graduate or higher		89%	91%	88%	84%	90%
% Who receive auto reimbursement/allowance		58%	54%	55%	57%	52%
% Ordained		96%	89%	97%	94%	88%
% Supervise one or more people		71%	60%	63%	60%	70%
Average % salary increase (for those who had an increase) this year		4.7%	3.4%	4.7%	4.1%	3.6%
COMPENSATION						
Base Salary	Highest 25%	$40,000	$39,475	$43,300	$48,500	$52,000
	Median	$30,000	$29,857	$32,840	$39,811	$40,000
	Lowest 25%	$20,600	$21,000	$25,800	$30,000	$30,000
	Average	$29,864	$30,551	$34,701	$39,161	$41,535
Housing	Highest 25%	$22,000	$24,000	$28,617	$27,600	$33,150
	Median	$14,400	$18,709	$24,000	$21,000	$26,000
	Lowest 25%	$10,000	$13,300	$19,686	$14,000	$20,000
	Average	$17,322	$19,380	$24,492	$21,058	$27,300
Parsonage	Highest 25%	-	-	-	-	$26,000
	Median	-	-	-	-	$16,800
	Lowest 25%	-	-	-	-	$9,600
	Average	-	-	-	-	$18,267
Total Compensation	**Highest 25%**	**$48,000**	**$54,310**	**$65,650**	**$66,516**	**$75,187**
	Median	**$43,000**	**$45,000**	**$55,500**	**$56,480**	**$63,000**
	Lowest 25%	**$36,091**	**$38,200**	**$48,705**	**$48,500**	**$50,250**
	Average	**$43,664**	**$46,999**	**$57,558**	**$58,596**	**$63,491**
BENEFITS						
Health Insurance	Highest 25%	$12,300	$10,800	$14,400	$14,800	$14,241
	Median	$6,726	$7,300	$9,500	$11,016	$11,455
	Lowest 25%	$3,800	$5,700	$5,000	$7,000	$6,423
	Average	$7,989	$7,834	$9,916	$10,991	$10,844
Life Insurance	Highest 25%	-	$650	$1,250	$500	$612
	Median	-	$410	$182	$360	$304
	Lowest 25%	-	$206	$93	$100	$132
	Average	-	$481	$937	$425	$545
Disability Insurance	Highest 25%	-	$740	$905	-	$650
	Median	-	$300	$530	-	$466
	Lowest 25%	-	$184	$202	-	$321
	Average	-	$504	$640	-	$628
Retirement	Highest 25%	$3,000	$5,872	$5,000	$5,927	$6,780
	Median	$2,000	$3,800	$3,086	$2,826	$4,100
	Lowest 25%	$1,500	$1,530	$1,500	$1,610	$2,400
	Average	$2,889	$3,851	$3,389	$4,146	$5,008
Continuing Education	Highest 25%	$1,000	$1,100	$1,500	$2,000	$2,550
	Median	$1,000	$1,000	$1,000	$1,500	$1,525
	Lowest 25%	$500	$500	$1,000	$750	$1,000
	Average	$955	$1,090	$1,205	$1,640	$1,976
Total Benefits	**Highest 25%**	**$12,055**	**$12,633**	**$15,600**	**$16,648**	**$18,925**
	Median	**$6,552**	**$8,625**	**$9,572**	**$9,286**	**$12,861**
	Lowest 25%	**$3,600**	**$4,540**	**$4,888**	**$5,293**	**$7,114**
	Average	**$8,365**	**$9,052**	**$11,158**	**$11,872**	**$13,699**
TOTAL COMPENSATION PLUS BENEFITS	**Highest 25%**	**$59,370**	**$63,630**	**$76,977**	**$76,428**	**$93,200**
	Median	**$48,725**	**$53,100**	**$63,938**	**$69,158**	**$73,000**
	Lowest 25%	**$37,500**	**$44,139**	**$55,679**	**$54,500**	**$59,500**
	Average	**$50,464**	**$54,868**	**$66,571**	**$69,052**	**$76,589**
Number of Respondents		45	95	78	53	248

- Not enough response to provide meaningful data.

* For detailed description and definitions of Data Distribution (Highest 25%, Median, Lowest 25%, and Average), see chapter 1, Explanation of Data Distribution.

Table 7-2: Annual Compensation of Full-Time Associate Pastors by Worship Attendance

	Data Distribution*	WORSHIP ATTENDANCE					
		100 or less	101-300	301-500	501-750	751-1,000	Over 1,000
CHARACTERISTICS							
Average weekend worship attendance		75	211	409	637	893	2,262
Average church income		$254,201	$484,678	$931,633	$1,269,650	$1,497,553	$3,366,290
Average # of years employed		7	6	8	7	10	7
Average # of paid vacation days		21	18	18	19	19	19
% College graduate or higher		75%	90%	87%	94%	89%	86%
% Who receive auto reimbursement/allowance		38%	54%	57%	65%	54%	40%
% Ordained		100%	90%	92%	97%	88%	87%
% Supervise one or more people		88%	60%	62%	72%	62%	74%
Average % salary increase (for those who had an increase) this year		-	3.8%	3.9%	3.3%	4.0%	3.9%
COMPENSATION							
Base Salary	Median	$28,000	$29,305	$35,000	$41,087	$39,500	$41,250
	Average	$26,812	$30,590	$36,312	$43,493	$40,305	$42,939
Housing	Median	$17,000	$20,000	$23,000	$25,000	$25,000	$25,500
	Average	$15,547	$21,069	$23,512	$25,996	$25,999	$26,976
Parsonage	Median	-	$14,000	$17,500	-	-	-
	Average	-	$18,959	$17,690	-	-	-
Total Compensation	**Median**	**$36,500**	**$45,057**	**$53,899**	**$60,109**	**$59,000**	**$64,704**
	Average	**$37,287**	**$49,283**	**$56,313**	**$64,141**	**$61,413**	**$64,435**
BENEFITS							
Health Insurance	Median	$5,950	$8,000	$11,140	$10,000	$10,090	$10,000
	Average	$7,136	$8,702	$11,088	$9,787	$10,310	$10,138
Life Insurance	Median	-	$403	$360	$213	$450	$251
	Average	-	$874	$459	$805	$575	$432
Disability	Median	-	$551	$640	$600	$388	$437
	Average	-	$610	$790	$777	$445	$600
Retirement	Median	-	$3,000	$3,388	$4,250	$3,163	$3,600
	Average	-	$4,000	$4,205	$4,708	$4,588	$4,655
Continuing Education	Median	-	$1,000	$1,450	$1,200	$1,000	$1,525
	Average	-	$1,183	$1,776	$1,694	$2,150	$1,903
Total Benefits	**Median**	**$7,085**	**$9,104**	**$10,028**	**$10,349**	**$14,044**	**$12,498**
	Average	**$8,870**	**$10,135**	**$12,420**	**$11,683**	**$13,487**	**$12,702**
TOTAL COMPENSATION PLUS BENEFITS	**Median**	**$49,600**	**$53,857**	**$65,033**	**$70,388**	**$71,115**	**$72,737**
	Average	**$44,695**	**$58,209**	**$66,861**	**$74,762**	**$74,498**	**$76,451**
Number of Respondents		16	138	135	66	59	120

- Not enough response to provide meaningful data.

** For detailed description and definitions of Data Distribution (Median and Average), see chapter 1, Explanation of Data Distribution.*

Table 7-3: Annual Compensation of Full-Time Associate Pastors by Church Setting

	Data Distribution*	CHURCH SETTING			
		Metro-politan city	Suburb of large city	Small town or rural city	Farming area
CHARACTERISTICS					
Average weekend worship attendance		1,153	883	684	328
Average church income		$1,995,693	$1,568,881	$1,063,173	$516,332
Average # of years employed		9	7	7	8
Average # of paid vacation days		19	19	18	20
% College graduate or higher		87%	89%	87%	87%
% Who receive auto reimbursement/allowance		39%	49%	62%	78%
% Ordained		91%	89%	94%	87%
% Supervise one or more people		62%	73%	62%	50%
Average % salary increase (for those who had an increase) this year		4.2%	3.8%	3.8%	2.7%
COMPENSATION					
Base Salary	Median	$37,124	$39,129	$32,715	$40,000
	Average	$37,824	$39,163	$34,627	$37,463
Housing	Median	$24,000	$26,000	$20,000	$19,600
	Average	$23,769	$27,820	$20,543	$18,965
Parsonage	Median	-	$20,000	$12,000	-
	Average	-	$20,723	$12,005	-
Total Compensation	**Median**	**$57,040**	**$60,008**	**$50,000**	**$52,333**
	Average	**$58,168**	**$61,447**	**$52,635**	**$50,694**
BENEFITS					
Health Insurance	Median	$10,140	$9,500	$9,294	$9,970
	Average	$10,119	$9,723	$10,075	$10,172
Life Insurance	Median	$372	$362	$351	-
	Average	$482	$569	$781	-
Disability Insurance	Median	$418	$450	$740	-
	Average	$475	$617	$782	-
Retirement	Median	$4,183	$3,625	$3,500	$1,800
	Average	$5,357	$4,467	$4,029	$2,166
Continuing Education	Median	$1,500	$1,000	$1,050	-
	Average	$1,848	$1,776	$1,482	-
Total Benefits	**Median**	**$11,065**	**$9,800**	**$11,000**	**$8,645**
	Average	**$12,346**	**$11,685**	**$12,196**	**$9,938**
TOTAL COMPENSATION PLUS BENEFITS	**Median**	**$69,200**	**$70,210**	**$59,120**	**$58,000**
	Average	**$69,217**	**$72,712**	**$62,891**	**$58,471**
Number of Respondents		104	225	177	23

- Not enough response to provide meaningful data.

* For detailed description and definitions of Data Distribution (Median and Average), see chapter 1, Explanation of Data Distribution.

Table 7-4: Annual Compensation of Full-Time Associate Pastors by Region

	Data Distribution*	REGION								
		New England	Middle Atlantic	South Atlantic	E-N Central	E-S Central	W-N Central	W-S Central	Mountain	Pacific
CHARACTERISTICS										
Average weekend worship attendance		682	850	875	651	873	521	1,363	966	712
Average church income		$1,263,375	$1,435,222	$1,646,853	$1,106,154	$1,704,977	$985,473	$2,014,433	$1,288,107	$1,334,921
Average # of years employed		9	6	8	7	7	8	8	6	9
Average # of paid vacation days		22	18	19	19	18	20	16	18	19
% College graduate or higher		100%	82%	92%	88%	89%	91%	84%	84%	89%
% Who receive auto reimbursement/allowance		75%	39%	54%	63%	35%	64%	53%	46%	49%
% Ordained		94%	88%	93%	88%	95%	91%	84%	88%	99%
% Supervise one or more people		94%	59%	63%	63%	78%	70%	57%	66%	74%
Average % salary increase (for those who had an increase) this year		4.5%	3.7%	3.8%	3.7%	5.1%	2.8%	3.9%	4.9%	4.0%
COMPENSATION										
Base Salary	Median	$33,000	$38,601	$40,000	$38,564	$36,500	$32,171	$38,900	$32,500	$36,000
	Average	$33,104	$40,655	$40,541	$37,779	$36,100	$32,270	$38,416	$34,277	$35,705
Housing	Median	$35,000	$22,000	$26,000	$20,000	$25,000	$24,000	$21,150	$22,079	$24,000
	Average	$32,875	$23,590	$24,885	$21,330	$24,696	$21,990	$22,835	$23,042	$26,439
Parsonage	Median	-	-	$9,600	-	-	-	-	-	-
	Average	-	-	$12,411	-	-	-	-	-	-
Total Compensation	**Median**	**$69,048**	**$54,000**	**$60,000**	**$53,921**	**$55,632**	**$51,000**	**$58,666**	**$50,000**	**$56,676**
	Average	**$66,924**	**$59,826**	**$61,086**	**$54,461**	**$55,020**	**$51,768**	**$58,742**	**$51,511**	**$58,057**
BENEFITS										
Health Insurance	Median	$10,952	$12,300	$8,500	$10,000	$8,384	$10,795	$9,291	$10,101	$7,519
	Average	$10,644	$11,369	$8,933	$10,287	$7,689	$10,696	$10,838	$10,296	$8,546
Life Insurance	Median	-	$382	$300	$156	-	$432	$586	$650	$132
	Average	-	$417	$674	$240	-	$449	$890	$542	$625
Disability Insurance	Median	-	$550	$364	$380	-	$400	$518	$660	$350
	Average	-	$568	$547	$580	-	$666	$608	$866	$744
Retirement	Median	$2,230	$3,500	$5,000	$3,282	$3,500	$2,765	$4,785	$3,639	$3,000
	Average	$2,765	$4,993	$5,214	$3,757	$3,948	$3,386	$4,978	$4,416	$4,119
Continuing Education	Median	-	$1,025	$1,150	$1,500	-	$1,000	$2,500	$850	$1,000
	Average	-	$1,313	$1,767	$1,876	-	$1,818	$2,156	$888	$1,300
Total Benefits	**Median**	**$10,952**	**$16,200**	**$10,543**	**$10,800**	**$8,434**	**$12,258**	**$9,395**	**$12,000**	**$9,000**
	Average	**$12,442**	**$14,742**	**$11,708**	**$12,217**	**$8,870**	**$12,588**	**$12,748**	**$10,938**	**$9,944**
TOTAL COMPENSATION PLUS BENEFITS	**Median**	**$80,542**	**$67,708**	**$68,509**	**$60,266**	**$64,500**	**$63,800**	**$65,500**	**$56,671**	**$65,879**
	Average	**$78,589**	**$72,570**	**$70,842**	**$64,822**	**$62,623**	**$63,553**	**$70,500**	**$59,868**	**$69,820**
Number of Respondents		16	59	112	79	21	47	64	57	80

- Not enough response to provide meaningful data.

* For detailed description and definitions of Data Distribution (Median and Average), see chapter 1, Explanation of Data Distribution.

Table 7-5: Annual Compensation of Full-Time Associate Pastors by Education

	Data Distribution*	EDUCATION			
		Less than Bachelor	Bachelor	Master	Doctorate
CHARACTERISTICS					
Average weekend worship attendance		1,014	881	776	812
Average church income		$1,441,085	$1,448,110	$1,406,515	$1,447,267
Average # of years employed		8	7	8	8
Average # of paid vacation days		17	17	20	19
% College graduate or higher		0%	100%	100%	100%
% Who receive auto reimbursement/allowance		29%	54%	57%	57%
% Ordained		76%	89%	95%	100%
% Supervise one or more people		66%	58%	70%	71%
Average % salary increase (for those who had an increase) this year		3.8%	3.8%	3.7%	4.7%
COMPENSATION					
Base Salary	Median	$32,500	$35,000	$37,324	$41,426
	Average	$35,110	$35,572	$38,373	$41,892
Housing	Median	$20,000	$24,000	$24,000	$27,750
	Average	$23,347	$23,829	$24,088	$27,557
Parsonage	Median	-	-	$16,000	-
	Average	-	-	$18,754	-
Total Compensation	**Median**	**$50,366**	**$53,921**	**$58,187**	**$68,492**
	Average	**$52,287**	**$53,510**	**$60,155**	**$65,775**
BENEFITS					
Health Insurance	Median	$7,100	$9,294	$10,000	$10,992
	Average	$7,685	$9,856	$10,085	$11,348
Life Insurance	Median	$432	$204	$382	$599
	Average	$564	$323	$729	$692
Disability Insurance	Median	$333	$350	$575	$540
	Average	$514	$476	$734	$786
Retirement	Median	$2,463	$2,695	$4,133	$5,250
	Average	$3,115	$3,484	$4,807	$5,902
Continuing Education	Median	$1,000	$1,600	$1,000	$2,000
	Average	$1,589	$1,999	$1,452	$2,300
Total Benefits	**Median**	**$7,100**	**$11,000**	**$10,440**	**$17,000**
	Average	**$7,876**	**$11,331**	**$12,454**	**$16,460**
TOTAL COMPENSATION PLUS BENEFITS	**Median**	**$53,058**	**$61,356**	**$68,115**	**$87,761**
	Average	**$59,373**	**$63,201**	**$71,534**	**$83,143**
Number of Respondents		62	171	261	30

- Not enough response to provide meaningful data.

* For detailed description and definitions of Data Distribution (Median and Average), see chapter 1, Explanation of Data Distribution.

Table 7-6: Annual Compensation of Full-Time Associate Pastors by Years Employed

	Data Distribution*	YEARS EMPLOYED			
		Less than 6 years	6-10 years	11-15 years	Over 15 years
CHARACTERISTICS					
Average weekend worship attendance		864	851	927	799
Average church income		$1,421,657	$1,325,762	$1,547,063	$1,647,132
Average # of years employed		3	8	13	22
Average # of paid vacation days		17	19	19	23
% College graduate or higher		91%	81%	87%	88%
% Who receive auto reimbursement/allowance		51%	51%	56%	53%
% Ordained		90%	92%	91%	97%
% Supervise one or more people		65%	65%	75%	73%
Average % salary increase (for those who had an increase) this year		4.4%	3.5%	2.9%	3.1%
COMPENSATION					
Base Salary	Median	$35,000	$35,000	$37,124	$42,328
	Average	$36,093	$36,984	$37,821	$44,637
Housing	Median	$22,500	$24,000	$24,000	$25,290
	Average	$23,093	$24,254	$24,797	$26,832
Parsonage	Median	$15,500	-	-	-
	Average	$17,883	-	-	-
Total Compensation	**Median**	**$52,604**	**$56,110**	**$57,338**	**$69,579**
	Average	**$54,381**	**$58,339**	**$58,495**	**$69,995**
BENEFITS					
Health Insurance	Median	$8,803	$9,576	$9,500	$10,040
	Average	$9,759	$10,079	$10,108	$9,009
Life Insurance	Median	$348	$263	$234	$374
	Average	$541	$409	$857	$758
Disability Insurance	Median	$446	$541	$600	$600
	Average	$504	$802	$681	$794
Retirement	Median	$3,147	$3,600	$3,684	$4,893
	Average	$3,875	$4,311	$4,113	$6,261
Continuing Education	Median	$1,200	$1,000	$1,000	$1,500
	Average	$1,751	$1,544	$1,207	$1,574
Total Benefits	**Median**	**$9,485**	**$10,000**	**$12,474**	**$12,237**
	Average	**$11,410**	**$11,921**	**$12,630**	**$12,650**
TOTAL COMPENSATION PLUS BENEFITS	**Median**	**$60,195**	**$66,800**	**$72,689**	**$77,575**
	Average	**$63,578**	**$70,479**	**$72,145**	**$80,595**
Number of Respondents		268	118	55	61

- Not enough response to provide meaningful data.

* For detailed description and definitions of Data Distribution (Median and Average), see chapter 1, Explanation of Data Distribution.

Table 7-7: Annual Compensation of Full-Time Associate Pastors by Denomination

	Data Distribution*	DENOMINATION					
		Assemblies of God	Baptist	Independent/ Nondenom.	Lutheran	Methodist	Presby-terian
CHARACTERISTICS							
Average weekend worship attendance		561	703	1,082	618	1,332	535
Average church income		$1,134,173	$1,263,963	$1,719,707	$1,038,770	$2,015,947	$1,524,316
Average # of years employed		9	8	7	10	6	7
Average # of paid vacation days		17	17	18	22	20	22
% College graduate or higher		71%	90%	80%	100%	96%	97%
% Who receive auto reimbursement/allowance		32%	65%	36%	80%	44%	59%
% Ordained		96%	90%	89%	93%	81%	91%
% Supervise one or more people		67%	60%	66%	60%	67%	70%
Average % salary increase (for those who had an increase) this year		3.8%	3.4%	4.4%	3.4%	3.4%	2.7%
COMPENSATION							
Base Salary	Median	$29,530	$32,840	$39,475	$40,000	$41,510	$36,414
	Average	$32,643	$35,577	$40,146	$42,730	$43,117	$40,513
Housing	Median	$24,000	$23,000	$24,000	$22,579	$15,000	$30,000
	Average	$23,109	$24,043	$24,293	$23,848	$16,859	$28,448
Parsonage	Median	-	-	-	-	-	-
	Average	-	-	-	-	-	-
Total Compensation	**Median**	**$46,944**	**$53,000**	**$57,000**	**$60,000**	**$49,450**	**$62,000**
	Average	**$51,961**	**$55,043**	**$59,839**	**$63,608**	**$57,282**	**$65,885**
BENEFITS							
Health Insurance	Median	$7,200	$10,000	$8,764	$17,272	$13,000	$12,972
	Average	$7,849	$9,676	$9,662	$14,977	$10,388	$12,993
Life Insurance	Median	-	$314	$364	-	-	$500
	Average	-	$765	$540	-	-	$1,045
Disability Insurance	Median	-	$457	$533	-	-	$560
	Average	-	$712	$602	-	-	$753
Retirement	Median	$1,542	$3,999	$2,600	$5,291	$4,200	$5,894
	Average	$2,272	$4,465	$3,947	$5,508	$5,505	$6,044
Continuing Education	Median	-	$1,000	$1,250	$1,000	$1,550	$2,000
	Average	-	$1,333	$1,826	$1,219	$2,025	$1,921
Total Benefits	**Median**	**$6,000**	**$11,214**	**$9,600**	**$23,032**	**$8,500**	**$14,661**
	Average	**$7,337**	**$11,736**	**$11,377**	**$19,055**	**$12,865**	**$16,368**
TOTAL COMPENSATION PLUS BENEFITS	**Median**	**$54,434**	**$65,500**	**$64,850**	**$75,700**	**$62,414**	**$79,045**
	Average	**$57,202**	**$65,056**	**$69,019**	**$81,393**	**$69,157**	**$83,906**
Number of Respondents		28	136	156	15	26	37

- Not enough response to provide meaningful data.

* For detailed description and definitions of Data Distribution (Median and Average), see chapter 1, Explanation of Data Distribution.

Table 7-8: Annual Compensation of Full-Time Associate Pastors by Gender

	Data Distribution*	GENDER	
		Male	Female
CHARACTERISTICS			
Average weekend worship attendance		847	833
Average church income		$1,430,664	$1,469,313
Average # of years employed		7	8
Average # of paid vacation days		18	19
% College graduate or higher		91%	74%
% Who receive auto reimbursement/allowance		53%	51%
% Ordained		93%	79%
% Supervise one or more people		66%	66%
Average % salary increase (for those who had an increase) this year		3.8%	3.8%
COMPENSATION			
Base Salary	Median	$35,994	$36,200
	Average	$37,330	$37,613
Housing	Median	$24,000	$24,500
	Average	$24,120	$23,911
Parsonage	Median	$12,360	$18,400
	Average	$16,555	$18,899
Total Compensation	**Median**	**$55,843**	**$52,625**
	Average	**$58,295**	**$52,477**
BENEFITS			
Health Insurance	Median	$9,802	$8,160
	Average	$10,089	$8,585
Life Insurance	Median	$285	$410
	Average	$577	$585
Disability Insurance	Median	$500	$426
	Average	$631	$623
Retirement	Median	$3,500	$4,443
	Average	$4,273	$5,114
Continuing Education	Median	$1,050	$1,425
	Average	$1,618	$1,825
Total Benefits	**Median**	**$11,000**	**$9,208**
	Average	**$12,048**	**$11,111**
TOTAL COMPENSATION PLUS BENEFITS	**Median**	**$65,912**	**$63,600**
	Average	**$69,091**	**$62,905**
Number of Respondents		451	78

- Not enough response to provide meaningful data.

* For detailed description and definitions of Data Distribution (Median and Average), see chapter 1, Explanation of Data Distribution.

Table 7-9: Annual Compensation of Part-Time Associate Pastors by Church Income

	Data Distribution*	CHURCH INCOME				
		$250K & Under	$251-$500K	$501-$750K	$751K-$1M	Over 1 Million
CHARACTERISTICS						
Average weekend worship attendance		136	264	316	451	1,065
Average church income		$146,990	$382,182	$617,781	$906,397	$2,100,206
Average # of years employed		4	5	6	9	8
Average # of paid vacation days		18	13	25	19	16
% College graduate or higher		84%	74%	89%	80%	77%
% Who receive auto reimbursement/allowance		38%	57%	47%	29%	56%
% Ordained		93%	86%	84%	76%	71%
% Supervise one or more people		51%	44%	21%	44%	38%
Average % salary increase (for those who had an increase) this year		5.0%	3.7%	-	-	4.3%
HOURLY RATE						
Base Rate	Average	$16	$15	$19	$16	$20
COMPENSATION						
Base Salary	Median	$13,200	$9,000	$20,868	$19,066	$19,275
	Average	$15,956	$11,148	$22,372	$18,326	$21,825
Housing	Median	$12,039	$8,100	$14,400	$12,180	$27,180
	Average	$13,191	$12,009	$16,324	$11,496	$24,603
Parsonage	Median	-	-	-	-	-
	Average	-	-	-	-	-
Total Compensation	**Median**	**$18,000**	**$12,520**	**$22,939**	**$24,085**	**$22,608**
	Average	**$21,190**	**$14,454**	**$28,291**	**$22,658**	**$27,941**
BENEFITS						
Health Insurance	Median	$6,000	-	-	-	-
	Average	$7,772	-	-	-	-
Life Insurance	Median	-	-	-	-	-
	Average	-	-	-	-	-
Disability Insurance	Median	-	-	-	-	-
	Average	-	-	-	-	-
Retirement	Median	-	-	-	-	-
	Average	-	-	-	-	-
Continuing Education	Median	$375	-	$813	-	-
	Average	$560	-	$878	-	-
Total Benefits	**Median**	**$5,376**	**$3,956**	**$3,000**	-	-
	Average	**$6,557**	**$4,292**	**$3,944**	-	-
TOTAL COMPENSATION PLUS BENEFITS	**Median**	**$17,100**	**$11,500**	**$26,000**	**$25,000**	**$22,608**
	Average	**$23,414**	**$15,144**	**$30,159**	**$26,950**	**$29,357**
Number of Respondents		43	35	19	17	34

- Not enough response to provide meaningful data.

* For detailed description and definitions of Data Distribution (Median and Average), see chapter 1, Explanation of Data Distribution.

Table 7-10: Annual Compensation of Part-Time Associate Pastors by Worship Attendance

	Data Distribution*	WORSHIP ATTENDANCE					
		100 or less	101-300	301-500	501-750	751-1,000	Over 1,000
CHARACTERISTICS							
Average weekend worship attendance		67	213	407	668	881	2,448
Average church income		$156,228	$404,825	$812,131	-	$1,272,687	$3,237,500
Average # of years employed		4	5	7	11	8	7
Average # of paid vacation days		20	19	16	17	12	16
% College graduate or higher		79%	89%	72%	86%	64%	89%
% Who receive auto reimbursement/allowance		43%	54%	38%	75%	36%	27%
% Ordained		96%	92%	68%	75%	55%	82%
% Supervise one or more people		42%	57%	18%	63%	27%	36%
Average % salary increase (for those who had an increase) this year		5.1%	3.3%	3.3%	-	-	-
HOURLY RATE							
Base Rate	Average	$16	$16	$17	-	$19	$19
COMPENSATION							
Base Salary	Median	$12,188	$12,000	$15,395	-	$15,775	$17,000
	Average	$14,834	$15,247	$17,580	-	$17,977	$18,480
Housing	Median	$12,000	$11,000	$16,200	-	-	-
	Average	$13,076	$12,975	$17,550	-	-	-
Parsonage	Median	-	-	-	-	-	-
	Average	-	-	-	-	-	-
Total Compensation	**Median**	**$18,000**	**$17,200**	**$19,035**	**$34,188**	**$18,324**	**$19,600**
	Average	**$20,717**	**$19,725**	**$21,964**	**$33,624**	**$20,349**	**$26,880**
BENEFITS							
Health Insurance	Median	-	$6,276	-	-	-	-
	Average	-	$8,668	-	-	-	-
Life Insurance	Median	-	-	-	-	-	-
	Average	-	-	-	-	-	-
Disability	Median	-	-	-	-	-	-
	Average	-	-	-	-	-	-
Retirement	Median	-	$2,250	-	-	-	-
	Average	-	$3,016	-	-	-	-
Continuing Education	Median	$475	$750	-	-	-	-
	Average	$633	$800	-	-	-	-
Total Benefits	**Median**	**$3,073**	**$5,473**	**$3,620**	**-**	**-**	**-**
	Average	**$5,667**	**$7,718**	**$5,110**	**-**	**-**	**-**
TOTAL COMPENSATION PLUS BENEFITS	**Median**	**$16,313**	**$17,600**	**$20,099**	**$34,608**	**$18,324**	**$19,600**
	Average	**$22,721**	**$22,165**	**$23,114**	**$36,769**	**$20,959**	**$26,971**
Number of Respondents		28	53	40	8	11	11

- Not enough response to provide meaningful data.

* For detailed description and definitions of Data Distribution (Median and Average), see chapter 1, Explanation of Data Distribution.

Table 7-11: Annual Compensation of Part-Time Associate Pastors by Church Setting

	Data Distribution*	CHURCH SETTING			
		Metro-politan city	Suburb of large city	Small town or rural city	Farming area
CHARACTERISTICS					
Average weekend worship attendance		470	666	314	-
Average church income		$801,108	$1,174,559	$503,393	-
Average # of years employed		6	7	5	-
Average # of paid vacation days		11	18	19	-
% College graduate or higher		86%	79%	83%	-
% Who receive auto reimbursement/allowance		43%	47%	41%	-
% Ordained		71%	87%	83%	-
% Supervise one or more people		43%	37%	44%	-
Average % salary increase (for those who had an increase) this year		4.1%	4.3%	3.9%	-
HOURLY RATE					
Base Rate	Average	$17	$20	$15	-
COMPENSATION					
Base Salary	Median	$10,750	$16,200	$12,532	-
	Average	$15,069	$19,284	$16,065	-
Housing	Median	$12,360	$14,871	$12,039	-
	Average	$12,822	$17,338	$14,169	-
Parsonage	Median	-	-	-	-
	Average	-	-	-	-
Total Compensation	**Median**	**$12,000**	**$20,475**	**$18,324**	-
	Average	**$18,382**	**$24,936**	**$21,157**	-
BENEFITS					
Health Insurance	Median	-	-	$6,000	-
	Average	-	-	$6,777	-
Life Insurance	Median	-	-	-	-
	Average	-	-	-	-
Disability Insurance	Median	-	-	-	-
	Average	-	-	-	-
Retirement	Median	-	$4,711	-	-
	Average	-	$3,961	-	-
Continuing Education	Median	-	-	$500	-
	Average	-	-	$517	-
Total Benefits	**Median**	-	**$4,420**	**$3,430**	-
	Average	-	**$8,376**	**$4,746**	-
TOTAL COMPENSATION PLUS BENEFITS	**Median**	**$12,000**	**$20,475**	**$19,603**	-
	Average	**$20,062**	**$26,838**	**$22,473**	-
Number of Respondents		24	62	59	7

- Not enough response to provide meaningful data.

* For detailed description and definitions of Data Distribution (Median and Average), see chapter 1, Explanation of Data Distribution.

Table 7-12: Annual Compensation of Part-Time Associate Pastors by Region

	Data Distribution*	REGION								
		New England	Middle Atlantic	South Atlantic	E-N Central	E-S Central	W-N Central	W-S Central	Mountain	Pacific
CHARACTERISTICS										
Average weekend worship attendance		-	648	707	369	-	465	-	239	292
Average church income		-	$1,142,505	$1,216,650	$594,844	-	$561,836	-	$551,098	$604,574
Average # of years employed		-	6	7	6	-	5	-	4	7
Average # of paid vacation days		-	21	25	14	-	17	-	12	18
% College graduate or higher		-	74%	90%	67%	-	88%	-	73%	87%
% Who receive auto reimbursement/allowance		-	35%	62%	63%	-	19%	-	33%	44%
% Ordained		-	78%	90%	86%	-	76%	-	83%	76%
% Supervise one or more people		-	57%	43%	32%	-	36%	-	50%	42%
Average % salary increase (for those who had an increase) this year		-	5.2%	4.9%	3.7%	-	4.5%	-	-	-
HOURLY RATE										
Base Rate	Average	-	$16	$19	$19	-	$16	-	$14	$17
COMPENSATION										
Base Salary	Median	-	$13,266	$18,450	$13,884	-	$11,396	-	$10,350	$14,400
	Average	-	$17,435	$20,984	$16,243	-	$14,845	-	$12,444	$17,219
Housing	Median	-	$12,078	$19,500	$10,000	-	-	-	-	$22,800
	Average	-	$13,454	$19,599	$11,557	-	-	-	-	$21,434
Parsonage	Median	-	-	-	-	-	-	-	-	-
	Average	-	-	-	-	-	-	-	-	-
Total Compensation	**Median**	-	**$20,000**	**$22,651**	**$16,575**	-	**$16,368**	-	**$13,581**	**$22,812**
	Average	-	**$22,463**	**$25,676**	**$20,513**	-	**$19,852**	-	**$17,147**	**$26,789**
BENEFITS										
Health Insurance	Median	-	-	-	-	-	-	-	-	-
	Average	-	-	-	-	-	-	-	-	-
Life Insurance	Median	-	-	-	-	-	-	-	-	-
	Average	-	-	-	-	-	-	-	-	-
Disability Insurance	Median	-	-	-	-	-	-	-	-	-
	Average	-	-	-	-	-	-	-	-	-
Retirement	Median	-	-	-	-	-	-	-	-	-
	Average	-	-	-	-	-	-	-	-	-
Continuing Education	Median	-	-	-	$613	-	-	-	-	-
	Average	-	-	-	$753	-	-	-	-	-
Total Benefits	**Median**	-	-	-	**$3,658**	-	-	-	-	**$3,393**
	Average	-	-	-	**$3,572**	-	-	-	-	**$4,650**
TOTAL COMPENSATION PLUS BENEFITS	**Median**	-	**$20,750**	**$22,788**	**$18,400**	-	**$16,868**	-	**$13,581**	**$21,075**
	Average	-	**$25,123**	**$29,605**	**$21,699**	-	**$21,554**	-	**$18,976**	**$26,544**
Number of Respondents		3	23	21	38	7	17	7	12	25

- Not enough response to provide meaningful data.

* For detailed description and definitions of Data Distribution (Median and Average), see chapter 1, Explanation of Data Distribution.

Table 7-13: Annual Compensation of Part-Time Associate Pastors by Education

	Data Distribution*	EDUCATION			
		Less than Bachelor	Bachelor	Master	Doctorate
CHARACTERISTICS					
Average weekend worship attendance		427	410	529	-
Average church income		$999,904	$685,739	$750,262	-
Average # of years employed		7	5	6	-
Average # of paid vacation days		19	16	17	-
% College graduate or higher		0%	100%	100%	-
% Who receive auto reimbursement/allowance		32%	50%	48%	-
% Ordained		58%	84%	89%	-
% Supervise one or more people		30%	40%	42%	-
Average % salary increase (for those who had an increase) this year		2.6%	4.1%	4.6%	-
HOURLY RATE					
Base Rate	Average	$18	$17	$16	-
COMPENSATION					
Base Salary	Median	$11,000	$16,150	$13,400	-
	Average	$14,986	$17,505	$17,677	-
Housing	Median	-	$17,450	$11,819	-
	Average	-	$17,367	$13,883	-
Parsonage	Median	-	-	-	-
	Average	-	-	-	-
Total Compensation	**Median**	**$11,000**	**$19,900**	**$21,957**	**-**
	Average	**$16,186**	**$23,294**	**$23,093**	**-**
BENEFITS					
Health Insurance	Median	-	-	$8,200	-
	Average	-	-	$9,787	-
Life Insurance	Median	-	-	-	-
	Average	-	-	-	-
Disability Insurance	Median	-	-	-	-
	Average	-	-	-	-
Retirement	Median	-	-	$3,509	-
	Average	-	-	$3,753	-
Continuing Education	Median	-	$900	$750	-
	Average	-	$921	$820	-
Total Benefits	**Median**	**-**	**$3,240**	**$4,700**	**-**
	Average	**-**	**$4,157**	**$8,075**	**-**
TOTAL COMPENSATION PLUS BENEFITS	**Median**	**$11,000**	**$20,300**	**$22,939**	**-**
	Average	**$17,126**	**$24,464**	**$26,043**	**-**
Number of Respondents		28	49	62	7

- Not enough response to provide meaningful data.

* For detailed description and definitions of Data Distribution (Median and Average), see chapter 1, Explanation of Data Distribution.

Table 7-14: Annual Compensation of Part-Time Associate Pastors by Years Employed

	Data Distribution*	YEARS EMPLOYED			
		Less than 6 years	6-10 years	11-15 years	Over 15 years
CHARACTERISTICS					
Average weekend worship attendance		377	517	1,069	562
Average church income		$565,530	$1,086,714	$1,525,557	$959,000
Average # of years employed		2	8	13	24
Average # of paid vacation days		16	15	23	32
% College graduate or higher		83%	78%	75%	75%
% Who receive auto reimbursement/allowance		43%	52%	43%	44%
% Ordained		85%	71%	86%	89%
% Supervise one or more people		38%	45%	43%	33%
Average % salary increase (for those who had an increase) this year		4.4%	4.1%	-	-
HOURLY RATE					
Base Rate	Average	$17	$18	$20	-
COMPENSATION					
Base Salary	Median	$11,500	$15,225	$19,531	$19,275
	Average	$15,195	$19,354	$18,834	$22,550
Housing	Median	$11,069	$16,500	$17,600	-
	Average	$12,734	$17,698	$17,156	-
Parsonage	Median	-	-	-	-
	Average	-	-	-	-
Total Compensation	**Median**	**$16,200**	**$20,000**	**$23,855**	**$34,175**
	Average	**$18,993**	**$23,321**	**$28,518**	**$34,797**
BENEFITS					
Health Insurance	Median	$6,000	-	-	-
	Average	$7,071	-	-	-
Life Insurance	Median	-	-	-	-
	Average	-	-	-	-
Disability Insurance	Median	-	-	-	-
	Average	-	-	-	-
Retirement	Median	$2,500	-	-	-
	Average	$3,111	-	-	-
Continuing Education	Median	$750	-	-	-
	Average	$781	-	-	-
Total Benefits	**Median**	**$2,970**	**$4,700**	**-**	**-**
	Average	**$5,722**	**$7,821**	**-**	**-**
TOTAL COMPENSATION PLUS BENEFITS	**Median**	**$16,450**	**$21,216**	**$27,832**	**$34,175**
	Average	**$20,246**	**$25,948**	**$31,355**	**$36,923**
Number of Respondents		89	34	14	9

- Not enough response to provide meaningful data.

* For detailed description and definitions of Data Distribution (Median and Average), see chapter 1, Explanation of Data Distribution.

Table 7-15: Annual Compensation of Part-Time Associate Pastors by Denomination

	Data Distribution*	DENOMINATION					
		Assemblies of God	Baptist	Independent/ Nondenom.	Lutheran	Methodist	Presby-terian
CHARACTERISTICS							
Average weekend worship attendance		327	524	594	-	664	218
Average church income		$594,991	$1,205,311	$986,844	-	$861,222	$636,719
Average # of years employed		4	4	9	-	7	4
Average # of paid vacation days		14	11	22	-	14	30
% College graduate or higher		73%	67%	86%	-	100%	100%
% Who receive auto reimbursement/allowance		13%	54%	25%	-	67%	67%
% Ordained		81%	74%	84%	-	100%	100%
% Supervise one or more people		57%	30%	42%	-	22%	25%
Average % salary increase (for those who had an increase) this year		3.5%	4.7%	4.2%	-	-	3.3%
HOURLY RATE							
Base Rate	Average	$11	$20	$18	-	$20	-
COMPENSATION							
Base Salary	Median	$11,000	$12,700	$16,000	-	$22,939	$15,095
	Average	$11,694	$18,598	$19,583	-	$19,211	$18,085
Housing	Median	$10,000	$13,539	$17,742	-	-	-
	Average	$10,943	$14,913	$18,371	-	-	-
Parsonage	Median	-	-	-	-	-	-
	Average	-	-	-	-	-	-
Total Compensation	**Median**	**$11,000**	**$16,550**	**$21,162**	**-**	**$22,939**	**$20,500**
	Average	**$14,412**	**$24,059**	**$25,097**	**-**	**$21,167**	**$24,863**
BENEFITS							
Health Insurance	Median	-	-	-	-	-	-
	Average	-	-	-	-	-	-
Life Insurance	Median	-	-	-	-	-	-
	Average	-	-	-	-	-	-
Disability Insurance	Median	-	-	-	-	-	-
	Average	-	-	-	-	-	-
Retirement	Median	-	-	-	-	-	-
	Average	-	-	-	-	-	-
Continuing Education	Median	-	-	-	-	-	-
	Average	-	-	-	-	-	-
Total Benefits	**Median**	**-**	**$2,088**	**-**	**-**	**-**	**-**
	Average	**-**	**$5,073**	**-**	**-**	**-**	**-**
TOTAL COMPENSATION PLUS BENEFITS	**Median**	**$11,000**	**$16,550**	**$21,162**	**-**	**$23,000**	**$22,360**
	Average	**$14,800**	**$25,675**	**$26,352**	**-**	**$23,939**	**$28,356**
Number of Respondents		16	27	32	2	9	12

- Not enough response to provide meaningful data.

* For detailed description and definitions of Data Distribution (Median and Average), see chapter 1, Explanation of Data Distribution.

Table 7-16: Annual Compensation of Part-Time Associate Pastors by Gender

	Data Distribution*	GENDER	
		Male	Female
CHARACTERISTICS			
Average weekend worship attendance		477	466
Average church income		$806,222	$787,108
Average # of years employed		5	7
Average # of paid vacation days		17	18
% College graduate or higher		85%	73%
% Who receive auto reimbursement/allowance		49%	38%
% Ordained		88%	73%
% Supervise one or more people		40%	42%
Average % salary increase (for those who had an increase) this year		4.3%	3.5%
HOURLY RATE			
Base Rate	Average	$18	$16
COMPENSATION			
Base Salary	Median	$15,225	$12,766
	Average	$18,168	$15,460
Housing	Median	$14,400	$12,039
	Average	$14,750	$16,870
Parsonage	Median	-	-
	Average	-	-
Total Compensation	**Median**	**$20,800**	**$16,162**
	Average	**$23,430**	**$19,954**
BENEFITS			
Health Insurance	Median	$6,000	-
	Average	$7,067	-
Life Insurance	Median	-	-
	Average	-	-
Disability Insurance	Median	-	-
	Average	-	-
Retirement	Median	$3,136	$2,450
	Average	$3,424	$2,942
Continuing Education	Median	$500	$750
	Average	$778	$743
Total Benefits	**Median**	**$4,758**	**$3,000**
	Average	**$5,969**	**$7,131**
TOTAL COMPENSATION PLUS BENEFITS	**Median**	**$20,800**	**$16,100**
	Average	**$25,311**	**$21,511**
Number of Respondents		97	56

- Not enough response to provide meaningful data.

* For detailed description and definitions of Data Distribution (Median and Average), see chapter 1, Explanation of Data Distribution.

Full-Time Associate Pastor Worksheet

	Enter your church data below	The 2014–2015 Compensation Handbook for Church Staff		Enter *Compensation Handbook* data below			
				Highest 25%	Median	Lowest 25%	Average
Church Income	$	Table 7-1	page 79	$	$	$	$
Worship Attendance		Table 7-2	page 80	n/a	$	n/a	$
Church Setting (metro, suburb, small town, or farming area)		Table 7-3	page 81	n/a	$	n/a	$
Region		Table 7-4	page 82	n/a	$	n/a	$
Person's Education		Table 7-5	page 83	n/a	$	n/a	$
Years Employed		Table 7-6	page 84	n/a	$	n/a	$
Denomination (if applicable)		Table 7-7	page 85	n/a	$	n/a	$

Looking at the table and page number references indicated in the *2014–2015 Compensation Handbook for Church Staff* columns above, locate the appropriate range for your church. Refer to the instructions below for step-by-step help.

FILLING OUT THE WORKSHEET

1. Fill in the gray boxes under *Enter your church data* with your church demographic information as follows:

   ▶ **Income** (Total annual church budget in past year)
   ▶ **Worship attendance** (Number of people, including children, who attend all weekend services)
   ▶ **Church setting** (Metropolitan city, suburb of large city, small town or rural city, or farming area)

   ▶ **Region** (Locate your state's region in the appendix on page 346.)
   ▶ **Education** (Highest level of education: less than bachelor, bachelor, master, or doctorate)

2. Use Table 7-1 (page 79) in your *2014–2015 Compensation Handbook for Church Staff* to enter data pertinent to your church. In the heading (top row), locate your church **income** from the five available ranges. Follow that column to the bottom rows, and copy the *Highest 25%*, *Median*, *Lowest 25%*, and *Average* amounts onto your worksheet.

3. Use Table 7-2 (page 80) on your *2014–2015 Compensation Handbook for Church Staff* to enter data pertinent to your church. In the heading (top row), locate your church's

worship attendance from the six available ranges. Follow that column to the bottom rows, and copy the *Median* and *Average* amounts onto your worksheet.

4. Use Table 7-3 (page 81) on your *2014–2015 Compensation Handbook for Church Staff* to enter data pertinent to your church. In the heading (top row), choose the **church setting** that best describes your church. Follow that column to the bottom rows, and copy the *Median* and *Average* amounts onto your worksheet.

5. Use Table 7-4 (page 82) on your *2014–2015 Compensation Handbook for Church Staff* to enter data pertinent to your church. In the heading (top row), look for the **region** where your church is located. Follow that column to the bottom rows, and copy the *Median* and *Average* amounts onto your worksheet.

6. Use Table 7-5 (page 83) on your *2014–2015 Compensation Handbook for Church Staff* to enter data pertinent to your Associate Pastor. In the heading (top row), look for **your Associate Pastor's highest level of education**. Follow that column to the bottom rows, and copy the *Median* and *Average* amounts onto your worksheet.

7. Use Table 7-6 (page 84) on your *2014–2015 Compensation Handbook for Church Staff* to enter data pertinent to your Associate Pastor. In the heading (top row), locate the **number of years your Associate Pastor has been employed**. Follow that column to the bottom rows, and copy the *Median* and *Average* amounts onto your worksheet.

8. Use Table 7-7 (page 85) on your *2014–2015 Compensation Handbook for Church Staff* to enter data pertinent to your church. In the heading (top row), look for **your church's denominational affiliation**. Follow that column to the bottom rows, and copy the *Median* and *Average* amounts onto your worksheet. If your church is not affiliated with a denomination, leave this section blank.

DETERMINING COMPENSATION

This tool will not provide you with a single compensation amount but rather with a range of values to help you determine the compensation appropriate to your situation.

1. Look at the values in the shaded *Median* column. Circle the **lowest** and the **highest** values. **This is the range of the median compensation plus benefits for churches similar to yours.**

2. For a variety of reasons, compensation plus benefits may be higher or lower than the range established in this table. Income and attendance are two significant factors affecting church compensation packages. If church income or attendance skews higher, you might want to consider moving toward or above the higher end of the range. Likewise, if church income or attendance skews lower, you may consider moving the package toward or below the lower end of the range.

3. Examine additional variables that might impact the compensation package you offer, such as years of service, education, and church setting.

4. Determine other circumstances unique to your situation, such as cost of living in your area, theological beliefs, pastoral performance, financial needs, the local economy, personal motivation, congregational goals, and others.

5. You now have a compensation package range based on the *2014–2015 Compensation Handbook*. Since each church and position are unique, your final compensation package will be based on additional factors unique to your situation.

Part-Time Associate Pastor Worksheet

	Enter your church data below	The 2014–2015 Compensation Handbook for Church Staff		Enter *Compensation Handbook* data below			
				Highest 25%	Median	Lowest 25%	Average
Church Income	$	Table 7-9	page 87	$	$	$	$
Worship Attendance		Table 7-10	page 88	n/a	$	n/a	$
Church Setting (metro, suburb, small town, or farming area)		Table 7-11	page 89	n/a	$	n/a	$
Region		Table 7-12	page 90	n/a	$	n/a	$
Person's Education		Table 7-13	page 91	n/a	$	n/a	$
Years Employed		Table 7-14	page 92	n/a	$	n/a	$
Denomination (if applicable)		Table 7-15	page 93	n/a	$	n/a	$

Looking at the table and page number references indicated in the *2014–2015 Compensation Handbook for Church Staff* columns above, locate the appropriate range for your church. Refer to the instructions below for step-by-step help.

FILLING OUT THE WORKSHEET

1. Fill in the gray boxes under *Enter your church data* with your church demographic information as follows:

   ▶ **Income** (Total annual church budget in past year)
   ▶ **Worship attendance** (Number of people, including children, who attend all weekend services)
   ▶ **Church setting** (Metropolitan city, suburb of large city, small town or rural city, or farming area)

   ▶ **Region** (Locate your state's region in the appendix on page 346.)
   ▶ **Education** (Highest level of education: less than bachelor, bachelor, master, or doctorate)

2. Use Table 7-9 (page 87) in your *2014–2015 Compensation Handbook for Church Staff* to enter data pertinent to your church. In the heading (top row), locate your church **income** from the five available ranges. Follow that column to the bottom rows, and copy the *Highest 25%*, *Median*, *Lowest 25%*, and *Average* amounts onto your worksheet.

3. Use Table 7-10 (page 88) on your *2014–2015 Compensation Handbook for Church Staff* to enter data pertinent to your church. In the heading (top row), locate your church's

worship attendance from the six available ranges. Follow that column to the bottom rows, and copy the *Median* and *Average* amounts onto your worksheet.

4. Use Table 7-11 (page 89) on your *2014–2015 Compensation Handbook for Church Staff* to enter data pertinent to your church. In the heading (top row), choose the **church setting** that best describes your church. Follow that column to the bottom rows, and copy the *Median* and *Average* amounts onto your worksheet.

5. Use Table 7-12 (page 90) on your *2014–2015 Compensation Handbook for Church Staff* to enter data pertinent to your church. In the heading (top row), look for the **region** where your church is located. Follow that column to the bottom rows, and copy the *Median* and *Average* amounts onto your worksheet.

6. Use Table 7-13 (page 91) on your *2014–2015 Compensation Handbook for Church Staff* to enter data pertinent to your Associate Pastor. In the heading (top row), look for **your Associate Pastor's highest level of education**. Follow that column to the bottom rows, and copy the *Median* and *Average* amounts onto your worksheet.

7. Use Table 7-14 (page 92) on your *2014–2015 Compensation Handbook for Church Staff* to enter data pertinent to your Associate Pastor. In the heading (top row), locate the **number of years your Associate Pastor has been employed**. Follow that column to the bottom rows, and copy the *Median* and *Average* amounts onto your worksheet.

8. Use Table 7-15 (page 93) on your *2014–2015 Compensation Handbook for Church Staff* to enter data pertinent to your church. In the heading (top row), look for **your church's denominational affiliation**. Follow that column to the bottom rows, and copy the *Median* and *Average* amounts onto your worksheet. If your church is not affiliated with a denomination, leave this section blank.

DETERMINING COMPENSATION

This tool will not provide you with a single compensation amount but rather with a range of values to help you determine the compensation appropriate to your situation.

1. Look at the values in the shaded *Median* column. Circle the **lowest** and the **highest** values. **This is the range of the median compensation plus benefits for churches similar to yours.**

2. For a variety of reasons, compensation plus benefits may be higher or lower than the range established in this table. Income and attendance are two significant factors affecting church compensation packages. If church income or attendance skews higher, you might want to consider moving toward or above the higher end of the range. Likewise, if church income or attendance skews lower, you may consider moving the package toward or below the lower end of the range.

3. Examine additional variables that might impact the compensation package you offer, such as years of service, education, and church setting.

4. Determine other circumstances unique to your situation, such as cost of living in your area, theological beliefs, pastoral performance, financial needs, the local economy, personal motivation, congregational goals, and others.

5. You now have a compensation package range based on the *2014–2015 Compensation Handbook*. Since each church and position are unique, your final compensation package will be based on additional factors unique to your situation.

8

ADULT MINISTRY/ CHRISTIAN EDUCATION PASTORS/ DIRECTORS

Employment Profile

For the purposes of this book, Adult Ministry and Christian Education Pastors/Directors have been reported together.

Adult Ministry Pastors/Directors include paid pastors and directors of church ministries for adults, married couples, men, singles, seniors, women, young adults, etc.

Christian Education Pastors/Directors include paid pastors and directors of educational ministries based on purpose rather than age gradation, such as Bible studies, cell groups, Christian education, discipleship, equipping, small groups, spiritual formation, etc.

Two-thirds of the full-time Adult Ministry/Christian Education Pastors/Directors who responded

are ordained ministers. This is an increase of 12 percentage points over the study conducted in 2011. More than nine in 10 of these ministers are employed by the church rather than self-employed. Nearly nine in 10 have at least a college degree, while four in 10 have a graduate degree.

Four in 10 survey participants work on a part-time basis. More than half of part-time Adult Ministry/Christian Education Pastors/Directors are ordained, which is 18 percentage points higher than in the previous survey.

The chart below provides a demographic profile of this sample.

	Full-Time	Part-Time
Number of respondents	**196**	**134**
Ordained	68%	49%
Average years employed	6%	6%
Male	66%	37%
Female	34%	63%
Self-employed (receives 1099)	7%	6%
Church employee (receives W-2)	93%	94%
High school diploma	8%	6%
Associate degree	6%	3%
Bachelor's degree	45%	53%
Master's degree	33%	31%
Doctoral degree	9%	7%

Total Compensation plus Benefits Package Analysis

The following analyses are based on data in the tables you will find later in this chapter. The tables show compensation plus benefits data for full-time and part-time Adult Ministry/Christian Education Pastors/Directors and are presented according to church income, church attendance, church setting, region, education, years employed, denomination, and gender. In this way, compensation plus benefits for Adult Ministry/Christian Education Pastors/Directors can be analyzed and compared from a variety of useful perspectives.

The total compensation plus benefits amount includes the base salary; housing allowance and/or parsonage amount; health, life, and disability insurance payments; retirement contribution; and educational funds.

A worksheet at the end of this chapter is provided to help you apply the data to your church's situation.

Full-timers in adult and education ministries receive benefits packages comparable to those of other professional and ministerial staff members within the church. More than half receive a housing allowance, health insurance, and retirement benefits. Fifty-six percent received salary increases, representing a 12-percentage-point increase over the 2011 study.

Part-timers receive few benefits, with the most common being paid vacation. More than four in 10 received paid vacation (48%) and a salary increase (46%).

Compensation Plus Benefits	Full-Time	Part-Time
Base Salary	97%	89%
Housing	55%	21%
Parsonage	3%	1%
Health Insurance*	56%	7%
Life Insurance*	31%	3%
Disability Insurance*	31%	4%
Retirement	57%	8%
Continuing Education	30%	15%
Received salary increase	56%	46%
Received paid vacation	97%	48%
Received auto reimbursement/allowance	45%	31%

* Only those reporting individual premiums for Health, Life, or Disability (not total insurance premiums) are included.

KEY POINTS

* Two-thirds of full-time Adult Ministry/Christian Education Pastors/Directors reporting serve churches with an income higher than $1,000,000 and a worship attendance of more than 500.

* Nearly six in 10 part-time Adult Ministry/Christian Education Pastors/Directors serve in churches with an income of $750,000 or less.

* In general, as church income increases, compensation and benefits for full-time Adult Ministry/Christian Education Pastors/Directors also increase.

* Full-time male Adult Ministry/Christian Education Pastors/Directors receive nearly 50% more in compensation plus benefits than their female counterparts.

Compensation & Benefits: National Averages for Full-Time Adult Ministry/Christian Education Pastors/Directors*	
2000	
2001	
2002	
2003	
2004	
2005	
2006	$67,711
2007	$59,791
2008	$60,312
2009	$58,877
2011	$56,495
2013	$63,320**

* No historical data available before 2006.

** The above trend is made available for your reference only. In addition to looking at this overall data, please refer to the detailed tables using your church's income, attendance, setting, region, and denomination as well as the person's education, gender, and years employed for guidance in compensating this position.

Table 8-1: Annual Compensation of Full-Time Adult Ministry/Christian Education Pastors/Directors by Church Income

CHARACTERISTICS	Data Distribution*	CHURCH INCOME				
		$250K & Under	$251-$500K	$501-$750K	$751K-$1M	Over $1 Million
Average weekend worship attendance		-	257	355	540	1,361
Average church income		-	$413,831	$612,137	$895,613	$2,350,710
Average # of years employed		-	10	8	7	8
Average # of paid vacation days		-	16	18	16	19
% College graduate or higher		-	53%	73%	95%	90%
% Who receive auto reimbursement/allowance		-	27%	50%	45%	48%
% Ordained		-	43%	73%	68%	65%
% Supervise one or more people		-	80%	64%	59%	66%
Average % salary increase (for those who had an increase) this year		-	3.0%	3.3%	3.0%	2.7%
COMPENSATION						
Base Salary	Highest 25%	-	$39,000	$42,000	$50,900	$48,750
	Median	-	$34,170	$35,085	$44,850	$40,600
	Lowest 25%	-	$30,000	$26,347	$37,569	$30,863
	Average	-	$31,503	$33,440	$44,837	$40,152
Housing	Highest 25%	-	-	$29,500	$32,000	$34,500
	Median	-	-	$23,945	$22,760	$29,010
	Lowest 25%	-	-	$16,500	$17,000	$21,000
	Average	-	-	$23,941	$26,737	$28,831
Parsonage	Highest 25%	-	-	-	-	-
	Median	-	-	-	-	-
	Lowest 25%	-	-	-	-	-
	Average	-	-	-	-	-
Total Compensation	**Highest 25%**	-	$40,068	$54,000	$66,095	$66,000
	Median	-	$34,585	$44,000	$51,450	$55,000
	Lowest 25%	-	$30,750	$38,582	$45,000	$45,000
	Average	-	$36,639	$46,971	$57,095	$56,594
BENEFITS						
Health Insurance	Highest 25%	-	-	$18,085	$14,086	$14,180
	Median	-	-	$8,648	$9,000	$10,603
	Lowest 25%	-	-	$5,288	$3,616	$5,004
	Average	-	-	$10,451	$8,532	$10,404
Life Insurance	Highest 25%	-	-	-	-	$400
	Median	-	-	-	-	$216
	Lowest 25%	-	-	-	-	$131
	Average	-	-	-	-	$499
Disability Insurance	Highest 25%	-	-	-	-	$534
	Median	-	-	-	-	$343
	Lowest 25%	-	-	-	-	$125
	Average	-	-	-	-	$392
Retirement	Highest 25%	-	-	$4,701	$6,469	$5,400
	Median	-	-	$3,600	$2,150	$3,800
	Lowest 25%	-	-	$2,400	$1,530	$2,249
	Average	-	-	$3,723	$3,446	$4,032
Continuing Education	Highest 25%	-	-	$1,500	$2,000	$2,000
	Median	-	-	$800	$1,800	$1,000
	Lowest 25%	-	-	$625	$1,000	$500
	Average	-	-	$1,019	$1,500	$1,350
Total Benefits	**Highest 25%**	-	$8,000	$12,075	$10,000	$18,522
	Median	-	$6,100	$8,273	$5,437	$10,468
	Lowest 25%	-	$1,050	$4,425	$2,136	$4,230
	Average	-	$4,913	$10,755	$7,369	$11,696
TOTAL COMPENSATION PLUS BENEFITS	**Highest 25%**	-	$52,293	$64,750	$72,250	$79,876
	Median	-	$35,200	$50,992	$60,146	$66,291
	Lowest 25%	-	$30,000	$42,930	$46,000	$48,066
	Average	-	$37,999	$55,771	$62,789	$66,449
Number of Respondents		4	15	22	22	120

- Not enough response to provide meaningful data.

* For detailed description and definitions of Data Distribution (Highest 25%, Median, Lowest 25%, and Average), see chapter 1, Explanation of Data Distribution.

Table 8-2: Annual Compensation of Full-Time Adult Ministry/Christian Education Pastors/Directors by Worship Attendance

	Data Distribution*	WORSHIP ATTENDANCE					
		100 or less	101-300	301-500	501-750	751-1,000	Over 1,000
CHARACTERISTICS							
Average weekend worship attendance	-		225	427	652	870	1,960
Average church income	-		$615,918	$966,536	$1,159,574	$1,522,377	$3,039,541
Average # of years employed	-		8	8	8	6	8
Average # of paid vacation days	-		17	17	20	18	18
% College graduate or higher	-		64%	84%	92%	89%	90%
% Who receive auto reimbursement/allowance	-		36%	46%	56%	37%	51%
% Ordained	-		61%	57%	67%	62%	71%
% Supervise one or more people	-		79%	58%	64%	50%	76%
Average % salary increase (for those who had an increase) this year	-		4.3%	2.9%	2.6%	2.7%	2.7%
COMPENSATION							
Base Salary	Median	-	$34,170	$42,200	$39,541	$34,828	$41,000
	Average	-	$31,091	$39,359	$40,216	$36,030	$42,312
Housing	Median	-	$16,750	$22,760	$31,300	$23,600	$30,000
	Average	-	$18,228	$24,009	$36,819	$24,284	$29,615
Parsonage	Median	-	-	-	-	-	-
	Average	-	-	-	-	-	-
Total Compensation	**Median**	-	**$42,000**	**$50,000**	**$50,400**	**$49,376**	**$59,300**
	Average	-	**$41,408**	**$50,754**	**$55,759**	**$50,040**	**$59,409**
BENEFITS							
Health Insurance	Median	-	$8,588	$9,590	$10,800	$7,513	$12,193
	Average	-	$8,753	$10,852	$9,335	$8,566	$11,318
Life Insurance	Median	-	-	$250	-	-	$174
	Average	-	-	$372	-	-	$488
Disability	Median	-	-	$461	$360	-	$282
	Average	-	-	$426	$386	-	$415
Retirement	Median	-	$3,091	$3,932	$3,390	$3,934	$3,173
	Average	-	$3,589	$4,115	$3,720	$3,933	$3,860
Continuing Education	Median	-	$600	$1,000	$1,000	-	$1,600
	Average	-	$809	$1,203	$909	-	$1,717
Total Benefits	**Median**	-	**$6,100**	**$8,503**	**$6,850**	**$8,252**	**$12,100**
	Average	-	**$7,586**	**$11,308**	**$9,417**	**$8,985**	**$12,502**
TOTAL COMPENSATION PLUS BENEFITS	**Median**	-	**$45,100**	**$59,806**	**$58,233**	**$56,178**	**$69,507**
	Average	-	**$45,531**	**$60,533**	**$62,541**	**$55,128**	**$70,597**
Number of Respondents		0	33	37	25	27	69

- Not enough response to provide meaningful data.

* For detailed description and definitions of Data Distribution (Median and Average), see chapter 1, Explanation of Data Distribution.

Table 8-3: Annual Compensation of Full-Time Adult Ministry/Christian Education Pastors/Directors by Church Setting

	Data Distribution*	CHURCH SETTING			
		Metro-politan city	Suburb of large city	Small town or rural city	Farming area
CHARACTERISTICS					
Average weekend worship attendance		1,004	1,235	730	-
Average church income		$1,910,078	$2,007,088	$1,257,203	-
Average # of years employed		8	9	6	-
Average # of paid vacation days		19	18	18	-
% College graduate or higher		92%	83%	81%	-
% Who receive auto reimbursement/allowance		49%	41%	53%	-
% Ordained		69%	64%	67%	-
% Supervise one or more people		78%	69%	61%	-
Average % salary increase (for those who had an increase) this year		3.5%	2.8%	3.1%	-
COMPENSATION					
Base Salary	Median	$42,000	$40,000	$38,000	-
	Average	$39,895	$38,084	$39,168	-
Housing	Median	$23,700	$29,255	$20,100	-
	Average	$24,901	$28,949	$24,293	-
Parsonage	Median	-	-	-	-
	Average	-	-	-	-
Total Compensation	**Median**	**$52,000**	**$53,740**	**$48,375**	**-**
	Average	**$53,413**	**$54,543**	**$50,798**	**-**
BENEFITS					
Health Insurance	Median	$11,190	$9,508	$10,200	-
	Average	$10,324	$10,344	$10,499	-
Life Insurance	Median	$200	$216	$237	-
	Average	$278	$628	$284	-
Disability Insurance	Median	$225	$324	$550	-
	Average	$247	$358	$582	-
Retirement	Median	$4,000	$3,250	$3,627	-
	Average	$4,334	$3,663	$3,834	-
Continuing Education	Median	$1,350	$1,000	$1,000	-
	Average	$1,256	$1,292	$1,221	-
Total Benefits	**Median**	**$12,440**	**$8,100**	**$9,200**	**-**
	Average	**$11,874**	**$10,144**	**$10,732**	**-**
TOTAL COMPENSATION PLUS BENEFITS	**Median**	**$58,334**	**$60,390**	**$59,806**	**-**
	Average	**$60,391**	**$61,950**	**$61,001**	**-**
Number of Respondents		37	98	57	1

- Not enough response to provide meaningful data.

* For detailed description and definitions of Data Distribution (Median and Average), see chapter 1, Explanation of Data Distribution.

Table 8-4: Annual Compensation of Full-Time Adult Ministry/Christian Education Pastors/Directors by Region

	Data Distribution*	REGION								
		New England	Middle Atlantic	South Atlantic	E-N Central	E-S Central	W-N Central	W-S Central	Mountain	Pacific
CHARACTERISTICS										
Average weekend worship attendance	-	948	834	1,116	1,027	913	1,009	1,147	1,444
Average church income	-	$1,898,163	$1,593,819	$1,542,904	$1,854,287	$1,548,724	$1,716,940	$1,681,552	$2,517,359
Average # of years employed	-	6	7	7	7	9	8	11	8
Average # of paid vacation days	-	18	19	17	16	19	16	21	17
% College graduate or higher	-	87%	93%	79%	90%	86%	90%	71%	73%
% Who receive auto reimbursement/allowance	-	13%	55%	47%	43%	43%	48%	42%	50%
% Ordained	-	47%	56%	56%	85%	67%	65%	88%	73%
% Supervise one or more people	-	57%	69%	65%	55%	81%	68%	79%	64%
Average % salary increase (for those who had an increase) this year	-	3.0%	2.7%	2.9%	5.3%	2.9%	2.9%	2.4%	2.4%
COMPENSATION										
Base Salary	Median	-	$32,000	$41,568	$42,200	$33,500	$36,000	$39,500	$39,661	$38,565
	Average	-	$34,681	$40,760	$42,293	$33,229	$40,292	$38,025	$38,760	$37,576
Housing	Median	-	$30,145	$29,500	$25,000	$21,000	$20,700	$25,000	$30,000	$29,010
	Average	-	$33,399	$26,393	$26,080	$23,227	$20,713	$24,324	$27,900	$33,202
Parsonage	Median	-	-	-	-	-	-	-	-	-
	Average	-	-	-	-	-	-	-	-	-
Total Compensation	**Median**	-	**$53,680**	**$51,450**	**$45,000**	**$51,400**	**$52,000**	**$45,000**	**$60,000**	**$55,000**
	Average	-	**$52,814**	**$53,957**	**$53,757**	**$49,819**	**$53,100**	**$50,111**	**$58,909**	**$53,407**
BENEFITS										
Health Insurance	Median	-	-	$8,967	$14,000	$7,670	$8,000	$17,400	$6,444	$9,169
	Average	-	-	$9,040	$13,411	$8,195	$10,519	$13,963	$9,120	$9,573
Life Insurance	Median	-	-	$258	$325	-	-	-	-	$132
	Average	-	-	$399	$786	-	-	-	-	$281
Disability Insurance	Median	-	-	$355	$225	-	-	-	-	$66
	Average	-	-	$367	$375	-	-	-	-	$241
Retirement	Median	-	$2,972	$3,934	$3,078	$5,719	$2,000	$3,268	$3,714	$3,553
	Average	-	$3,474	$4,346	$3,552	$5,356	$2,655	$3,601	$3,955	$3,883
Continuing Education	Median	-	-	$875	$900	-	$1,750	-	-	-
	Average	-	-	$1,049	$1,020	-	$1,485	-	-	-
Total Benefits	**Median**	-	**$9,035**	**$10,299**	**$11,175**	**$10,338**	**$4,835**	**$6,810**	**$9,722**	**$7,630**
	Average	-	**$10,801**	**$11,307**	**$12,924**	**$10,874**	**$7,517**	**$10,057**	**$11,357**	**$9,552**
TOTAL COMPENSATION PLUS BENEFITS	**Median**	-	**$66,292**	**$58,535**	**$48,500**	**$59,806**	**$60,486**	**$48,000**	**$67,354**	**$59,881**
	Average	-	**$60,737**	**$62,628**	**$61,388**	**$58,622**	**$60,259**	**$57,107**	**$65,378**	**$64,616**
Number of Respondents		1	15	40	34	21	21	23	19	22

- Not enough response to provide meaningful data.

* For detailed description and definitions of Data Distribution (Median and Average), see chapter 1, Explanation of Data Distribution.

Table 8-5: Annual Compensation of Full-Time Adult Ministry/Christian Education Pastors/Directors by Education

	Data Distribution*	EDUCATION			
		Less than Bachelor	Bachelor	Master	Doctorate
CHARACTERISTICS					
Average weekend worship attendance		693	1,289	936	752
Average church income		$999,461	$2,073,195	$1,672,096	$1,750,959
Average # of years employed		8	8	7	9
Average # of paid vacation days		16	18	19	16
% College graduate or higher		0%	100%	100%	100%
% Who receive auto reimbursement/allowance		13%	48%	55%	50%
% Ordained		59%	60%	74%	64%
% Supervise one or more people		80%	58%	72%	75%
Average % salary increase (for those who had an increase) this year		2.9%	2.9%	2.7%	5.7%
COMPENSATION					
Base Salary	Median	$33,100	$41,000	$41,000	$39,925
	Average	$32,264	$40,123	$40,463	$39,463
Housing	Median	$15,000	$23,700	$29,250	-
	Average	$20,129	$26,556	$28,339	-
Parsonage	Median	-	-	-	-
	Average	-	-	-	-
Total Compensation	**Median**	**$35,000**	**$51,750**	**$53,685**	**$54,347**
	Average	**$39,851**	**$54,731**	**$56,693**	**$54,503**
BENEFITS					
Health Insurance	Median	-	$12,193	$9,672	$9,203
	Average	-	$11,544	$10,303	$9,282
Life Insurance	Median	-	$177	$329	-
	Average	-	$518	$531	-
Disability Insurance	Median	-	$334	$245	-
	Average	-	$432	$334	-
Retirement	Median	$2,200	$3,435	$4,000	$2,511
	Average	$2,874	$3,538	$4,544	$3,226
Continuing Education	Median	-	$1,500	$1,000	-
	Average	-	$1,370	$1,228	-
Total Benefits	**Median**	**$2,000**	**$9,835**	**$10,338**	**$11,606**
	Average	**$2,991**	**$11,106**	**$12,303**	**$10,476**
TOTAL COMPENSATION PLUS BENEFITS	**Median**	**$34,700**	**$60,104**	**$64,278**	**$72,187**
	Average	**$40,024**	**$63,791**	**$67,335**	**$64,106**
Number of Respondents		30	81	69	12

- Not enough response to provide meaningful data.

* For detailed description and definitions of Data Distribution (Median and Average), see chapter 1, Explanation of Data Distribution.

Table 8-6: Annual Compensation of Full-Time Adult Ministry/Christian Education Pastors/Directors by Years Employed

	Data Distribution*	YEARS EMPLOYED			
		Less than 6 years	6-10 years	11-15 years	Over 15 years
CHARACTERISTICS					
Average weekend worship attendance		1,062	1,058	1,050	970
Average church income		$1,823,586	$1,728,750	$1,823,262	$1,597,450
Average # of years employed		3	8	13	23
Average # of paid vacation days		16	18	20	22
% College graduate or higher		85%	85%	80%	84%
% Who receive auto reimbursement/allowance		42%	40%	62%	37%
% Ordained		63%	63%	62%	94%
% Supervise one or more people		63%	69%	67%	79%
Average % salary increase (for those who had an increase) this year		3.2%	3.1%	2.4%	2.5%
COMPENSATION					
Base Salary	Median	$39,750	$40,161	$38,185	$42,000
	Average	$39,547	$37,319	$41,379	$37,728
Housing	Median	$24,777	$27,200	$24,805	$27,500
	Average	$26,995	$25,727	$28,166	$26,207
Parsonage	Median	-	-	-	-
	Average	-	-	-	-
Total Compensation	**Median**	**$50,200**	**$47,029**	**$54,369**	**$58,000**
	Average	**$52,061**	**$52,033**	**$55,503**	**$57,081**
BENEFITS					
Health Insurance	Median	$11,190	$9,172	$6,677	$14,920
	Average	$10,467	$9,078	$7,692	$13,339
Life Insurance	Median	$200	$242	$227	-
	Average	$521	$237	$775	-
Disability Insurance	Median	$208	$276	-	$600
	Average	$273	$329	-	$846
Retirement	Median	$3,899	$3,306	$2,703	$4,055
	Average	$4,097	$3,939	$3,142	$4,072
Continuing Education	Median	$1,500	$750	-	-
	Average	$1,362	$998	-	-
Total Benefits	**Median**	**$8,200**	**$8,550**	**$6,369**	**$10,962**
	Average	**$10,255**	**$10,397**	**$8,169**	**$12,826**
TOTAL COMPENSATION PLUS BENEFITS	**Median**	**$57,100**	**$58,080**	**$62,326**	**$60,962**
	Average	**$61,256**	**$58,703**	**$62,508**	**$68,557**
Number of Respondents		84	55	21	19

- Not enough response to provide meaningful data.

* For detailed description and definitions of Data Distribution (Median and Average), see chapter 1, Explanation of Data Distribution.

Table 8-7: Annual Compensation of Full-Time Adult Ministry/Christian Education Pastors/Directors by Denomination

	Data Distribution*	DENOMINATION					
		Assemblies of God	Baptist	Independent/ Nondenom.	Lutheran	Methodist	Presby-terian
CHARACTERISTICS							
Average weekend worship attendance		801	938	1,538	1,170	800	538
Average church income		$1,233,181	$1,771,183	$2,341,923	$1,935,754	$1,270,214	$1,460,906
Average # of years employed		5	8	7	13	7	8
Average # of paid vacation days		13	19	17	19	15	20
% College graduate or higher		50%	96%	79%	91%	73%	100%
% Who receive auto reimbursement/allowance		38%	67%	31%	9%	13%	56%
% Ordained		63%	82%	75%	55%	7%	29%
% Supervise one or more people		50%	73%	74%	55%	67%	67%
Average % salary increase (for those who had an increase) this year		3.0%	2.4%	3.8%	2.8%	3.1%	2.3%
COMPENSATION							
Base Salary	Median	$28,868	$39,750	$40,161	$34,000	$41,000	$43,840
	Average	$31,340	$38,275	$39,283	$36,891	$38,994	$42,329
Housing	Median	-	$24,877	$27,000	-	-	-
	Average	-	$25,936	$30,276	-	-	-
Parsonage	Median	-	-	-	-	-	-
	Average	-	-	-	-	-	-
Total Compensation	**Median**	**$40,467**	**$55,000**	**$55,000**	**$44,600**	**$41,000**	**$50,490**
	Average	**$44,164**	**$58,016**	**$55,152**	**$49,280**	**$38,994**	**$50,274**
BENEFITS							
Health Insurance	Median	-	$11,400	$11,192	-	-	$8,754
	Average	-	$11,387	$10,904	-	-	$8,873
Life Insurance	Median	-	$190	$174	-	-	-
	Average	-	$509	$581	-	-	-
Disability Insurance	Median	-	$66	$420	-	-	-
	Average	-	$192	$449	-	-	-
Retirement	Median	-	$4,135	$3,371	$3,390	-	$3,300
	Average	-	$4,432	$4,224	$3,141	-	$3,930
Continuing Education	Median	-	$1,000	-	-	-	$800
	Average	-	$1,537	-	-	-	$941
Total Benefits	**Median**	**-**	**$11,391**	**$10,070**	**$5,560**	**$5,500**	**$7,635**
	Average	**-**	**$12,423**	**$12,699**	**$10,207**	**$7,452**	**$8,975**
TOTAL COMPENSATION PLUS BENEFITS	**Median**	**$46,835**	**$67,900**	**$68,321**	**$45,796**	**$44,300**	**$58,713**
	Average	**$51,012**	**$69,708**	**$65,668**	**$53,424**	**$43,465**	**$58,750**
Number of Respondents		8	52	48	11	15	18

- Not enough response to provide meaningful data.

* For detailed description and definitions of Data Distribution (Median and Average), see chapter 1, Explanation of Data Distribution.

Table 8-8: Annual Compensation of Full-Time Adult Ministry/Christian Education Pastors/Directors by Gender

	Data Distribution*	GENDER	
		Male	Female
CHARACTERISTICS			
Average weekend worship attendance		1,137	909
Average church income		$1,912,708	$1,549,859
Average # of years employed		7	8
Average # of paid vacation days		18	18
% College graduate or higher		92%	75%
% Who receive auto reimbursement/allowance		54%	34%
% Ordained		87%	37%
% Supervise one or more people		72%	63%
Average % salary increase (for those who had an increase) this year		2.9%	3.0%
COMPENSATION			
Base Salary	Median	$39,875	$40,000
	Average	$39,394	$37,944
Housing	Median	$26,551	$22,000
	Average	$27,388	$24,169
Parsonage	Median	-	-
	Average	-	-
Total Compensation	**Median**	**$59,700**	**$42,200**
	Average	**$60,473**	**$43,693**
BENEFITS			
Health Insurance	Median	$11,191	$7,670
	Average	$11,151	$8,359
Life Insurance	Median	$200	$242
	Average	$550	$313
Disability Insurance	Median	$316	$454
	Average	$392	$416
Retirement	Median	$4,000	$2,778
	Average	$4,218	$3,394
Continuing Education	Median	$1,500	$500
	Average	$1,527	$832
Total Benefits	**Median**	**$11,079**	**$4,949**
	Average	**$12,316**	**$7,784**
TOTAL COMPENSATION PLUS BENEFITS	**Median**	**$71,000**	**$46,198**
	Average	**$71,632**	**$48,064**
Number of Respondents		111	85

- Not enough response to provide meaningful data.

* For detailed description and definitions of Data Distribution (Median and Average), see chapter 1, Explanation of Data Distribution.

Table 8-9: Annual Compensation of Part-Time Adult Ministry/Christian Education Pastors/Directors by Church Income

	Data Distribution*	CHURCH INCOME				
		$250K & Under	$251-$500K	$501-$750K	$751K-$1M	Over 1 Million
CHARACTERISTICS						
Average weekend worship attendance		156	278	378	508	1,076
Average church income		$159,652	$363,542	$625,896	$892,674	$1,814,506
Average # of years employed		5	5	8	8	6
Average # of paid vacation days		14	12	11	12	14
% College graduate or higher		76%	73%	96%	93%	97%
% Who receive auto reimbursement/allowance		29%	38%	36%	19%	24%
% Ordained		37%	23%	38%	25%	51%
% Supervise one or more people		76%	50%	36%	50%	34%
Average % salary increase (for those who had an increase) this year		-	2.0%	5.1%	3.1%	3.1%
HOURLY RATE						
Base Rate	Average	$15	$17	$17	$18	$18
COMPENSATION						
Base Salary	Median	$11,624	$17,629	$11,000	$16,500	$16,292
	Average	$13,747	$17,586	$12,789	$16,990	$17,970
Housing	Median	-	-	-	-	$26,000
	Average	-	-	-	-	$24,785
Parsonage	Median	-	-	-	-	-
	Average	-	-	-	-	-
Total Compensation	**Median**	**$12,000**	**$17,629**	**$12,775**	**$16,500**	**$16,700**
	Average	**$15,650**	**$18,103**	**$14,222**	**$16,990**	**$20,339**
BENEFITS						
Health Insurance	Median	-	-	-	-	-
	Average	-	-	-	-	-
Life Insurance	Median	-	-	-	-	-
	Average	-	-	-	-	-
Disability Insurance	Median	-	-	-	-	-
	Average	-	-	-	-	-
Retirement	Median	-	-	-	-	-
	Average	-	-	-	-	-
Continuing Education	Median	-	-	-	-	-
	Average	-	-	-	-	-
Total Benefits	**Median**	-	**$800**	-	-	**$1,870**
	Average	-	**$821**	-	-	**$2,317**
TOTAL COMPENSATION PLUS BENEFITS	**Median**	**$12,000**	**$19,336**	**$12,775**	**$18,000**	**$19,000**
	Average	**$15,840**	**$21,677**	**$15,269**	**$17,655**	**$22,772**
Number of Respondents		21	26	26	16	38

- Not enough response to provide meaningful data.

* For detailed description and definitions of Data Distribution (Median and Average), see chapter 1, Explanation of Data Distribution.

Table 8-10: Annual Compensation of Part-Time Adult Ministry/Christian Education Pastors/Directors by Worship Attendance

	Data Distribution*	WORSHIP ATTENDANCE					
		100 or less	101-300	301-500	501-750	751-1,000	Over 1,000
CHARACTERISTICS							
Average weekend worship attendance		-	198	425	628	870	1,714
Average church income		-	$358,372	$884,034	$1,003,872	$1,406,341	$2,244,227
Average # of years employed		-	5	9	6	6	5
Average # of paid vacation days		-	12	11	12	15	15
% College graduate or higher		-	84%	87%	95%	92%	100%
% Who receive auto reimbursement/allowance		-	32%	30%	32%	25%	14%
% Ordained		-	32%	26%	48%	58%	53%
% Supervise one or more people		-	61%	33%	36%	25%	40%
Average % salary increase (for those who had an increase) this year		-	3.3%	4.9%	2.8%	2.8%	-
HOURLY RATE							
Base Rate	Average	-	$17	$16	$17	$16	$20
COMPENSATION							
Base Salary	Median	-	$15,000	$11,337	$16,465	$15,396	$19,500
	Average	-	$15,400	$14,709	$18,314	$14,390	$21,267
Housing	Median	-	$12,000	-	-	-	-
	Average	-	$12,571	-	-	-	-
Parsonage	Median	-	-	-	-	-	-
	Average	-	-	-	-	-	-
Total Compensation	**Median**	-	**$14,218**	**$14,700**	**$16,465**	**$15,977**	**$19,500**
	Average	-	**$15,666**	**$17,492**	**$19,348**	**$17,057**	**$23,231**
BENEFITS							
Health Insurance	Median	-	-	-	-	-	-
	Average	-	-	-	-	-	-
Life Insurance	Median	-	-	-	-	-	-
	Average	-	-	-	-	-	-
Disability	Median	-	-	-	-	-	-
	Average	-	-	-	-	-	-
Retirement	Median	-	-	-	-	-	-
	Average	-	-	-	-	-	-
Continuing Education	Median	-	$500	-	-	-	-
	Average	-	$1,103	-	-	-	-
Total Benefits	**Median**	-	**$1,000**	-	-	-	-
	Average	-	**$1,314**	-	-	-	-
TOTAL COMPENSATION PLUS BENEFITS	**Median**	-	**$14,218**	**$15,000**	**$17,160**	**$15,977**	**$19,500**
	Average	-	**$16,148**	**$20,644**	**$23,974**	**$17,414**	**$23,967**
Number of Respondents		5	49	31	22	12	15

- Not enough response to provide meaningful data.

* For detailed description and definitions of Data Distribution (Median and Average), see chapter 1, Explanation of Data Distribution.

Table 8-11: Annual Compensation of Part-Time Adult Ministry/Christian Education Pastors/Directors by Church Setting

	Data Distribution*	CHURCH SETTING			
		Metro-politan city	Suburb of large city	Small town or rural city	Farming area
CHARACTERISTICS					
Average weekend worship attendance		587	588	514	-
Average church income		$795,547	$1,122,756	$746,151	-
Average # of years employed		6	6	6	-
Average # of paid vacation days		15	13	11	-
% College graduate or higher		85%	90%	88%	-
% Who receive auto reimbursement/allowance		29%	25%	31%	-
% Ordained		52%	40%	31%	-
% Supervise one or more people		48%	55%	38%	-
Average % salary increase (for those who had an increase) this year		3.1%	2.6%	4.1%	
HOURLY RATE					
Base Rate	Average	$17	$18	$16	-
COMPENSATION					
Base Salary	Median	$15,921	$18,000	$13,015	-
	Average	$16,453	$18,603	$14,809	-
Housing	Median	$13,436	-	$18,150	-
	Average	$15,486	-	$20,563	-
Parsonage	Median	-	-	-	-
	Average	-	-	-	-
Total Compensation	**Median**	**$14,700**	**$19,500**	**$15,000**	**-**
	Average	**$18,768**	**$20,256**	**$15,965**	**-**
BENEFITS					
Health Insurance	Median	-	-	-	-
	Average	-	-	-	-
Life Insurance	Median	-	-	-	-
	Average	-	-	-	-
Disability Insurance	Median	-	-	-	-
	Average	-	-	-	-
Retirement	Median	-	-	-	-
	Average	-	-	-	-
Continuing Education	Median	-	$678	$500	-
	Average	-	$958	$763	-
Total Benefits	**Median**	**-**	**$1,000**	**$975**	**-**
	Average	**-**	**$1,424**	**$1,640**	**-**
TOTAL COMPENSATION PLUS BENEFITS	**Median**	**$14,700**	**$19,651**	**$15,600**	**-**
	Average	**$20,380**	**$20,889**	**$18,767**	**-**
Number of Respondents		21	50	61	2

- Not enough response to provide meaningful data.

* For detailed description and definitions of Data Distribution (Median and Average), see chapter 1, Explanation of Data Distribution.

Table 8-12: Annual Compensation of Part-Time Adult Ministry/Christian Education Pastors/Directors by Region

	Data Distribution*	New England	Middle Atlantic	South Atlantic	E-N Central	E-S Central	W-N Central	W-S Central	Mountain	Pacific
						REGION				
CHARACTERISTICS										
Average weekend worship attendance		-	606	449	459	-	416	1,368	-	491
Average church income		-	$1,200,721	$672,994	$863,105	-	$573,528	$1,878,842	-	$654,527
Average # of years employed		-	5	4	6	-	7	8	-	7
Average # of paid vacation days		-	8	11	12	-	12	18	-	15
% College graduate or higher		-	95%	80%	77%	-	100%	100%	-	93%
% Who receive auto reimbursement/allowance		-	10%	13%	34%	-	33%	44%	-	28%
% Ordained		-	26%	53%	33%	-	25%	70%	-	28%
% Supervise one or more people		-	50%	47%	50%	-	58%	20%	-	52%
Average % salary increase (for those who had an increase) this year		-	-	5.0%	2.8%	-	3.3%	4.7%	-	4.8%
HOURLY RATE										
Base Rate	Average	-	$16	$17	$16	-	$16	$24	-	$16
COMPENSATION										
Base Salary	Median	-	$10,600	$15,498	$17,687	-	$16,618	$23,520	-	$10,163
	Average	-	$14,434	$16,525	$15,680	-	$17,011	$24,048	-	$14,498
Housing	Median	-	-	-	-	-	-	-	-	$19,140
	Average	-	-	-	-	-	-	-	-	$21,793
Parsonage	Median	-	-	-	-	-	-	-	-	$1,200
	Average	-	-	-	-	-	-	-	-	$1,200
Total Compensation	**Median**	-	$10,700	$15,600	$19,000	-	$16,618	$25,060	-	$13,436
	Average	-	$14,464	$17,994	$17,203	-	$17,011	$29,159	-	$16,993
BENEFITS										
Health Insurance	Median	-	-	-	-	-	-	-	-	-
	Average	-	-	-	-	-	-	-	-	-
Life Insurance	Median	-	-	-	-	-	-	-	-	-
	Average	-	-	-	-	-	-	-	-	-
Disability Insurance	Median	-	-	-	-	-	-	-	-	-
	Average	-	-	-	-	-	-	-	-	-
Retirement	Median	-	-	-	-	-	-	-	-	-
	Average	-	-	-	-	-	-	-	-	-
Continuing Education	Median	-	-	-	$500	-	-	-	-	-
	Average	-	-	-	$700	-	-	-	-	-
Total Benefits	**Median**	-	-	-	$950	-	-	-	-	$2,720
	Average	-	-	-	$1,303	-	-	-	-	$2,466
TOTAL COMPENSATION PLUS BENEFITS	**Median**	-	$10,850	$15,600	$19,500	-	$16,718	$25,060	-	$15,298
	Average	-	$18,774	$18,171	$17,653	-	$18,103	$31,364	-	$19,964
Number of Respondents		6	20	15	30	4	12	10	7	30

- Not enough response to provide meaningful data.

* For detailed description and definitions of Data Distribution (Median and Average), see chapter 1, Explanation of Data Distribution.

Table 8-13: Annual Compensation of Part-Time Adult Ministry/Christian Education Pastors/Directors by Education

	Data Distribution*	EDUCATION			
		Less than Bachelor	Bachelor	Master	Doctorate
CHARACTERISTICS					
Average weekend worship attendance		316	547	536	958
Average church income		$434,533	$984,414	$829,190	$1,169,000
Average # of years employed		7	6	6	5
Average # of paid vacation days		13	12	14	11
% College graduate or higher		0%	100%	100%	100%
% Who receive auto reimbursement/allowance		27%	29%	33%	33%
% Ordained		23%	26%	53%	89%
% Supervise one or more people		40%	44%	60%	11%
Average % salary increase (for those who had an increase) this year		3.7%	4.0%	2.9%	-
HOURLY RATE					
Base Rate	Average	$15	$17	$18	-
COMPENSATION					
Base Salary	Median	$10,573	$13,000	$16,700	-
	Average	$12,800	$16,592	$17,986	-
Housing	Median	-	$19,140	$15,000	-
	Average	-	$18,482	$18,887	-
Parsonage	Median	-	-	-	-
	Average	-	-	-	-
Total Compensation	**Median**	**$11,145**	**$17,344**	**$18,580**	**-**
	Average	**$12,842**	**$18,271**	**$19,824**	**-**
BENEFITS					
Health Insurance	Median	-	-	-	-
	Average	-	-	-	-
Life Insurance	Median	-	-	-	-
	Average	-	-	-	-
Disability Insurance	Median	-	-	-	-
	Average	-	-	-	-
Retirement	Median	-	-	-	-
	Average	-	-	-	-
Continuing Education	Median	-	$500	$878	-
	Average	-	$1,083	$1,228	-
Total Benefits	**Median**	**-**	**$988**	**$1,870**	**-**
	Average	**-**	**$1,374**	**$2,096**	**-**
TOTAL COMPENSATION PLUS BENEFITS	**Median**	**$11,145**	**$17,687**	**$20,000**	**$20,000**
	Average	**$12,929**	**$20,214**	**$22,309**	**$18,089**
Number of Respondents		15	66	41	9

- Not enough response to provide meaningful data.

* For detailed description and definitions of Data Distribution (Median and Average), see chapter 1, Explanation of Data Distribution.

Table 8-14: Annual Compensation of Part-Time Adult Ministry/Christian Education Pastors/Directors by Years Employed

	Data Distribution*	YEARS EMPLOYED			
		Less than 6 years	6-10 years	11-15 years	Over 15 years
CHARACTERISTICS					
Average weekend worship attendance		521	644	521	385
Average church income		$839,162	$963,186	$799,924	$758,303
Average # of years employed		2	8	13	23
Average # of paid vacation days		10	15	14	14
% College graduate or higher		90%	89%	85%	88%
% Who receive auto reimbursement/allowance		25%	41%	15%	38%
% Ordained		32%	44%	50%	50%
% Supervise one or more people		42%	50%	54%	25%
Average % salary increase (for those who had an increase) this year		3.4%	2.8%	-	-
HOURLY RATE					
Base Rate	Average	$16	$19	$16	-
COMPENSATION					
Base Salary	Median	$10,500	$20,095	$17,783	-
	Average	$13,062	$20,389	$19,368	-
Housing	Median	$15,000	-	-	-
	Average	$16,282	-	-	-
Parsonage	Median	-	-	-	-
	Average	-	-	-	-
Total Compensation	**Median**	**$12,250**	**$20,189**	**$20,668**	**$16,000**
	Average	**$14,562**	**$22,966**	**$20,482**	**$18,570**
BENEFITS					
Health Insurance	Median	-	-	-	-
	Average	-	-	-	-
Life Insurance	Median	-	-	-	-
	Average	-	-	-	-
Disability Insurance	Median	-	-	-	-
	Average	-	-	-	-
Retirement	Median	-	-	-	-
	Average	-	-	-	-
Continuing Education	Median	$500	$533	-	-
	Average	$764	$1,254	-	-
Total Benefits	**Median**	**$900**	**$1,600**	**-**	**-**
	Average	**$1,023**	**$1,869**	**-**	**-**
TOTAL COMPENSATION PLUS BENEFITS	**Median**	**$12,550**	**$21,500**	**$23,125**	**$16,000**
	Average	**$16,175**	**$23,660**	**$27,021**	**$18,570**
Number of Respondents		74	35	13	8

- Not enough response to provide meaningful data.

* For detailed description and definitions of Data Distribution (Median and Average), see chapter 1, Explanation of Data Distribution.

Table 8-15: Annual Compensation of Part-Time Adult Ministry/Christian Education Pastors/Directors by Denomination

	Data Distribution*	DENOMINATION					
		Assemblies of God	Baptist	Independent/ Nondenom.	Lutheran	Methodist	Presby- terian
CHARACTERISTICS							
Average weekend worship attendance		-	600	635	-	562	246
Average church income		-	$1,043,386	$947,124	-	$1,143,091	$568,856
Average # of years employed		-	7	8	-	4	6
Average # of paid vacation days		-	11	13	-	13	11
% College graduate or higher		-	92%	76%	-	95%	80%
% Who receive auto reimbursement/allowance		-	32%	18%	-	16%	50%
% Ordained		-	48%	48%	-	25%	20%
% Supervise one or more people		-	36%	52%	-	35%	50%
Average % salary increase (for those who had an increase) this year		-	2.9%	-	-	2.7%	-
HOURLY RATE							
Base Rate	Average	-	$16	$17	-	$19	$16
COMPENSATION							
Base Salary	Median	-	$10,920	$15,600	-	$20,100	$19,200
	Average	-	$13,302	$18,738	-	$18,239	$15,994
Housing	Median	-	-	-	-	-	-
	Average	-	-	-	-	-	-
Parsonage	Median	-	-	-	-	-	-
	Average	-	-	-	-	-	-
Total Compensation	**Median**	-	$11,960	$21,700	-	$20,100	$21,200
	Average	-	$14,299	$19,879	-	$19,930	$18,961
BENEFITS							
Health Insurance	Median	-	-	-	-	-	-
	Average	-	-	-	-	-	-
Life Insurance	Median	-	-	-	-	-	-
	Average	-	-	-	-	-	-
Disability Insurance	Median	-	-	-	-	-	-
	Average	-	-	-	-	-	-
Retirement	Median	-	-	-	-	-	-
	Average	-	-	-	-	-	-
Continuing Education	Median	-	-	-	-	-	-
	Average	-	-	-	-	-	-
Total Benefits	**Median**	-	-	-	-	-	-
	Average	-	-	-	-	-	-
TOTAL COMPENSATION PLUS BENEFITS	**Median**	-	$13,000	$22,188	-	$21,525	$21,700
	Average	-	$17,551	$20,489	-	$20,292	$20,134
Number of Respondents		3	28	22	4	20	10

- Not enough response to provide meaningful data.

* For detailed description and definitions of Data Distribution (Median and Average), see chapter 1, Explanation of Data Distribution.

Table 8-16: Annual Compensation of Part-Time Adult Ministry/Christian Education Pastors/Directors by Gender

	Data Distribution*	GENERALLY GENDER	
		Male	Female
CHARACTERISTICS			
Average weekend worship attendance		716	491
Average church income		$1,065,592	$824,804
Average # of years employed		6	6
Average # of paid vacation days		12	12
% College graduate or higher		91%	88%
% Who receive auto reimbursement/allowance		46%	23%
% Ordained		79%	23%
% Supervise one or more people		21%	54%
Average % salary increase (for those who had an increase) this year		3.5%	3.5%
HOURLY RATE			
Base Rate	Average	$19	$17
COMPENSATION			
Base Salary	Median	$15,198	$15,600
	Average	$15,704	$16,579
Housing	Median	$12,000	$19,570
	Average	$15,797	$20,130
Parsonage	Median	-	-
	Average	-	-
Total Compensation	**Median**	**$14,400**	**$18,000**
	Average	**$16,248**	**$18,431**
BENEFITS			
Health Insurance	Median	-	-
	Average	-	-
Life Insurance	Median	-	-
	Average	-	-
Disability Insurance	Median	-	-
	Average	-	-
Retirement	Median	-	$1,095
	Average	-	$1,299
Continuing Education	Median	-	$500
	Average	-	$990
Total Benefits	**Median**	-	**$1,000**
	Average	-	**$1,409**
TOTAL COMPENSATION PLUS BENEFITS	**Median**	**$14,700**	**$19,268**
	Average	**$19,116**	**$19,866**
Number of Respondents		35	98

- Not enough response to provide meaningful data.

* For detailed description and definitions of Data Distribution (Median and Average), see chapter 1, Explanation of Data Distribution.

Full-Time Adult Ministry/Christian Education Pastor/Director Worksheet

	Enter your church data below	The 2014–2015 Compensation Handbook for Church Staff		Enter *Compensation Handbook* data below			
				Highest 25%	Median	Lowest 25%	Average
Church Income	$	Table 8-1	page 103	$	$	$	$
Worship Attendance		Table 8-2	page 104	n/a	$	n/a	$
Church Setting (metro, suburb, small town, or farming area)		Table 8-3	page 105	n/a	$	n/a	$
Region		Table 8-4	page 106	n/a	$	n/a	$
Person's Education		Table 8-5	page 107	n/a	$	n/a	$
Years Employed		Table 8-6	page 108	n/a	$	n/a	$
Denomination (if applicable)		Table 8-7	page 109	n/a	$	n/a	$

Looking at the table and page number references indicated in the *2014–2015 Compensation Handbook for Church Staff* columns above, locate the appropriate range for your church. Refer to the instructions below for step-by-step help.

FILLING OUT THE WORKSHEET

1. Fill in the gray boxes under *Enter your church data* with your church demographic information as follows:

   ▶ **Income** (Total annual church budget in past year)
   ▶ **Worship attendance** (Number of people, including children, who attend all weekend services)
   ▶ **Church setting** (Metropolitan city, suburb of large city, small town or rural city, or farming area)

   ▶ **Region** (Locate your state's region in the appendix on page 346.)
   ▶ **Education** (Highest level of education: less than bachelor, bachelor, master, or doctorate)

2. Use Table 8-1 (page 103) in your *2014–2015 Compensation Handbook for Church Staff* to enter data pertinent to your church. In the heading (top row), locate your church **income** from the five available ranges. Follow that column to the bottom rows, and copy the *Highest 25%*, *Median*, *Lowest 25%*, and *Average* amounts onto your worksheet.

3. Use Table 8-2 (page 104) on your *2014–2015 Compensation Handbook for Church Staff* to enter data pertinent to your church. In the heading (top row), locate your church's

worship attendance from the six available ranges. Follow that column to the bottom rows, and copy the *Median* and *Average* amounts onto your worksheet.

4. Use Table 8-3 (page 105) on your *2014–2015 Compensation Handbook for Church Staff* to enter data pertinent to your church. In the heading (top row), choose the **church setting** that best describes your church. Follow that column to the bottom rows, and copy the *Median* and *Average* amounts onto your worksheet.

5. Use Table 8-4 (page 106) on your *2014–2015 Compensation Handbook for Church Staff* to enter data pertinent to your church. In the heading (top row), look for the **region** where your church is located. Follow that column to the bottom rows, and copy the *Median* and *Average* amounts onto your worksheet.

6. Use Table 8-5 (page 107) on your *2014–2015 Compensation Handbook for Church Staff* to enter data pertinent to your Adult Ministry/ Christian Education Pastor/Director. In the heading (top row), look for **your Adult Ministry/Christian Education Pastor/Director's highest level of education**. Follow that column to the bottom rows, and copy the *Median* and *Average* amounts onto your worksheet.

7. Use Table 8-6 (page 108) on your *2014–2015 Compensation Handbook for Church Staff* to enter data pertinent to your Adult Ministry/Christian Education Pastor/Director. In the heading (top row), locate the **number of years your Adult Ministry/Christian Education Pastor/Director has been employed**. Follow that column to the bottom rows, and copy the *Median* and *Average* amounts onto your worksheet.

8. Use Table 8-7 (page 109) on your *2014–2015 Compensation Handbook for Church Staff* to enter data pertinent to your church. In the heading (top row), look for **your church's denominational affiliation**. Follow that column to the bottom rows, and copy the *Median* and *Average* amounts onto your worksheet. If your church is not affiliated with a denomination, leave this section blank.

DETERMINING COMPENSATION

This tool will not provide you with a single compensation amount but rather with a range of values to help you determine the compensation appropriate to your situation.

1. Look at the values in the shaded *Median* column. Circle the **lowest** and the **highest** values. **This is the range of the median compensation plus benefits for churches similar to yours.**

2. For a variety of reasons, compensation plus benefits may be higher or lower than the range established in this table. Income and attendance are two significant factors affecting church compensation packages. If church income or attendance skews higher, you might want to consider moving toward or above the higher end of the range. Likewise, if church income or attendance skews lower, you may consider moving the package toward or below the lower end of the range.

3. Examine additional variables that might impact the compensation package you offer, such as years of service, education, and church setting.

4. Determine other circumstances unique to your situation, such as cost of living in your area, theological beliefs, pastoral performance, financial needs, the local economy, personal motivation, congregational goals, and others.

5. You now have a compensation package range based on the *2014–2015 Compensation Handbook*. Since each church and position are unique, your final compensation package will be based on additional factors unique to your situation.

Part-Time Adult Ministry/Christian Education Pastor/Director Worksheet

	Enter your church data below	The 2014–2015 Compensation Handbook for Church Staff		Enter *Compensation Handbook* data below			
				Highest 25%	Median	Lowest 25%	Average
Church Income	$	Table 8-9	page 111	$	$	$	$
Worship Attendance		Table 8-10	page 112	n/a	$	n/a	$
Church Setting (metro, suburb, small town, or farming area)		Table 8-11	page 113	n/a	$	n/a	$
Region		Table 8-12	page 114	n/a	$	n/a	$
Person's Education		Table 8-13	page 115	n/a	$	n/a	$
Years Employed		Table 8-14	page 116	n/a	$	n/a	$
Denomination (if applicable)		Table 8-15	page 117	n/a	$	n/a	$

Looking at the table and page number references indicated in the **2014–2015 Compensation Handbook for Church Staff** columns above, locate the appropriate range for your church. Refer to the instructions below for step-by-step help.

FILLING OUT THE WORKSHEET

1. Fill in the gray boxes under *Enter your church data* with your church demographic information as follows:

   ▶ **Income** (Total annual church budget in past year)
   ▶ **Worship attendance** (Number of people, including children, who attend all weekend services)
   ▶ **Church setting** (Metropolitan city, suburb of large city, small town or rural city, or farming area)

   ▶ **Region** (Locate your state's region in the appendix on page 346.)
   ▶ **Education** (Highest level of education: less than bachelor, bachelor, master, or doctorate)

2. Use Table 8-9 (page 111) in your *2014–2015 Compensation Handbook for Church Staff* to enter data pertinent to your church. In the heading (top row), locate your church **income** from the five available ranges. Follow that column to the bottom rows, and copy the *Highest 25%*, *Median*, *Lowest 25%*, and *Average* amounts onto your worksheet.

3. Use Table 8-10 (page 112) on your *2014–2015 Compensation Handbook for Church Staff* to enter data pertinent to your church. In the heading (top row), locate your church's

worship attendance from the six available ranges. Follow that column to the bottom rows, and copy the *Median* and *Average* amounts onto your worksheet.

4. Use Table 8-11 (page 113) on your *2014–2015 Compensation Handbook for Church Staff* to enter data pertinent to your church. In the heading (top row), choose the **church setting** that best describes your church. Follow that column to the bottom rows, and copy the *Median* and *Average* amounts onto your worksheet.

5. Use Table 8-12 (page 114) on your *2014–2015 Compensation Handbook for Church Staff* to enter data pertinent to your church. In the heading (top row), look for the **region** where your church is located. Follow that column to the bottom rows, and copy the *Median* and *Average* amounts onto your worksheet.

6. Use Table 8-13 (page 115) on your *2014–2015 Compensation Handbook for Church Staff* to enter data pertinent to your Adult Ministry/ Christian Education Pastor/Director. In the heading (top row), look for **your Adult Ministry/Christian Education Pastor/Director's highest level of education**. Follow that column to the bottom rows, and copy the *Median* and *Average* amounts onto your worksheet.

7. Use Table 8-14 (page 116) on your *2014–2015 Compensation Handbook for Church Staff* to enter data pertinent to your Adult Ministry/Christian Education Pastor/Director. In the heading (top row), locate the **number of years your Adult Ministry/Christian Education Pastor/Director has been employed**. Follow that column to the bottom rows, and copy the *Median* and *Average* amounts onto your worksheet.

8. Use Table 8-15 (page 117) on your *2014–2015 Compensation Handbook for Church Staff* to enter data pertinent to your church. In the

heading (top row), look for **your church's denominational affiliation**. Follow that column to the bottom rows, and copy the *Median* and *Average* amounts onto your worksheet. If your church is not affiliated with a denomination, leave this section blank.

DETERMINING COMPENSATION

This tool will not provide you with a single compensation amount but rather with a range of values to help you determine the compensation appropriate to your situation.

1. Look at the values in the shaded *Median* column. Circle the **lowest** and the **highest** values. **This is the range of the median compensation plus benefits for churches similar to yours.**

2. For a variety of reasons, compensation plus benefits may be higher or lower than the range established in this table. Income and attendance are two significant factors affecting church compensation packages. If church income or attendance skews higher, you might want to consider moving toward or above the higher end of the range. Likewise, if church income or attendance skews lower, you may consider moving the package toward or below the lower end of the range.

3. Examine additional variables that might impact the compensation package you offer, such as years of service, education, and church setting.

4. Determine other circumstances unique to your situation, such as cost of living in your area, theological beliefs, pastoral performance, financial needs, the local economy, personal motivation, congregational goals, and others.

5. You now have a compensation package range based on the *2014–2015 Compensation Handbook*. Since each church and position are unique, your final compensation package will be based on additional factors unique to your situation.

9

YOUTH PASTORS/
DIRECTORS

Employment Profile

Youth Pastors/Directors include paid pastors and directors of junior high, senior high, or college students. This category may include such titles as Campus Pastor, College Minister, Junior High Pastor/Director, Senior High Pastor/Director, Youth Center Director, Youth Pastor/Director, etc.

On average, Youth Pastors/Directors have been employed in their current position for fewer years than other church staff. An equal percentage of full-time and part-time Youth Pastors/Directors are considered church employees (94% each) rather than self-employed. Among full-timers, about nine in 10 have a college degree and are male.

Three-fourths of full-time Youth Pastors are ordained, which is seven percentage points higher than in 2011. Approximately one-fourth of the Youth Pastors/Directors in this sample work part-time. Of this part-time group, females account for 32% compared to 9% of full-timers.

The chart below provides a demographic profile of this sample.

	Full-Time	Part-Time
Number of respondents	**418**	**124**
Ordained	74%	33%
Average years employed	5	4
Male	91%	68%
Female	9%	32%
Self-employed (receives 1099)	6%	6%
Church employee (receives W-2)	94%	94%
High school diploma	8%	17%
Associate degree	6%	13%
Bachelor's degree	58%	54%
Master's degree	28%	16%
Doctoral degree	<1%	0%

Total Compensation plus Benefits Package Analysis

The following analyses are based on data in the tables you will find later in this chapter. The tables show compensation plus benefits data for full-time and part-time Youth Pastors/Directors and are presented according to church income, church attendance, church setting, region, education, years employed, denomination, and gender. In this way, the compensation plus benefits of Youth Pastors/Directors can be analyzed and compared from a variety of useful perspectives.

The total compensation plus benefits amount includes the base salary; housing allowance and/or parsonage amount; health, life, and disability insurance payments; retirement contribution; and educational funds.

A worksheet at the end of this chapter is provided to help you apply the data to your church's situation.

More than six in 10 full-time Youth Pastors receive housing (67%) and health insurance (68%) benefits as well as salary increases (61%). Each of these benefits reflects an increase of more than 10 percentage points over the 2011 numbers.

One-fourth of part-time Youth Pastors receive housing benefits, about triple the number in 2011.

Compensation Plus Benefits	Full-Time	Part-Time
Base Salary	99%	90%
Housing	67%	26%
Parsonage	7%	2%
Health Insurance*	68%	5%
Life Insurance*	25%	1%
Disability Insurance*	24%	0%
Retirement	55%	2%
Continuing Education	33%	8%
Received salary increase	61%	31%
Received paid vacation	94%	46%
Received auto reimbursement/allowance	51%	28%

Only those reporting individual premiums for Health, Life, or Disability (not total insurance premiums) are included.

KEY POINTS

* About six in 10 part-time Youth Pastors/Directors serve in churches with 300 or less in attendance.

* In general, as church attendance, years employed, and the minister's education level increase, compensation and benefits for full-time Youth Pastors/Directors also increase.

* The vast majority of full-time Youth Pastors/ Directors in this report serve in churches set in a suburb of a large city or a small town/rural city. Youth Pastors/Directors in metropolitan cities and suburbs of large cities have higher compensation packages than their counterparts in small towns/rural cities or farming areas.

* Male full-time Youth Pastors receive 23% more in compensation and benefits than their female counterparts.

Compensation & Benefits: National Averages for Full-Time Youth Pastors/Directors	
2000	$42,561
2001	$43,288
2002	$45,043
2003	$47,058
2004	$47,302
2005	$50,371
2006	$51,640
2007	$50,824
2008	$51,484
2009	$50,540
2011	$51,825
2013	$57,254*

The above trend is made available for your reference only. In addition to looking at this overall data, please refer to the detailed tables using your church's income, attendance, setting, region, and denomination as well as the person's education, gender, and years employed for guidance in compensating this position.

Table 9-1: Annual Compensation of Full-Time Youth Pastors/Directors by Church Income

CHARACTERISTICS	Data Distribution*	CHURCH INCOME				
		$250K & Under	$251-$500K	$501-$750K	$751K-$1M	Over $1 Million
Average weekend worship attendance		401	268	359	514	1,093
Average church income		$163,662	$387,928	$623,782	$897,626	$2,144,846
Average # of years employed		4	5	4	5	5
Average # of paid vacation days		13	14	16	16	17
% College graduate or higher		75%	82%	87%	79%	91%
% Who receive auto reimbursement/allowance		46%	56%	50%	43%	54%
% Ordained		67%	72%	71%	77%	77%
% Supervise one or more people		67%	43%	37%	37%	64%
Average % salary increase (for those who had an increase) this year		4.3%	4.3%	4.2%	4.0%	3.5%
COMPENSATION						
Base Salary	Highest 25%	$31,000	$40,000	$40,745	$40,000	$45,000
	Median	$27,300	$30,000	$32,000	$35,000	$33,018
	Lowest 25%	$23,000	$23,000	$24,532	$27,379	$25,729
	Average	$25,663	$31,853	$33,344	$34,117	$35,196
Housing	Highest 25%	$27,300	$20,000	$23,103	$20,514	$29,705
	Median	$18,900	$16,000	$17,835	$17,474	$23,050
	Lowest 25%	$12,000	$13,080	$11,500	$14,200	$15,480
	Average	$20,253	$16,644	$17,925	$17,918	$23,097
Parsonage	Highest 25%	-	-	$15,528	-	-
	Median	-	-	$9,600	-	-
	Lowest 25%	-	-	$2,764	-	-
	Average	-	-	$9,644	-	-
Total Compensation	**Highest 25%**	**$45,000**	**$50,000**	**$52,250**	**$49,550**	**$60,000**
	Median	**$33,000**	**$42,230**	**$43,200**	**$43,655**	**$50,500**
	Lowest 25%	**$26,000**	**$35,690**	**$39,344**	**$38,510**	**$42,000**
	Average	**$35,366**	**$43,627**	**$46,127**	**$45,196**	**$52,772**
BENEFITS						
Health Insurance	Highest 25%	$9,082	$10,359	$12,500	$12,480	$14,437
	Median	$6,370	$7,083	$9,600	$8,076	$10,189
	Lowest 25%	$4,300	$3,179	$4,200	$4,200	$6,540
	Average	$7,656	$7,249	$8,967	$8,267	$10,598
Life Insurance	Highest 25%	-	$509	$391	-	$364
	Median	-	$302	$207	-	$216
	Lowest 25%	-	$150	$120	-	$99
	Average	-	$486	$269	-	$370
Disability Insurance	Highest 25%	-	-	$931	-	$538
	Median	-	-	$500	-	$350
	Lowest 25%	-	-	$261	-	$191
	Average	-	-	$623	-	$389
Retirement	Highest 25%	$1,625	$3,500	$3,196	$3,610	$4,241
	Median	$890	$2,445	$2,050	$1,584	$2,750
	Lowest 25%	$698	$1,470	$1,460	$1,153	$1,759
	Average	$1,278	$2,679	$2,719	$2,396	$3,232
Continuing Education	Highest 25%	-	$1,250	$1,500	$1,200	$2,000
	Median	-	$1,000	$1,000	$1,000	$1,000
	Lowest 25%	-	$800	$500	$750	$600
	Average	-	$1,461	$1,318	$2,183	$1,760
Total Benefits	**Highest 25%**	**$8,200**	**$12,000**	**$14,588**	**$12,863**	**$17,236**
	Median	**$5,000**	**$6,600**	**$8,000**	**$7,893**	**$11,250**
	Lowest 25%	**$1,100**	**$2,150**	**$4,100**	**$2,687**	**$5,678**
	Average	**$5,880**	**$7,351**	**$9,967**	**$8,598**	**$11,711**
TOTAL COMPENSATION PLUS BENEFITS	**Highest 25%**	**$45,618**	**$55,176**	**$61,023**	**$59,055**	**$73,938**
	Median	**$38,550**	**$49,195**	**$51,896**	**$49,407**	**$60,549**
	Lowest 25%	**$31,300**	**$39,910**	**$42,600**	**$41,264**	**$50,456**
	Average	**$41,076**	**$48,970**	**$53,958**	**$52,471**	**$63,971**
Number of Respondents		24	62	70	52	203

- Not enough response to provide meaningful data.

* For detailed description and definitions of Data Distribution (Highest 25%, Median, Lowest 25%, and Average), see chapter 1, Explanation of Data Distribution.

Table 9-2: Annual Compensation of Full-Time Youth Pastors/Directors by Worship Attendance

	Data Distribution*	100 or less	101-300	301-500	501-750	751-1,000	Over 1,000
CHARACTERISTICS							
Average weekend worship attendance	-		219	406	640	892	1,815
Average church income	-		$474,557	$842,886	$1,136,123	$1,725,154	$3,057,862
Average # of years employed	-		4	4	6	5	6
Average # of paid vacation days	-		14	17	16	16	16
% College graduate or higher	-		80%	89%	85%	84%	90%
% Who receive auto reimbursement/allowance	-		54%	56%	49%	42%	51%
% Ordained	-		67%	72%	70%	89%	79%
% Supervise one or more people	-		43%	35%	53%	63%	81%
Average % salary increase (for those who had an increase) this year	-		4.7%	3.7%	3.3%	3.0%	4.3%
COMPENSATION							
Base Salary	Median	-	$30,000	$31,860	$35,000	$33,628	$34,000
	Average	-	$30,424	$32,513	$36,191	$34,427	$36,843
Housing	Median	-	$16,804	$18,000	$20,184	$24,000	$25,245
	Average	-	$17,418	$18,094	$20,088	$22,554	$25,700
Parsonage	Median	-	$9,600	$10,000	-	-	-
	Average	-	$8,311	$11,459	-	-	-
Total Compensation	**Median**	-	**$42,000**	**$42,840**	**$45,931**	**$51,923**	**$52,750**
	Average	-	**$42,100**	**$45,101**	**$48,660**	**$53,420**	**$55,797**
BENEFITS							
Health Insurance	Median	-	$6,500	$8,038	$10,424	$8,500	$10,964
	Average	-	$7,318	$8,749	$10,240	$9,245	$11,415
Life Insurance	Median	-	$184	$200	$219	$190	$250
	Average	-	$350	$224	$275	$263	$491
Disability	Median	-	$500	$375	$495	$363	$302
	Average	-	$579	$475	$508	$345	$363
Retirement	Median	-	$1,850	$2,294	$2,750	$2,250	$2,725
	Average	-	$2,649	$2,624	$2,808	$3,199	$3,402
Continuing Education	Median	-	$1,000	$1,000	$1,000	$1,500	$1,500
	Average	-	$1,192	$1,536	$1,759	$2,462	$2,257
Total Benefits	**Median**	-	**$7,183**	**$6,900**	**$10,600**	**$10,638**	**$13,600**
	Average	-	**$7,804**	**$8,864**	**$10,480**	**$11,028**	**$13,099**
TOTAL COMPENSATION PLUS BENEFITS	**Median**	-	**$47,575**	**$51,291**	**$58,481**	**$59,934**	**$64,850**
	Average	-	**$48,467**	**$52,250**	**$58,582**	**$63,377**	**$68,557**
Number of Respondents		7	101	93	75	57	77

- Not enough response to provide meaningful data.

* For detailed description and definitions of Data Distribution (Median and Average), see chapter 1, Explanation of Data Distribution.

Table 9-3: Annual Compensation of Full-Time Youth Pastors/Directors by Church Setting

	Data Distribution*	CHURCH SETTING			
		Metro-politan city	Suburb of large city	Small town or rural city	Farming area
CHARACTERISTICS					
Average weekend worship attendance		895	799	608	466
Average church income		$2,048,291	$1,484,599	$950,847	$714,054
Average # of years employed		5	5	4	3
Average # of paid vacation days		16	16	15	13
% College graduate or higher		88%	89%	83%	67%
% Who receive auto reimbursement/allowance		48%	53%	51%	56%
% Ordained		78%	71%	76%	78%
% Supervise one or more people		61%	53%	51%	33%
Average % salary increase (for those who had an increase) this year		3.6%	3.9%	3.9%	-
COMPENSATION					
Base Salary	Median	$32,900	$34,000	$30,000	$30,895
	Average	$33,699	$35,550	$31,482	$31,392
Housing	Median	$23,500	$21,295	$18,180	-
	Average	$24,460	$21,832	$18,208	-
Parsonage	Median	-	$12,600	$4,000	-
	Average	-	$12,502	$7,146	-
Total Compensation	**Median**	**$48,000**	**$48,688**	**$42,737**	**$43,432**
	Average	**$50,876**	**$51,139**	**$44,295**	**$41,845**
BENEFITS					
Health Insurance	Median	$7,165	$10,000	$9,146	-
	Average	$8,677	$10,153	$9,120	-
Life Insurance	Median	$229	$222	$205	-
	Average	$262	$436	$313	-
Disability Insurance	Median	$293	$342	$415	-
	Average	$354	$430	$458	-
Retirement	Median	$2,773	$2,510	$2,300	-
	Average	$3,535	$2,930	$2,643	-
Continuing Education	Median	$1,000	$1,000	$1,000	-
	Average	$1,066	$1,912	$1,666	-
Total Benefits	**Median**	**$7,165**	**$10,359**	**$8,200**	**-**
	Average	**$9,216**	**$10,915**	**$9,794**	**-**
TOTAL COMPENSATION PLUS BENEFITS	**Median**	**$55,726**	**$58,106**	**$50,799**	**$44,000**
	Average	**$58,902**	**$60,970**	**$52,882**	**$46,481**
Number of Respondents		68	176	159	9

- Not enough response to provide meaningful data.

* For detailed description and definitions of Data Distribution (Median and Average), see chapter 1, Explanation of Data Distribution.

Table 9-4: Annual Compensation of Full-Time Youth Pastors/Directors by Region

	Data Distribution*	REGION								
		New England	Middle Atlantic	South Atlantic	E-N Central	E-S Central	W-N Central	W-S Central	Mountain	Pacific
CHARACTERISTICS										
Average weekend worship attendance		545	742	738	732	796	612	792	657	770
Average church income		$1,042,267	$1,129,031	$1,605,174	$1,079,446	$1,548,045	$1,025,487	$1,577,751	$1,040,998	$1,616,185
Average # of years employed		5	4	5	5	5	6	5	5	5
Average # of paid vacation days		16	16	16	16	15	16	15	17	17
% College graduate or higher		75%	84%	85%	88%	88%	89%	88%	81%	83%
% Who receive auto reimbursement/allowance		100%	42%	53%	61%	45%	42%	46%	45%	50%
% Ordained		44%	63%	66%	72%	85%	70%	90%	81%	78%
% Supervise one or more people		78%	50%	57%	42%	61%	61%	53%	48%	55%
Average % salary increase (for those who had an increase) this year		-	3.6%	4.4%	3.4%	4.1%	3.2%	4.7%	3.7%	3.5%
COMPENSATION										
Base Salary	Median	$38,000	$31,295	$38,124	$31,930	$30,565	$28,493	$34,622	$30,000	$30,000
	Average	$36,292	$32,876	$36,529	$32,720	$33,011	$30,844	$37,185	$30,709	$32,422
Housing	Median	-	$15,370	$20,626	$16,625	$21,000	$17,750	$20,000	$21,500	$22,000
	Average	-	$17,033	$23,071	$18,548	$19,939	$17,886	$20,990	$22,167	$22,893
Parsonage	Median	-	-	-	-	-	-	-	-	-
	Average	-	-	-	-	-	-	-	-	-
Total Compensation	**Median**	**$42,000**	**$42,737**	**$48,250**	**$42,250**	**$50,750**	**$42,768**	**$49,567**	**$44,480**	**$47,063**
	Average	**$46,976**	**$45,163**	**$50,329**	**$45,534**	**$48,737**	**$43,012**	**$53,858**	**$46,280**	**$51,487**
BENEFITS										
Health Insurance	Median	-	$11,555	$9,000	$12,000	$7,000	$6,600	$8,646	$10,600	$7,583
	Average	-	$10,799	$9,753	$11,792	$7,290	$7,724	$9,545	$9,640	$8,158
Life Insurance	Median	-	$300	$271	$214	-	$266	$244	-	$156
	Average	-	$307	$331	$486	-	$435	$362	-	$189
Disability Insurance	Median	-	$382	$440	$279	$242	$327	$474	-	$261
	Average	-	$384	$444	$438	$328	$314	$558	-	$328
Retirement	Median	-	$2,089	$3,000	$2,281	$3,500	$1,800	$3,000	$2,530	$2,000
	Average	-	$2,261	$3,448	$2,530	$3,848	$2,387	$3,188	$3,264	$2,616
Continuing Education	Median	-	$1,000	$1,000	$1,000	-	$1,050	$1,000	$1,000	$1,000
	Average	-	$1,143	$1,522	$1,280	-	$1,969	$2,044	$1,142	$2,375
Total Benefits	**Median**	**$3,675**	**$9,737**	**$7,536**	**$12,169**	**$6,630**	**$7,200**	**$10,825**	**$10,950**	**$7,940**
	Average	**$7,064**	**$11,206**	**$9,815**	**$11,913**	**$7,953**	**$9,103**	**$10,621**	**$10,825**	**$9,139**
TOTAL COMPENSATION PLUS BENEFITS	**Median**	**$48,600**	**$53,537**	**$57,750**	**$51,500**	**$59,560**	**$49,885**	**$60,162**	**$51,500**	**$54,000**
	Average	**$53,255**	**$56,369**	**$59,222**	**$55,309**	**$57,291**	**$51,494**	**$63,253**	**$55,136**	**$58,669**
Number of Respondents		9	33	75	78	34	44	52	33	60

- Not enough response to provide meaningful data.

* For detailed description and definitions of Data Distribution (Median and Average), see chapter 1, Explanation of Data Distribution.

Table 9-5: Annual Compensation of Full-Time Youth Pastors/Directors by Education

	Data Distribution*	EDUCATION			
		Less than Bachelor	Bachelor	Master	Doctorate
CHARACTERISTICS					
Average weekend worship attendance		619	738	727	-
Average church income		$1,150,587	$1,274,599	$1,503,971	-
Average # of years employed		4	5	5	-
Average # of paid vacation days		13	16	17	-
% College graduate or higher		0%	100%	100%	-
% Who receive auto reimbursement/allowance		40%	52%	55%	-
% Ordained		71%	72%	81%	-
% Supervise one or more people		60%	50%	55%	-
Average % salary increase (for those who had an increase) this year		3.7%	4.2%	3.2%	-
COMPENSATION					
Base Salary	Median	$33,500	$31,930	$33,500	-
	Average	$33,560	$32,727	$35,669	-
Housing	Median	$19,000	$18,900	$24,000	-
	Average	$18,012	$19,923	$23,492	-
Parsonage	Median	-	$8,000	-	-
	Average	-	$8,428	-	-
Total Compensation	**Median**	**$43,770**	**$44,000**	**$52,431**	**-**
	Average	**$44,767**	**$46,692**	**$53,442**	**-**
BENEFITS					
Health Insurance	Median	$7,688	$10,000	$8,291	-
	Average	$8,083	$9,804	$9,218	-
Life Insurance	Median	$170	$202	$320	-
	Average	$442	$341	$368	-
Disability Insurance	Median	-	$322	$470	-
	Average	-	$360	$541	-
Retirement	Median	$1,998	$2,000	$3,300	-
	Average	$2,057	$2,516	$3,920	-
Continuing Education	Median	$1,500	$1,000	$1,000	-
	Average	$1,977	$1,828	$1,356	-
Total Benefits	**Median**	**$5,750**	**$10,633**	**$7,879**	**-**
	Average	**$7,384**	**$10,722**	**$10,062**	**-**
TOTAL COMPENSATION PLUS BENEFITS	**Median**	**$48,500**	**$52,594**	**$60,092**	**-**
	Average	**$51,458**	**$55,892**	**$62,790**	**-**
Number of Respondents		58	236	113	2

- Not enough response to provide meaningful data.

* For detailed description and definitions of Data Distribution (Median and Average), see chapter 1, Explanation of Data Distribution.

Table 9-6: Annual Compensation of Full-Time Youth Pastors/Directors by Years Employed

	Data Distribution*	YEARS EMPLOYED			
		Less than 6 years	6-10 years	11-15 years	Over 15 years
CHARACTERISTICS					
Average weekend worship attendance		697	848	615	1,089
Average church income		$1,287,559	$1,496,119	$1,261,614	$2,023,285
Average # of years employed		3	8	13	20
Average # of paid vacation days		14	18	21	23
% College graduate or higher		84%	89%	81%	100%
% Who receive auto reimbursement/allowance		52%	46%	48%	40%
% Ordained		69%	87%	76%	100%
% Supervise one or more people		49%	63%	67%	60%
Average % salary increase (for those who had an increase) this year		4.1%	3.8%	3.0%	-
COMPENSATION					
Base Salary	Median	$32,000	$30,670	$36,000	$36,500
	Average	$32,777	$34,308	$41,278	$40,819
Housing	Median	$17,639	$24,000	$22,000	$25,200
	Average	$18,539	$24,143	$24,617	$28,466
Parsonage	Median	$10,000	-	-	-
	Average	$10,288	-	-	-
Total Compensation	**Median**	**$43,860**	**$51,500**	**$54,195**	**$54,000**
	Average	**$45,170**	**$53,581**	**$59,133**	**$66,438**
BENEFITS					
Health Insurance	Median	$7,977	$10,698	$9,000	$15,835
	Average	$8,373	$10,919	$9,426	$15,046
Life Insurance	Median	$206	$230	-	$380
	Average	$290	$474	-	$443
Disability Insurance	Median	$352	$338	-	$380
	Average	$409	$410	-	$443
Retirement	Median	$2,228	$2,617	$3,300	$2,719
	Average	$2,681	$3,144	$3,146	$3,000
Continuing Education	Median	$1,000	$1,500	-	-
	Average	$1,290	$2,558	-	-
Total Benefits	**Median**	**$7,400**	**$11,152**	**$10,900**	**$19,025**
	Average	**$8,739**	**$11,648**	**$11,015**	**$18,906**
TOTAL COMPENSATION PLUS BENEFITS	**Median**	**$51,246**	**$61,120**	**$64,980**	**$74,025**
	Average	**$52,688**	**$64,493**	**$69,624**	**$85,344**
Number of Respondents		255	95	21	10

- Not enough response to provide meaningful data.

* For detailed description and definitions of Data Distribution (Median and Average), see chapter 1, Explanation of Data Distribution.

Table 9-7: Annual Compensation of Full-Time Youth Pastors/Directors by Denomination

	Data Distribution*	DENOMINATION					
		Assemblies of God	Baptist	Independent/ Nondenom.	Lutheran	Methodist	Presby-terian
CHARACTERISTICS							
Average weekend worship attendance		582	619	970	701	647	630
Average church income		$998,941	$1,323,158	$1,595,185	$1,298,654	$1,337,680	$1,468,131
Average # of years employed		4	5	5	6	5	3
Average # of paid vacation days		14	15	16	19	17	17
% College graduate or higher		64%	90%	84%	92%	88%	86%
% Who receive auto reimbursement/allowance		31%	60%	42%	46%	48%	59%
% Ordained		85%	88%	82%	42%	15%	32%
% Supervise one or more people		55%	53%	56%	46%	42%	45%
Average % salary increase (for those who had an increase) this year		3.4%	3.6%	4.3%	3.1%	4.0%	3.0%
COMPENSATION							
Base Salary	Median	$27,324	$31,389	$33,480	$34,549	$37,428	$38,272
	Average	$28,998	$31,986	$35,354	$37,953	$40,037	$39,153
Housing	Median	$17,750	$20,000	$19,400	-	-	-
	Average	$18,935	$21,379	$20,498	-	-	-
Parsonage	Median	-	-	-	-	-	-
	Average	-	-	-	-	-	-
Total Compensation	**Median**	**$41,795**	**$48,000**	**$50,000**	**$41,000**	**$40,404**	**$47,210**
	Average	**$43,037**	**$49,696**	**$51,996**	**$43,514**	**$43,772**	**$47,305**
BENEFITS							
Health Insurance	Median	$8,938	$9,432	$9,600	-	$6,259	$7,794
	Average	$7,908	$9,466	$9,608	-	$7,026	$9,951
Life Insurance	Median	-	$222	$212	-	-	$216
	Average	-	$330	$491	-	-	$227
Disability Insurance	Median	-	$342	$384	-	-	-
	Average	-	$467	$350	-	-	-
Retirement	Median	$1,554	$3,260	$1,767	$3,091	$1,625	$2,847
	Average	$1,691	$3,556	$2,620	$2,862	$1,917	$3,621
Continuing Education	Median	$1,350	$1,000	$1,000	$600	$800	$1,200
	Average	$2,872	$1,796	$1,956	$1,260	$973	$1,382
Total Benefits	**Median**	**$7,312**	**$10,100**	**$9,918**	**$4,796**	**$5,006**	**$9,007**
	Average	**$7,878**	**$10,609**	**$10,769**	**$8,771**	**$6,163**	**$11,125**
TOTAL COMPENSATION PLUS BENEFITS	**Median**	**$48,435**	**$58,950**	**$59,101**	**$43,600**	**$46,229**	**$52,875**
	Average	**$49,602**	**$59,464**	**$61,860**	**$51,610**	**$49,461**	**$57,418**
Number of Respondents		42	106	98	13	26	22

- Not enough response to provide meaningful data.

* For detailed description and definitions of Data Distribution (Median and Average), see chapter 1, Explanation of Data Distribution.

Table 9-8: Annual Compensation of Full-Time Youth Pastors/Directors by Gender

	Data Distribution*	GENDER	
		Male	Female
CHARACTERISTICS			
Average weekend worship attendance		729	655
Average church income		$1,353,392	$1,215,221
Average # of years employed		5	5
Average # of paid vacation days		16	18
% College graduate or higher		86%	84%
% Who receive auto reimbursement/allowance		51%	56%
% Ordained		79%	33%
% Supervise one or more people		54%	47%
Average % salary increase (for those who had an increase) this year		3.8%	4.5%
COMPENSATION			
Base Salary	Median	$32,000	$37,886
	Average	$33,401	$36,230
Housing	Median	$20,000	$13,060
	Average	$20,933	$14,400
Parsonage	Median	$9,800	-
	Average	$9,941	-
Total Compensation	**Median**	**$46,982**	**$39,044**
	Average	**$49,033**	**$41,515**
BENEFITS			
Health Insurance	Median	$9,853	$6,429
	Average	$9,539	$6,798
Life Insurance	Median	$215	$248
	Average	$331	$322
Disability Insurance	Median	$365	-
	Average	$411	-
Retirement	Median	$2,425	$2,100
	Average	$2,955	$2,677
Continuing Education	Median	$1,000	$775
	Average	$1,781	$863
Total Benefits	**Median**	**$10,000**	**$5,103**
	Average	**$10,473**	**$6,045**
TOTAL COMPENSATION PLUS BENEFITS	**Median**	**$55,614**	**$46,534**
	Average	**$58,206**	**$47,396**
Number of Respondents		373	39

- Not enough response to provide meaningful data.

* For detailed description and definitions of Data Distribution (Median and Average), see chapter 1, Explanation of Data Distribution.

Table 9-9: Annual Compensation of Part-Time Youth Pastors/Directors by Church Income

	Data Distribution*	CHURCH INCOME				
		$250K & Under	$251-$500K	$501-$750K	$751K-$1M	Over 1 Million
CHARACTERISTICS						
Average weekend worship attendance		125	205	313	393	1,216
Average church income		$141,983	$369,149	$612,138	$856,558	$1,880,000
Average # of years employed		4	5	4	5	3
Average # of paid vacation days		11	9	10	7	11
% College graduate or higher		59%	75%	76%	100%	30%
% Who receive auto reimbursement/allowance		24%	23%	43%	40%	0%
% Ordained		32%	38%	25%	33%	30%
% Supervise one or more people		29%	37%	28%	40%	30%
Average % salary increase (for those who had an increase) this year		-	7.8%	4.3%	-	-
HOURLY RATE						
Base Rate	Average	$14	$16	$16	$19	$18
COMPENSATION						
Base Salary	Median	$7,200	$14,000	$17,585	$12,011	$15,600
	Average	$7,574	$13,941	$16,007	$12,480	$16,840
Housing	Median	$7,200	$11,426	-	-	-
	Average	$9,599	$11,820	-	-	-
Parsonage	Median	-	-	-	-	-
	Average	-	-	-	-	-
Total Compensation	**Median**	**$7,668**	**$14,700**	**$18,000**	**$17,886**	**$22,775**
	Average	**$10,013**	**$15,047**	**$18,191**	**$15,632**	**$21,390**
BENEFITS						
Health Insurance	Median	-	-	-	-	-
	Average	-	-	-	-	-
Life Insurance	Median	-	-	-	-	-
	Average	-	-	-	-	-
Disability Insurance	Median	-	-	-	-	-
	Average	-	-	-	-	-
Retirement	Median	-	-	-	-	-
	Average	-	-	-	-	-
Continuing Education	Median	-	-	-	-	-
	Average	-	-	-	-	-
Total Benefits	**Median**	-	-	-	-	-
	Average	-	-	-	-	-
TOTAL COMPENSATION PLUS BENEFITS	**Median**	**$7,668**	**$15,000**	**$18,000**	**$19,073**	**$22,775**
	Average	**$10,109**	**$15,313**	**$18,380**	**$16,174**	**$21,440**
Number of Respondents		33	40	29	10	10

- Not enough response to provide meaningful data.

* For detailed description and definitions of Data Distribution (Median and Average), see chapter 1, Explanation of Data Distribution.

Table 9-10: Annual Compensation of Part-Time Youth Pastors/Directors by Worship Attendance

	Data Distribution*	WORSHIP ATTENDANCE					
		100 or less	101-300	301-500	501-750	751-1,000	Over 1,000
CHARACTERISTICS							
Average weekend worship attendance		75	196	387	608	-	-
Average church income		$162,336	$404,660	$591,629	$1,085,316	-	-
Average # of years employed		4	5	4	3	-	-
Average # of paid vacation days		10	10	8	13	-	-
% College graduate or higher		65%	72%	83%	56%	-	-
% Who receive auto reimbursement/allowance		24%	29%	35%	22%	-	-
% Ordained		35%	40%	10%	13%	-	-
% Supervise one or more people		30%	30%	40%	33%	-	-
Average % salary increase (for those who had an increase) this year		-	4.3%	5.4%	-	-	-
HOURLY RATE							
Base Rate	Average	$14	$17	$16	$14	-	-
COMPENSATION							
Base Salary	Median	$7,240	$10,900	$15,885	$15,000	-	-
	Average	$8,669	$12,186	$15,613	$15,819	-	-
Housing	Median	-	$11,460	-	-	-	-
	Average	-	$11,774	-	-	-	-
Parsonage	Median	-	-	-	-	-	-
	Average	-	-	-	-	-	-
Total Compensation	**Median**	$7,440	$15,000	$15,885	$15,000	-	-
	Average	$10,740	$14,868	$15,613	$17,523	-	-
BENEFITS							
Health Insurance	Median	-	-	-	-	-	-
	Average	-	-	-	-	-	-
Life Insurance	Median	-	-	-	-	-	-
	Average	-	-	-	-	-	-
Disability Insurance	Median	-	-	-	-	-	-
	Average	-	-	-	-	-	-
Retirement	Median	-	-	-	-	-	-
	Average	-	-	-	-	-	-
Continuing Education	Median	-	-	-	-	-	-
	Average	-	-	-	-	-	-
Total Benefits	**Median**	-	$1,500	-	-	-	-
	Average	-	$1,760	-	-	-	-
TOTAL COMPENSATION PLUS BENEFITS	**Median**	$7,440	$15,600	$15,885	$15,000	-	-
	Average	$10,833	$15,166	$15,757	$17,567	-	-
Number of Respondents		21	66	20	9	1	6

- Not enough response to provide meaningful data.

* For detailed description and definitions of Data Distribution (Median and Average), see chapter 1, Explanation of Data Distribution.

Table 9-11: Annual Compensation of Part-Time Youth Pastors/Directors by Church Setting

	Data Distribution*	CHURCH SETTING			
		Metro-politan city	Suburb of large city	Small town or rural city	Farming area
CHARACTERISTICS					
Average weekend worship attendance		273	404	242	-
Average church income		$557,400	$662,120	$388,864	-
Average # of years employed		5	5	4	-
Average # of paid vacation days		9	9	11	-
% College graduate or higher		89%	73%	61%	-
% Who receive auto reimbursement/allowance		33%	27%	21%	-
% Ordained		43%	27%	34%	-
% Supervise one or more people		38%	36%	28%	-
Average % salary increase (for those who had an increase) this year		-	4.5%	2.9%	-
HOURLY RATE					
Base Rate	Average	$16	$17	$16	-
COMPENSATION					
Base Salary	Median	$9,500	$13,180	$12,500	-
	Average	$12,821	$13,442	$13,630	-
Housing	Median	-	$16,262	$7,200	-
	Average	-	$17,510	$9,445	-
Parsonage	Median	-	-	-	-
	Average	-	-	-	-
Total Compensation	**Median**	**$12,000**	**$16,000**	**$14,200**	**-**
	Average	**$14,870**	**$15,546**	**$15,125**	**-**
BENEFITS					
Health Insurance	Median	-	-	-	-
	Average	-	-	-	-
Life Insurance	Median	-	-	-	-
	Average	-	-	-	-
Disability Insurance	Median	-	-	-	-
	Average	-	-	-	-
Retirement	Median	-	-	-	-
	Average	-	-	-	-
Continuing Education	Median	-	-	-	-
	Average	-	-	-	-
Total Benefits	**Median**	**-**	**-**	**$1,250**	**-**
	Average	**-**	**-**	**$1,280**	**-**
TOTAL COMPENSATION PLUS BENEFITS	**Median**	**$13,000**	**$16,100**	**$14,500**	**-**
	Average	**$15,228**	**$16,580**	**$15,369**	**-**
Number of Respondents		21	53	43	6

- *Not enough response to provide meaningful data.*

* *For detailed description and definitions of Data Distribution (Median and Average), see chapter 1, Explanation of Data Distribution.*

Table 9-12: Annual Compensation of Part-Time Youth Pastors/Directors by Region

	Data Distribution*	New England	Middle Atlantic	South Atlantic	E-N Central	E-S Central	W-N Central	W-S Central	Mountain	Pacific
						REGION				
CHARACTERISTICS										
Average weekend worship attendance		-	410	233	243	217	315	-	283	409
Average church income		-	$600,722	$500,391	$471,903	$491,881	$512,552	-	$491,960	$582,332
Average # of years employed		-	4	4	6	2	4	-	2	5
Average # of paid vacation days		-	11	8	10	9	14	-	8	11
% College graduate or higher		-	80%	64%	76%	86%	70%	-	62%	59%
% Who receive auto reimbursement/allowance		-	40%	23%	28%	33%	30%	-	8%	33%
% Ordained		-	40%	14%	44%	13%	33%	-	31%	50%
% Supervise one or more people		-	40%	32%	40%	0%	63%	-	23%	35%
Average % salary increase (for those who had an increase) this year		-	4.5%	-	6.0%	-	5.8%	-	3.6%	-
HOURLY RATE										
Base Rate	Average	-	$19	$16	$16	-	$15	-	$17	$13
COMPENSATION										
Base Salary	Median	-	$17,000	$12,500	$6,000	$12,000	$20,800	-	$13,531	$10,800
	Average	-	$16,151	$11,914	$9,634	$15,736	$17,092	-	$15,034	$10,402
Housing	Median	-	-	-	$14,700	-	-	-	-	$12,500
	Average	-	-	-	$15,699	-	-	-	-	$13,270
Parsonage	Median	-	-	-	-	-	-	-	-	-
	Average	-	-	-	-	-	-	-	-	-
Total Compensation	**Median**	-	**$16,500**	**$12,360**	**$11,000**	**$18,646**	**$20,800**	-	**$15,061**	**$13,200**
	Average	-	$17,296	$11,448	$13,730	$18,238	$19,402	-	$15,354	$14,302
BENEFITS										
Health Insurance	Median	-	-	-	-	-	-	-	-	-
	Average	-	-	-	-	-	-	-	-	-
Life Insurance	Median	-	-	-	-	-	-	-	-	-
	Average	-	-	-	-	-	-	-	-	-
Disability Insurance	Median	-	-	-	-	-	-	-	-	-
	Average	-	-	-	-	-	-	-	-	-
Retirement	Median	-	-	-	-	-	-	-	-	-
	Average	-	-	-	-	-	-	-	-	-
Continuing Education	Median	-	-	-	-	-	-	-	-	-
	Average	-	-	-	-	-	-	-	-	-
Total Benefits	**Median**	-	-	-	-	-	-	-	-	-
	Average	-	-	-	-	-	-	-	-	-
TOTAL COMPENSATION PLUS BENEFITS	**Median**	-	**$16,500**	**$12,500**	**$11,760**	**$18,646**	**$20,800**	-	**$15,061**	**$13,829**
	Average	-	**$17,296**	**$11,489**	**$14,020**	**$18,585**	**$19,558**	-	**$15,430**	**$14,737**
Number of Respondents		3	10	22	26	9	10	7	13	24

- Not enough response to provide meaningful data.

* For detailed description and definitions of Data Distribution (Median and Average), see chapter 1, Explanation of Data Distribution.

Table 9-13: Annual Compensation of Part-Time Youth Pastors/Directors by Education

	Data Distribution*	EDUCATION			
		Less than Bachelor	Bachelor	Master	Doctorate
CHARACTERISTICS					
Average weekend worship attendance		405	264	317	-
Average church income		$613,245	$480,515	$541,588	-
Average # of years employed		5	4	4	-
Average # of paid vacation days		11	9	9	-
% College graduate or higher		0%	100%	100%	-
% Who receive auto reimbursement/allowance		25%	27%	42%	-
% Ordained		31%	31%	47%	-
% Supervise one or more people		37%	31%	42%	-
Average % salary increase (for those who had an increase) this year		-	5.2%	6.4%	-
HOURLY RATE					
Base Rate	Average	$16	$16	$17	-
COMPENSATION					
Base Salary	Median	$11,600	$12,000	$12,500	-
	Average	$11,981	$13,280	$15,393	-
Housing	Median	$9,300	$12,500	-	-
	Average	$11,049	$12,525	-	-
Parsonage	Median	-	-	-	-
	Average	-	-	-	-
Total Compensation	**Median**	**$15,000**	**$14,700**	**$15,000**	-
	Average	**$15,095**	**$14,961**	**$16,213**	-
BENEFITS					
Health Insurance	Median	-	-	-	-
	Average	-	-	-	-
Life Insurance	Median	-	-	-	-
	Average	-	-	-	-
Disability Insurance	Median	-	-	-	-
	Average	-	-	-	-
Retirement	Median	-	-	-	-
	Average	-	-	-	-
Continuing Education	Median	-	-	-	-
	Average	-	-	-	-
Total Benefits	**Median**	-	**$1,250**	-	-
	Average	-	**$1,871**	-	-
TOTAL COMPENSATION PLUS BENEFITS	**Median**	**$15,000**	**$15,000**	**$15,900**	-
	Average	**$15,186**	**$15,254**	**$18,935**	-
Number of Respondents		36	64	19	0

- Not enough response to provide meaningful data.

* For detailed description and definitions of Data Distribution (Median and Average), see chapter 1, Explanation of Data Distribution.

Table 9-14: Annual Compensation of Part-Time Youth Pastors/Directors by Years Employed

	Data Distribution*	YEARS EMPLOYED			
		Less than 6 years	6-10 years	11-15 years	Over 15 years
CHARACTERISTICS					
Average weekend worship attendance		297	447	-	-
Average church income		$528,736	$634,399	-	-
Average # of years employed		2	8	-	-
Average # of paid vacation days		9	11	-	-
% College graduate or higher		71%	76%	-	-
% Who receive auto reimbursement/allowance		28%	14%	-	-
% Ordained		26%	52%	-	-
% Supervise one or more people		26%	55%	-	-
Average % salary increase (for those who had an increase) this year		5.6%	-	-	-
HOURLY RATE					
Base Rate	Average	$16	$18	-	-
COMPENSATION					
Base Salary	Median	$12,000	$8,608	-	-
	Average	$13,154	$12,193	-	-
Housing	Median	$10,185	$16,524	-	-
	Average	$10,692	$17,951	-	-
Parsonage	Median	-	-	-	-
	Average	-	-	-	-
Total Compensation	**Median**	$14,200	$12,850	-	-
	Average	$14,654	$14,728	-	-
BENEFITS					
Health Insurance	Median	-	-	-	-
	Average	-	-	-	-
Life Insurance	Median	-	-	-	-
	Average	-	-	-	-
Disability Insurance	Median	-	-	-	-
	Average	-	-	-	-
Retirement	Median	-	-	-	-
	Average	-	-	-	-
Continuing Education	Median	-	-	-	-
	Average	-	-	-	-
Total Benefits	**Median**	$1,000	-	-	-
	Average	$1,579	-	-	-
TOTAL COMPENSATION PLUS BENEFITS	**Median**	$14,500	$14,000	-	-
	Average	$14,951	$17,007	-	-
Number of Respondents		82	21	5	3

- Not enough response to provide meaningful data.

* For detailed description and definitions of Data Distribution (Median and Average), see chapter 1, Explanation of Data Distribution.

Table 9-15: Annual Compensation of Part-Time Youth Pastors/Directors by Denomination

	Data Distribution*	DENOMINATION					
		Assemblies of God	Baptist	Independent/ Nondenom.	Lutheran	Methodist	Presby- terian
CHARACTERISTICS							
Average weekend worship attendance		212	289	297	-	182	408
Average church income		$379,761	$479,832	$468,646	-	$433,573	$936,200
Average # of years employed		2	4	4	-	5	3
Average # of paid vacation days		11	9	12	-	9	7
% College graduate or higher		69%	71%	68%	-	89%	50%
% Who receive auto reimbursement/allowance		15%	28%	28%	-	33%	13%
% Ordained		62%	43%	30%	-	11%	0%
% Supervise one or more people		38%	34%	35%	-	33%	22%
Average % salary increase (for those who had an increase) this year		-	-	4.1%	-	5.8%	-
HOURLY RATE							
Base Rate	Average	$14	$16	$15	-	-	$15
COMPENSATION							
Base Salary	Median	$10,200	$15,061	$11,850	-	$11,289	$15,000
	Average	$10,767	$14,596	$12,373	-	$12,862	$13,479
Housing	Median	-	-	-	-	-	-
	Average	-	-	-	-	-	-
Parsonage	Median	-	-	-	-	-	-
	Average	-	-	-	-	-	-
Total Compensation	**Median**	**$15,000**	**$15,600**	**$14,000**	-	**$11,289**	**$15,000**
	Average	$14,403	$16,398	$15,831	-	$13,290	$15,096
BENEFITS							
Health Insurance	Median	-	-	-	-	-	-
	Average	-	-	-	-	-	-
Life Insurance	Median	-	-	-	-	-	-
	Average	-	-	-	-	-	-
Disability Insurance	Median	-	-	-	-	-	-
	Average	-	-	-	-	-	-
Retirement	Median	-	-	-	-	-	-
	Average	-	-	-	-	-	-
Continuing Education	Median	-	-	-	-	-	-
	Average	-	-	-	-	-	-
Total Benefits	**Median**	-	-	-	-	-	-
	Average	-	-	-	-	-	-
TOTAL COMPENSATION PLUS BENEFITS	**Median**	**$15,800**	**$15,600**	**$14,000**	-	**$11,539**	**$15,000**
	Average	$15,088	$16,442	$15,971	-	$13,353	$15,221
Number of Respondents		13	29	25	3	9	9

- Not enough response to provide meaningful data.

* For detailed description and definitions of Data Distribution (Median and Average), see chapter 1, Explanation of Data Distribution.

Table 9-16: Annual Compensation of Part-Time Youth Pastors/Directors by Gender

	Data Distribution*	GENDER	
		Male	Female
CHARACTERISTICS			
Average weekend worship attendance		280	384
Average church income		$484,254	$628,727
Average # of years employed		4	4
Average # of paid vacation days		10	9
% College graduate or higher		66%	77%
% Who receive auto reimbursement/allowance		27%	28%
% Ordained		41%	15%
% Supervise one or more people		33%	35%
Average % salary increase (for those who had an increase) this year		5.6%	3.8%
HOURLY RATE			
Base Rate	Average	$16	$17
COMPENSATION			
Base Salary	Median	$12,000	$12,191
	Average	$13,328	$13,233
Housing	Median	$11,460	-
	Average	$11,983	-
Parsonage	Median	-	-
	Average	-	-
Total Compensation	**Median**	**$15,000**	**$15,000**
	Average	**$15,556**	**$14,281**
BENEFITS			
Health Insurance	Median	-	-
	Average	-	-
Life Insurance	Median	-	-
	Average	-	-
Disability Insurance	Median	-	-
	Average	-	-
Retirement	Median	-	-
	Average	-	-
Continuing Education	Median	-	-
	Average	-	-
Total Benefits	**Median**	**$857**	**-**
	Average	**$1,474**	**-**
TOTAL COMPENSATION PLUS BENEFITS	**Median**	**$15,300**	**$15,000**
	Average	**$15,819**	**$15,614**
Number of Respondents		84	40

- Not enough response to provide meaningful data.

* For detailed description and definitions of Data Distribution (Median and Average), see chapter 1, Explanation of Data Distribution.

Full-Time Youth Pastor/Director Worksheet

	Enter your church data below	The 2014–2015 Compensation Handbook for Church Staff		Enter *Compensation Handbook* data below			
				Highest 25%	Median	Lowest 25%	Average
Church Income	$	Table 9-1	page 127	$	$	$	$
Worship Attendance		Table 9-2	page 128	n/a	$	n/a	$
Church Setting (metro, suburb, small town, or farming area)		Table 9-3	page 129	n/a	$	n/a	$
Region		Table 9-4	page 130	n/a	$	n/a	$
Person's Education		Table 9-5	page 131	n/a	$	n/a	$
Years Employed		Table 9-6	page 132	n/a	$	n/a	$
Denomination (if applicable)		Table 9-7	page 133	n/a	$	n/a	$

Looking at the table and page number references indicated in the *2014–2015 Compensation Handbook for Church Staff* columns above, locate the appropriate range for your church. Refer to the instructions below for step-by-step help.

FILLING OUT THE WORKSHEET

1. Fill in the gray boxes under *Enter your church data* with your church demographic information as follows:

   ▶ **Income** (Total annual church budget in past year)
   ▶ **Worship attendance** (Number of people, including children, who attend all weekend services)
   ▶ **Church setting** (Metropolitan city, suburb of large city, small town or rural city, or farming area)

   ▶ **Region** (Locate your state's region in the appendix on page 346.)
   ▶ **Education** (Highest level of education: less than bachelor, bachelor, master, or doctorate)

2. Use Table 9-1 (page 127) in your *2014–2015 Compensation Handbook for Church Staff* to enter data pertinent to your church. In the heading (top row), locate your church **income** from the five available ranges. Follow that column to the bottom rows, and copy the *Highest 25%*, *Median*, *Lowest 25%*, and *Average* amounts onto your worksheet.

3. Use Table 9-2 (page 128) on your *2014–2015 Compensation Handbook for Church Staff* to enter data pertinent to your church. In the heading (top row), locate your church's

worship attendance from the six available ranges. Follow that column to the bottom rows, and copy the *Median* and *Average* amounts onto your worksheet.

4. Use Table 9-3 (page 129) on your *2014–2015 Compensation Handbook for Church Staff* to enter data pertinent to your church. In the heading (top row), choose the **church setting** that best describes your church. Follow that column to the bottom rows, and copy the *Median* and *Average* amounts onto your worksheet.

5. Use Table 9-4 (page 130) on your *2014–2015 Compensation Handbook for Church Staff* to enter data pertinent to your church. In the heading (top row), look for the **region** where your church is located. Follow that column to the bottom rows, and copy the *Median* and *Average* amounts onto your worksheet.

6. Use Table 9-5 (page 131) on your *2014–2015 Compensation Handbook for Church Staff* to enter data pertinent to your Youth Pastor/Director. In the heading (top row), look for **your Youth Pastor/Director's highest level of education**. Follow that column to the bottom rows, and copy the *Median* and *Average* amounts onto your worksheet.

7. Use Table 9-6 (page 132) on your *2014–2015 Compensation Handbook for Church Staff* to enter data pertinent to your Youth Pastor/Director. In the heading (top row), locate the **number of years your Youth Pastor/Director has been employed**. Follow that column to the bottom rows, and copy the *Median* and *Average* amounts onto your worksheet.

8. Use Table 9-7 (page 133) on your *2014–2015 Compensation Handbook for Church Staff* to enter data pertinent to your church. In the heading (top row), look for **your church's denominational affiliation**. Follow that column to the bottom rows, and copy the *Median* and *Average* amounts onto your worksheet. If your church is not affiliated with a denomination, leave this section blank.

DETERMINING COMPENSATION

This tool will not provide you with a single compensation amount but rather with a range of values to help you determine the compensation appropriate to your situation.

1. Look at the values in the shaded *Median* column. Circle the **lowest** and the **highest** values. **This is the range of the median compensation plus benefits for churches similar to yours.**

2. For a variety of reasons, compensation plus benefits may be higher or lower than the range established in this table. Income and attendance are two significant factors affecting church compensation packages. If church income or attendance skews higher, you might want to consider moving toward or above the higher end of the range. Likewise, if church income or attendance skews lower, you may consider moving the package toward or below the lower end of the range.

3. Examine additional variables that might impact the compensation package you offer, such as years of service, education, and church setting.

4. Determine other circumstances unique to your situation, such as cost of living in your area, theological beliefs, pastoral performance, financial needs, the local economy, personal motivation, congregational goals, and others.

5. You now have a compensation package range based on the *2014–2015 Compensation Handbook*. Since each church and position are unique, your final compensation package will be based on additional factors unique to your situation.

Part-Time Youth Pastor/Director Worksheet

	Enter your church data below	The 2014–2015 Compensation Handbook for Church Staff		Enter *Compensation Handbook* data below			
				Highest 25%	Median	Lowest 25%	Average
Church Income	$	Table 9-9	page 135	$	$	$	$
Worship Attendance		Table 9-10	page 136	n/a	$	n/a	$
Church Setting (metro, suburb, small town, or farming area)		Table 9-11	page 137	n/a	$	n/a	$
Region		Table 9-12	page 138	n/a	$	n/a	$
Person's Education		Table 9-13	page 139	n/a	$	n/a	$
Years Employed		Table 9-14	page 140	n/a	$	n/a	$
Denomination (if applicable)		Table 9-15	page 141	n/a	$	n/a	$

Looking at the table and page number references indicated in the ***2014–2015 Compensation Handbook for Church Staff*** columns above, locate the appropriate range for your church. Refer to the instructions below for step-by-step help.

FILLING OUT THE WORKSHEET

1. Fill in the gray boxes under ***Enter your church data*** with your church demographic information as follows:

   ▶ **Income** (Total annual church budget in past year)
   ▶ **Worship attendance** (Number of people, including children, who attend all weekend services)
   ▶ **Church setting** (Metropolitan city, suburb of large city, small town or rural city, or farming area)

   ▶ **Region** (Locate your state's region in the appendix on page 346.)
   ▶ **Education** (Highest level of education: less than bachelor, bachelor, master, or doctorate)

2. Use Table 9-9 (page 135) in your *2014–2015 Compensation Handbook for Church Staff* to enter data pertinent to your church. In the heading (top row), locate your church **income** from the five available ranges. Follow that column to the bottom rows, and copy the ***Highest 25%***, ***Median***, ***Lowest 25%***, and ***Average*** amounts onto your worksheet.

3. Use Table 9-10 (page 136) on your *2014–2015 Compensation Handbook for Church Staff* to enter data pertinent to your church. In the heading (top row), locate your church's

worship attendance from the six available ranges. Follow that column to the bottom rows, and copy the *Median* and *Average* amounts onto your worksheet.

4. Use Table 9-11 (page 137) on your *2014–2015 Compensation Handbook for Church Staff* to enter data pertinent to your church. In the heading (top row), choose the **church setting** that best describes your church. Follow that column to the bottom rows, and copy the *Median* and *Average* amounts onto your worksheet.

5. Use Table 9-12 (page 138) on your *2014–2015 Compensation Handbook for Church Staff* to enter data pertinent to your church. In the heading (top row), look for the **region** where your church is located. Follow that column to the bottom rows, and copy the *Median* and *Average* amounts onto your worksheet.

6. Use Table 9-13 (page 139) on your *2014–2015 Compensation Handbook for Church Staff* to enter data pertinent to your Youth Pastor/ Director. In the heading (top row), look for **your Youth Pastor/Director's highest level of education**. Follow that column to the bottom rows, and copy the *Median* and *Average* amounts onto your worksheet.

7. Use Table 9-14 (page 140) on your *2014–2015 Compensation Handbook for Church Staff* to enter data pertinent to your Youth Pastor/ Director. In the heading (top row), locate the **number of years your Youth Pastor/Director has been employed**. Follow that column to the bottom rows, and copy the *Median* and *Average* amounts onto your worksheet.

8. Use Table 9-15 (page 141) on your *2014–2015 Compensation Handbook for Church Staff* to enter data pertinent to your church. In the heading (top row), look for **your church's denominational affiliation**. Follow that column to the bottom rows, and copy the *Median* and *Average* amounts onto your worksheet. If your church is not affiliated with a denomination, leave this section blank.

DETERMINING COMPENSATION

This tool will not provide you with a single compensation amount but rather with a range of values to help you determine the compensation appropriate to your situation.

1. Look at the values in the shaded *Median* column. Circle the **lowest** and the **highest** values. **This is the range of the median compensation plus benefits for churches similar to yours.**

2. For a variety of reasons, compensation plus benefits may be higher or lower than the range established in this table. Income and attendance are two significant factors affecting church compensation packages. If church income or attendance skews higher, you might want to consider moving toward or above the higher end of the range. Likewise, if church income or attendance skews lower, you may consider moving the package toward or below the lower end of the range.

3. Examine additional variables that might impact the compensation package you offer, such as years of service, education, and church setting.

4. Determine other circumstances unique to your situation, such as cost of living in your area, theological beliefs, pastoral performance, financial needs, the local economy, personal motivation, congregational goals, and others.

5. You now have a compensation package range based on the *2014–2015 Compensation Handbook*. Since each church and position are unique, your final compensation package will be based on additional factors unique to your situation.

10

CHILDREN'S/ PRESCHOOL PASTORS/ DIRECTORS

Employment Profile

Children's/Preschool Pastors/Directors are paid pastors and directors for children's ministries from nursery through elementary school age. (They are church staff, not school staff.) This category may include such positions as Early Childhood Pastor, Elementary School Pastor, Preschool Pastor/Director, Child-Care Director, Day-Care Director, etc.

Of the children's ministry leaders who responded to our survey, nearly six in 10 work full-time. More than nine in 10 full-time and part-time children's

ministry leaders are employed by the church rather than self-employed. Nearly three-fourths of full-time children's ministry leaders are female, and 80% have at least a bachelor's degree. Women hold more than 90% of the part-time positions.

The chart below provides a demographic profile of this sample.

	Full-Time	Part-Time
Number of respondents	**276**	**188**
Ordained	49%	11%
Average years employed	8	5
Male	28%	7%
Female	72%	93%
Self-employed (receives 1099)	2%	5%
Church employee (receives W-2)	98%	95%
High school diploma	10%	18%
Associate degree	11%	10%
Bachelor's degree	53%	59%
Master's degree	26%	12%
Doctoral degree	1%	1%

Total Compensation plus Benefits Package Analysis

The following analyses are based on data in the tables you will find later in this chapter. The tables show compensation plus benefits data for full-time and part-time Children's/Preschool Pastors/Directors and are presented according to church income, church attendance, church setting, region, education, years employed, denomination, and gender. In this way, the compensation plus benefits of children's ministry leaders can be analyzed and compared from a variety of useful perspectives.

The total compensation plus benefits amount includes the base salary; housing allowance and/or parsonage amount; health, life, and disability insurance payments; retirement contribution; and educational funds.

A worksheet at the end of this chapter is provided to help you apply the data to your church's situation.

Almost none of the paid children's ministry leaders live in church-provided parsonages; however, about four in 10 full-timers receive a housing allowance. The percentage of those receiving benefits such as health insurance, retirement, and continuing education is comparable to other pastors, not including Solo or Senior Pastors, for full-time positions.

Nearly six in 10 full-time Children's/Preschool Pastors/Directors received a salary increase, a 14-percentage-point increase from the previous study.

Compensation Plus Benefits	Full-Time	Part-Time
Base Salary	99%	96%
Housing	39%	6%
Parsonage	1%	1%
Health Insurance*	58%	5%
Life Insurance*	29%	1%
Disability Insurance*	23%	3%
Retirement	54%	7%
Continuing Education	29%	10%
Received salary increase	58%	46%
Received paid vacation	94%	48%
Received auto reimbursement/allowance	37%	22%

Only those reporting individual premiums for Health, Life, or Disability (not total insurance premiums) are included.

KEY POINTS

* More than six in 10 full-time Children's/Preschool Pastors/Directors in this sample serve in larger churches with an income of over $1,000,000 and a worship attendance of more than 500.

* For the most part, as worship attendance and the minister's education level and years employed increase, average compensation and benefits for full-time children's ministry leaders also increase.

* About half of the full-time Children's/Preschool Pastors/Directors in this sample serve in churches set in a suburb of a large city; another three in 10 serve in a small town or rural city. Church setting does not seem to have a significant impact in compensation and benefits of full-time children's ministry leaders.

* Nearly three-fourths of full-time Children's/Preschool Pastors/Directors in this sample are female. However, the 77 reported full-time males in these positions receive 26% more in average compensation and benefits packages than their female counterparts.

Compensation & Benefits: National Averages for Full-Time Children's/Preschool Pastors/Directors*	
2000	
2001	
2002	
2003	
2004	
2005	
2006	$46,361
2007	$52,434
2008	$53,033
2009	$50,782
2011	$50,611
2013	$54,246**

No historical data available before 2006.

**The above trend is made available for your reference only. In addition to looking at this overall data, please refer to the detailed tables using your church's income, attendance, setting, region, and denomination as well as the person's education, gender, and years employed for guidance in compensating this position.*

Table 10-1: Annual Compensation of Full-Time Children's/Preschool Pastors/Directors by Church Income

CHARACTERISTICS	Data Distribution*	CHURCH INCOME				
		$250K & Under	$251-$500K	$501-$750K	$751K-$1M	Over $1 Million
Average weekend worship attendance		327	274	360	595	1,324
Average church income		$112,938	$416,526	$646,220	$908,878	$2,775,296
Average # of years employed		4	6	7	8	9
Average # of paid vacation days		16	16	15	17	17
% College graduate or higher		75%	62%	88%	69%	84%
% Who receive auto reimbursement/allowance		25%	24%	24%	28%	45%
% Ordained		75%	67%	42%	47%	48%
% Supervise one or more people		75%	71%	74%	67%	83%
Average % salary increase (for those who had an increase) this year		-	4.2%	3.1%	3.8%	3.8%
COMPENSATION						
Base Salary	Highest 25%	-	$32,500	$45,550	$44,100	$49,854
	Median	-	$26,057	$39,792	$35,200	$38,000
	Lowest 25%	-	$19,500	$31,170	$27,000	$30,000
	Average	-	$26,753	$38,187	$35,485	$39,459
Housing	Highest 25%	-	-	$25,500	$24,000	$30,000
	Median	-	-	$14,200	$18,000	$24,887
	Lowest 25%	-	-	$12,000	$13,500	$20,000
	Average	-	-	$17,956	$19,300	$25,259
Parsonage	Highest 25%	-	-	-	-	-
	Median	-	-	-	-	-
	Lowest 25%	-	-	-	-	-
	Average	-	-	-	-	-
Total Compensation	**Highest 25%**	-	**$40,000**	**$49,778**	**$49,500**	**$59,000**
	Median	-	**$33,040**	**$42,000**	**$44,606**	**$50,000**
	Lowest 25%	-	**$24,113**	**$34,600**	**$35,600**	**$40,000**
	Average	-	**$32,845**	**$43,162**	**$43,927**	**$50,377**
BENEFITS						
Health Insurance	Highest 25%	-	$5,000	$8,965	$10,410	$12,172
	Median	-	$2,891	$5,409	$6,886	$7,754
	Lowest 25%	-	$1,020	$3,000	$4,737	$4,895
	Average	-	$4,178	$6,764	$7,655	$8,809
Life Insurance	Highest 25%	-	-	$254	-	$446
	Median	-	-	$103	-	$212
	Lowest 25%	-	-	$89	-	$100
	Average	-	-	$176	-	$336
Disability Insurance	Highest 25%	-	-	-	-	$527
	Median	-	-	-	-	$373
	Lowest 25%	-	-	-	-	$236
	Average	-	-	-	-	$483
Retirement	Highest 25%	-	-	$2,400	$2,439	$4,430
	Median	-	-	$2,132	$1,298	$2,653
	Lowest 25%	-	-	$1,300	$900	$1,541
	Average	-	-	$2,246	$1,994	$3,101
Continuing Education	Highest 25%	-	-	$1,500	$1,000	$1,860
	Median	-	-	$750	$1,000	$1,000
	Lowest 25%	-	-	$500	$625	$600
	Average	-	-	$1,067	$875	$1,474
Total Benefits	**Highest 25%**	-	**$7,000**	**$10,506**	**$12,273**	**$13,733**
	Median	-	**$3,615**	**$5,599**	**$5,150**	**$8,250**
	Lowest 25%	-	**$2,400**	**$2,632**	**$1,000**	**$3,451**
	Average	-	**$5,116**	**$7,232**	**$6,031**	**$9,400**
TOTAL COMPENSATION PLUS BENEFITS	**Highest 25%**	**$43,850**	**$47,150**	**$56,000**	**$56,452**	**$70,443**
	Median	**$28,650**	**$33,500**	**$47,195**	**$49,531**	**$58,462**
	Lowest 25%	**$22,000**	**$26,400**	**$40,740**	**$37,750**	**$44,200**
	Average	**$36,750**	**$36,305**	**$49,040**	**$48,450**	**$58,668**
Number of Respondents		8	21	34	36	161

- Not enough response to provide meaningful data.

* For detailed description and definitions of Data Distribution (Highest 25%, Median, Lowest 25%, and Average), see chapter 1, Explanation of Data Distribution.

Table 10-2: Annual Compensation of Full-Time Children's/Preschool Pastors/Directors by Worship Attendance

	Data Distribution*	WORSHIP ATTENDANCE					
		100 or less	101-300	301-500	501-750	751-1,000	Over 1,000
CHARACTERISTICS							
Average weekend worship attendance	-		242	408	625	890	2,223
Average church income	-		$561,610	$1,382,484	$1,151,760	$1,937,108	$4,054,530
Average # of years employed	-		7	7	7	8	10
Average # of paid vacation days	-		16	16	16	18	18
% College graduate or higher	-		71%	76%	84%	84%	81%
% Who receive auto reimbursement/allowance	-		30%	29%	39%	42%	39%
% Ordained	-		53%	38%	45%	67%	47%
% Supervise one or more people	-		79%	69%	74%	76%	86%
Average % salary increase (for those who had an increase) this year	-		3.6%	4.3%	3.1%	4.0%	4.0%
COMPENSATION							
Base Salary	Median	-	$35,000	$33,000	$35,000	$37,567	$40,648
	Average	-	$34,471	$34,236	$35,342	$38,572	$42,165
Housing	Median	-	$14,200	$20,340	$22,500	$22,000	$25,000
	Average	-	$16,336	$21,119	$23,714	$21,867	$25,658
Parsonage	Median	-	-	-	-	-	-
	Average	-	-	-	-	-	-
Total Compensation	**Median**	-	**$36,599**	**$42,000**	**$45,404**	**$48,952**	**$50,767**
	Average	-	**$38,101**	**$42,769**	**$44,746**	**$51,807**	**$52,936**
BENEFITS							
Health Insurance	Median	-	$4,000	$8,090	$6,545	$10,838	$7,100
	Average	-	$5,742	$7,977	$7,926	$9,982	$8,526
Life Insurance	Median	-	-	$76	$155	$250	$270
	Average	-	-	$225	$364	$270	$265
Disability	Median	-	$543	-	$421	$384	$387
	Average	-	$1,039	-	$583	$630	$373
Retirement	Median	-	$2,274	$1,215	$2,100	$2,288	$3,010
	Average	-	$2,922	$2,063	$2,561	$3,006	$3,458
Continuing Education	Median	-	$875	$1,000	$1,000	$1,550	$1,500
	Average	-	$1,031	$1,135	$929	$2,333	$1,754
Total Benefits	**Median**	-	**$5,569**	**$5,800**	**$5,152**	**$10,666**	**$8,890**
	Average	-	**$6,590**	**$6,532**	**$6,813**	**$11,651**	**$10,043**
TOTAL COMPENSATION PLUS BENEFITS	**Median**	-	**$42,005**	**$48,073**	**$51,750**	**$58,306**	**$61,154**
	Average	-	**$43,215**	**$47,943**	**$50,384**	**$61,312**	**$61,805**
Number of Respondents		4	43	48	58	38	80

- Not enough response to provide meaningful data.

* For detailed description and definitions of Data Distribution (Median and Average), see chapter 1, Explanation of Data Distribution.

Table 10-3: Annual Compensation of Full-Time Children's/Preschool Pastors/Directors by Church Setting

	Data Distribution*	CHURCH SETTING			
		Metro-politan city	Suburb of large city	Small town or rural city	Farming area
CHARACTERISTICS					
Average weekend worship attendance		1,352	1,125	700	-
Average church income		$2,922,219	$2,167,607	$1,118,477	-
Average # of years employed		9	8	7	-
Average # of paid vacation days		17	17	16	-
% College graduate or higher		76%	83%	75%	-
% Who receive auto reimbursement/allowance		25%	40%	43%	-
% Ordained		54%	48%	48%	-
% Supervise one or more people		87%	75%	80%	-
Average % salary increase (for those who had an increase) this year		4.6%	3.5%	2.9%	-
COMPENSATION					
Base Salary	Median	$38,342	$36,000	$36,000	-
	Average	$39,372	$37,826	$35,672	-
Housing	Median	$26,700	$24,870	$22,000	-
	Average	$26,334	$23,030	$21,134	-
Parsonage	Median	-	-	-	-
	Average	-	-	-	-
Total Compensation	**Median**	**$48,000**	**$45,808**	**$43,580**	**-**
	Average	**$49,063**	**$47,047**	**$45,177**	**-**
BENEFITS					
Health Insurance	Median	$6,570	$7,254	$7,061	-
	Average	$8,459	$8,484	$7,624	-
Life Insurance	Median	$385	$130	$295	-
	Average	$447	$224	$474	-
Disability Insurance	Median	$388	$352	$829	-
	Average	$373	$481	$946	-
Retirement	Median	$3,175	$2,400	$1,901	-
	Average	$3,349	$2,861	$2,672	-
Continuing Education	Median	$1,250	$1,000	$1,000	-
	Average	$1,293	$1,553	$1,193	-
Total Benefits	**Median**	**$7,105**	**$6,914**	**$7,975**	**-**
	Average	**$9,137**	**$8,161**	**$8,648**	**-**
TOTAL COMPENSATION PLUS BENEFITS	**Median**	**$58,800**	**$54,100**	**$49,871**	**-**
	Average	**$56,979**	**$53,963**	**$51,895**	**-**
Number of Respondents		55	130	83	5

- Not enough response to provide meaningful data.

* For detailed description and definitions of Data Distribution (Median and Average), see chapter 1, Explanation of Data Distribution.

Table 10-4: Annual Compensation of Full-Time Children's/Preschool Pastors/Directors by Region

	Data Distribution*	New England	Middle Atlantic	South Atlantic	E-N Central	E-S Central	W-N Central	W-S Central	Mountain	Pacific
CHARACTERISTICS										
Average weekend worship attendance	-	776	753	950	1,035	981	1,184	1,226	1,426
Average church income	-	$1,100,605	$1,583,803	$1,956,580	$2,025,994	$2,394,090	$2,367,129	$1,551,778	$2,402,403
Average # of years employed	-	7	7	8	9	8	8	8	9
Average # of paid vacation days	-	18	16	17	16	17	15	20	17
% College graduate or higher	-	70%	96%	79%	68%	79%	77%	70%	76%
% Who receive auto reimbursement/allowance	-	30%	52%	35%	25%	21%	46%	30%	29%
% Ordained	-	35%	37%	53%	42%	71%	56%	25%	61%
% Supervise one or more people	-	83%	75%	63%	85%	82%	77%	90%	88%
Average % salary increase (for those who had an increase) this year	-	2.5%	3.8%	3.0%	6.3%	3.4%	5.5%	2.8%	3.2%
COMPENSATION										
Base Salary	Median	-	$36,050	$37,724	$37,079	$37,019	$34,171	$35,200	$37,250	$39,900
	Average	-	$36,993	$40,332	$37,263	$36,554	$32,979	$36,855	$36,893	$38,703
Housing	Median	-	-	$21,534	$20,340	-	$25,000	$21,930	-	$27,000
	Average	-	-	$21,768	$20,720	-	$24,499	$22,906	-	$27,042
Parsonage	Median	-	-	-	-	-	-	-	-	-
	Average	-	-	-	-	-	-	-	-	-
Total Compensation	**Median**	-	**$40,000**	**$46,000**	**$48,000**	**$45,200**	**$47,750**	**$44,500**	**$42,754**	**$46,781**
	Average	-	**$42,804**	**$47,888**	**$48,519**	**$44,890**	**$45,994**	**$46,115**	**$43,041**	**$49,495**
BENEFITS										
Health Insurance	Median	-	$5,568	$8,690	$9,900	$9,000	$5,608	$6,024	$12,125	$5,053
	Average	-	$6,479	$8,899	$10,075	$8,821	$7,765	$8,078	$9,794	$5,642
Life Insurance	Median	-	-	$224	$125	-	$137	$378	-	$187
	Average	-	-	$264	$279	-	$360	$488	-	$211
Disability Insurance	Median	-	-	$400	$500	-	-	-	-	$119
	Average	-	-	$455	$539	-	-	-	-	$306
Retirement	Median	-	$2,920	$2,750	$1,780	$2,745	$1,789	$3,098	$2,420	$2,367
	Average	-	$3,430	$3,460	$2,602	$2,812	$2,407	$3,154	$2,303	$2,541
Continuing Education	Median	-	$750	$750	$1,100	$1,110	$1,500	$1,000	$350	$750
	Average	-	$872	$1,166	$1,287	$1,180	$2,045	$1,250	$350	$1,690
Total Benefits	**Median**	-	**$5,569**	**$9,517**	**$9,825**	**$8,570**	**$8,000**	**$5,599**	**$10,714**	**$4,446**
	Average	-	**$6,930**	**$9,703**	**$10,250**	**$9,589**	**$8,796**	**$6,696**	**$10,153**	**$6,159**
TOTAL COMPENSATION PLUS BENEFITS	**Median**	-	**$48,222**	**$55,889**	**$57,104**	**$56,197**	**$55,050**	**$51,000**	**$51,107**	**$52,703**
	Average	-	**$48,851**	**$55,772**	**$57,910**	**$58,484**	**$52,842**	**$51,957**	**$49,641**	**$54,748**
Number of Respondents		6	23	48	43	21	34	47	20	34

- Not enough response to provide meaningful data.

* For detailed description and definitions of Data Distribution (Median and Average), see chapter 1, Explanation of Data Distribution.

Table 10-5: Annual Compensation of Full-Time Children's/Preschool Pastors/Directors by Education

	Data Distribution*	EDUCATION			
		Less than Bachelor	Bachelor	Master	Doctorate
CHARACTERISTICS					
Average weekend worship attendance		1,091	983	1,097	-
Average church income		$1,713,531	$1,742,354	$2,675,476	-
Average # of years employed		9	8	7	-
Average # of paid vacation days		17	17	16	-
% College graduate or higher		0%	100%	100%	-
% Who receive auto reimbursement/allowance		25%	35%	51%	-
% Ordained		34%	50%	59%	-
% Supervise one or more people		80%	75%	83%	-
Average % salary increase (for those who had an increase) this year		3.1%	3.6%	3.8%	-
COMPENSATION					
Base Salary	Median	$34,710	$35,200	$38,258	-
	Average	$34,486	$36,957	$40,584	-
Housing	Median	$18,000	$22,748	$21,965	-
	Average	$18,265	$22,613	$23,559	-
Parsonage	Median	-	-	-	-
	Average	-	-	-	-
Total Compensation	**Median**	**$40,890**	**$45,000**	**$50,232**	**-**
	Average	**$39,809**	**$46,151**	**$52,233**	**-**
BENEFITS					
Health Insurance	Median	$6,000	$6,650	$8,000	-
	Average	$8,159	$8,104	$8,321	-
Life Insurance	Median	-	$202	$350	-
	Average	-	$321	$370	-
Disability Insurance	Median	-	$368	$738	-
	Average	-	$464	$1,087	-
Retirement	Median	$1,441	$2,300	$2,400	-
	Average	$2,055	$2,957	$3,103	-
Continuing Education	Median	$750	$1,000	$1,500	-
	Average	$948	$1,238	$1,973	-
Total Benefits	**Median**	**$5,150**	**$6,825**	**$8,967**	**-**
	Average	**$6,716**	**$8,444**	**$9,020**	**-**
TOTAL COMPENSATION PLUS BENEFITS	**Median**	**$43,200**	**$51,900**	**$58,748**	**-**
	Average	**$44,723**	**$53,268**	**$60,093**	**-**
Number of Respondents		55	142	70	2

- Not enough response to provide meaningful data.

* For detailed description and definitions of Data Distribution (Median and Average), see chapter 1, Explanation of Data Distribution.

Table 10-6: Annual Compensation of Full-Time Children's/Preschool Pastors/Directors by Years Employed

	Data Distribution*	YEARS EMPLOYED			
		Less than 6 years	6-10 years	11-15 years	Over 15 years
CHARACTERISTICS					
Average weekend worship attendance		900	994	1,098	1,675
Average church income		$1,848,858	$1,546,111	$2,364,394	$3,407,393
Average # of years employed		3	8	13	20
Average # of paid vacation days		15	17	19	21
% College graduate or higher		82%	80%	76%	66%
% Who receive auto reimbursement/allowance		42%	39%	38%	27%
% Ordained		57%	41%	47%	42%
% Supervise one or more people		76%	74%	85%	94%
Average % salary increase (for those who had an increase) this year		4.4%	3.1%	3.0%	2.4%
COMPENSATION					
Base Salary	Median	$33,200	$38,383	$42,000	$46,157
	Average	$33,189	$37,268	$43,745	$46,905
Housing	Median	$22,000	$25,000	$20,000	$23,000
	Average	$22,610	$24,493	$19,948	$22,634
Parsonage	Median	-	-	-	-
	Average	-	-	-	-
Total Compensation	**Median**	**$41,000**	**$48,000**	**$46,000**	**$52,000**
	Average	**$43,786**	**$47,637**	**$50,322**	**$53,764**
BENEFITS					
Health Insurance	Median	$6,186	$8,364	$9,240	$6,000
	Average	$7,507	$8,893	$8,534	$7,512
Life Insurance	Median	$258	$153	$206	$270
	Average	$337	$363	$330	$317
Disability Insurance	Median	$349	$400	-	$403
	Average	$462	$822	-	$555
Retirement	Median	$2,121	$2,334	$2,088	$3,000
	Average	$2,800	$2,739	$2,670	$3,409
Continuing Education	Median	$1,000	$1,000	$500	$1,040
	Average	$1,383	$1,418	$709	$1,488
Total Benefits	**Median**	**$6,040**	**$8,967**	**$6,200**	**$7,384**
	Average	**$7,639**	**$9,515**	**$7,498**	**$8,346**
TOTAL COMPENSATION PLUS BENEFITS	**Median**	**$49,500**	**$56,452**	**$51,000**	**$59,240**
	Average	**$49,888**	**$55,775**	**$56,862**	**$61,857**
Number of Respondents		113	77	34	33

- Not enough response to provide meaningful data.

* For detailed description and definitions of Data Distribution (Median and Average), see chapter 1, Explanation of Data Distribution.

Table 10-7: Annual Compensation of Full-Time Children's/Preschool Pastors/Directors by Denomination

	Data Distribution*	DENOMINATION					
		Assemblies of God	Baptist	Independent/ Nondenom.	Lutheran	Methodist	Presby- terian
CHARACTERISTICS							
Average weekend worship attendance		697	888	1,547	-	1,072	699
Average church income		$1,074,348	$2,716,625	$2,285,174	-	$1,522,420	$1,545,268
Average # of years employed		6	9	9	-	11	8
Average # of paid vacation days		15	16	17	-	18	17
% College graduate or higher		61%	83%	81%	-	88%	82%
% Who receive auto reimbursement/allowance		26%	63%	17%	-	29%	32%
% Ordained		81%	53%	51%	-	13%	0%
% Supervise one or more people		74%	78%	76%	-	82%	82%
Average % salary increase (for those who had an increase) this year		3.6%	3.3%	4.6%	-	2.7%	2.7%
COMPENSATION							
Base Salary	Median	$31,575	$37,800	$40,000	-	$38,000	$40,000
	Average	$30,602	$39,196	$40,419	-	$38,534	$40,020
Housing	Median	$20,170	$22,000	$22,000	-	-	-
	Average	$20,790	$22,226	$22,733	-	-	-
Parsonage	Median	-	-	-	-	-	-
	Average	-	-	-	-	-	-
Total Compensation	**Median**	**$45,000**	**$49,996**	**$47,500**	**-**	**$38,000**	**$40,000**
	Average	**$44,789**	**$49,334**	**$50,524**	**-**	**$38,534**	**$40,020**
BENEFITS							
Health Insurance	Median	$10,796	$6,000	$6,856	-	-	$8,996
	Average	$8,903	$7,431	$7,816	-	-	$9,817
Life Insurance	Median	-	$324	$174	-	-	-
	Average	-	$404	$323	-	-	-
Disability Insurance	Median	-	$391	$275	-	-	-
	Average	-	$811	$339	-	-	-
Retirement	Median	$1,616	$3,175	$2,331	-	$1,884	$2,125
	Average	$1,740	$3,320	$2,633	-	$2,237	$2,894
Continuing Education	Median	$1,000	$2,000	$1,000	-	$750	-
	Average	$1,005	$2,206	$983	-	$802	-
Total Benefits	**Median**	**$6,105**	**$8,286**	**$7,548**	**-**	**$2,365**	**$7,070**
	Average	**$7,927**	**$9,664**	**$8,440**	**-**	**$3,947**	**$7,078**
TOTAL COMPENSATION PLUS BENEFITS	**Median**	**$51,000**	**$57,537**	**$56,000**	**-**	**$45,485**	**$44,675**
	Average	**$51,410**	**$57,628**	**$57,256**	**-**	**$42,249**	**$45,811**
Number of Respondents		38	65	67	3	17	22

- Not enough response to provide meaningful data.

* For detailed description and definitions of Data Distribution (Median and Average), see chapter 1, Explanation of Data Distribution.

Table 10-8: Annual Compensation of Full-Time Children's/Preschool Pastors/Directors by Gender

	Data Distribution*	GENDER	
		Male	Female
CHARACTERISTICS			
Average weekend worship attendance		1,096	998
Average church income		$2,198,250	$1,872,399
Average # of years employed		7	8
Average # of paid vacation days		16	17
% College graduate or higher		81%	79%
% Who receive auto reimbursement/allowance		39%	36%
% Ordained		91%	33%
% Supervise one or more people		73%	81%
Average % salary increase (for those who had an increase) this year		3.0%	3.8%
COMPENSATION			
Base Salary	Median	$32,728	$38,000
	Average	$35,303	$38,179
Housing	Median	$22,500	$22,000
	Average	$22,615	$22,883
Parsonage	Median	-	-
	Average	-	-
Total Compensation	**Median**	**$50,960**	**$42,000**
	Average	**$54,001**	**$43,853**
BENEFITS			
Health Insurance	Median	$10,733	$6,000
	Average	$9,597	$7,410
Life Insurance	Median	$212	$223
	Average	$358	$321
Disability Insurance	Median	$358	$399
	Average	$472	$639
Retirement	Median	$2,324	$2,297
	Average	$2,970	$2,870
Continuing Education	Median	$1,000	$1,000
	Average	$1,647	$1,283
Total Benefits	**Median**	**$10,871**	**$6,000**
	Average	**$10,971**	**$7,393**
TOTAL COMPENSATION PLUS BENEFITS	**Median**	**$61,400**	**$48,907**
	Average	**$63,119**	**$50,007**
Number of Respondents		77	198

- Not enough response to provide meaningful data.

* For detailed description and definitions of Data Distribution (Median and Average), see chapter 1, Explanation of Data Distribution.

Table 10-9: Annual Compensation of Part-Time Children's/Preschool Pastors/Directors by Church Income

	Data Distribution*	CHURCH INCOME				
		$250K & Under	$251-$500K	$501-$750K	$751K-$1M	Over 1 Million
CHARACTERISTICS						
Average weekend worship attendance		233	237	400	449	770
Average church income		$169,674	$373,300	$635,118	$876,789	$1,461,372
Average # of years employed		3	4	5	4	5
Average # of paid vacation days		9	10	9	10	15
% College graduate or higher		58%	81%	76%	75%	65%
% Who receive auto reimbursement/allowance		6%	15%	29%	20%	30%
% Ordained		6%	25%	9%	14%	7%
% Supervise one or more people		68%	66%	54%	54%	47%
Average % salary increase (for those who had an increase) this year		-	3.7%	5.4%	6.6%	3.4%
HOURLY RATE						
Base Rate	Average	$16	$16	$17	$16	$15
COMPENSATION						
Base Salary	Median	$7,843	$12,600	$16,817	$18,943	$16,000
	Average	$11,158	$13,828	$16,851	$18,472	$17,907
Housing	Median	-	-	-	-	-
	Average	-	-	-	-	-
Parsonage	Median	-	-	-	-	-
	Average	-	-	-	-	-
Total Compensation	**Median**	$7,843	$12,600	$16,817	$18,943	$17,300
	Average	$11,158	$14,093	$17,080	$18,021	$18,784
BENEFITS						
Health Insurance	Median	-	-	-	-	-
	Average	-	-	-	-	-
Life Insurance	Median	-	-	-	-	-
	Average	-	-	-	-	-
Disability Insurance	Median	-	-	-	-	-
	Average	-	-	-	-	-
Retirement	Median	-	-	-	-	-
	Average	-	-	-	-	-
Continuing Education	Median	-	-	-	-	-
	Average	-	-	-	-	-
Total Benefits	**Median**	-	-	$773	-	$1,123
	Average	-	-	$2,384	-	$2,838
TOTAL COMPENSATION PLUS BENEFITS	**Median**	$7,843	$12,600	$17,000	$19,018	$17,300
	Average	$11,221	$14,232	$17,761	$18,256	$19,582
Number of Respondents		19	33	35	35	57

- Not enough response to provide meaningful data.

* For detailed description and definitions of Data Distribution (Median and Average), see chapter 1, Explanation of Data Distribution.

Table 10-10: Annual Compensation of Part-Time Children's/Preschool Pastors/Directors by Worship Attendance

	Data Distribution*	WORSHIP ATTENDANCE					
		100 or less	101-300	301-500	501-750	751-1,000	Over 1,000
CHARACTERISTICS							
Average weekend worship attendance		-	211	416	628	867	1,265
Average church income		-	$431,739	$877,609	$1,032,966	$1,289,860	$1,900,000
Average # of years employed		-	4	4	5	6	4
Average # of paid vacation days		-	10	11	11	17	12
% College graduate or higher		-	78%	75%	67%	56%	80%
% Who receive auto reimbursement/allowance		-	19%	40%	9%	9%	20%
% Ordained		-	19%	11%	3%	9%	0%
% Supervise one or more people		-	62%	61%	55%	48%	20%
Average % salary increase (for those who had an increase) this year		-	5.4%	3.9%	4.0%	5.1%	-
HOURLY RATE							
Base Rate	Average	-	$16	$16	$16	$14	$16
COMPENSATION							
Base Salary	Median	-	$14,000	$18,768	$15,870	$14,449	$17,070
	Average	-	$14,194	$18,250	$17,352	$14,905	$18,382
Housing	Median	-	-	-	-	-	-
	Average	-	-	-	-	-	-
Parsonage	Median	-	-	-	-	-	-
	Average	-	-	-	-	-	-
Total Compensation	**Median**	-	$13,500	$20,000	$15,870	$15,950	$17,070
	Average	-	$14,115	$19,119	$17,435	$15,602	$18,382
BENEFITS							
Health Insurance	Median	-	-	-	-	-	-
	Average	-	-	-	-	-	-
Life Insurance	Median	-	-	-	-	-	-
	Average	-	-	-	-	-	-
Disability	Median	-	-	-	-	-	-
	Average	-	-	-	-	-	-
Retirement	Median	-	-	-	-	-	-
	Average	-	-	-	-	-	-
Continuing Education	Median	-	-	$500	-	-	-
	Average	-	-	$594	-	-	-
Total Benefits	**Median**	-	-	$500	$800	-	-
	Average	-	-	$611	$2,908	-	-
TOTAL COMPENSATION PLUS BENEFITS	**Median**	-	$13,500	$20,000	$15,875	$15,950	$17,105
	Average	-	$14,289	$19,239	$18,435	$16,637	$18,578
Number of Respondents		4	59	57	32	22	10

- Not enough response to provide meaningful data.

* For detailed description and definitions of Data Distribution (Median and Average), see chapter 1, Explanation of Data Distribution.

Table 10-11: Annual Compensation of Part-Time Children's/Preschool Pastors/Directors by Church Setting

	Data Distribution*	CHURCH SETTING			
		Metro-politan city	Suburb of large city	Small town or rural city	Farming area
CHARACTERISTICS					
Average weekend worship attendance		418	484	496	-
Average church income		$783,833	$950,842	$758,918	-
Average # of years employed		7	4	4	-
Average # of paid vacation days		12	12	11	-
% College graduate or higher		77%	78%	65%	-
% Who receive auto reimbursement/allowance		30%	22%	18%	-
% Ordained		4%	11%	14%	-
% Supervise one or more people		58%	51%	59%	-
Average % salary increase (for those who had an increase) this year		5.5%	5.1%	3.4%	-
HOURLY RATE					
Base Rate	Average	$17	$16	$15	-
COMPENSATION					
Base Salary	Median	$19,036	$16,320	$16,000	-
	Average	$17,334	$16,914	$15,752	-
Housing	Median	-	-	-	-
	Average	-	-	-	-
Parsonage	Median	-	-	-	-
	Average	-	-	-	-
Total Compensation	**Median**	**$19,268**	**$16,320**	**$16,490**	**-**
	Average	**$17,668**	**$17,110**	**$15,946**	**-**
BENEFITS					
Health Insurance	Median	-	-	-	-
	Average	-	-	-	-
Life Insurance	Median	-	-	-	-
	Average	-	-	-	-
Disability Insurance	Median	-	-	-	-
	Average	-	-	-	-
Retirement	Median	-	-	-	-
	Average	-	-	-	-
Continuing Education	Median	-	-	$500	-
	Average	-	-	$575	-
Total Benefits	**Median**	**-**	**$500**	**$500**	**-**
	Average	**-**	**$1,542**	**$1,232**	**-**
TOTAL COMPENSATION PLUS BENEFITS	**Median**	**$19,268**	**$16,320**	**$16,537**	**-**
	Average	**$19,008**	**$17,387**	**$16,178**	**-**
Number of Respondents		24	85	73	6

- Not enough response to provide meaningful data.

* For detailed description and definitions of Data Distribution (Median and Average), see chapter 1, Explanation of Data Distribution.

Table 10-12: Annual Compensation of Part-Time Children's/Preschool Pastors/Directors by Region

	Data Distribution*	REGION								
		New England	Middle Atlantic	South Atlantic	E-N Central	E-S Central	W-N Central	W-S Central	Mountain	Pacific
CHARACTERISTICS										
Average weekend worship attendance	-		535	431	538	561	460	479	498	465
Average church income	-		$813,675	$896,434	$924,037	$981,391	$732,815	$1,168,539	$751,657	$692,264
Average # of years employed	-		3	3	4	8	5	4	5	5
Average # of paid vacation days	-		11	10	14	9	9	14	13	11
% College graduate or higher	-		56%	80%	64%	69%	84%	80%	53%	74%
% Who receive auto reimbursement/allowance	-		13%	22%	34%	29%	25%	38%	0%	13%
% Ordained	-		6%	3%	7%	14%	24%	7%	13%	17%
% Supervise one or more people	-		56%	57%	45%	43%	75%	63%	50%	53%
Average % salary increase (for those who had an increase) this year	-		3.2%	6.1%	4.2%	4.3%	4.6%	4.8%	3.1%	3.3%
HOURLY RATE										
Base Rate	Average	-	$15	$15	$14	$16	$15	$17	$16	$17
COMPENSATION										
Base Salary	Median	-	$13,000	$14,780	$17,160	$17,740	$16,000	$23,605	$15,300	$15,870
	Average	-	$14,608	$14,897	$16,057	$19,384	$14,089	$23,592	$15,906	$15,947
Housing	Median	-	-	-	-	-	-	-	-	-
	Average	-	-	-	-	-	-	-	-	-
Parsonage	Median	-	-	-	-	-	-	-	-	-
	Average	-	-	-	-	-	-	-	-	-
Total Compensation	**Median**	-	**$14,454**	**$15,300**	**$18,000**	**$16,670**	**$16,190**	**$23,605**	**$15,000**	**$15,870**
	Average	-	**$16,188**	**$15,425**	**$17,080**	**$18,704**	**$14,228**	**$23,592**	**$15,645**	**$15,762**
BENEFITS										
Health Insurance	Median	-	-	-	-	-	-	-	-	-
	Average	-	-	-	-	-	-	-	-	-
Life Insurance	Median	-	-	-	-	-	-	-	-	-
	Average	-	-	-	-	-	-	-	-	-
Disability Insurance	Median	-	-	-	-	-	-	-	-	-
	Average	-	-	-	-	-	-	-	-	-
Retirement	Median	-	-	-	-	-	-	-	-	-
	Average	-	-	-	-	-	-	-	-	-
Continuing Education	Median	-	-	-	-	-	-	-	-	-
	Average	-	-	-	-	-	-	-	-	-
Total Benefits	**Median**	-	-	$500	-	-	-	-	-	-
	Average	-	-	$1,503	-	-	-	-	-	-
TOTAL COMPENSATION PLUS BENEFITS	**Median**	-	**$14,677**	**$15,300**	**$18,000**	**$16,670**	**$16,190**	**$23,771**	**$15,000**	**$15,875**
	Average	-	**$16,982**	**$15,758**	**$17,686**	**$18,982**	**$14,363**	**$24,610**	**$15,713**	**$16,308**
Number of Respondents		7	16	36	29	14	25	16	15	30

- Not enough response to provide meaningful data.

* For detailed description and definitions of Data Distribution (Median and Average), see chapter 1, Explanation of Data Distribution.

Table 10-13: Annual Compensation of Part-Time Children's/Preschool Pastors/Directors by Education

	Data Distribution*	EDUCATION			
		Less than Bachelor	Bachelor	Master	Doctorate
CHARACTERISTICS					
Average weekend worship attendance		522	447	479	-
Average church income		$878,210	$805,799	$939,958	-
Average # of years employed		6	4	4	-
Average # of paid vacation days		12	11	12	-
% College graduate or higher		0%	100%	100%	-
% Who receive auto reimbursement/allowance		16%	23%	32%	-
% Ordained		12%	11%	18%	-
% Supervise one or more people		45%	64%	59%	-
Average % salary increase (for those who had an increase) this year		3.0%	5.3%	2.7%	-
HOURLY RATE					
Base Rate	Average	$15	$16	$17	-
COMPENSATION					
Base Salary	Median	$13,500	$16,320	$16,460	-
	Average	$14,306	$16,574	$19,787	-
Housing	Median	-	-	-	-
	Average	-	-	-	-
Parsonage	Median	-	-	-	-
	Average	-	-	-	-
Total Compensation	**Median**	**$13,250**	**$16,380**	**$20,000**	**-**
	Average	**$14,256**	**$16,722**	**$22,104**	**-**
BENEFITS					
Health Insurance	Median	-	-	-	-
	Average	-	-	-	-
Life Insurance	Median	-	-	-	-
	Average	-	-	-	-
Disability Insurance	Median	-	-	-	-
	Average	-	-	-	-
Retirement	Median	-	$1,080	-	-
	Average	-	$1,268	-	-
Continuing Education	Median	-	$500	-	-
	Average	-	$692	-	-
Total Benefits	**Median**	**$800**	**$550**	**-**	**-**
	Average	**$2,033**	**$2,294**	**-**	**-**
TOTAL COMPENSATION PLUS BENEFITS	**Median**	**$13,250**	**$16,380**	**$20,000**	**-**
	Average	**$14,622**	**$17,252**	**$22,499**	**-**
Number of Respondents		50	104	22	1

- Not enough response to provide meaningful data.

* For detailed description and definitions of Data Distribution (Median and Average), see chapter 1, Explanation of Data Distribution.

Table 10-14: Annual Compensation of Part-Time Children's/Preschool Pastors/Directors by Years Employed

	Data Distribution*	YEARS EMPLOYED			
		Less than 6 years	6-10 years	11-15 years	Over 15 years
CHARACTERISTICS					
Average weekend worship attendance		471	504	518	-
Average church income		$797,930	$987,839	$971,018	-
Average # of years employed		2	8	13	-
Average # of paid vacation days		10	16	12	-
% College graduate or higher		77%	58%	69%	-
% Who receive auto reimbursement/allowance		22%	23%	23%	-
% Ordained		10%	13%	15%	-
% Supervise one or more people		54%	65%	46%	-
Average % salary increase (for those who had an increase) this year		4.9%	4.0%	3.2%	-
HOURLY RATE					
Base Rate	Average	$16	$15	$18	-
COMPENSATION					
Base Salary	Median	$14,846	$18,193	$16,150	-
	Average	$15,270	$17,739	$19,863	-
Housing	Median	-	-	-	-
	Average	-	-	-	-
Parsonage	Median	-	-	-	-
	Average	-	-	-	-
Total Compensation	**Median**	**$14,923**	**$19,350**	**$16,150**	**-**
	Average	**$15,404**	**$19,345**	**$19,863**	**-**
BENEFITS					
Health Insurance	Median	-	-	-	-
	Average	-	-	-	-
Life Insurance	Median	-	-	-	-
	Average	-	-	-	-
Disability Insurance	Median	-	-	-	-
	Average	-	-	-	-
Retirement	Median	-	-	-	-
	Average	-	-	-	-
Continuing Education	Median	$500	-	-	-
	Average	$586	-	-	-
Total Benefits	**Median**	**$500**	**$1,323**	**-**	**-**
	Average	**$1,995**	**$2,567**	**-**	**-**
TOTAL COMPENSATION PLUS BENEFITS	**Median**	**$15,146**	**$19,500**	**$16,150**	**-**
	Average	**$15,737**	**$20,008**	**$20,701**	**-**
Number of Respondents		127	31	13	3

- Not enough response to provide meaningful data.

* For detailed description and definitions of Data Distribution (Median and Average), see chapter 1, Explanation of Data Distribution.

Table 10-15: Annual Compensation of Part-Time Children's/Preschool Pastors/Directors by Denomination

	Data Distribution*	DENOMINATION					
		Assemblies of God	Baptist	Independent/ Nondenom.	Lutheran	Methodist	Presby-terian
CHARACTERISTICS							
Average weekend worship attendance		398	475	533	-	319	476
Average church income		$624,970	$933,392	$786,513	-	$573,263	$1,145,499
Average # of years employed		5	4	5	-	3	5
Average # of paid vacation days		11	12	11	-	8	18
% College graduate or higher		50%	83%	58%	-	92%	54%
% Who receive auto reimbursement/allowance		8%	34%	12%	-	0%	23%
% Ordained		33%	8%	6%	-	0%	8%
% Supervise one or more people		67%	55%	67%	-	83%	25%
Average % salary increase (for those who had an increase) this year		-	4.8%	5.4%	-	-	4.1%
HOURLY RATE							
Base Rate	Average	$16	$17	$16	-	$17	$13
COMPENSATION							
Base Salary	Median	$14,250	$18,138	$12,780	-	$16,320	$12,800
	Average	$14,336	$18,187	$14,677	-	$17,750	$13,877
Housing	Median	-	-	-	-	-	-
	Average	-	-	-	-	-	-
Parsonage	Median	-	-	-	-	-	-
	Average	-	-	-	-	-	-
Total Compensation	**Median**	**$14,250**	**$18,943**	**$14,560**	**-**	**$16,320**	**$13,500**
	Average	**$13,813**	**$18,609**	**$14,994**	**-**	**$17,750**	**$16,014**
BENEFITS							
Health Insurance	Median	-	-	-	-	-	-
	Average	-	-	-	-	-	-
Life Insurance	Median	-	-	-	-	-	-
	Average	-	-	-	-	-	-
Disability Insurance	Median	-	-	-	-	-	-
	Average	-	-	-	-	-	-
Retirement	Median	-	-	-	-	-	-
	Average	-	-	-	-	-	-
Continuing Education	Median	-	-	-	-	-	-
	Average	-	-	-	-	-	-
Total Benefits	**Median**	**-**	**$600**	**$828**	**-**	**-**	**-**
	Average	**-**	**$2,813**	**$2,124**	**-**	**-**	**-**
TOTAL COMPENSATION PLUS BENEFITS	**Median**	**$14,250**	**$19,500**	**$14,560**	**-**	**$16,445**	**$13,500**
	Average	**$13,813**	**$19,259**	**$15,511**	**-**	**$17,813**	**$16,014**
Number of Respondents		12	65	34	1	12	13

- Not enough response to provide meaningful data.

* For detailed description and definitions of Data Distribution (Median and Average), see chapter 1, Explanation of Data Distribution.

Table 10-16: Annual Compensation of Part-Time Children's/Preschool Pastors/Directors by Gender

	Data Distribution*	GENDER	
		Male	Female
CHARACTERISTICS			
Average weekend worship attendance		393	486
Average church income		$679,805	$862,244
Average # of years employed		4	5
Average # of paid vacation days		8	12
% College graduate or higher		69%	72%
% Who receive auto reimbursement/allowance		0%	24%
% Ordained		54%	8%
% Supervise one or more people		58%	56%
Average % salary increase (for those who had an increase) this year		-	4.2%
HOURLY RATE			
Base Rate	Average	$17	$16
COMPENSATION			
Base Salary	Median	$12,500	$16,320
	Average	$14,043	$16,371
Housing	Median	-	$12,000
	Average	-	$13,393
Parsonage	Median	-	-
	Average	-	-
Total Compensation	**Median**	**$13,000**	**$16,350**
	Average	**$14,600**	**$16,654**
BENEFITS			
Health Insurance	Median	-	$5,201
	Average	-	$5,600
Life Insurance	Median	-	-
	Average	-	-
Disability Insurance	Median	-	-
	Average	-	-
Retirement	Median	-	$910
	Average	-	$1,144
Continuing Education	Median	-	$500
	Average	-	$639
Total Benefits	**Median**	**-**	**$675**
	Average	**-**	**$2,119**
TOTAL COMPENSATION PLUS BENEFITS	**Median**	**$13,000**	**$16,390**
	Average	**$15,478**	**$17,070**
Number of Respondents		13	174

- Not enough response to provide meaningful data.

* For detailed description and definitions of Data Distribution (Median and Average), see chapter 1, Explanation of Data Distribution.

Full-Time Children's/Preschool Pastor/Director Worksheet

	Enter your church data below	The 2014–2015 Compensation Handbook for Church Staff		Enter *Compensation Handbook* data below			
				Highest 25%	Median	Lowest 25%	Average
Church Income	$	Table 10-1	page 151	$	$	$	$
Worship Attendance		Table 10-2	page 152	n/a	$	n/a	$
Church Setting (metro, suburb, small town, or farming area)		Table 10-3	page 153	n/a	$	n/a	$
Region		Table 10-4	page 154	n/a	$	n/a	$
Person's Education		Table 10-5	page 155	n/a	$	n/a	$
Years Employed		Table 10-6	page 156	n/a	$	n/a	$
Denomination (if applicable)		Table 10-7	page 157	n/a	$	n/a	$

Looking at the table and page number references indicated in the *2014–2015 Compensation Handbook for Church Staff* columns above, locate the appropriate range for your church. Refer to the instructions below for step-by-step help.

FILLING OUT THE WORKSHEET

1. Fill in the gray boxes under *Enter your church data* with your church demographic information as follows:

   ▶ **Income** (Total annual church budget in past year)
   ▶ **Worship attendance** (Number of people, including children, who attend all weekend services)
   ▶ **Church setting** (Metropolitan city, suburb of large city, small town or rural city, or farming area)

   ▶ **Region** (Locate your state's region in the appendix on page 346.)
   ▶ **Education** (Highest level of education: less than bachelor, bachelor, master, or doctorate)

2. Use Table 10-1 (page 151) in your *2014–2015 Compensation Handbook for Church Staff* to enter data pertinent to your church. In the heading (top row), locate your church **income** from the five available ranges. Follow that column to the bottom rows, and copy the *Highest 25%*, *Median*, *Lowest 25%*, and *Average* amounts onto your worksheet.

3. Use Table 10-2 (page 152) on your *2014–2015 Compensation Handbook for Church Staff* to enter data pertinent to your church. In the heading (top row), locate your church's

worship attendance from the six available ranges. Follow that column to the bottom rows, and copy the *Median* and *Average* amounts onto your worksheet.

4. Use Table 10-3 (page 153) on your *2014–2015 Compensation Handbook for Church Staff* to enter data pertinent to your church. In the heading (top row), choose the **church setting** that best describes your church. Follow that column to the bottom rows, and copy the *Median* and *Average* amounts onto your worksheet.

5. Use Table 10-4 (page 154) on your *2014–2015 Compensation Handbook for Church Staff* to enter data pertinent to your church. In the heading (top row), look for the **region** where your church is located. Follow that column to the bottom rows, and copy the *Median* and *Average* amounts onto your worksheet.

6. Use Table 10-5 (page 155) on your *2014–2015 Compensation Handbook for Church Staff* to enter data pertinent to your Children's/Preschool Pastor/Director. In the heading (top row), look for **your Children's/Preschool Pastor/Director's highest level of education**. Follow that column to the bottom rows, and copy the *Median* and *Average* amounts onto your worksheet.

7. Use Table 10-6 (page 156) on your *2014–2015 Compensation Handbook for Church Staff* to enter data pertinent to your Children's/Preschool Pastor/Director. In the heading (top row), locate the **number of years your Children's/Preschool Pastor/Director has been employed**. Follow that column to the bottom rows, and copy the *Median* and *Average* amounts onto your worksheet.

8. Use Table 10-7 (page 157) on your *2014–2015 Compensation Handbook for Church Staff* to enter data pertinent to your church. In the

heading (top row), look for **your church's denominational affiliation**. Follow that column to the bottom rows, and copy the *Median* and *Average* amounts onto your worksheet. If your church is not affiliated with a denomination, leave this section blank.

DETERMINING COMPENSATION

This tool will not provide you with a single compensation amount but rather with a range of values to help you determine the compensation appropriate to your situation.

1. Look at the values in the shaded *Median* column. Circle the **lowest** and the **highest** values. **This is the range of the median compensation plus benefits for churches similar to yours.**

2. For a variety of reasons, compensation plus benefits may be higher or lower than the range established in this table. Income and attendance are two significant factors affecting church compensation packages. If church income or attendance skews higher, you might want to consider moving toward or above the higher end of the range. Likewise, if church income or attendance skews lower, you may consider moving the package toward or below the lower end of the range.

3. Examine additional variables that might impact the compensation package you offer, such as years of service, education, and church setting.

4. Determine other circumstances unique to your situation, such as cost of living in your area, theological beliefs, pastoral performance, financial needs, the local economy, personal motivation, congregational goals, and others.

5. You now have a compensation package range based on the *2014–2015 Compensation Handbook*. Since each church and position are unique, your final compensation package will be based on additional factors unique to your situation.

Part-Time Children's/Preschool Pastor/Director Worksheet

	Enter your church data below	The 2014–2015 Compensation Handbook for Church Staff		Enter Compensation Handbook data below			
				Highest 25%	Median	Lowest 25%	Average
Church Income	$	Table 10-9	page 159	$	$	$	$
Worship Attendance		Table 10-10	page 160	n/a	$	n/a	$
Church Setting (metro, suburb, small town, or farming area)		Table 10-11	page 161	n/a	$	n/a	$
Region		Table 10-12	page 162	n/a	$	n/a	$
Person's Education		Table 10-13	page 163	n/a	$	n/a	$
Years Employed		Table 10-14	page 164	n/a	$	n/a	$
Denomination (if applicable)		Table 10-15	page 165	n/a	$	n/a	$

Looking at the table and page number references indicated in the **2014–2015 Compensation Handbook for Church Staff** columns above, locate the appropriate range for your church. Refer to the instructions below for step-by-step help.

FILLING OUT THE WORKSHEET

1. Fill in the gray boxes under **Enter your church data** with your church demographic information as follows:

   ▶ **Income** (Total annual church budget in past year)
   ▶ **Worship attendance** (Number of people, including children, who attend all weekend services)
   ▶ **Church setting** (Metropolitan city, suburb of large city, small town or rural city, or farming area)

   ▶ **Region** (Locate your state's region in the appendix on page 346.)
   ▶ **Education** (Highest level of education: less than bachelor, bachelor, master, or doctorate)

2. Use Table 10-9 (page 159) in your *2014–2015 Compensation Handbook for Church Staff* to enter data pertinent to your church. In the heading (top row), locate your church **income** from the five available ranges. Follow that column to the bottom rows, and copy the **Highest 25%**, **Median**, **Lowest 25%**, and **Average** amounts onto your worksheet.

3. Use Table 10-10 (page 160) on your *2014–2015 Compensation Handbook for Church Staff* to enter data pertinent to your church. In the heading (top row), locate your church's

worship attendance from the six available ranges. Follow that column to the bottom rows, and copy the *Median* and *Average* amounts onto your worksheet.

4. Use Table 10-11 (page 161) on your *2014–2015 Compensation Handbook for Church Staff* to enter data pertinent to your church. In the heading (top row), choose the **church setting** that best describes your church. Follow that column to the bottom rows, and copy the *Median* and *Average* amounts onto your worksheet.

5. Use Table 10-12 (page 162) on your *2014–2015 Compensation Handbook for Church Staff* to enter data pertinent to your church. In the heading (top row), look for the **region** where your church is located. Follow that column to the bottom rows, and copy the *Median* and *Average* amounts onto your worksheet.

6. Use Table 10-13 (page 163) on your *2014–2015 Compensation Handbook for Church Staff* to enter data pertinent to your Children's/Preschool Pastor/Director. In the heading (top row), look for **your Children's/Preschool Pastor/Director's highest level of education**. Follow that column to the bottom rows, and copy the *Median* and *Average* amounts onto your worksheet.

7. Use Table 10-14 (page 164) on your *2014–2015 Compensation Handbook for Church Staff* to enter data pertinent to your Children's/Preschool Pastor/Director. In the heading (top row), locate the **number of years your Children's/Preschool Pastor/Director has been employed**. Follow that column to the bottom rows, and copy the *Median* and *Average* amounts onto your worksheet.

8. Use Table 10-15 (page 165) on your *2014–2015 Compensation Handbook for Church Staff* to enter data pertinent to your church. In the

heading (top row), look for **your church's denominational affiliation**. Follow that column to the bottom rows, and copy the *Median* and *Average* amounts onto your worksheet. If your church is not affiliated with a denomination, leave this section blank.

DETERMINING COMPENSATION

This tool will not provide you with a single compensation amount but rather with a range of values to help you determine the compensation appropriate to your situation.

1. Look at the values in the shaded *Median* column. Circle the **lowest** and the **highest** values. **This is the range of the median compensation plus benefits for churches similar to yours.**

2. For a variety of reasons, compensation plus benefits may be higher or lower than the range established in this table. Income and attendance are two significant factors affecting church compensation packages. If church income or attendance skews higher, you might want to consider moving toward or above the higher end of the range. Likewise, if church income or attendance skews lower, you may consider moving the package toward or below the lower end of the range.

3. Examine additional variables that might impact the compensation package you offer, such as years of service, education, and church setting.

4. Determine other circumstances unique to your situation, such as cost of living in your area, theological beliefs, pastoral performance, financial needs, the local economy, personal motivation, congregational goals, and others.

5. You now have a compensation package range based on the *2014–2015 Compensation Handbook*. Since each church and position are unique, your final compensation package will be based on additional factors unique to your situation.

11

MUSIC/CHOIR/ WORSHIP PASTORS/ DIRECTORS

Employment Profile

Music/Choir/Worship Pastors/Directors include paid pastors and directors of church music programs, including band, bell/chimes choir, music ministry, orchestra, praise and worship team, vocal choir, etc. This category may include such positions as Music Pastor, Worship Pastor, Worship Leader, Choir Director, Choir Master, Director of Music Ministries, etc.

While full-time music ministry positions are mostly held by males, part-time positions are almost evenly split between males and females. Nearly nine in 10 full-time music ministry leaders hold at least a bachelor's degree. Two-thirds of full-time music ministry leaders are ordained. More than nine in 10 full-time and part-time music ministers are considered church employees rather than self-employed.

The chart below provides a demographic profile of this sample.

	Full-Time	Part-Time
Number of respondents	**295**	**213**
Ordained	66%	19%
Average years employed	8	9
Male	85%	49%
Female	15%	51%
Self-employed (receives 1099)	3%	6%
Church employee (receives W-2)	97%	94%
High school diploma	5%	14%
Associate degree	7%	10%
Bachelor's degree	51%	49%
Master's degree	31%	20%
Doctoral degree	6%	6%

Total Compensation plus Benefits Package Analysis

The following analyses are based on data in the tables you will find later in this chapter. The tables show compensation plus benefits data for full-time and part-time Music/Choir/Worship Pastors/Directors and are presented according to church income, church attendance, church setting, region, education, years employed, denomination, and gender. In this way, the compensation plus benefits of music ministry leaders can be analyzed and compared from a variety of useful perspectives.

The total compensation plus benefits amount includes the base salary; housing allowance and/or parsonage amount; health, life, and disability insurance payments; retirement contribution; and educational funds.

A worksheet at the end of this chapter is provided to help you apply the data to your church's situation.

Most benefits reported by music ministry leaders are comparable to those of Youth Pastors/Directors, Adult Ministry/Christian Education Pastors/Directors, and Children's/Preschool Pastors/Directors. Only 1% of full-time music ministry leaders live in church-provided parsonages, but the majority (60%) of them receive housing allowances. Fifty-nine percent of full-time worship ministers received a salary increase in the past year.

Compensation Plus Benefits	Full-Time	Part-Time
Base Salary	99%	98%
Housing	60%	5%
Parsonage	1%	0%
Health Insurance*	71%	2%
Life Insurance*	35%	2%
Disability Insurance*	32%	2%
Retirement	67%	5%
Continuing Education	31%	8%
Received salary increase	59%	45%
Received paid vacation	96%	44%
Received auto reimbursement/allowance	47%	13%

Only those reporting individual premiums for Health, Life, or Disability (not total insurance premiums) are included.

KEY POINTS

✷ About six in 10 full-time Music/Choir/Worship Pastors/Directors serve in larger congregations (those with more than $1 million in church income) and more than 500 in worship attendance.

✷ The vast majority of Music/Choir/Worship Pastors/Directors, both full-time and part-time, serve in churches set in a suburb of a large city or in a small town or rural city.

✷ Full-time male Music/Choir/Worship Pastors/Directors earn 31% more than their female counterparts.

✷ For the most part, as worship attendance, minister's education level, and years employed increase, average compensation and benefits for full-time music ministry leaders also increase.

Compensation & Benefits: National Averages for Full-Time Music/Choir/Worship Pastors/Directors	
2000	$50,911
2001	$53,200
2002	$55,046
2003	$56,875
2004	$57,279
2005	$60,316
2006	$64,075
2007	$65,133
2008	$61,373
2009	$61,754
2011	$60,392
2013	$68,597*

The above trend is made available for your reference only. In addition to looking at this overall data, please refer to the detailed tables using your church's income, attendance, setting, region, and denomination as well as the person's education, gender, and years employed for guidance in compensating this position.

Table 11-1: Annual Compensation of Full-Time Music/Choir/Worship Pastors/Directors by Church Income

CHARACTERISTICS	Data Distribution*	$250K & Under	$251-$500K	$501-$750K	$751K-$1M	Over $1 Million
Average weekend worship attendance	-		233	332	542	1,160
Average church income	-		$418,735	$628,244	$906,183	$2,278,333
Average # of years employed	-		9	8	6	9
Average # of paid vacation days	-		18	17	17	18
% College graduate or higher	-		85%	80%	94%	91%
% Who receive auto reimbursement/allowance	-		42%	50%	39%	51%
% Ordained	-		69%	57%	84%	64%
% Supervise one or more people	-		54%	50%	57%	73%
Average % salary increase (for those who had an increase) this year	-		5.3%	3.4%	3.2%	3.8%
COMPENSATION						
Base Salary	Highest 25%	-	$41,313	$41,736	$50,000	$59,332
	Median	-	$31,350	$35,500	$40,500	$44,811
	Lowest 25%	-	$24,100	$27,495	$29,649	$32,305
	Average	-	$33,039	$36,071	$40,007	$45,746
Housing	Highest 25%	-	$24,000	$28,000	$27,112	$34,416
	Median	-	$18,860	$22,000	$20,000	$26,983
	Lowest 25%	-	$15,098	$16,505	$15,700	$20,000
	Average	-	$19,190	$22,190	$21,220	$27,956
Parsonage	Highest 25%	-	-	-	-	-
	Median	-	-	-	-	-
	Lowest 25%	-	-	-	-	-
	Average	-	-	-	-	-
Total Compensation	**Highest 25%**	-	**$51,737**	**$57,400**	**$60,200**	**$72,788**
	Median	-	**$45,000**	**$48,301**	**$50,000**	**$61,880**
	Lowest 25%	-	**$37,250**	**$39,020**	**$43,000**	**$51,000**
	Average	-	**$45,642**	**$49,130**	**$51,495**	**$63,198**
BENEFITS						
Health Insurance	Highest 25%	-	$8,796	$11,943	$14,172	$14,603
	Median	-	$5,580	$9,240	$10,000	$11,212
	Lowest 25%	-	$3,720	$3,310	$7,975	$6,783
	Average	-	$6,340	$8,291	$10,721	$11,078
Life Insurance	Highest 25%	-	-	$262	$480	$400
	Median	-	-	$111	$200	$227
	Lowest 25%	-	-	$42	$88	$100
	Average	-	-	$202	$315	$435
Disability Insurance	Highest 25%	-	-	$858	$535	$532
	Median	-	-	$600	$527	$399
	Lowest 25%	-	-	$47	$330	$226
	Average	-	-	$763	$524	$417
Retirement	Highest 25%	-	$4,624	$5,740	$2,988	$6,136
	Median	-	$3,635	$3,000	$1,610	$3,298
	Lowest 25%	-	$1,963	$1,620	$1,200	$1,930
	Average	-	$3,605	$3,435	$2,292	$4,222
Continuing Education	Highest 25%	-	$1,500	$1,350	$1,750	$1,800
	Median	-	$1,000	$900	$1,350	$1,000
	Lowest 25%	-	$800	$500	$550	$750
	Average	-	$1,073	$1,103	$1,280	$1,479
Total Benefits	**Highest 25%**	-	**$11,539**	**$12,105**	**$16,541**	**$19,087**
	Median	-	**$6,000**	**$7,848**	**$12,027**	**$12,950**
	Lowest 25%	-	**$3,722**	**$4,211**	**$8,000**	**$6,086**
	Average	-	**$7,299**	**$9,268**	**$12,097**	**$13,399**
TOTAL COMPENSATION PLUS BENEFITS	**Highest 25%**	-	**$55,000**	**$67,805**	**$73,400**	**$89,811**
	Median	-	**$50,381**	**$58,321**	**$60,831**	**$75,052**
	Lowest 25%	-	**$41,670**	**$46,500**	**$52,000**	**$60,840**
	Average	-	**$51,481**	**$57,935**	**$61,111**	**$75,464**
Number of Respondents		6	26	40	39	174

- Not enough response to provide meaningful data.

* For detailed description and definitions of Data Distribution (Highest 25%, Median, Lowest 25%, and Average), see chapter 1, Explanation of Data Distribution.

Table 11-2: Annual Compensation of Full-Time Music/Choir/Worship Pastors/Directors by Worship Attendance

	Data Distribution*	WORSHIP ATTENDANCE					
		100 or less	101-300	301-500	501-750	751-1,000	Over 1,000
CHARACTERISTICS							
Average weekend worship attendance	-		239	417	641	897	1,930
Average church income	-		$704,834	$978,626	$1,279,541	$1,536,157	$3,425,885
Average # of years employed	-		9	8	8	7	8
Average # of paid vacation days	-		18	18	17	17	18
% College graduate or higher	-		91%	88%	87%	82%	91%
% Who receive auto reimbursement/allowance	-		44%	52%	50%	39%	50%
% Ordained	-		60%	67%	63%	65%	70%
% Supervise one or more people	-		62%	58%	62%	64%	84%
Average % salary increase (for those who had an increase) this year	-		4.3%	3.4%	3.1%	4.3%	4.0%
COMPENSATION							
Base Salary	Median	-	$38,290	$35,893	$45,000	$42,743	$44,811
	Average	-	$40,464	$37,115	$45,872	$43,633	$46,173
Housing	Median	-	$18,860	$21,946	$27,810	$24,500	$30,000
	Average	-	$20,615	$24,540	$26,042	$25,332	$31,139
Parsonage	Median	-	-	-	-	-	-
	Average	-	-	-	-	-	-
Total Compensation	**Median**	-	**$51,369**	**$50,000**	**$60,771**	**$58,607**	**$61,880**
	Average	-	**$51,042**	**$52,624**	**$60,133**	**$60,024**	**$65,578**
BENEFITS							
Health Insurance	Median	-	$9,057	$8,450	$12,000	$10,500	$11,516
	Average	-	$8,675	$9,364	$11,800	$10,659	$11,470
Life Insurance	Median	-	$177	$227	$216	$362	$227
	Average	-	$326	$369	$284	$448	$454
Disability	Median	-	$384	$530	$330	$415	$332
	Average	-	$503	$574	$406	$473	$815
Retirement	Median	-	$4,200	$2,921	$2,669	$2,820	$3,231
	Average	-	$3,990	$3,553	$3,609	$3,773	$4,446
Continuing Education	Median	-	$1,000	$1,000	$1,000	$1,000	$1,138
	Average	-	$1,131	$1,309	$1,410	$1,431	$1,769
Total Benefits	**Median**	-	**$8,812**	**$9,231**	**$11,664**	**$12,800**	**$14,705**
	Average	-	**$10,407**	**$10,491**	**$12,475**	**$12,894**	**$14,356**
TOTAL COMPENSATION PLUS BENEFITS	**Median**	-	**$57,562**	**$60,586**	**$74,103**	**$67,500**	**$77,004**
	Average	-	**$60,448**	**$61,110**	**$72,310**	**$70,895**	**$78,587**
Number of Respondents		6	53	68	42	51	70

- Not enough response to provide meaningful data.

* For detailed description and definitions of Data Distribution (Median and Average), see chapter 1, Explanation of Data Distribution.

Table 11-3: Annual Compensation of Full-Time Music/Choir/Worship Pastors/Directors by Church Setting

	Data Distribution*	CHURCH SETTING			
		Metro-politan city	Suburb of large city	Small town or rural city	Farming area
CHARACTERISTICS					
Average weekend worship attendance		1,010	994	606	-
Average church income		$2,127,160	$1,889,829	$1,065,448	-
Average # of years employed		10	8	8	-
Average # of paid vacation days		19	17	18	-
% College graduate or higher		96%	91%	81%	-
% Who receive auto reimbursement/allowance		39%	52%	46%	-
% Ordained		62%	65%	70%	-
% Supervise one or more people		77%	70%	58%	-
Average % salary increase (for those who had an increase) this year		4.2%	4.2%	3.1%	-
COMPENSATION					
Base Salary	Median	$46,214	$40,000	$36,828	-
	Average	$46,446	$42,483	$39,388	-
Housing	Median	$28,007	$27,400	$20,000	-
	Average	$29,405	$27,809	$22,182	-
Parsonage	Median	-	-	-	-
	Average	-	-	-	-
Total Compensation	**Median**	**$59,197**	**$58,756**	**$53,153**	**-**
	Average	**$61,656**	**$59,103**	**$54,176**	**-**
BENEFITS					
Health Insurance	Median	$9,682	$11,882	$9,018	-
	Average	$9,992	$11,365	$9,294	-
Life Insurance	Median	$270	$204	$264	-
	Average	$457	$421	$313	-
Disability Insurance	Median	$326	$400	$530	-
	Average	$348	$442	$632	-
Retirement	Median	$4,161	$2,572	$3,300	-
	Average	$4,910	$3,675	$3,640	-
Continuing Education	Median	$1,500	$1,000	$1,000	-
	Average	$1,579	$1,233	$1,397	-
Total Benefits	**Median**	**$10,083**	**$12,109**	**$10,238**	**-**
	Average	**$12,690**	**$12,620**	**$11,497**	**-**
TOTAL COMPENSATION PLUS BENEFITS	**Median**	**$70,090**	**$69,025**	**$64,114**	**-**
	Average	**$73,689**	**$70,117**	**$64,158**	**-**
Number of Respondents		58	132	100	2

- Not enough response to provide meaningful data.

* For detailed description and definitions of Data Distribution (Median and Average), see chapter 1, Explanation of Data Distribution.

Table 11-4: Annual Compensation of Full-Time Music/Choir/Worship Pastors/Directors by Region

	Data Distribution*	New England	Middle Atlantic	South Atlantic	E-N Central	E-S Central	W-N Central	W-S Central	Mountain	Pacific
					REGION					
CHARACTERISTICS										
Average weekend worship attendance	-	913	840	819	870	773	903	717	1,057	
Average church income	-	$1,866,277	$1,943,140	$1,299,262	$1,668,497	$1,397,129	$1,710,501	$1,179,537	$2,007,205
Average # of years employed	-	10	9	8	8	6	9	9	7
Average # of paid vacation days	-	20	19	18	16	18	17	19	16
% College graduate or higher	-	92%	97%	81%	83%	93%	83%	88%	81%
% Who receive auto reimbursement/allowance	-	21%	47%	58%	41%	41%	55%	46%	41%
% Ordained	-	29%	57%	67%	75%	57%	86%	70%	74%
% Supervise one or more people	-	71%	68%	48%	70%	79%	70%	63%	71%
Average % salary increase (for those who had an increase) this year	-	2.6%	3.7%	3.4%	3.1%	4.0%	3.5%	3.1%	6.5%
COMPENSATION										
Base Salary	Median	-	$46,500	$44,930	$37,414	$42,000	$42,436	$38,491	$35,930	$32,916
	Average	-	$48,037	$47,335	$38,796	$42,892	$42,987	$40,768	$39,226	$36,789
Housing	Median	-	-	$28,483	$22,946	$25,500	$23,000	$20,670	$25,000	$24,000
	Average	-	-	$31,058	$23,482	$24,389	$22,388	$25,701	$25,609	$25,879
Parsonage	Median	-	-	-	-	-	-	-	-	-
	Average	-	-	-	-	-	-	-	-	-
Total Compensation	**Median**	-	$56,315	$63,036	$50,550	$55,926	$51,725	$60,837	$52,000	$50,990
	Average	-	$54,653	$64,220	$53,125	$57,526	$54,981	$61,687	$54,221	$54,736
BENEFITS										
Health Insurance	Median	-	$12,976	$10,000	$12,583	$8,700	$10,078	$7,900	$9,999	$8,341
	Average	-	$11,338	$10,142	$12,987	$9,883	$9,237	$9,346	$10,828	$8,817
Life Insurance	Median	-	-	$240	$173	$226	$256	$311	-	$132
	Average	-	-	$356	$518	$325	$430	$505	-	$216
Disability Insurance	Median	-	-	$392	$315	$438	$400	$487	-	$238
	Average	-	-	$455	$355	$432	$463	$474	-	$400
Retirement	Median	-	$2,750	$4,000	$2,572	$3,500	$1,909	$5,100	$3,293	$2,519
	Average	-	$4,065	$4,527	$3,496	$3,749	$2,867	$4,744	$3,785	$3,245
Continuing Education	Median	-	-	$1,000	$1,200	-	$2,000	-	$1,000	-
	Average	-	-	$1,052	$1,531	-	$1,889	-	$972	-
Total Benefits	**Median**	-	$16,041	$10,114	$13,942	$7,869	$12,096	$8,860	$11,516	$8,800
	Average	-	$14,365	$12,145	$14,576	$12,086	$11,981	$10,688	$12,841	$9,929
TOTAL COMPENSATION PLUS BENEFITS	**Median**	-	$70,104	$75,632	$65,069	$68,169	$67,150	$66,330	$59,091	$63,938
	Average	-	$69,017	$75,804	$65,369	$68,806	$66,086	$71,380	$62,128	$63,205
Number of Respondents		5	14	66	50	30	29	43	24	34

- Not enough response to provide meaningful data.

* For detailed description and definitions of Data Distribution (Median and Average), see chapter 1, Explanation of Data Distribution.

Table 11-5: Annual Compensation of Full-Time Music/Choir/Worship Pastors/Directors by Education

CHARACTERISTICS	Data Distribution*	EDUCATION			
		Less than Bachelor	Bachelor	Master	Doctorate
Average weekend worship attendance		730	965	794	588
Average church income		$1,132,771	$1,786,500	$1,649,545	$1,547,826
Average # of years employed		7	7	10	12
Average # of paid vacation days		17	17	19	18
% College graduate or higher		0%	100%	100%	100%
% Who receive auto reimbursement/allowance		29%	48%	56%	53%
% Ordained		65%	66%	71%	47%
% Supervise one or more people		71%	63%	69%	75%
Average % salary increase (for those who had an increase) this year		4.4%	4.1%	3.5%	2.3%
COMPENSATION					
Base Salary	Median	$30,775	$39,056	$43,222	$55,505
	Average	$32,292	$41,337	$44,965	$55,283
Housing	Median	$21,495	$24,500	$25,500	-
	Average	$22,390	$25,552	$26,787	-
Parsonage	Median	-	-	-	-
	Average	-	-	-	-
Total Compensation	**Median**	**$45,500**	**$54,988**	**$61,307**	**$66,300**
	Average	**$46,780**	**$56,708**	**$61,707**	**$68,145**
BENEFITS					
Health Insurance	Median	$7,238	$10,000	$11,081	$9,488
	Average	$7,988	$10,683	$10,598	$9,304
Life Insurance	Median	-	$202	$290	-
	Average	-	$365	$405	-
Disability Insurance	Median	-	$399	$391	-
	Average	-	$447	$492	-
Retirement	Median	$2,505	$2,600	$4,000	$6,294
	Average	$3,642	$3,261	$4,513	$6,152
Continuing Education	Median	-	$1,000	$1,000	-
	Average	-	$1,307	$1,553	-
Total Benefits	**Median**	**$5,931**	**$11,845**	**$9,804**	**$13,754**
	Average	**$9,322**	**$12,415**	**$12,733**	**$12,755**
TOTAL COMPENSATION PLUS BENEFITS	**Median**	**$52,238**	**$67,323**	**$73,027**	**$80,736**
	Average	**$53,344**	**$67,448**	**$73,861**	**$80,900**
Number of Respondents		35	146	88	17

- Not enough response to provide meaningful data.

* For detailed description and definitions of Data Distribution (Median and Average), see chapter 1, Explanation of Data Distribution.

Table 11-6: Annual Compensation of Full-Time Music/Choir/Worship Pastors/Directors by Years Employed

	Data Distribution*	YEARS EMPLOYED			
		Less than 6 years	6-10 years	11-15 years	Over 15 years
CHARACTERISTICS					
Average weekend worship attendance		868	951	896	786
Average church income		$1,651,487	$1,836,755	$1,699,371	$1,548,895
Average # of years employed		3	8	13	23
Average # of paid vacation days		15	19	19	24
% College graduate or higher		86%	89%	86%	94%
% Who receive auto reimbursement/allowance		48%	40%	51%	53%
% Ordained		66%	57%	66%	67%
% Supervise one or more people		58%	75%	65%	71%
Average % salary increase (for those who had an increase) this year		5.0%	3.3%	2.9%	3.0%
COMPENSATION					
Base Salary	Median	$37,000	$40,000	$47,733	$49,603
	Average	$40,011	$41,422	$47,467	$46,722
Housing	Median	$22,320	$26,406	$25,000	$27,905
	Average	$24,788	$27,168	$25,595	$26,071
Parsonage	Median	-	-	-	-
	Average	-	-	-	-
Total Compensation	**Median**	**$50,381**	**$55,991**	**$60,080**	**$62,218**
	Average	**$54,259**	**$58,205**	**$61,994**	**$64,103**
BENEFITS					
Health Insurance	Median	$8,321	$11,424	$12,000	$12,744
	Average	$9,384	$10,956	$10,921	$10,793
Life Insurance	Median	$208	$105	$226	$375
	Average	$466	$353	$287	$519
Disability Insurance	Median	$388	$399	$373	$500
	Average	$489	$414	$373	$601
Retirement	Median	$2,505	$2,850	$2,500	$5,740
	Average	$3,184	$4,289	$3,489	$5,552
Continuing Education	Median	$1,000	$1,025	$1,000	$1,000
	Average	$1,135	$1,469	$1,566	$1,265
Total Benefits	**Median**	**$9,630**	**$13,300**	**$13,100**	**$12,800**
	Average	**$10,619**	**$12,714**	**$13,427**	**$13,510**
TOTAL COMPENSATION PLUS BENEFITS	**Median**	**$61,000**	**$68,169**	**$74,100**	**$78,289**
	Average	**$63,330**	**$70,213**	**$74,332**	**$77,238**
Number of Respondents		119	72	37	36

- Not enough response to provide meaningful data.

* For detailed description and definitions of Data Distribution (Median and Average), see chapter 1, Explanation of Data Distribution.

Table 11-7: Annual Compensation of Full-Time Music/Choir/Worship Pastors/Directors by Denomination

	Data Distribution*	DENOMINATION					
		Assemblies of God	Baptist	Independent/ Nondenom.	Lutheran	Methodist	Presby- terian
CHARACTERISTICS							
Average weekend worship attendance		760	716	1,175	-	1,089	549
Average church income		$1,198,471	$1,556,291	$2,051,069	-	$2,065,247	$1,622,203
Average # of years employed		5	9	7	-	9	8
Average # of paid vacation days		15	18	17	-	17	20
% College graduate or higher		88%	91%	73%	-	96%	100%
% Who receive auto reimbursement/allowance		35%	66%	30%	-	18%	43%
% Ordained		88%	87%	73%	-	18%	19%
% Supervise one or more people		65%	68%	56%	-	74%	68%
Average % salary increase (for those who had an increase) this year		-	3.3%	4.8%	-	2.7%	4.4%
COMPENSATION							
Base Salary	Median	$39,467	$37,156	$38,640	-	$47,733	$57,002
	Average	$38,028	$40,702	$40,178	-	$48,952	$53,733
Housing	Median	$19,140	$25,250	$21,074	-	-	-
	Average	$21,601	$26,700	$24,243	-	-	-
Parsonage	Median	-	-	-	-	-	-
	Average	-	-	-	-	-	-
Total Compensation	**Median**	**$50,000**	**$57,893**	**$54,996**	**-**	**$49,500**	**$62,000**
	Average	**$54,546**	**$61,643**	**$55,356**	**-**	**$49,799**	**$61,576**
BENEFITS							
Health Insurance	Median	$11,642	$10,000	$10,138	-	$7,499	$11,161
	Average	$11,125	$10,150	$10,657	-	$7,594	$11,698
Life Insurance	Median	-	$302	$200	-	-	$240
	Average	-	$480	$510	-	-	$228
Disability Insurance	Median	-	$430	$361	-	-	$294
	Average	-	$544	$356	-	-	$309
Retirement	Median	$1,980	$3,702	$2,519	-	$2,689	$4,261
	Average	$3,490	$4,179	$3,668	-	$3,168	$4,622
Continuing Education	Median	-	$1,500	$1,000	-	$500	$1,200
	Average	-	$1,502	$1,363	-	$1,043	$1,525
Total Benefits	**Median**	**$9,600**	**$12,500**	**$13,100**	**-**	**$5,477**	**$13,277**
	Average	**$10,399**	**$13,127**	**$13,304**	**-**	**$7,159**	**$14,012**
TOTAL COMPENSATION PLUS BENEFITS	**Median**	**$61,800**	**$72,579**	**$68,264**	**-**	**$55,114**	**$78,720**
	Average	**$62,498**	**$73,612**	**$67,493**	**-**	**$56,647**	**$75,069**
Number of Respondents		17	102	57	6	23	28

- Not enough response to provide meaningful data.

* For detailed description and definitions of Data Distribution (Median and Average), see chapter 1, Explanation of Data Distribution.

Table 11-8: Annual Compensation of Full-Time Music/Choir/Worship Pastors/Directors by Gender

	Data Distribution*	GENDER	
		Male	Female
CHARACTERISTICS			
Average weekend worship attendance		872	798
Average church income		$1,689,572	$1,414,676
Average # of years employed		8	10
Average # of paid vacation days		18	18
% College graduate or higher		88%	86%
% Who receive auto reimbursement/allowance		51%	26%
% Ordained		71%	38%
% Supervise one or more people		68%	55%
Average % salary increase (for those who had an increase) this year		3.9%	3.4%
COMPENSATION			
Base Salary	Median	$40,000	$40,800
	Average	$42,271	$41,523
Housing	Median	$25,000	$24,133
	Average	$26,124	$23,959
Parsonage	Median	-	-
	Average	-	-
Total Compensation	**Median**	**$58,548**	**$45,900**
	Average	**$59,839**	**$46,524**
BENEFITS			
Health Insurance	Median	$10,196	$8,386
	Average	$10,543	$8,611
Life Insurance	Median	$227	$214
	Average	$424	$250
Disability Insurance	Median	$400	$442
	Average	$426	$621
Retirement	Median	$3,101	$3,298
	Average	$4,095	$3,070
Continuing Education	Median	$1,000	$1,000
	Average	$1,404	$1,176
Total Benefits	**Median**	**$12,027**	**$7,756**
	Average	**$12,673**	**$9,410**
TOTAL COMPENSATION PLUS BENEFITS	**Median**	**$70,129**	**$53,152**
	Average	**$71,152**	**$54,353**
Number of Respondents		250	43

- Not enough response to provide meaningful data.

* For detailed description and definitions of Data Distribution (Median and Average), see chapter 1, Explanation of Data Distribution.

Table 11-9: Annual Compensation of Part-Time Music/Choir/Worship Pastors/Directors by Church Income

	Data Distribution*	CHURCH INCOME				
		$250K & Under	$251-$500K	$501-$750K	$751K-$1M	Over 1 Million
CHARACTERISTICS						
Average weekend worship attendance		130	209	345	402	901
Average church income		$167,206	$377,989	$628,676	$855,805	$1,543,314
Average # of years employed		9	8	9	11	9
Average # of paid vacation days		9	12	9	16	12
% College graduate or higher		65%	81%	88%	76%	83%
% Who receive auto reimbursement/allowance		10%	14%	12%	28%	7%
% Ordained		22%	22%	9%	19%	13%
% Supervise one or more people		48%	55%	42%	48%	26%
Average % salary increase (for those who had an increase) this year		4.8%	3.4%	4.3%	-	3.0%
HOURLY RATE						
Base Rate	Average	$25	$25	$24	$28	$23
COMPENSATION						
Base Salary	Median	$7,000	$10,960	$15,600	$17,325	$14,118
	Average	$8,786	$12,014	$16,697	$19,269	$17,161
Housing	Median	-	-	-	-	-
	Average	-	-	-	-	-
Parsonage	Median	-	-	-	-	-
	Average	-	-	-	-	-
Total Compensation	**Median**	$7,015	$11,000	$15,600	$17,325	$14,209
	Average	$8,798	$12,254	$17,411	$19,269	$16,724
BENEFITS						
Health Insurance	Median	-	-	-	-	-
	Average	-	-	-	-	-
Life Insurance	Median	-	-	-	-	-
	Average	-	-	-	-	-
Disability Insurance	Median	-	-	-	-	-
	Average	-	-	-	-	-
Retirement	Median	-	-	-	-	-
	Average	-	-	-	-	-
Continuing Education	Median	-	-	-	-	-
	Average	-	-	-	-	-
Total Benefits	**Median**	-	$1,000	-	-	-
	Average	-	$1,925	-	-	-
TOTAL COMPENSATION PLUS BENEFITS	**Median**	$7,015	$11,500	$16,800	$17,325	$14,209
	Average	$8,921	$12,516	$17,563	$19,785	$17,711
Number of Respondents		54	60	35	26	31

- Not enough response to provide meaningful data.

* For detailed description and definitions of Data Distribution (Median and Average), see chapter 1, Explanation of Data Distribution.

Table 11-10: Annual Compensation of Part-Time Music/Choir/Worship Pastors/Directors by Worship Attendance

	Data Distribution*	WORSHIP ATTENDANCE					
		100 or less	101-300	301-500	501-750	751-1,000	Over 1,000
CHARACTERISTICS							
Average weekend worship attendance		70	199	409	618	890	2,068
Average church income		$205,283	$402,918	$789,899	$939,839	$1,377,429	$2,396,429
Average # of years employed		8	9	7	10	12	15
Average # of paid vacation days		14	9	14	12	10	16
% College graduate or higher		73%	76%	79%	81%	75%	75%
% Who receive auto reimbursement/allowance		6%	13%	18%	9%	14%	0%
% Ordained		29%	18%	14%	14%	0%	38%
% Supervise one or more people		42%	49%	56%	41%	25%	50%
Average % salary increase (for those who had an increase) this year		3.8%	3.9%	4.3%	4.2%	-	-
HOURLY RATE							
Base Rate	Average	$24	$27	$21	$23	-	$19
COMPENSATION							
Base Salary	Median	$6,425	$10,842	$14,500	$16,500	$16,887	$12,000
	Average	$8,411	$12,891	$15,224	$18,596	$19,452	$17,858
Housing	Median	-	-	-	-	-	-
	Average	-	-	-	-	-	-
Parsonage	Median	-	-	-	-	-	-
	Average	-	-	-	-	-	-
Total Compensation	**Median**	$6,500	$10,920	$14,500	$17,500	$16,887	-
	Average	$8,392	$13,377	$15,666	$19,367	$19,452	-
BENEFITS							
Health Insurance	Median	-	-	-	-	-	-
	Average	-	-	-	-	-	-
Life Insurance	Median	-	-	-	-	-	-
	Average	-	-	-	-	-	-
Disability	Median	-	-	-	-	-	-
	Average	-	-	-	-	-	-
Retirement	Median	-	-	-	-	-	-
	Average	-	-	-	-	-	-
Continuing Education	Median	-	$575	-	-	-	-
	Average	-	$633	-	-	-	-
Total Benefits	**Median**	-	$825	-	-	-	-
	Average	-	$1,509	-	-	-	-
TOTAL COMPENSATION PLUS BENEFITS	**Median**	$6,775	$11,000	$14,500	$17,500	$16,887	$12,000
	Average	$8,652	$13,590	$15,975	$20,111	$21,142	$13,105
Number of Respondents		35	101	36	22	8	8

- Not enough response to provide meaningful data.

* For detailed description and definitions of Data Distribution (Median and Average), see chapter 1, Explanation of Data Distribution.

Table 11-11: Annual Compensation of Part-Time Music/Choir/Worship Pastors/Directors by Church Setting

	Data Distribution*	CHURCH SETTING			
		Metro-politan city	Suburb of large city	Small town or rural city	Farming area
CHARACTERISTICS					
Average weekend worship attendance		361	380	334	-
Average church income		$618,835	$700,286	$518,519	-
Average # of years employed		7	9	11	-
Average # of paid vacation days		11	14	9	-
% College graduate or higher		74%	79%	76%	-
% Who receive auto reimbursement/allowance		9%	14%	12%	-
% Ordained		12%	21%	19%	-
% Supervise one or more people		54%	46%	43%	-
Average % salary increase (for those who had an increase) this year		5.2%	4.2%	3.8%	-
HOURLY RATE					
Base Rate	Average	$21	$26	$25	-
COMPENSATION					
Base Salary	Median	$13,000	$15,000	$10,240	-
	Average	$13,509	$16,950	$11,498	-
Housing	Median	-	-	-	-
	Average	-	-	-	-
Parsonage	Median	-	-	-	-
	Average	-	-	-	-
Total Compensation	**Median**	**$13,260**	**$14,780**	**$10,450**	**-**
	Average	**$14,051**	**$16,742**	**$11,870**	**-**
BENEFITS					
Health Insurance	Median	-	-	-	-
	Average	-	-	-	-
Life Insurance	Median	-	-	-	-
	Average	-	-	-	-
Disability Insurance	Median	-	-	-	-
	Average	-	-	-	-
Retirement	Median	-	-	-	-
	Average	-	-	-	-
Continuing Education	Median	-	-	$700	-
	Average	-	-	$800	-
Total Benefits	**Median**	**-**	**$520**	**$625**	**-**
	Average	**-**	**$1,518**	**$863**	**-**
TOTAL COMPENSATION PLUS BENEFITS	**Median**	**$13,260**	**$14,780**	**$10,638**	**-**
	Average	**$14,593**	**$17,271**	**$11,974**	**-**
Number of Respondents		35	84	85	6

- Not enough response to provide meaningful data.

* For detailed description and definitions of Data Distribution (Median and Average), see chapter 1, Explanation of Data Distribution.

Table 11-12: Annual Compensation of Part-Time Music/Choir/Worship Pastors/Directors by Region

	Data Distribution*	REGION								
		New England	Middle Atlantic	South Atlantic	E-N Central	E-S Central	W-N Central	W-S Central	Mountain	Pacific
CHARACTERISTICS										
Average weekend worship attendance		282	397	276	303	335	306	637	322	503
Average church income		$654,812	$734,819	$590,126	$554,712	$632,540	$516,437	$903,514	$488,352	$513,013
Average # of years employed		11	11	10	8	12	8	9	6	7
Average # of paid vacation days		12	20	9	8	8	11	15	15	12
% College graduate or higher		89%	83%	69%	73%	79%	89%	75%	67%	71%
% Who receive auto reimbursement/allowance		10%	6%	9%	26%	10%	11%	0%	8%	24%
% Ordained		20%	0%	19%	9%	25%	17%	44%	25%	25%
% Supervise one or more people		22%	56%	38%	38%	57%	57%	25%	67%	62%
Average % salary increase (for those who had an increase) this year		2.7%	2.8%	4.4%	2.4%	4.1%	3.3%	4.8%	4.6%	-
HOURLY RATE										
Base Rate	Average	$25	$22	$30	$27	$24	$17	$24	$30	$22
COMPENSATION										
Base Salary	Median	-	$11,500	$13,367	$10,382	$12,500	$7,390	$15,600	$15,080	$16,000
	Average	-	$14,606	$14,898	$11,677	$14,221	$9,680	$14,110	$14,110	$17,855
Housing	Median	-	-	-	-	-	-	-	-	-
	Average	-	-	-	-	-	-	-	-	-
Parsonage	Median	-	-	-	-	-	-	-	-	-
	Average	-	-	-	-	-	-	-	-	-
Total Compensation	**Median**	-	$11,000	$13,630	$10,382	$12,250	$7,000	$15,600	$15,080	$17,000
	Average	-	$11,751	$15,583	$11,677	$13,930	$10,367	$14,904	$15,221	$17,569
BENEFITS										
Health Insurance	Median	-	-	-	-	-	-	-	-	-
	Average	-	-	-	-	-	-	-	-	-
Life Insurance	Median	-	-	-	-	-	-	-	-	-
	Average	-	-	-	-	-	-	-	-	-
Disability Insurance	Median	-	-	-	-	-	-	-	-	-
	Average	-	-	-	-	-	-	-	-	-
Retirement	Median	-	-	-	-	-	-	-	-	-
	Average	-	-	-	-	-	-	-	-	-
Continuing Education	Median	-	-	$825	-	-	-	-	-	-
	Average	-	-	$706	-	-	-	-	-	-
Total Benefits	**Median**	-	-	$1,000	-	-	-	-	-	-
	Average	-	-	$1,647	-	-	-	-	-	-
TOTAL COMPENSATION PLUS BENEFITS	**Median**	-	$11,000	$13,630	$10,632	$12,250	$7,179	$15,600	$15,080	$17,000
	Average	-	$12,016	$16,293	$11,695	$14,611	$10,609	$14,984	$15,295	$17,925
Number of Respondents		10	18	45	38	22	31	16	12	21

- Not enough response to provide meaningful data.

* For detailed description and definitions of Data Distribution (Median and Average), see chapter 1, Explanation of Data Distribution.

Table 11-13: Annual Compensation of Part-Time Music/Choir/Worship Pastors/Directors by Education

	Data Distribution*	EDUCATION			
		Less than Bachelor	Bachelor	Master	Doctorate
CHARACTERISTICS					
Average weekend worship attendance		350	386	282	397
Average church income		$543,568	$610,242	$541,862	$932,008
Average # of years employed		9	9	11	11
Average # of paid vacation days		13	10	11	14
% College graduate or higher		0%	100%	100%	100%
% Who receive auto reimbursement/allowance		17%	15%	7%	0%
% Ordained		17%	12%	36%	25%
% Supervise one or more people		46%	43%	51%	62%
Average % salary increase (for those who had an increase) this year		4.5%	3.7%	4.2%	-
HOURLY RATE					
Base Rate	Average	$24	$21	$31	$39
COMPENSATION					
Base Salary	Median	$11,460	$11,375	$13,630	$21,500
	Average	$12,329	$13,257	$14,775	$21,833
Housing	Median	-	-	-	-
	Average	-	-	-	-
Parsonage	Median	-	-	-	-
	Average	-	-	-	-
Total Compensation	**Median**	**$12,000**	**$11,653**	**$13,630**	**$18,750**
	Average	**$12,790**	**$13,707**	**$15,385**	**$18,391**
BENEFITS					
Health Insurance	Median	-	-	-	-
	Average	-	-	-	-
Life Insurance	Median	-	-	-	-
	Average	-	-	-	-
Disability Insurance	Median	-	-	-	-
	Average	-	-	-	-
Retirement	Median	-	-	-	-
	Average	-	-	-	-
Continuing Education	Median	-	-	-	-
	Average	-	-	-	-
Total Benefits	**Median**	-	**$490**	-	-
	Average	-	**$763**	-	-
TOTAL COMPENSATION PLUS BENEFITS	**Median**	**$12,000**	**$11,653**	**$13,630**	**$18,750**
	Average	**$13,077**	**$13,822**	**$16,024**	**$20,065**
Number of Respondents		49	101	42	13

- Not enough response to provide meaningful data.

* For detailed description and definitions of Data Distribution (Median and Average), see chapter 1, Explanation of Data Distribution.

Table 11-14: Annual Compensation of Part-Time Music/Choir/Worship Pastors/Directors by Years Employed

	Data Distribution*	YEARS EMPLOYED			
		Less than 6 years	6-10 years	11-15 years	Over 15 years
CHARACTERISTICS					
Average weekend worship attendance		333	377	261	402
Average church income		$570,173	$635,368	$526,501	$596,493
Average # of years employed		2	8	13	25
Average # of paid vacation days		9	11	12	10
% College graduate or higher		76%	79%	67%	78%
% Who receive auto reimbursement/allowance		12%	16%	5%	13%
% Ordained		18%	15%	14%	23%
% Supervise one or more people		41%	50%	45%	50%
Average % salary increase (for those who had an increase) this year		5.0%	3.9%	-	3.3%
HOURLY RATE					
Base Rate	Average	$21	$23	$27	$37
COMPENSATION					
Base Salary	Median	$10,400	$13,104	$10,460	$11,500
	Average	$12,584	$15,270	$13,194	$13,051
Housing	Median	-	-	-	-
	Average	-	-	-	-
Parsonage	Median	-	-	-	-
	Average	-	-	-	-
Total Compensation	**Median**	**$9,393**	**$12,717**	**$10,920**	**$11,500**
	Average	**$12,643**	**$14,296**	**$13,856**	**$13,186**
BENEFITS					
Health Insurance	Median	-	-	-	-
	Average	-	-	-	-
Life Insurance	Median	-	-	-	-
	Average	-	-	-	-
Disability Insurance	Median	-	-	-	-
	Average	-	-	-	-
Retirement	Median	-	-	-	-
	Average	-	-	-	-
Continuing Education	Median	-	-	-	-
	Average	-	-	-	-
Total Benefits	**Median**	**$1,000**	**$520**	**-**	**-**
	Average	**$2,434**	**$654**	**-**	**-**
TOTAL COMPENSATION PLUS BENEFITS	**Median**	**$10,400**	**$12,817**	**$10,920**	**$11,500**
	Average	**$13,039**	**$14,437**	**$13,909**	**$14,130**
Number of Respondents		85	48	21	32

- *Not enough response to provide meaningful data.*

* *For detailed description and definitions of Data Distribution (Median and Average), see chapter 1, Explanation of Data Distribution.*

Table 11-15: Annual Compensation of Part-Time Music/Choir/Worship Pastors/Directors by Denomination

	Data Distribution*	DENOMINATION					
		Assemblies of God	Baptist	Independent/ Nondenom.	Lutheran	Methodist	Presby- terian
CHARACTERISTICS							
Average weekend worship attendance		403	348	326	237	499	235
Average church income		$689,431	$605,547	$558,263	$406,022	$741,091	$533,407
Average # of years employed		7	9	8	14	10	7
Average # of paid vacation days		12	9	13	18	13	16
% College graduate or higher		50%	84%	73%	67%	73%	74%
% Who receive auto reimbursement/allowance		17%	10%	9%	11%	13%	9%
% Ordained		42%	25%	28%	0%	0%	0%
% Supervise one or more people		73%	38%	73%	44%	47%	38%
Average % salary increase (for those who had an increase) this year		-	4.2%	4.4%	-	-	4.8%
HOURLY RATE							
Base Rate	Average	$17	$27	$21	$32	$19	$30
COMPENSATION							
Base Salary	Median	$13,498	$13,260	$9,733	$17,000	$13,750	$15,104
	Average	$12,662	$13,932	$12,688	$15,466	$15,201	$17,343
Housing	Median	-	-	-	-	-	-
	Average	-	-	-	-	-	-
Parsonage	Median	-	-	-	-	-	-
	Average	-	-	-	-	-	-
Total Compensation	**Median**	**$13,498**	**$13,445**	**$10,500**	**$17,000**	**$13,750**	**$15,104**
	Average	**$13,987**	**$14,429**	**$12,801**	**$15,466**	**$15,201**	**$17,343**
BENEFITS							
Health Insurance	Median	-	-	-	-	-	-
	Average	-	-	-	-	-	-
Life Insurance	Median	-	-	-	-	-	-
	Average	-	-	-	-	-	-
Disability Insurance	Median	-	-	-	-	-	-
	Average	-	-	-	-	-	-
Retirement	Median	-	-	-	-	-	-
	Average	-	-	-	-	-	-
Continuing Education	Median	-	-	-	-	-	-
	Average	-	-	-	-	-	-
Total Benefits	**Median**	-	-	-	-	-	-
	Average	-	-	-	-	-	-
TOTAL COMPENSATION PLUS BENEFITS	**Median**	**$13,536**	**$13,445**	**$10,600**	**$17,000**	**$14,000**	**$15,104**
	Average	**$14,308**	**$14,480**	**$12,867**	**$15,744**	**$15,367**	**$18,004**
Number of Respondents		12	53	33	9	15	24

- Not enough response to provide meaningful data.

* For detailed description and definitions of Data Distribution (Median and Average), see chapter 1, Explanation of Data Distribution.

Table 11-16: Annual Compensation of Part-Time Music/Choir/Worship Pastors/Directors by Gender

	Data Distribution*	GENDER	
		Male	Female
CHARACTERISTICS			
Average weekend worship attendance		348	362
Average church income		$555,635	$649,744
Average # of years employed		9	10
Average # of paid vacation days		11	11
% College graduate or higher		77%	75%
% Who receive auto reimbursement/allowance		11%	14%
% Ordained		28%	10%
% Supervise one or more people		56%	37%
Average % salary increase (for those who had an increase) this year		4.4%	3.8%
HOURLY RATE			
Base Rate	Average	$26	$23
COMPENSATION			
Base Salary	Median	$13,445	$10,500
	Average	$15,016	$12,642
Housing	Median	$11,665	-
	Average	$14,642	-
Parsonage	Median	-	-
	Average	-	-
Total Compensation	**Median**	**$13,630**	**$10,600**
	Average	**$15,060**	**$12,983**
BENEFITS			
Health Insurance	Median	-	-
	Average	-	-
Life Insurance	Median	-	-
	Average	-	-
Disability Insurance	Median	-	-
	Average	-	-
Retirement	Median	-	-
	Average	-	-
Continuing Education	Median	-	$575
	Average	-	$576
Total Benefits	**Median**	**$425**	**$773**
	Average	**$1,341**	**$1,566**
TOTAL COMPENSATION PLUS BENEFITS	**Median**	**$13,630**	**$10,876**
	Average	**$15,510**	**$13,223**
Number of Respondents		104	107

- Not enough response to provide meaningful data.

* For detailed description and definitions of Data Distribution (Median and Average), see chapter 1, Explanation of Data Distribution.

Full-Time Music/Choir/Worship Pastor/Director Worksheet

	Enter your church data below	The 2014–2015 Compensation Handbook for Church Staff		Enter *Compensation Handbook* data below			
				Highest 25%	Median	Lowest 25%	Average
Church Income	$	Table 11-1	page 175	$	$	$	$
Worship Attendance		Table 11-2	page 176	n/a	$	n/a	$
Church Setting (metro, suburb, small town, or farming area)		Table 11-3	page 177	n/a	$	n/a	$
Region		Table 11-4	page 178	n/a	$	n/a	$
Person's Education		Table 11-5	page 179	n/a	$	n/a	$
Years Employed		Table 11-6	page 180	n/a	$	n/a	$
Denomination (if applicable)		Table 11-7	page 181	n/a	$	n/a	$

Looking at the table and page number references indicated in the ***2014–2015 Compensation Handbook for Church Staff*** columns above, locate the appropriate range for your church. Refer to the instructions below for step-by-step help.

FILLING OUT THE WORKSHEET

1. Fill in the gray boxes under *Enter your church data* with your church demographic information as follows:

   ▶ **Income** (Total annual church budget in past year)
   ▶ **Worship attendance** (Number of people, including children, who attend all weekend services)
   ▶ **Church setting** (Metropolitan city, suburb of large city, small town or rural city, or farming area)

   ▶ **Region** (Locate your state's region in the appendix on page 346.)
   ▶ **Education** (Highest level of education: less than bachelor, bachelor, master, or doctorate)

2. Use Table 11-1 (page 175) in your *2014–2015 Compensation Handbook for Church Staff* to enter data pertinent to your church. In the heading (top row), locate your church **income** from the five available ranges. Follow that column to the bottom rows, and copy the *Highest 25%*, *Median*, *Lowest 25%*, and *Average* amounts onto your worksheet.

3. Use Table 11-2 (page 176) on your *2014–2015 Compensation Handbook for Church Staff* to enter data pertinent to your church. In the heading (top row), locate your church's

worship attendance from the six available ranges. Follow that column to the bottom rows, and copy the *Median* and *Average* amounts onto your worksheet.

4. Use Table 11-3 (page 177) on your *2014–2015 Compensation Handbook for Church Staff* to enter data pertinent to your church. In the heading (top row), choose the **church setting** that best describes your church. Follow that column to the bottom rows, and copy the *Median* and *Average* amounts onto your worksheet.

5. Use Table 11-4 (page 178) on your *2014–2015 Compensation Handbook for Church Staff* to enter data pertinent to your church. In the heading (top row), look for the **region** where your church is located. Follow that column to the bottom rows, and copy the *Median* and *Average* amounts onto your worksheet.

6. Use Table 11-5 (page 179) on your *2014–2015 Compensation Handbook for Church Staff* to enter data pertinent to your Music/Choir/ Worship Pastor/Director. In the heading (top row), look for **your Music/Choir/Worship Pastor/Director's highest level of education**. Follow that column to the bottom rows, and copy the *Median* and *Average* amounts onto your worksheet.

7. Use Table 11-6 (page 180) on your *2014–2015 Compensation Handbook for Church Staff* to enter data pertinent to your Music/Choir/ Worship Pastor/Director. In the heading (top row), locate the **number of years your Music/ Choir/Worship Pastor/Director has been employed**. Follow that column to the bottom rows, and copy the *Median* and *Average* amounts onto your worksheet.

8. Use Table 11-7 (page 181) on your *2014–2015 Compensation Handbook for Church Staff* to enter data pertinent to your church. In the

heading (top row), look for **your church's denominational affiliation**. Follow that column to the bottom rows, and copy the *Median* and *Average* amounts onto your worksheet. If your church is not affiliated with a denomination, leave this section blank.

DETERMINING COMPENSATION

This tool will not provide you with a single compensation amount but rather with a range of values to help you determine the compensation appropriate to your situation.

1. Look at the values in the shaded *Median* column. Circle the **lowest** and the **highest** values. **This is the range of the median compensation plus benefits for churches similar to yours.**

2. For a variety of reasons, compensation plus benefits may be higher or lower than the range established in this table. Income and attendance are two significant factors affecting church compensation packages. If church income or attendance skews higher, you might want to consider moving toward or above the higher end of the range. Likewise, if church income or attendance skews lower, you may consider moving the package toward or below the lower end of the range.

3. Examine additional variables that might impact the compensation package you offer, such as years of service, education, and church setting.

4. Determine other circumstances unique to your situation, such as cost of living in your area, theological beliefs, pastoral performance, financial needs, the local economy, personal motivation, congregational goals, and others.

5. You now have a compensation package range based on the *2014–2015 Compensation Handbook*. Since each church and position are unique, your final compensation package will be based on additional factors unique to your situation.

Part-Time Music/Choir/Worship Pastor/Director Worksheet

	Enter your church data below	The 2014–2015 Compensation Handbook for Church Staff		Enter Compensation Handbook data below			
				Highest 25%	Median	Lowest 25%	Average
Church Income	$	Table 11-9	page 183	$	$	$	$
Worship Attendance		Table 11-10	page 184	n/a	$	n/a	$
Church Setting (metro, suburb, small town, or farming area)		Table 11-11	page 185	n/a	$	n/a	$
Region		Table 11-12	page 186	n/a	$	n/a	$
Person's Education		Table 11-13	page 187	n/a	$	n/a	$
Years Employed		Table 11-14	page 188	n/a	$	n/a	$
Denomination (if applicable)		Table 11-15	page 189	n/a	$	n/a	$

Looking at the table and page number references indicated in the *2014–2015 Compensation Handbook for Church Staff* columns above, locate the appropriate range for your church. Refer to the instructions below for step-by-step help.

FILLING OUT THE WORKSHEET

1. Fill in the gray boxes under *Enter your church data* with your church demographic information as follows:

   ▷ **Income** (Total annual church budget in past year)
   ▷ **Worship attendance** (Number of people, including children, who attend all weekend services)
   ▷ **Church setting** (Metropolitan city, suburb of large city, small town or rural city, or farming area)

   ▷ **Region** (Locate your state's region in the appendix on page 346.)
   ▷ **Education** (Highest level of education: less than bachelor, bachelor, master, or doctorate)

2. Use Table 11-9 (page 183) in your *2014–2015 Compensation Handbook for Church Staff* to enter data pertinent to your church. In the heading (top row), locate your church **income** from the five available ranges. Follow that column to the bottom rows, and copy the *Highest 25%*, *Median*, *Lowest 25%*, and *Average* amounts onto your worksheet.

3. Use Table 11-10 (page 184) on your *2014–2015 Compensation Handbook for Church Staff* to enter data pertinent to your church. In the heading (top row), locate your church's

worship attendance from the six available ranges. Follow that column to the bottom rows, and copy the *Median* and *Average* amounts onto your worksheet.

4. Use Table 11-11 (page 185) on your *2014–2015 Compensation Handbook for Church Staff* to enter data pertinent to your church. In the heading (top row), choose the **church setting** that best describes your church. Follow that column to the bottom rows, and copy the *Median* and *Average* amounts onto your worksheet.

5. Use Table 11-12 (page 186) on your *2014–2015 Compensation Handbook for Church Staff* to enter data pertinent to your church. In the heading (top row), look for the **region** where your church is located. Follow that column to the bottom rows, and copy the *Median* and *Average* amounts onto your worksheet.

6. Use Table 11-13 (page 187) on your *2014–2015 Compensation Handbook for Church Staff* to enter data pertinent to your Children's/Preschool Pastor/Director. In the heading (top row), look for **your Music/Choir/Worship Pastor/Director's highest level of education**. Follow that column to the bottom rows, and copy the *Median* and *Average* amounts onto your worksheet.

7. Use Table 11-14 (page 188) on your *2014–2015 Compensation Handbook for Church Staff* to enter data pertinent to your Children's/Preschool Pastor/Director. In the heading (top row), locate the **number of years your Music/Choir/Worship Pastor/Director has been employed**. Follow that column to the bottom rows, and copy the *Median* and *Average* amounts onto your worksheet.

8. Use Table 11-15 (page 189) on your *2014–2015 Compensation Handbook for Church Staff* to enter data pertinent to your church. In the

heading (top row), look for **your church's denominational affiliation**. Follow that column to the bottom rows, and copy the *Median* and *Average* amounts onto your worksheet. If your church is not affiliated with a denomination, leave this section blank.

DETERMINING COMPENSATION

This tool will not provide you with a single compensation amount but rather with a range of values to help you determine the compensation appropriate to your situation.

1. Look at the values in the shaded *Median* column. Circle the **lowest** and the **highest** values. **This is the range of the median compensation plus benefits for churches similar to yours.**

2. For a variety of reasons, compensation plus benefits may be higher or lower than the range established in this table. Income and attendance are two significant factors affecting church compensation packages. If church income or attendance skews higher, you might want to consider moving toward or above the higher end of the range. Likewise, if church income or attendance skews lower, you may consider moving the package toward or below the lower end of the range.

3. Examine additional variables that might impact the compensation package you offer, such as years of service, education, and church setting.

4. Determine other circumstances unique to your situation, such as cost of living in your area, theological beliefs, pastoral performance, financial needs, the local economy, personal motivation, congregational goals, and others.

5. You now have a compensation package range based on the *2014–2015 Compensation Handbook*. Since each church and position are unique, your final compensation package will be based on additional factors unique to your situation.

12

ADMINISTRATORS

Employment Profile

Administrators include paid but usually not ordained staff who supervise the business aspects of church operations, such as financial management, business operations, and some staff oversight. This may include such positions as Business Administrator, Business Manager, Chief Financial Officer, Chief Operating Officer, etc.

Three-quarters of Administrators who reported serve in a full-time capacity. Two in 10 full-time Administrators are ordained ministers. Six in 10 full-time Administrators are female. More than six in 10 full- and part-time Administrators have a minimum of a bachelor's degree. Nearly all are employed by the church rather than self-employed.

The chart below provides a demographic profile of this sample.

	Full-Time	Part-Time
Number of respondents	**351**	**110**
Ordained	18%	12%
Average years employed	8	5
Male	41%	32%
Female	59%	68%
Self-employed (receives 1099)	1%	8%
Church employee (receives W-2)	99%	92%
High school diploma	14%	22%
Associate degree	18%	17%
Bachelor's degree	46%	41%
Master's degree	20%	15%
Doctoral degree	2%	5%

Total Compensation plus Benefits Package Analysis

The following analyses are based on data in the tables you will find later in this chapter. The tables show compensation plus benefits data for full-time and part-time Administrators and are presented according to church income, church attendance, church setting, region, education, years employed, denomination, and gender. In this way, the Administrator's compensation plus benefits can be analyzed and compared from a variety of useful perspectives.

The total compensation plus benefits amount includes the base salary; housing allowance and/ or parsonage amount; health, life, and disability

insurance payments; retirement contribution; and educational funds.

A worksheet at the end of this chapter is provided to help you apply the data to your church's situation.

More than half of full-time Administrators receive health insurance and retirement benefits as well as salary increases. Most church administrators do not receive housing or parsonage allowances.

Compensation Plus Benefits	Full-Time	Part-Time
Base Salary	100%	97%
Housing	13%	5%
Parsonage	0%	0%
Health Insurance*	57%	10%
Life Insurance*	32%	1%
Disability Insurance*	26%	3%
Retirement	53%	9%
Continuing Education	24%	6%
Received salary increase	54%	51%
Received paid vacation	98%	53%
Received auto reimbursement/allowance	27%	15%

Only those reporting individual premiums for Health, Life, or Disability (not total insurance premiums) are included.

KEY POINTS

* About half of the full-time Administrators who responded to the survey serve in larger churches with an income of over $1,000,000 and a worship attendance of more than 500.

* In general, as church income, worship attendance, and the minister's education level increase, compensation and benefits for full-time Administrators also increase.

* More than four in 10 full-time Administrators in this survey serve in churches set in a suburb of a large city.

* Full-time male Administrators receive higher compensation and benefits packages (39% higher) than their female counterparts.

Compensation & Benefits: National Averages for Full-Time Administrators	
2000	$44,768
2001	$48,064
2002	$47,305
2003	$50,615
2004	$49,907
2005	$53,153
2006	$52,036
2007	$57,639
2008	$54,237
2009	$56,637
2011	$54,400
2013	$57,145*

The above trend is made available for your reference only. In addition to looking at this overall data, please refer to the detailed tables using your church's income, attendance, setting, region, and denomination as well as the person's education, gender, and years employed for guidance in compensating this position.

Table 12-1: Annual Compensation of Full-Time Administrators by Church Income

CHARACTERISTICS	Data Distribution*	CHURCH INCOME				
		$250K & Under	$251-$500K	$501-$750K	$751K-$1M	Over $1 Million
Average weekend worship attendance		-	233	332	463	1,405
Average church income		$129,677	$392,206	$640,281	$882,730	$2,526,990
Average # of years employed		6	9	9	9	8
Average # of paid vacation days		13	17	18	16	18
% College graduate or higher		38%	64%	55%	57%	79%
% Who receive auto reimbursement/allowance		8%	17%	29%	26%	30%
% Ordained		8%	6%	12%	21%	22%
% Supervise one or more people		38%	67%	81%	95%	92%
Average % salary increase (for those who had an increase) this year		-	3.4%	3.2%	3.9%	3.6%
COMPENSATION						
Base Salary	Highest 25%	$44,000	$43,051	$44,096	$49,432	$65,000
	Median	$36,000	$35,000	$38,110	$40,000	$50,805
	Lowest 25%	$28,000	$29,300	$30,500	$33,652	$42,250
	Average	$32,505	$35,920	$39,033	$41,341	$54,698
Housing	Highest 25%	-	-	-	-	$35,646
	Median	-	-	-	-	$29,400
	Lowest 25%	-	-	-	-	$25,000
	Average	-	-	-	-	$29,915
Parsonage	Highest 25%	-	-	-	-	-
	Median	-	-	-	-	-
	Lowest 25%	-	-	-	-	-
	Average	-	-	-	-	-
Total Compensation	**Highest 25%**	**$44,100**	**$44,646**	**$47,563**	**$51,000**	**$70,383**
	Median	**$38,000**	**$35,121**	**$39,353**	**$42,000**	**$57,628**
	Lowest 25%	**$29,500**	**$30,250**	**$31,825**	**$35,000**	**$45,606**
	Average	**$35,163**	**$37,077**	**$41,370**	**$45,040**	**$59,742**
BENEFITS						
Health Insurance	Highest 25%	-	$11,573	$10,850	$10,260	$12,168
	Median	-	$5,400	$7,705	$7,320	$7,865
	Lowest 25%	-	$4,000	$4,257	$6,540	$4,550
	Average	-	$7,351	$7,634	$8,707	$8,835
Life Insurance	Highest 25%	-	$300	-	$650	$500
	Median	-	$199	-	$456	$250
	Lowest 25%	-	$70	-	$300	$100
	Average	-	$209	-	$591	$409
Disability Insurance	Highest 25%	-	-	-	-	$600
	Median	-	-	-	-	$414
	Lowest 25%	-	-	-	-	$256
	Average	-	-	-	-	$519
Retirement	Highest 25%	-	$3,275	$2,500	$5,219	$5,244
	Median	-	$2,300	$1,622	$2,490	$3,053
	Lowest 25%	-	$1,400	$1,210	$1,659	$2,000
	Average	-	$2,717	$2,350	$3,370	$3,853
Continuing Education	Highest 25%	-	$875	$625	$1,400	$1,500
	Median	-	$500	$500	$550	$1,000
	Lowest 25%	-	$375	$350	$500	$500
	Average	-	$636	$615	$1,288	$1,054
Total Benefits	**Highest 25%**	**-**	**$10,023**	**$9,661**	**$12,870**	**$15,514**
	Median	**-**	**$5,387**	**$5,351**	**$8,566**	**$8,750**
	Lowest 25%	**-**	**$3,798**	**$2,010**	**$3,600**	**$4,800**
	Average	**-**	**$7,440**	**$6,609**	**$8,995**	**$10,739**
TOTAL COMPENSATION PLUS BENEFITS	**Highest 25%**	**$46,660**	**$49,408**	**$56,100**	**$57,442**	**$82,825**
	Median	**$38,263**	**$38,495**	**$43,581**	**$49,700**	**$65,960**
	Lowest 25%	**$31,300**	**$31,535**	**$34,380**	**$39,590**	**$51,861**
	Average	**$37,603**	**$41,242**	**$46,091**	**$50,313**	**$69,296**
Number of Respondents		13	53	42	58	172

- Not enough response to provide meaningful data.

* For detailed description and definitions of Data Distribution (Highest 25%, Median, Lowest 25%, and Average), see chapter 1, Explanation of Data Distribution.

Table 12-2: Annual Compensation of Full-Time Administrators by Worship Attendance

	Data Distribution*	WORSHIP ATTENDANCE					
		100 or less	101-300	301-500	501-750	751-1,000	Over 1,000
CHARACTERISTICS							
Average weekend worship attendance		77	216	414	629	888	2,775
Average church income		$393,464	$618,794	$950,887	$1,298,645	$1,612,572	$3,859,237
Average # of years employed		6	10	9	8	7	7
Average # of paid vacation days		14	18	18	17	17	18
% College graduate or higher		64%	68%	64%	63%	62%	83%
% Who receive auto reimbursement/allowance		9%	21%	36%	28%	19%	28%
% Ordained		9%	6%	19%	23%	28%	20%
% Supervise one or more people		40%	73%	93%	95%	81%	91%
Average % salary increase (for those who had an increase) this year		-	3.8%	3.2%	4.0%	3.4%	3.5%
COMPENSATION							
Base Salary	Median	$36,000	$37,470	$41,000	$44,280	$45,606	$56,811
	Average	$33,509	$39,908	$43,807	$46,212	$46,236	$59,196
Housing	Median	-	-	$25,134	$33,600	$29,297	$28,150
	Average	-	-	$24,333	$29,056	$28,456	$30,941
Parsonage	Median	-	-	-	-	-	-
	Average	-	-	-	-	-	-
Total Compensation	**Median**	**$37,000**	**$38,220**	**$46,468**	**$49,150**	**$47,660**	**$62,000**
	Average	**$36,800**	**$41,007**	**$48,198**	**$50,235**	**$51,139**	**$64,425**
BENEFITS							
Health Insurance	Median	-	$7,600	$7,705	$7,320	$6,592	$8,319
	Average	-	$8,613	$8,654	$8,106	$7,428	$9,224
Life Insurance	Median	-	$278	$234	$288	$324	$247
	Average	-	$349	$447	$518	$467	$382
Disability	Median	-	$354	$460	$350	$398	$455
	Average	-	$478	$522	$546	$464	$521
Retirement	Median	-	$2,200	$2,500	$2,700	$2,560	$3,550
	Average	-	$3,376	$2,980	$3,312	$3,033	$4,206
Continuing Education	Median	-	$625	$725	$500	-	$1,200
	Average	-	$820	$1,065	$875	-	$1,380
Total Benefits	**Median**	-	**$7,175**	**$6,916**	**$7,597**	**$7,419**	**$9,667**
	Average	-	**$8,769**	**$7,824**	**$9,006**	**$10,076**	**$11,715**
TOTAL COMPENSATION PLUS BENEFITS	**Median**	**$39,263**	**$43,178**	**$50,000**	**$56,403**	**$58,160**	**$77,250**
	Average	**$39,264**	**$46,983**	**$52,900**	**$57,994**	**$58,765**	**$74,655**
Number of Respondents		11	82	83	65	37	71

- Not enough response to provide meaningful data.

* For detailed description and definitions of Data Distribution (Median and Average), see chapter 1, Explanation of Data Distribution.

Table 12-3: Annual Compensation of Full-Time Administrators by Church Setting

	Data Distribution*	CHURCH SETTING			
		Metro-politan city	Suburb of large city	Small town or rural city	Farming area
CHARACTERISTICS					
Average weekend worship attendance		1,122	996	737	-
Average church income		$2,291,380	$1,694,456	$1,018,971	-
Average # of years employed		7	9	8	-
Average # of paid vacation days		17	18	17	-
% College graduate or higher		78%	70%	60%	-
% Who receive auto reimbursement/allowance		20%	33%	25%	-
% Ordained		16%	19%	18%	-
% Supervise one or more people		84%	85%	86%	-
Average % salary increase (for those who had an increase) this year		3.5%	3.9%	3.5%	-
COMPENSATION					
Base Salary	Median	$44,365	$44,737	$41,137	-
	Average	$48,524	$48,192	$42,903	-
Housing	Median	$20,916	$26,450	$29,447	-
	Average	$24,494	$26,690	$28,314	-
Parsonage	Median	-	-	-	-
	Average	-	-	-	-
Total Compensation	**Median**	**$46,988**	**$48,328**	**$44,000**	**-**
	Average	**$53,137**	**$51,837**	**$46,733**	**-**
BENEFITS					
Health Insurance	Median	$6,531	$7,824	$7,320	-
	Average	$7,218	$8,422	$9,098	-
Life Insurance	Median	$255	$250	$300	-
	Average	$337	$380	$588	-
Disability Insurance	Median	$403	$390	$541	-
	Average	$464	$493	$613	-
Retirement	Median	$2,600	$2,980	$2,501	-
	Average	$3,541	$3,530	$3,119	-
Continuing Education	Median	$600	$700	$550	-
	Average	$947	$947	$1,038	-
Total Benefits	**Median**	**$6,210**	**$9,000**	**$7,033**	**-**
	Average	**$7,879**	**$10,455**	**$8,885**	**-**
TOTAL COMPENSATION PLUS BENEFITS	**Median**	**$54,514**	**$55,362**	**$50,240**	**-**
	Average	**$58,838**	**$59,834**	**$53,305**	**-**
Number of Respondents		76	153	118	2

- Not enough response to provide meaningful data.

* For detailed description and definitions of Data Distribution (Median and Average), see chapter 1, Explanation of Data Distribution.

Table 12-4: Annual Compensation of Full-Time Administrators by Region

	Data Distribution*	REGION								
		New England	Middle Atlantic	South Atlantic	E-N Central	E-S Central	W-N Central	W-S Central	Mountain	Pacific
CHARACTERISTICS										
Average weekend worship attendance		674	1,154	1,005	724	659	919	987	1,004	888
Average church income		$1,295,250	$2,404,006	$1,739,705	$1,303,525	$1,430,124	$1,145,457	$1,655,114	$1,284,105	$1,533,229
Average # of years employed		10	9	9	9	12	6	8	10	7
Average # of paid vacation days		19	18	18	18	18	17	17	19	16
% College graduate or higher		75%	65%	71%	79%	63%	63%	73%	67%	58%
% Who receive auto reimbursement/allowance		11%	26%	21%	43%	40%	26%	29%	33%	19%
% Ordained		0%	10%	21%	13%	15%	14%	20%	5%	31%
% Supervise one or more people		67%	84%	87%	86%	75%	86%	84%	95%	88%
Average % salary increase (for those who had an increase) this year		3.0%	3.1%	3.2%	2.8%	3.0%	4.1%	5.3%	3.3%	4.5%
COMPENSATION										
Base Salary	Median	$44,100	$44,491	$44,280	$42,750	$37,282	$40,340	$43,788	$44,000	$45,000
	Average	$47,797	$49,515	$47,207	$45,036	$45,590	$43,221	$45,757	$46,127	$46,613
Housing	Median	-	-	$29,100	-	-	-	-	-	$33,600
	Average	-	-	$28,095	-	-	-	-	-	$29,390
Parsonage	Median	-	-	-	-	-	-	-	-	-
	Average	-	-	-	-	-	-	-	-	-
Total Compensation	**Median**	$47,660	$44,491	$47,000	$44,258	$45,451	$41,149	$50,000	$44,725	$50,466
	Average	$50,463	$49,902	$52,235	$46,890	$48,776	$45,181	$52,274	$47,318	$52,702
BENEFITS										
Health Insurance	Median	-	$8,500	$7,410	$8,000	$7,670	$7,838	$6,000	$8,484	$6,000
	Average	-	$9,453	$8,137	$9,296	$7,103	$8,693	$7,345	$8,316	$7,332
Life Insurance	Median	-	$295	$237	$168	$360	$400	$330	-	$175
	Average	-	$308	$300	$207	$687	$680	$575	-	$397
Disability Insurance	Median	-	-	$500	$350	-	$560	$520	-	$211
	Average	-	-	$549	$498	-	$712	$542	-	$302
Retirement	Median	-	$1,919	$2,980	$3,522	$2,696	$3,000	$2,550	$2,500	$2,550
	Average	-	$3,497	$3,674	$3,443	$3,842	$3,471	$2,964	$3,116	$2,950
Continuing Education	Median	-	-	$650	$850	-	$500	$600	-	-
	Average	-	-	$945	$954	-	$916	$1,183	-	-
Total Benefits	**Median**	-	$10,075	$6,779	$8,200	$9,911	$7,383	$8,250	$4,565	$6,038
	Average	-	$10,835	$8,909	$10,028	$11,193	$8,599	$8,626	$8,803	$7,738
TOTAL COMPENSATION PLUS BENEFITS	**Median**	$53,000	$49,150	$55,485	$49,515	$53,695	$49,220	$55,100	$49,622	$55,650
	Average	$63,297	$57,242	$59,924	$53,582	$56,975	$52,585	$57,547	$53,186	$58,316
Number of Respondents		9	31	95	42	20	36	45	21	52

- Not enough response to provide meaningful data.

* For detailed description and definitions of Data Distribution (Median and Average), see chapter 1, Explanation of Data Distribution.

Table 12-5: Annual Compensation of Full-Time Administrators by Education

	Data Distribution*	EDUCATION			
		Less than Bachelor	Bachelor	Master	Doctorate
CHARACTERISTICS					
Average weekend worship attendance		677	877	1,425	1,352
Average church income		$967,467	$1,626,666	$2,343,834	-
Average # of years employed		10	8	8	4
Average # of paid vacation days		17	17	18	17
% College graduate or higher		0%	100%	100%	100%
% Who receive auto reimbursement/allowance		19%	29%	34%	25%
% Ordained		8%	17%	34%	38%
% Supervise one or more people		83%	86%	85%	88%
Average % salary increase (for those who had an increase) this year		3.2%	3.6%	4.4%	-
COMPENSATION					
Base Salary	Median	$40,000	$45,000	$45,500	$49,000
	Average	$41,108	$47,624	$50,685	$49,313
Housing	Median	-	$28,450	$27,200	-
	Average	-	$26,864	$27,499	-
Parsonage	Median	-	-	-	-
	Average	-	-	-	-
Total Compensation	**Median**	**$40,340**	**$50,000**	**$56,562**	**$51,750**
	Average	**$42,623**	**$51,428**	**$58,828**	**$55,188**
BENEFITS					
Health Insurance	Median	$7,740	$6,500	$8,500	-
	Average	$8,290	$7,848	$8,941	-
Life Insurance	Median	$320	$245	$250	-
	Average	$439	$398	$455	-
Disability Insurance	Median	$378	$400	$500	-
	Average	$515	$506	$551	-
Retirement	Median	$2,253	$2,845	$3,661	-
	Average	$2,730	$3,384	$4,257	-
Continuing Education	Median	$500	$650	$1,100	-
	Average	$617	$968	$1,150	-
Total Benefits	**Median**	**$7,870**	**$7,342**	**$9,250**	**-**
	Average	**$8,595**	**$8,864**	**$10,588**	**-**
TOTAL COMPENSATION PLUS BENEFITS	**Median**	**$45,000**	**$54,607**	**$60,394**	**$59,219**
	Average	**$48,695**	**$58,483**	**$66,220**	**$66,250**
Number of Respondents		109	159	68	8

- Not enough response to provide meaningful data.

* For detailed description and definitions of Data Distribution (Median and Average), see chapter 1, Explanation of Data Distribution.

Table 12-6: Annual Compensation of Full-Time Administrators by Years Employed

CHARACTERISTICS	Data Distribution*	Less than 6 years	6-10 years	11-15 years	Over 15 years
Average weekend worship attendance		1,267	819	566	774
Average church income		$1,822,530	$1,640,508	$1,216,946	$1,344,676
Average # of years employed		3	8	13	22
Average # of paid vacation days		15	18	19	21
% College graduate or higher		77%	65%	59%	56%
% Who receive auto reimbursement/allowance		22%	26%	30%	41%
% Ordained		18%	14%	14%	20%
% Supervise one or more people		85%	86%	84%	90%
Average % salary increase (for those who had an increase) this year		4.2%	3.5%	3.0%	2.9%
COMPENSATION					
Base Salary	Median	$44,140	$44,725	$42,000	$43,830
	Average	$45,810	$47,727	$46,978	$44,564
Housing	Median	$24,000	$26,000	-	-
	Average	$24,663	$28,202	-	-
Parsonage	Median	-	-	-	-
	Average	-	-	-	-
Total Compensation	**Median**	**$46,000**	**$49,000**	**$44,346**	**$44,165**
	Average	**$49,302**	**$51,258**	**$50,553**	**$48,571**
BENEFITS					
Health Insurance	Median	$6,912	$7,140	$8,400	$8,500
	Average	$8,376	$7,157	$9,981	$8,681
Life Insurance	Median	$247	$234	$347	$203
	Average	$450	$363	$449	$490
Disability Insurance	Median	$439	$350	$500	$481
	Average	$564	$511	$493	$491
Retirement	Median	$2,642	$2,783	$3,057	$2,550
	Average	$3,468	$3,074	$3,601	$3,660
Continuing Education	Median	$500	$875	$500	-
	Average	$980	$1,097	$871	-
Total Benefits	**Median**	**$6,500**	**$6,989**	**$9,546**	**$9,920**
	Average	**$8,772**	**$7,826**	**$12,064**	**$10,687**
TOTAL COMPENSATION PLUS BENEFITS	**Median**	**$50,915**	**$53,750**	**$54,019**	**$52,640**
	Average	**$55,832**	**$57,153**	**$59,605**	**$56,512**
Number of Respondents		134	101	60	41

- Not enough response to provide meaningful data.

* For detailed description and definitions of Data Distribution (Median and Average), see chapter 1, Explanation of Data Distribution.

Table 12-7: Annual Compensation of Full-Time Administrators by Denomination

	Data Distribution*	Assemblies of God	Baptist	Independent/ Nondenom.	Lutheran	Methodist	Presby- terian
CHARACTERISTICS							
Average weekend worship attendance		577	969	1,272	571	869	470
Average church income		$911,498	$1,930,778	$2,226,491	$1,360,323	$1,049,695	$1,314,906
Average # of years employed		10	9	8	6	8	7
Average # of paid vacation days		16	17	18	17	17	20
% College graduate or higher		52%	74%	71%	74%	49%	81%
% Who receive auto reimbursement/allowance		30%	32%	21%	37%	18%	43%
% Ordained		17%	24%	30%	5%	3%	7%
% Supervise one or more people		73%	93%	80%	95%	84%	85%
Average % salary increase (for those who had an increase) this year		5.9%	4.2%	3.9%	3.3%	3.2%	2.4%
COMPENSATION							
Base Salary	Median	$34,155	$44,100	$45,000	$44,737	$42,000	$48,277
	Average	$37,166	$48,386	$48,002	$49,000	$41,747	$51,471
Housing	Median	-	$25,067	$26,450	-	-	-
	Average	-	$23,158	$30,243	-	-	-
Parsonage	Median	-	-	-	-	-	-
	Average	-	-	-	-	-	-
Total Compensation	**Median**	$35,000	$52,000	$50,000	$44,737	$42,000	$48,880
	Average	$40,463	$54,472	$54,667	$50,052	$41,747	$52,756
BENEFITS							
Health Insurance	Median	-	$7,080	$9,906	$7,294	$7,200	$7,880
	Average	-	$8,280	$9,862	$10,191	$6,745	$8,418
Life Insurance	Median	-	$225	$364	$445	-	$258
	Average	-	$450	$495	$824	-	$251
Disability Insurance	Median	-	$396	$381	$1,000	-	-
	Average	-	$393	$478	$1,110	-	-
Retirement	Median	-	$2,500	$2,000	$3,827	$2,406	$3,761
	Average	-	$3,297	$3,334	$4,532	$2,300	$4,096
Continuing Education	Median	-	$1,000	$1,000	$500	$500	$1,200
	Average	-	$1,085	$1,169	$637	$556	$1,182
Total Benefits	**Median**	$3,575	$6,577	$10,000	$11,500	$5,000	$10,098
	Average	$7,015	$9,128	$10,607	$12,376	$6,016	$10,441
TOTAL COMPENSATION PLUS BENEFITS	**Median**	$38,000	$57,626	$56,261	$57,497	$47,392	$62,403
	Average	$43,220	$61,385	$62,183	$60,474	$46,837	$61,706
Number of Respondents		23	75	71	19	39	28

- Not enough response to provide meaningful data.

* For detailed description and definitions of Data Distribution (Median and Average), see chapter 1, Explanation of Data Distribution.

Table 12-8: Annual Compensation of Full-Time Administrators by Gender

	Data Distribution*	GENDER	
		Male	Female
CHARACTERISTICS			
Average weekend worship attendance		1,208	737
Average church income		$2,172,706	$1,168,280
Average # of years employed		8	9
Average # of paid vacation days		17	17
% College graduate or higher		84%	58%
% Who receive auto reimbursement/allowance		34%	22%
% Ordained		36%	5%
% Supervise one or more people		89%	83%
Average % salary increase (for those who had an increase) this year		3.5%	3.8%
COMPENSATION			
Base Salary	Median	$50,000	$40,370
	Average	$52,402	$42,155
Housing	Median	$26,900	-
	Average	$26,917	-
Parsonage	Median	-	-
	Average	-	-
Total Compensation	**Median**	**$57,382**	**$41,137**
	Average	**$60,163**	**$43,339**
BENEFITS			
Health Insurance	Median	$8,500	$6,656
	Average	$9,513	$7,443
Life Insurance	Median	$245	$294
	Average	$403	$445
Disability Insurance	Median	$400	$402
	Average	$449	$582
Retirement	Median	$3,000	$2,501
	Average	$4,059	$2,876
Continuing Education	Median	$875	$500
	Average	$1,234	$859
Total Benefits	**Median**	**$9,510**	**$7,175**
	Average	**$10,647**	**$8,321**
TOTAL COMPENSATION PLUS BENEFITS	**Median**	**$65,575**	**$46,904**
	Average	**$68,456**	**$49,373**
Number of Respondents		143	207

- Not enough response to provide meaningful data.

* For detailed description and definitions of Data Distribution (Median and Average), see chapter 1, Explanation of Data Distribution.

Table 12-9: Annual Compensation of Part-Time Administrators by Church Income

	Data Distribution*	CHURCH INCOME				
		$250K & Under	$251-$500K	$501-$750K	$751K-$1M	Over 1 Million
CHARACTERISTICS						
Average weekend worship attendance		127	209	342	602	805
Average church income		$139,642	$364,638	$620,365	$902,670	$1,657,414
Average # of years employed		6	6	5	5	4
Average # of paid vacation days		12	13	10	10	18
% College graduate or higher		53%	46%	76%	60%	75%
% Who receive auto reimbursement/allowance		13%	8%	14%	30%	25%
% Ordained		17%	8%	5%	10%	25%
% Supervise one or more people		28%	54%	63%	80%	69%
Average % salary increase (for those who had an increase) this year		8.1%	6.4%	4.5%	5.5%	4.8%
HOURLY RATE						
Base Rate	Average	$14	$15	$18	$18	$26
COMPENSATION						
Base Salary	Median	$10,075	$22,035	$22,360	$25,993	$31,212
	Average	$11,228	$20,803	$23,117	$26,175	$30,919
Housing	Median	-	-	-	-	-
	Average	-	-	-	-	-
Parsonage	Median	-	-	-	-	-
	Average	-	-	-	-	-
Total Compensation	**Median**	**$9,750**	**$21,500**	**$22,360**	**$29,230**	**$31,212**
	Average	**$10,982**	**$20,459**	**$23,117**	**$27,925**	**$34,253**
BENEFITS						
Health Insurance	Median	-	-	-	-	-
	Average	-	-	-	-	-
Life Insurance	Median	-	-	-	-	-
	Average	-	-	-	-	-
Disability Insurance	Median	-	-	-	-	-
	Average	-	-	-	-	-
Retirement	Median	-	-	-	-	-
	Average	-	-	-	-	-
Continuing Education	Median	-	-	-	-	-
	Average	-	-	-	-	-
Total Benefits	**Median**	-	-	-	-	-
	Average	-	-	-	-	-
TOTAL COMPENSATION PLUS BENEFITS	**Median**	**$10,400**	**$22,570**	**$23,544**	**$30,478**	**$31,840**
	Average	**$11,304**	**$21,111**	**$24,389**	**$28,615**	**$35,876**
Number of Respondents		32	26	21	10	16

- Not enough response to provide meaningful data.

* For detailed description and definitions of Data Distribution (Median and Average), see chapter 1, Explanation of Data Distribution.

Table 12-10: Annual Compensation of Part-Time Administrators by Worship Attendance

	Data Distribution*	WORSHIP ATTENDANCE					
		100 or less	101-300	301-500	501-750	751-1,000	Over 1,000
CHARACTERISTICS							
Average weekend worship attendance		77	202	389	605	870	-
Average church income		$136,997	$379,371	$770,909	$1,134,062	$1,413,400	-
Average # of years employed		7	5	5	7	3	-
Average # of paid vacation days		8	13	10	10	13	-
% College graduate or higher		48%	58%	78%	40%	78%	-
% Who receive auto reimbursement/allowance		9%	7%	28%	40%	22%	-
% Ordained		14%	11%	11%	10%	22%	-
% Supervise one or more people		22%	59%	61%	67%	56%	-
Average % salary increase (for those who had an increase) this year		7.1%	5.2%	6.8%	3.0%	-	-
HOURLY RATE							
Base Rate	Average	$12	$16	$17	$19	-	-
COMPENSATION							
Base Salary	Median	$10,400	$22,570	$19,916	$25,602	$31,206	-
	Average	$10,947	$20,813	$21,839	$25,018	$29,564	-
Housing	Median	-	-	-	-	-	-
	Average	-	-	-	-	-	-
Parsonage	Median	-	-	-	-	-	-
	Average	-	-	-	-	-	-
Total Compensation	**Median**	**$10,400**	**$21,500**	**$22,360**	**$29,021**	**$31,206**	**-**
	Average	**$10,947**	**$20,213**	**$22,673**	**$26,768**	**$33,939**	**-**
BENEFITS		-	-	-	-	-	
Health Insurance	Median	-	-	-	-	-	-
	Average	-	-	-	-	-	-
Life Insurance	Median	-	-	-	-	-	-
	Average	-	-	-	-	-	-
Disability	Median	-	-	-	-	-	-
	Average	-	-	-	-	-	-
Retirement	Median	-	-	-	-	-	-
	Average	-	-	-	-	-	-
Continuing Education	Median	-	-	-	-	-	-
	Average	-	-	-	-	-	-
Total Benefits	**Median**	**-**	**$1,225**	**-**	**-**	**-**	**-**
	Average	**-**	**$3,742**	**-**	**-**	**-**	**-**
TOTAL COMPENSATION PLUS BENEFITS	**Median**	**$10,400**	**$21,500**	**$23,544**	**$29,547**	**$31,206**	**-**
	Average	**$11,323**	**$20,752**	**$24,547**	**$27,548**	**$35,184**	**-**
Number of Respondents		23	45	18	10	9	5

- Not enough response to provide meaningful data.

* For detailed description and definitions of Data Distribution (Median and Average), see chapter 1, Explanation of Data Distribution.

Table 12-11: Annual Compensation of Part-Time Administrators by Church Setting

	Data Distribution*	CHURCH SETTING			
		Metro-politan city	Suburb of large city	Small town or rural city	Farming area
CHARACTERISTICS					
Average weekend worship attendance		369	466	283	-
Average church income		$442,690	$793,303	$479,042	-
Average # of years employed		5	5	6	-
Average # of paid vacation days		10	16	11	-
% College graduate or higher		53%	68%	57%	-
% Who receive auto reimbursement/allowance		18%	15%	15%	-
% Ordained		12%	9%	17%	-
% Supervise one or more people		47%	53%	55%	-
Average % salary increase (for those who had an increase) this year		-	4.8%	7.6%	-
HOURLY RATE					
Base Rate	Average	$15	$20	$15	-
COMPENSATION					
Base Salary	Median	$14,000	$24,000	$17,050	-
	Average	$19,140	$23,179	$18,449	-
Housing	Median	-	-	-	-
	Average	-	-	-	-
Parsonage	Median	-	-	-	-
	Average	-	-	-	-
Total Compensation	**Median**	$14,000	$24,000	$17,300	-
	Average	$19,140	$23,179	$19,609	-
BENEFITS					
Health Insurance	Median	-	-	-	-
	Average	-	-	-	-
Life Insurance	Median	-	-	-	-
	Average	-	-	-	-
Disability Insurance	Median	-	-	-	-
	Average	-	-	-	-
Retirement	Median	-	-	-	-
	Average	-	-	-	-
Continuing Education	Median	-	-	-	-
	Average	-	-	-	-
Total Benefits	**Median**	-	$2,280	$4,209	-
	Average	-	$3,901	$4,422	-
TOTAL COMPENSATION PLUS BENEFITS	**Median**	$14,000	$25,000	$18,000	-
	Average	$19,961	$23,743	$20,700	-
Number of Respondents		17	47	42	3

- Not enough response to provide meaningful data.

* For detailed description and definitions of Data Distribution (Median and Average), see chapter 1, Explanation of Data Distribution.

Table 12-12: Annual Compensation of Part-Time Administrators by Region

	Data Distribution*	New England	Middle Atlantic	South Atlantic	E-N Central	E-S Central	W-N Central	W-S Central	Mountain	Pacific
CHARACTERISTICS										
Average weekend worship attendance	-	-	516	233	469	-	309	-	331	398
Average church income	-	-	$657,509	$485,934	$828,271	-	$514,812	-	$499,927	$415,647
Average # of years employed	-	-	7	6	6	-	3	-	3	5
Average # of paid vacation days	-	-	7	12	19	-	12	-	11	13
% College graduate or higher	-	-	50%	63%	74%	-	50%	-	78%	44%
% Who receive auto reimbursement/allowance	-	-	8%	17%	11%	-	0%	-	0%	17%
% Ordained	-	-	0%	17%	11%	-	0%	-	11%	18%
% Supervise one or more people	-	-	50%	47%	67%	-	67%	-	56%	41%
Average % salary increase (for those who had an increase) this year	-	-	-	7.1%	6.3%	-	-	-	-	4.2%
HOURLY RATE										
Base Rate	Average	-	$20	$16	$17	-	$17	-	$16	$18
COMPENSATION										
Base Salary	Median	-	$19,500	$19,750	$21,500	-	$24,960	-	$15,184	$18,700
	Average	-	$19,434	$21,151	$22,755	-	$25,235	-	$14,695	$19,037
Housing	Median	-	-	-	-	-	-	-	-	-
	Average	-	-	-	-	-	-	-	-	-
Parsonage	Median	-	-	-	-	-	-	-	-	-
	Average	-	-	-	-	-	-	-	-	-
Total Compensation	**Median**	-	$19,500	$17,000	$21,500	-	$24,960	-	$15,184	$19,550
	Average	-	$19,434	$20,819	$24,597	-	$25,235	-	$14,695	$19,151
BENEFITS										
Health Insurance	Median	-	-	-	-	-	-	-	-	-
	Average	-	-	-	-	-	-	-	-	-
Life Insurance	Median	-	-	-	-	-	-	-	-	-
	Average	-	-	-	-	-	-	-	-	-
Disability Insurance	Median	-	-	-	-	-	-	-	-	-
	Average	-	-	-	-	-	-	-	-	-
Retirement	Median	-	-	-	-	-	-	-	-	-
	Average	-	-	-	-	-	-	-	-	-
Continuing Education	Median	-	-	-	-	-	-	-	-	-
	Average	-	-	-	-	-	-	-	-	-
Total Benefits	**Median**	-	-	-	-	-	-	-	-	-
	Average	-	-	-	-	-	-	-	-	-
TOTAL COMPENSATION PLUS BENEFITS	**Median**	-	$19,500	$17,000	$21,500	-	$24,960	-	$15,184	$22,524
	Average	-	$19,842	$21,227	$25,396	-	$26,189	-	$15,412	$20,688
Number of Respondents		4	12	30	19	1	12	5	9	18

- Not enough response to provide meaningful data.

* For detailed description and definitions of Data Distribution (Median and Average), see chapter 1, Explanation of Data Distribution.

Table 12-13: Annual Compensation of Part-Time Administrators by Education

	Data Distribution*	EDUCATION			
		Less than Bachelor	Bachelor	Master	Doctorate
CHARACTERISTICS					
Average weekend worship attendance		271	396	570	-
Average church income		$489,898	$641,485	$778,539	-
Average # of years employed		6	5	5	-
Average # of paid vacation days		11	15	11	-
% College graduate or higher		0%	100%	100%	-
% Who receive auto reimbursement/allowance		14%	11%	13%	-
% Ordained		7%	13%	13%	-
% Supervise one or more people		44%	58%	56%	-
Average % salary increase (for those who had an increase) this year		4.8%	6.6%	-	-
HOURLY RATE					
Base Rate	Average	$15	$19	$18	-
COMPENSATION					
Base Salary	Median	$17,500	$19,750	$22,500	-
	Average	$18,706	$22,943	$22,834	-
Housing	Median	-	-	-	-
	Average	-	-	-	-
Parsonage	Median	-	-	-	-
	Average	-	-	-	-
Total Compensation	**Median**	**$20,400**	**$19,100**	**$24,000**	-
	Average	**$19,133**	**$22,259**	**$23,834**	-
BENEFITS					
Health Insurance	Median	-	-	-	-
	Average	-	-	-	-
Life Insurance	Median	-	-	-	-
	Average	-	-	-	-
Disability Insurance	Median	-	-	-	-
	Average	-	-	-	-
Retirement	Median	-	-	-	-
	Average	-	-	-	-
Continuing Education	Median	-	-	-	-
	Average	-	-	-	-
Total Benefits	**Median**	**$1,280**	-	-	-
	Average	**$2,536**	-	-	-
TOTAL COMPENSATION PLUS BENEFITS	**Median**	**$21,500**	**$20,500**	**$24,000**	-
	Average	**$19,737**	**$23,196**	**$24,343**	-
Number of Respondents		43	45	16	6

- Not enough response to provide meaningful data.

* For detailed description and definitions of Data Distribution (Median and Average), see chapter 1, Explanation of Data Distribution.

Table 12-14: Annual Compensation of Part-Time Administrators by Years Employed

	Data Distribution*	YEARS EMPLOYED			
		Less than 6 years	6-10 years	11-15 years	Over 15 years
CHARACTERISTICS					
Average weekend worship attendance		390	314	355	-
Average church income		$593,491	$606,553	$475,455	-
Average # of years employed		3	7	13	-
Average # of paid vacation days		13	14	7	-
% College graduate or higher		67%	50%	45%	-
% Who receive auto reimbursement/allowance		13%	14%	18%	-
% Ordained		12%	18%	0%	-
% Supervise one or more people		53%	55%	50%	-
Average % salary increase (for those who had an increase) this year		6.7%	6.2%	-	-
HOURLY RATE					
Base Rate	Average	$18	$16	$14	-
COMPENSATION					
Base Salary	Median	$16,524	$22,570	$20,000	-
	Average	$19,836	$23,177	$18,475	-
Housing	Median	-	-	-	-
	Average	-	-	-	-
Parsonage	Median	-	-	-	-
	Average	-	-	-	-
Total Compensation	**Median**	**$16,848**	**$22,101**	**$20,000**	**-**
	Average	**$20,207**	**$23,948**	**$18,475**	**-**
BENEFITS					
Health Insurance	Median	-	-	-	-
	Average	-	-	-	-
Life Insurance	Median	-	-	-	-
	Average	-	-	-	-
Disability Insurance	Median	-	-	-	-
	Average	-	-	-	-
Retirement	Median	-	-	-	-
	Average	-	-	-	-
Continuing Education	Median	-	-	-	-
	Average	-	-	-	-
Total Benefits	**Median**	**$4,429**	**-**	**-**	**-**
	Average	**$5,474**	**-**	**-**	**-**
TOTAL COMPENSATION PLUS BENEFITS	**Median**	**$18,000**	**$23,785**	**$20,000**	**-**
	Average	**$20,821**	**$25,418**	**$18,828**	**-**
Number of Respondents		69	22	11	4

- Not enough response to provide meaningful data.

* For detailed description and definitions of Data Distribution (Median and Average), see chapter 1, Explanation of Data Distribution.

Table 12-15: Annual Compensation of Part-Time Administrators by Denomination

CHARACTERISTICS	Data Distribution*	Assemblies of God	Baptist	Independent/ Nondenom.	Lutheran	Methodist	Presby- terian
Average weekend worship attendance		246	408	312	-	-	274
Average church income		$448,750	$777,858	$351,859	-	-	$628,699
Average # of years employed		10	4	4	-	-	6
Average # of paid vacation days		12	12	11	-	-	14
% College graduate or higher		38%	48%	50%	-	-	90%
% Who receive auto reimbursement/allowance		50%	22%	4%	-	-	10%
% Ordained		25%	18%	13%	-	-	0%
% Supervise one or more people		75%	70%	38%	-	-	44%
Average % salary increase (for those who had an increase) this year		-	5.8%	-	-	-	-
HOURLY RATE							
Base Rate	Average	-	$21	$14	-	-	$17
COMPENSATION							
Base Salary	Median	$22,250	$24,960	$14,200	-	-	$18,000
	Average	$19,751	$23,887	$16,184	-	-	$21,580
Housing	Median	-	-	-	-	-	-
	Average	-	-	-	-	-	-
Parsonage	Median	-	-	-	-	-	-
	Average	-	-	-	-	-	-
Total Compensation	**Median**	**$22,250**	**$26,650**	**$14,000**	**-**	**-**	**$18,000**
	Average	**$19,751**	**$25,364**	**$16,011**	**-**	**-**	**$21,580**
BENEFITS							
Health Insurance	Median	-	-	-	-	-	-
	Average	-	-	-	-	-	-
Life Insurance	Median	-	-	-	-	-	-
	Average	-	-	-	-	-	-
Disability Insurance	Median	-	-	-	-	-	-
	Average	-	-	-	-	-	-
Retirement	Median	-	-	-	-	-	-
	Average	-	-	-	-	-	-
Continuing Education	Median	-	-	-	-	-	-
	Average	-	-	-	-	-	-
Total Benefits	**Median**	**-**	**-**	**-**	**-**	**-**	**-**
	Average	**-**	**-**	**-**	**-**	**-**	**-**
TOTAL COMPENSATION PLUS BENEFITS	**Median**	**$22,250**	**$27,512**	**$14,000**	**-**	**-**	**$18,000**
	Average	**$20,417**	**$25,819**	**$16,788**	**-**	**-**	**$22,429**
Number of Respondents		8	23	24	3	1	10

- Not enough response to provide meaningful data.

* For detailed description and definitions of Data Distribution (Median and Average), see chapter 1, Explanation of Data Distribution.

Table 12-16: Annual Compensation of Part-Time Administrators by Gender

	Data Distribution*	GENDER	
		Male	Female
CHARACTERISTICS			
Average weekend worship attendance		331	385
Average church income		$563,707	$610,649
Average # of years employed		4	6
Average # of paid vacation days		14	13
% College graduate or higher		71%	56%
% Who receive auto reimbursement/allowance		31%	7%
% Ordained		24%	7%
% Supervise one or more people		60%	48%
Average % salary increase (for those who had an increase) this year		6.2%	5.6%
HOURLY RATE			
Base Rate	Average	$19	$16
COMPENSATION			
Base Salary	Median	$17,500	$20,000
	Average	$20,101	$20,981
Housing	Median	-	-
	Average	-	-
Parsonage	Median	-	-
	Average	-	-
Total Compensation	**Median**	**$18,000**	**$20,000**
	Average	**$21,332**	**$20,981**
BENEFITS			
Health Insurance	Median	-	-
	Average	-	-
Life Insurance	Median	-	-
	Average	-	-
Disability Insurance	Median	-	-
	Average	-	-
Retirement	Median	-	-
	Average	-	-
Continuing Education	Median	-	-
	Average	-	-
Total Benefits	**Median**	**$3,440**	**$2,800**
	Average	**$3,784**	**$4,564**
TOTAL COMPENSATION PLUS BENEFITS	**Median**	**$21,960**	**$21,000**
	Average	**$22,413**	**$21,616**
Number of Respondents		35	75

- Not enough response to provide meaningful data.

* For detailed description and definitions of Data Distribution (Median and Average), see chapter 1, Explanation of Data Distribution.

Full-Time Administrator Worksheet

	Enter your church data below	The 2014–2015 Compensation Handbook for Church Staff		Enter *Compensation Handbook* data below			
				Highest 25%	Median	Lowest 25%	Average
Church Income	$	Table 12-1	page 199	$	$	$	$
Worship Attendance		Table 12-2	page 200	n/a	$	n/a	$
Church Setting (metro, suburb, small town, or farming area)		Table 12-3	page 201	n/a	$	n/a	$
Region		Table 12-4	page 202	n/a	$	n/a	$
Person's Education		Table 12-5	page 203	n/a	$	n/a	$
Years Employed		Table 12-6	page 204	n/a	$	n/a	$
Denomination (if applicable)		Table 12-7	page 205	n/a	$	n/a	$

Looking at the table and page number references indicated in the *2014–2015 Compensation Handbook for Church Staff* columns above, locate the appropriate range for your church. Refer to the instructions below for step-by-step help.

FILLING OUT THE WORKSHEET

1. Fill in the gray boxes under *Enter your church data* with your church demographic information as follows:

   ▶ **Income** (Total annual church budget in past year)
   ▶ **Worship attendance** (Number of people, including children, who attend all weekend services)
   ▶ **Church setting** (Metropolitan city, suburb of large city, small town or rural city, or farming area)

   ▶ **Region** (Locate your state's region in the appendix on page 346.)
   ▶ **Education** (Highest level of education: less than bachelor, bachelor, master, or doctorate)

2. Use Table 12-1 (page 199) in your *2014–2015 Compensation Handbook for Church Staff* to enter data pertinent to your church. In the heading (top row), locate your church **income** from the five available ranges. Follow that column to the bottom rows, and copy the *Highest 25%*, *Median*, *Lowest 25%*, and *Average* amounts onto your worksheet.

3. Use Table 12-2 (page 200) on your *2014–2015 Compensation Handbook for Church Staff* to enter data pertinent to your church. In the heading (top row), locate your church's

worship attendance from the six available ranges. Follow that column to the bottom rows, and copy the *Median* and *Average* amounts onto your worksheet.

4. Use Table 12-3 (page 201) on your *2014–2015 Compensation Handbook for Church Staff* to enter data pertinent to your church. In the heading (top row), choose the **church setting** that best describes your church. Follow that column to the bottom rows, and copy the *Median* and *Average* amounts onto your worksheet.

5. Use Table 12-4 (page 202) on your *2014–2015 Compensation Handbook for Church Staff* to enter data pertinent to your church. In the heading (top row), look for the **region** where your church is located. Follow that column to the bottom rows, and copy the *Median* and *Average* amounts onto your worksheet.

6. Use Table 12-5 (page 203) on your *2014–2015 Compensation Handbook for Church Staff* to enter data pertinent to your Administrator. In the heading (top row), look for **your Administrator's highest level of education**. Follow that column to the bottom rows, and copy the *Median* and *Average* amounts onto your worksheet.

7. Use Table 12-6 (page 204) on your *2014–2015 Compensation Handbook for Church Staff* to enter data pertinent to your Administrator. In the heading (top row), locate the **number of years your Administrator has been employed**. Follow that column to the bottom rows, and copy the *Median* and *Average* amounts onto your worksheet.

8. Use Table 12-7 (page 205) on your *2014–2015 Compensation Handbook for Church Staff* to enter data pertinent to your church. In the heading (top row), look for **your church's denominational affiliation**. Follow that column to the bottom rows, and copy the *Median* and *Average* amounts onto your worksheet. If your church is not affiliated with a denomination, leave this section blank.

DETERMINING COMPENSATION

This tool will not provide you with a single compensation amount but rather with a range of values to help you determine the compensation appropriate to your situation.

1. Look at the values in the shaded *Median* column. Circle the **lowest** and the **highest** values. **This is the range of the median compensation plus benefits for churches similar to yours.**

2. For a variety of reasons, compensation plus benefits may be higher or lower than the range established in this table. Income and attendance are two significant factors affecting church compensation packages. If church income or attendance skews higher, you might want to consider moving toward or above the higher end of the range. Likewise, if church income or attendance skews lower, you may consider moving the package toward or below the lower end of the range.

3. Examine additional variables that might impact the compensation package you offer, such as years of service, education, and church setting.

4. Determine other circumstances unique to your situation, such as cost of living in your area, theological beliefs, pastoral performance, financial needs, the local economy, personal motivation, congregational goals, and others.

5. You now have a compensation package range based on the *2014–2015 Compensation Handbook*. Since each church and position are unique, your final compensation package will be based on additional factors unique to your situation.

Part-Time Administrator Worksheet

	Enter your church data below	The 2014–2015 Compensation Handbook for Church Staff		Enter *Compensation Handbook* data below			
				Highest 25%	Median	Lowest 25%	Average
Church Income	$	Table 12-9	page 207	$	$	$	$
Worship Attendance		Table 12-10	page 208	n/a	$	n/a	$
Church Setting (metro, suburb, small town, or farming area)		Table 12-11	page 209	n/a	$	n/a	$
Region		Table 12-12	page 210	n/a	$	n/a	$
Person's Education		Table 12-13	page 211	n/a	$	n/a	$
Years Employed		Table 12-14	page 212	n/a	$	n/a	$
Denomination (if applicable)		Table 12-15	page 213	n/a	$	n/a	$

Looking at the table and page number references indicated in the *2014–2015 Compensation Handbook for Church Staff* columns above, locate the appropriate range for your church. Refer to the instructions below for step-by-step help.

FILLING OUT THE WORKSHEET

1. Fill in the gray boxes under *Enter your church data* with your church demographic information as follows:

   ▶ **Income** (Total annual church budget in past year)
   ▶ **Worship attendance** (Number of people, including children, who attend all weekend services)
   ▶ **Church setting** (Metropolitan city, suburb of large city, small town or rural city, or farming area)

   ▶ **Region** (Locate your state's region in the appendix on page 346.)
   ▶ **Education** (Highest level of education: less than bachelor, bachelor, master, or doctorate)

2. Use Table 12-9 (page 207) in your *2014–2015 Compensation Handbook for Church Staff* to enter data pertinent to your church. In the heading (top row), locate your church **income** from the five available ranges. Follow that column to the bottom rows, and copy the *Highest 25%*, *Median*, *Lowest 25%*, and *Average* amounts onto your worksheet.

3. Use Table 12-10 (page 208) on your *2014–2015 Compensation Handbook for Church Staff* to enter data pertinent to your church. In the heading (top row), locate your church's

worship attendance from the six available ranges. Follow that column to the bottom rows, and copy the *Median* and *Average* amounts onto your worksheet.

4. Use Table 12-11 (page 209) on your *2014–2015 Compensation Handbook for Church Staff* to enter data pertinent to your church. In the heading (top row), choose the **church setting** that best describes your church. Follow that column to the bottom rows, and copy the *Median* and *Average* amounts onto your worksheet.

5. Use Table 12-12 (page 210) on your *2014–2015 Compensation Handbook for Church Staff* to enter data pertinent to your church. In the heading (top row), look for the **region** where your church is located. Follow that column to the bottom rows, and copy the *Median* and *Average* amounts onto your worksheet.

6. Use Table 12-13 (page 211) on your *2014–2015 Compensation Handbook for Church Staff* to enter data pertinent to your Administrator. In the heading (top row), look for **your Administrator's highest level of education**. Follow that column to the bottom rows, and copy the *Median* and *Average* amounts onto your worksheet.

7. Use Table 12-14 (page 212) on your *2014–2015 Compensation Handbook for Church Staff* to enter data pertinent to your Administrator. In the heading (top row), locate the **number of years your Administrator has been employed**. Follow that column to the bottom rows, and copy the *Median* and *Average* amounts onto your worksheet.

8. Use Table 12-15 (page 213) on your *2014–2015 Compensation Handbook for Church Staff* to enter data pertinent to your church. In the heading (top row), look for **your church's denominational affiliation**. Follow that column to the bottom rows, and copy the *Median* and *Average* amounts onto your worksheet. If your church is not affiliated with a denomination, leave this section blank.

DETERMINING COMPENSATION

This tool will not provide you with a single compensation amount but rather with a range of values to help you determine the compensation appropriate to your situation.

1. Look at the values in the shaded *Median* column. Circle the **lowest** and the **highest** values. **This is the range of the median compensation plus benefits for churches similar to yours.**

2. For a variety of reasons, compensation plus benefits may be higher or lower than the range established in this table. Income and attendance are two significant factors affecting church compensation packages. If church income or attendance skews higher, you might want to consider moving toward or above the higher end of the range. Likewise, if church income or attendance skews lower, you may consider moving the package toward or below the lower end of the range.

3. Examine additional variables that might impact the compensation package you offer, such as years of service, education, and church setting.

4. Determine other circumstances unique to your situation, such as cost of living in your area, theological beliefs, pastoral performance, financial needs, the local economy, personal motivation, congregational goals, and others.

5. You now have a compensation package range based on the *2014–2015 Compensation Handbook*. Since each church and position are unique, your final compensation package will be based on additional factors unique to your situation.

13

BOOKKEEPERS/ ACCOUNTANTS

Employment Profile

Bookkeepers/Accountants include paid personnel who assist with day-to-day financial matters in the church. This category may include such positions as Accountant, Controller, Financial Administrative Assistant, Financial Secretary, Payroll Secretary, Treasurer, etc.

Six in 10 Bookkeeper/Accountant positions reported are part-time. In general, most Bookkeepers/

Accountants are female and are employed by the church rather than self-employed. About half of full- and part-time Bookkeepers/Accountants have a minimum of a bachelor's degree.

The chart below provides a demographic profile of this sample.

	Full-Time	Part-Time
Number of respondents	**202**	**304**
Ordained	4%	3%
Average years employed	11	9
Male	11%	17%
Female	89%	83%
Self-employed (receives 1099)	0	8%
Church employee (receives W-2)	100%	92%
High school diploma	27%	24%
Associate degree	27%	22%
Bachelor's degree	39%	47%
Master's degree	8%	7%
Doctoral degree	0%	0%

Total Compensation plus Benefits Package Analysis

The following analyses are based on data in the tables you will find later in this chapter. The tables show compensation plus benefits data for full-time and part-time Bookkeepers/Accountants and are presented according to church income, church attendance, church setting, region, education, years employed, denomination, and gender. In this way, the compensation plus benefits of Bookkeepers/Accountants can be analyzed and compared from a variety of useful perspectives.

The total compensation plus benefits amount includes the base salary; housing allowance and/

or parsonage amount; health, life, and disability insurance payments; retirement contribution; and educational funds.

A worksheet at the end of this chapter is provided to help you apply the data to your church's situation.

Nearly all full-time Bookkeepers/Accountants receive paid vacation. More than half receive health insurance benefits and salary increases. Few part-time Bookkeepers/Accountants reported fringe benefits other than paid vacation, which more than four in 10 of those reporting receive.

Compensation Plus Benefits	Full-Time	Part-Time
Base Salary	100%	99%
Housing	2%	2%
Parsonage	0%	1%
Health Insurance*	52%	5%
Life Insurance*	33%	2%
Disability Insurance*	25%	3%
Retirement	49%	11%
Continuing Education	9%	5%
Received salary increase	56%	47%
Received paid vacation	98%	42%
Received auto reimbursement/allowance	23%	10%

Only those reporting individual premiums for Health, Life, or Disability (not total insurance premiums) are included.

221

KEY POINTS

* Larger churches are more likely to employ full-time financial assistants, while small churches account for more than half of part-time positions. Nearly six in 10 full-time Bookkeepers/Accountants serve in churches with an income of more than $1,000,000 and more than 500 in worship attendance. More than six in 10 part-time Bookkeepers/Accountants serve in churches with an income of $750,000 or less.

* In general, as church income, church attendance, and the staff member's education level increase, compensation and benefits for full-time Bookkeepers/Accountants also increase.

* Full-time Bookkeepers/Accountants serving in churches in a suburb of a large city or in a metropolitan city have higher compensation and benefits packages compared to those serving in small towns.

Compensation & Benefits: National Averages for Full-Time Bookkeepers/Accountants	
2000	$27,992
2001	$29,220
2002	$29,398
2003	$30,457
2004	$32,765
2005	$33,336
2006	$36,122
2007	$38,185
2008	$37,631
2009	$38,809
2011	$41,207
2013	$43,214*

The above trend is made available for your reference only. In addition to looking at this overall data, please refer to the detailed tables using your church's income, attendance, setting, region, and denomination as well as the person's education, gender, and years employed for guidance in compensating this position.

Table 13-1: Annual Compensation of Full-Time Bookkeepers/Accountants by Church Income

CHARACTERISTICS	Data Distribution*	CHURCH INCOME				
		$250K & Under	$251-$500K	$501-$750K	$751K-$1M	Over $1 Million
Average weekend worship attendance		-	211	381	529	1,445
Average church income		-	$385,031	$640,020	$906,191	$2,625,057
Average # of years employed		-	11	18	11	10
Average # of paid vacation days		-	16	18	16	16
% College graduate or higher		-	27%	21%	48%	56%
% Who receive auto reimbursement/allowance		-	18%	26%	24%	23%
% Ordained		-	14%	4%	0%	3%
% Supervise one or more people		-	45%	48%	41%	50%
Average % salary increase (for those who had an increase) this year		-	4.1%	3.4%	2.7%	3.4%
COMPENSATION						
Base Salary	Highest 25%	-	$33,199	$36,596	$38,835	$47,000
	Median	-	$29,500	$32,428	$34,013	$40,000
	Lowest 25%	-	$22,552	$28,500	$27,957	$35,000
	Average	-	$29,282	$32,070	$34,775	$43,090
Housing	Highest 25%	-	-	-	-	-
	Median	-	-	-	-	-
	Lowest 25%	-	-	-	-	-
	Average	-	-	-	-	-
Parsonage	Highest 25%	-	-	-	-	-
	Median	-	-	-	-	-
	Lowest 25%	-	-	-	-	-
	Average	-	-	-	-	-
Total Compensation	**Highest 25%**	-	$33,800	$36,596	$38,835	$48,000
	Median	-	$31,113	$32,428	$34,013	$40,131
	Lowest 25%	-	$23,500	$28,500	$27,957	$35,000
	Average	-	$31,372	$32,070	$34,775	$43,400
BENEFITS						
Health Insurance	Highest 25%	-	-	$8,400	$10,300	$9,670
	Median	-	-	$5,783	$7,080	$5,803
	Lowest 25%	-	-	$3,727	$3,750	$3,800
	Average	-	-	$6,235	$7,111	$6,907
Life Insurance	Highest 25%	-	-	-	-	$409
	Median	-	-	-	-	$156
	Lowest 25%	-	-	-	-	$57
	Average	-	-	-	-	$272
Disability Insurance	Highest 25%	-	-	-	-	$392
	Median	-	-	-	-	$240
	Lowest 25%	-	-	-	-	$175
	Average	-	-	-	-	$336
Retirement	Highest 25%	-	-	$1,541	$2,880	$3,340
	Median	-	-	$1,300	$1,793	$2,087
	Lowest 25%	-	-	$1,000	$1,260	$1,410
	Average	-	-	$1,655	$2,210	$2,289
Continuing Education	Highest 25%	-	-	-	-	$1,750
	Median	-	-	-	-	$1,100
	Lowest 25%	-	-	-	-	$500
	Average	-	-	-	-	$1,230
Total Benefits	**Highest 25%**	-	$5,400	$7,800	$9,200	$10,869
	Median	-	$3,336	$4,941	$5,719	$6,011
	Lowest 25%	-	$2,436	$1,000	$3,600	$2,325
	Average	-	$3,644	$5,350	$6,620	$7,298
TOTAL COMPENSATION PLUS BENEFITS	**Highest 25%**	-	$35,336	$41,808	$44,200	$54,921
	Median	-	$32,386	$35,438	$39,600	$45,363
	Lowest 25%	-	$27,300	$30,201	$33,000	$39,030
	Average	-	$32,933	$36,082	$38,370	$48,915
Number of Respondents		6	22	28	29	111

- Not enough response to provide meaningful data.

* For detailed description and definitions of Data Distribution (Highest 25%, Median, Lowest 25%, and Average), see chapter 1, Explanation of Data Distribution.

Table 13-2: Annual Compensation of Full-Time Bookkeepers/Accountants by Worship Attendance

	Data Distribution*	WORSHIP ATTENDANCE					
		100 or less	101-300	301-500	501-750	751-1,000	Over 1,000
CHARACTERISTICS							
Average weekend worship attendance	-		223	420	627	896	2,285
Average church income	-		$536,146	$942,553	$1,291,346	$1,708,043	$3,804,985
Average # of years employed	-		13	11	15	10	9
Average # of paid vacation days	-		17	16	17	17	16
% College graduate or higher	-		30%	49%	45%	36%	63%
% Who receive auto reimbursement/allowance	-		24%	29%	13%	21%	26%
% Ordained	-		10%	0%	0%	4%	4%
% Supervise one or more people	-		39%	49%	47%	40%	57%
Average % salary increase (for those who had an increase) this year	-		3.7%	2.7%	4.0%	3.1%	3.4%
COMPENSATION							
Base Salary	Median	-	$31,113	$33,250	$37,633	$34,900	$44,000
	Average	-	$30,022	$36,301	$38,436	$36,562	$47,265
Housing	Median	-	-	-	-	-	-
	Average	-	-	-	-	-	-
Parsonage	Median	-	-	-	-	-	-
	Average	-	-	-	-	-	-
Total Compensation	**Median**	-	**$32,193**	**$33,250**	**$37,633**	**$35,000**	**$44,500**
	Average	-	**$31,138**	**$36,301**	**$38,436**	**$37,562**	**$47,547**
BENEFITS							
Health Insurance	Median	-	$5,124	$5,018	$7,500	$5,981	$5,623
	Average	-	$6,464	$6,057	$7,212	$6,526	$7,030
Life Insurance	Median	-	-	-	$100	$200	$200
	Average	-	-	-	$338	$256	$274
Disability Insurance	Median	-	-	-	-	$305	$232
	Average	-	-	-	-	$349	$456
Retirement	Median	-	$1,793	$2,000	$1,590	$2,220	$2,249
	Average	-	$2,241	$2,438	$1,706	$2,279	$2,326
Continuing Education	Median	-	-	-	-	-	-
	Average	-	-	-	-	-	-
Total Benefits	**Median**	-	**$4,941**	**$4,100**	**$6,346**	**$5,550**	**$6,204**
	Average	-	**$5,933**	**$5,498**	**$6,512**	**$6,958**	**$7,589**
TOTAL COMPENSATION PLUS BENEFITS	**Median**	-	**$33,820**	**$35,890**	**$43,075**	**$39,974**	**$50,795**
	Average	-	**$34,550**	**$39,110**	**$42,397**	**$42,849**	**$54,034**
Number of Respondents		4	41	36	38	25	55

- Not enough response to provide meaningful data.

* For detailed description and definitions of Data Distribution (Median and Average), see chapter 1, Explanation of Data Distribution.

Table 13-3: Annual Compensation of Full-Time Bookkeepers/Accountants by Church Setting

	Data Distribution*	CHURCH SETTING			
		Metro-politan city	Suburb of large city	Small town or rural city	Farming area
CHARACTERISTICS					
Average weekend worship attendance		928	1,481	565	-
Average church income		$2,026,203	$2,402,185	$1,016,258	-
Average # of years employed		9	10	13	-
Average # of paid vacation days		15	17	17	-
% College graduate or higher		73%	41%	38%	-
% Who receive auto reimbursement/allowance		14%	21%	31%	-
% Ordained		4%	4%	3%	-
% Supervise one or more people		36%	53%	46%	-
Average % salary increase (for those who had an increase) this year		2.7%	3.3%	3.7%	-
COMPENSATION					
Base Salary	Median	$39,396	$38,453	$33,000	-
	Average	$41,018	$42,084	$33,270	-
Housing	Median	-	-	-	-
	Average	-	-	-	-
Parsonage	Median	-	-	-	-
	Average	-	-	-	-
Total Compensation	**Median**	**$39,396**	**$38,750**	**$33,046**	**-**
	Average	**$41,229**	**$42,422**	**$33,969**	**-**
BENEFITS					
Health Insurance	Median	$5,410	$5,268	$6,153	-
	Average	$6,091	$6,641	$6,937	-
Life Insurance	Median	$144	$275	$122	-
	Average	$230	$404	$234	-
Disability Insurance	Median	$245	$300	$305	-
	Average	$240	$443	$574	-
Retirement	Median	$2,024	$1,808	$1,929	-
	Average	$2,188	$2,136	$2,227	-
Continuing Education	Median	-	-	$500	-
	Average	-	-	$722	-
Total Benefits	**Median**	**$3,988**	**$5,400**	**$6,004**	**-**
	Average	**$5,556**	**$6,739**	**$7,137**	**-**
TOTAL COMPENSATION PLUS BENEFITS	**Median**	**$43,016**	**$44,315**	**$39,200**	**-**
	Average	**$44,329**	**$46,799**	**$39,160**	**-**
Number of Respondents		45	75	78	1

- Not enough response to provide meaningful data.

* For detailed description and definitions of Data Distribution (Median and Average), see chapter 1, Explanation of Data Distribution.

Table 13-4: Annual Compensation of Full-Time Bookkeepers/Accountants by Region

	Data Distribution*	New England	Middle Atlantic	South Atlantic	E-N Central	E-S Central	W-N Central	W-S Central	Mountain	Pacific
CHARACTERISTICS										
Average weekend worship attendance	-	1,053	887	1,821	663	500	812	1,187	862
Average church income	-	$2,106,872	$1,836,018	$2,369,438	$1,307,470	$831,820	$1,667,253	$2,000,800	$1,669,854
Average # of years employed	-	12	10	11	11	11	11	19	9
Average # of paid vacation days	-	20	16	17	14	19	16	16	16
% College graduate or higher	-	40%	47%	42%	43%	46%	51%	60%	44%
% Who receive auto reimbursement/allowance	-	0%	31%	16%	26%	38%	28%	31%	8%
% Ordained	-	0%	5%	0%	0%	0%	8%	7%	4%
% Supervise one or more people	-	30%	58%	53%	23%	75%	36%	36%	50%
Average % salary increase (for those who had an increase) this year	-	3.3%	3.0%	2.9%	4.3%	4.3%	3.1%	3.6%	3.2%
COMPENSATION										
Base Salary	Median	-	$36,450	$38,000	$36,732	$33,250	$36,000	$35,449	$37,000	$39,868
	Average	-	$37,478	$39,470	$39,948	$32,430	$37,178	$35,956	$38,593	$44,034
Housing	Median	-	-	-	-	-	-	-	-	-
	Average	-	-	-	-	-	-	-	-	-
Parsonage	Median	-	-	-	-	-	-	-	-	-
	Average	-	-	-	-	-	-	-	-	-
Total Compensation	**Median**	-	**$36,450**	**$38,000**	**$36,732**	**$33,914**	**$36,000**	**$35,630**	**$37,000**	**$39,868**
	Average	-	**$37,478**	**$39,830**	**$39,948**	**$33,886**	**$37,178**	**$37,037**	**$38,593**	**$44,034**
BENEFITS										
Health Insurance	Median	-	-	$5,769	$6,355	$5,300	-	$5,378	$10,000	$4,500
	Average	-	-	$6,306	$8,903	$5,465	-	$5,655	$9,306	$5,121
Life Insurance	Median	-	-	$252	$217	-	-	$89	-	$70
	Average	-	-	$447	$257	-	-	$186	-	$139
Disability Insurance	Median	-	-	$380	$233	-	-	$300	-	$259
	Average	-	-	$782	$235	-	-	$371	-	$259
Retirement	Median	-	-	$2,000	$2,298	$1,504	-	$2,450	-	$1,470
	Average	-	-	$2,219	$2,294	$2,049	-	$2,574	-	$2,438
Continuing Education	Median	-	-	-	-	-	-	-	-	-
	Average	-	-	-	-	-	-	-	-	-
Total Benefits	**Median**	-	-	**$6,842**	**$5,839**	**$3,975**	**$2,528**	**$4,941**	**$8,500**	**$3,648**
	Average	-	-	**$6,836**	**$9,151**	**$5,641**	**$3,970**	**$5,696**	**$8,676**	**$4,804**
TOTAL COMPENSATION PLUS BENEFITS	**Median**	-	**$42,725**	**$41,646**	**$38,049**	**$35,053**	**$39,140**	**$39,883**	**$44,062**	**$43,075**
	Average	-	**$43,279**	**$45,394**	**$45,852**	**$37,732**	**$39,926**	**$41,194**	**$44,955**	**$44,516**
Number of Respondents		4	10	43	31	23	13	37	15	26

- Not enough response to provide meaningful data.

* For detailed description and definitions of Data Distribution (Median and Average), see chapter 1, Explanation of Data Distribution.

Table 13-5: Annual Compensation of Full-Time Bookkeepers/Accountants by Education

	Data Distribution*	EDUCATION			
		Less than Bachelor	Bachelor	Master	Doctorate
CHARACTERISTICS					
Average weekend worship attendance		864	1,125	1,242	-
Average church income		$1,514,240	$2,067,881	$2,046,867	-
Average # of years employed		13	10	6	-
Average # of paid vacation days		17	17	13	-
% College graduate or higher		0%	100%	100%	-
% Who receive auto reimbursement/allowance		22%	24%	20%	-
% Ordained		5%	1%	7%	-
% Supervise one or more people		46%	45%	60%	-
Average % salary increase (for those who had an increase) this year		3.3%	3.4%	3.3%	-
COMPENSATION					
Base Salary	Median	$35,000	$39,500	$43,200	-
	Average	$35,087	$41,382	$47,391	-
Housing	Median	-	-	-	-
	Average	-	-	-	-
Parsonage	Median	-	-	-	-
	Average	-	-	-	-
Total Compensation	**Median**	**$35,050**	**$39,500**	**$45,000**	**-**
	Average	**$35,792**	**$41,382**	**$48,424**	**-**
BENEFITS					
Health Insurance	Median	$5,773	$5,574	$6,807	-
	Average	$6,189	$6,904	$8,579	-
Life Insurance	Median	$144	$153	-	-
	Average	$347	$262	-	-
Disability Insurance	Median	$288	$275	-	-
	Average	$378	$315	-	-
Retirement	Median	$1,869	$1,869	$2,690	-
	Average	$2,189	$2,189	$2,770	-
Continuing Education	Median	$500	-	-	-
	Average	$778	-	-	-
Total Benefits	**Median**	**$6,048**	**$4,529**	**$7,714**	**-**
	Average	**$6,406**	**$6,413**	**$8,637**	**-**
TOTAL COMPENSATION PLUS BENEFITS	**Median**	**$39,647**	**$43,998**	**$55,170**	**-**
	Average	**$39,962**	**$46,342**	**$52,591**	**-**
Number of Respondents		107	77	15	0

- Not enough response to provide meaningful data.

* For detailed description and definitions of Data Distribution (Median and Average), see chapter 1, Explanation of Data Distribution.

Table 13-6: Annual Compensation of Full-Time Bookkeepers/Accountants by Years Employed

	Data Distribution*	YEARS EMPLOYED			
		Less than 6 years	6-10 years	11-15 years	Over 15 years
CHARACTERISTICS					
Average weekend worship attendance		1,179	1,143	815	762
Average church income		$2,087,712	$1,736,382	$1,536,590	$1,670,156
Average # of years employed		3	8	13	24
Average # of paid vacation days		13	17	19	19
% College graduate or higher		54%	47%	47%	36%
% Who receive auto reimbursement/allowance		22%	23%	27%	24%
% Ordained		7%	4%	3%	0%
% Supervise one or more people		41%	49%	56%	39%
Average % salary increase (for those who had an increase) this year		3.3%	3.7%	4.0%	2.6%
COMPENSATION					
Base Salary	Median	$36,393	$38,500	$35,000	$34,484
	Average	$37,888	$38,986	$39,914	$37,245
Housing	Median	-	-	-	-
	Average	-	-	-	-
Parsonage	Median	-	-	-	-
	Average	-	-	-	-
Total Compensation	**Median**	**$36,393**	**$38,500**	**$35,911**	**$34,484**
	Average	**$38,414**	**$38,986**	**$41,931**	**$37,245**
BENEFITS					
Health Insurance	Median	$5,510	$5,605	$4,328	$7,472
	Average	$5,375	$6,622	$6,520	$8,167
Life Insurance	Median	$96	$144	$183	$300
	Average	$219	$332	$333	$360
Disability Insurance	Median	$324	$223	-	$300
	Average	$644	$317	-	$296
Retirement	Median	$1,969	$2,000	$1,590	$2,000
	Average	$2,131	$2,267	$1,968	$2,144
Continuing Education	Median	-	-	-	-
	Average	-	-	-	-
Total Benefits	**Median**	**$4,529**	**$6,048**	**$5,000**	**$6,220**
	Average	**$5,491**	**$6,693**	**$6,534**	**$7,578**
TOTAL COMPENSATION PLUS BENEFITS	**Median**	**$39,883**	**$42,108**	**$41,600**	**$41,466**
	Average	**$41,490**	**$43,489**	**$46,006**	**$42,846**
Number of Respondents		58	55	34	46

- Not enough response to provide meaningful data.

* For detailed description and definitions of Data Distribution (Median and Average), see chapter 1, Explanation of Data Distribution.

Table 13-7: Annual Compensation of Full-Time Bookkeepers/Accountants by Denomination

	Data Distribution*	DENOMINATION					
		Assemblies of God	Baptist	Independent/ Nondenom.	Lutheran	Methodist	Presby- terian
CHARACTERISTICS							
Average weekend worship attendance		920	860	1,355	-	812	522
Average church income		$1,494,407	$1,559,200	$2,221,851	-	$1,686,734	$1,797,773
Average # of years employed		12	11	12	-	10	12
Average # of paid vacation days		15	16	16	-	18	19
% College graduate or higher		29%	51%	41%	-	63%	50%
% Who receive auto reimbursement/allowance		20%	30%	12%	-	6%	31%
% Ordained		12%	2%	6%	-	0%	0%
% Supervise one or more people		35%	44%	51%	-	20%	56%
Average % salary increase (for those who had an increase) this year		3.3%	3.1%	3.5%	-	3.2%	3.4%
COMPENSATION							
Base Salary	Median	$35,100	$34,269	$38,000	-	$37,633	$38,135
	Average	$33,731	$34,603	$40,565	-	$39,137	$42,987
Housing	Median	-	-	-	-	-	-
	Average	-	-	-	-	-	-
Parsonage	Median	-	-	-	-	-	-
	Average	-	-	-	-	-	-
Total Compensation	**Median**	**$36,050**	**$34,269**	**$38,400**	**-**	**$37,633**	**$38,135**
	Average	**$35,814**	**$34,756**	**$41,467**	**-**	**$39,137**	**$42,987**
BENEFITS							
Health Insurance	Median	-	$5,938	$5,520	-	$6,425	-
	Average	-	$6,814	$6,799	-	$6,215	-
Life Insurance	Median	-	$200	$240	-	-	$210
	Average	-	$411	$284	-	-	$391
Disability Insurance	Median	-	$331	$220	-	-	-
	Average	-	$447	$533	-	-	-
Retirement	Median	-	$2,000	$1,554	-	$1,471	$2,150
	Average	-	$2,185	$1,922	-	$1,939	$2,402
Continuing Education	Median	-	$600	-	-	-	-
	Average	-	$678	-	-	-	-
Total Benefits	**Median**	**-**	**$6,107**	**$4,499**	**-**	**$5,802**	**$4,940**
	Average	**-**	**$6,624**	**$6,549**	**-**	**$6,067**	**$7,437**
TOTAL COMPENSATION PLUS BENEFITS	**Median**	**$36,050**	**$39,887**	**$42,000**	**-**	**$40,819**	**$44,522**
	Average	**$36,862**	**$40,099**	**$46,348**	**-**	**$43,687**	**$48,100**
Number of Respondents		17	62	51	1	16	16

- Not enough response to provide meaningful data.

* For detailed description and definitions of Data Distribution (Median and Average), see chapter 1, Explanation of Data Distribution.

Table 13-8: Annual Compensation of Full-Time Bookkeepers/Accountants by Gender

	Data Distribution*	GENDER	
		Male	Female
CHARACTERISTICS			
Average weekend worship attendance		1,095	931
Average church income		$1,913,543	$1,709,810
Average # of years employed		7	12
Average # of paid vacation days		15	17
% College graduate or higher		62%	45%
% Who receive auto reimbursement/allowance		19%	23%
% Ordained		5%	3%
% Supervise one or more people		62%	44%
Average % salary increase (for those who had an increase) this year		2.4%	3.5%
COMPENSATION			
Base Salary	Median	$39,600	$36,000
	Average	$44,688	$37,631
Housing	Median	-	-
	Average	-	-
Parsonage	Median	-	-
	Average	-	-
Total Compensation	**Median**	**$39,600**	**$36,000**
	Average	**$44,974**	**$38,123**
BENEFITS			
Health Insurance	Median	$6,000	$5,758
	Average	$7,360	$6,606
Life Insurance	Median	-	$200
	Average	-	$308
Disability Insurance	Median	-	$288
	Average	-	$343
Retirement	Median	$2,097	$1,938
	Average	$2,250	$2,178
Continuing Education	Median	-	$600
	Average	-	$924
Total Benefits	**Median**	**$5,719**	**$5,400**
	Average	**$7,138**	**$6,586**
TOTAL COMPENSATION PLUS BENEFITS	**Median**	**$44,989**	**$41,014**
	Average	**$49,394**	**$42,568**
Number of Respondents		21	178

- Not enough response to provide meaningful data.

* For detailed description and definitions of Data Distribution (Median and Average), see chapter 1, Explanation of Data Distribution.

Table 13-9: Annual Compensation of Part-Time Bookkeepers/Accountants by Church Income

	Data Distribution*	CHURCH INCOME				
		$250K & Under	$251-$500K	$501-$750K	$751K-$1M	Over 1 Million
CHARACTERISTICS						
Average weekend worship attendance		115	233	340	425	1,069
Average church income		$143,487	$383,075	$607,198	$850,344	$1,939,492
Average # of years employed		10	9	7	8	8
Average # of paid vacation days		11	11	10	10	14
% College graduate or higher		36%	42%	71%	55%	74%
% Who receive auto reimbursement/allowance		5%	9%	11%	15%	13%
% Ordained		3%	1%	4%	3%	3%
% Supervise one or more people		15%	11%	15%	13%	23%
Average % salary increase (for those who had an increase) this year		4.4%	4.9%	4.6%	4.6%	3.0%
HOURLY RATE						
Base Rate	Average	$14	$15	$16	$16	$20
COMPENSATION						
Base Salary	Median	$5,200	$10,070	$12,100	$16,744	$22,724
	Average	$8,647	$11,767	$14,833	$16,653	$23,590
Housing	Median	-	-	-	-	-
	Average	-	-	-	-	-
Parsonage	Median	-	-	-	-	-
	Average	-	-	-	-	-
Total Compensation	**Median**	**$5,480**	**$10,140**	**$12,100**	**$16,744**	**$22,000**
	Average	**$9,425**	**$11,924**	**$14,833**	**$16,653**	**$23,372**
BENEFITS						
Health Insurance	Median	-	-	-	-	-
	Average	-	-	-	-	-
Life Insurance	Median	-	-	-	-	-
	Average	-	-	-	-	-
Disability Insurance	Median	-	-	-	-	-
	Average	-	-	-	-	-
Retirement	Median	-	-	-	-	$1,715
	Average	-	-	-	-	$1,605
Continuing Education	Median	-	-	-	-	-
	Average	-	-	-	-	-
Total Benefits	**Median**	-	-	-	-	**$1,430**
	Average	-	-	-	-	**$2,460**
TOTAL COMPENSATION PLUS BENEFITS	**Median**	**$5,480**	**$10,140**	**$12,100**	**$16,744**	**$22,000**
	Average	**$7,917**	**$12,091**	**$14,967**	**$17,045**	**$24,392**
Number of Respondents		66	74	48	41	69

- Not enough response to provide meaningful data.

* For detailed description and definitions of Data Distribution (Median and Average), see chapter 1, Explanation of Data Distribution.

Table 13-10: Annual Compensation of Part-Time Bookkeepers/Accountants by Worship Attendance

	Data Distribution*	WORSHIP ATTENDANCE					
		100 or less	101-300	301-500	501-750	751-1,000	Over 1,000
CHARACTERISTICS							
Average weekend worship attendance		72	209	402	623	887	2,042
Average church income		$339,654	$404,219	$831,025	$1,036,148	$1,630,381	$2,773,849
Average # of years employed		13	9	7	9	9	7
Average # of paid vacation days		12	10	11	14	13	15
% College graduate or higher		30%	49%	58%	68%	89%	71%
% Who receive auto reimbursement/allowance		5%	11%	7%	8%	17%	19%
% Ordained		0%	3%	6%	0%	6%	0%
% Supervise one or more people		14%	14%	14%	20%	11%	43%
Average % salary increase (for those who had an increase) this year		4.2%	4.9%	4.0%	3.6%	3.1%	3.4%
HOURLY RATE							
Base Rate	Average	$13	$16	$15	$17	$21	$21
COMPENSATION							
Base Salary	Median	$3,660	$11,200	$15,163	$14,760	$18,000	$27,250
	Average	$8,504	$12,673	$16,591	$15,182	$20,188	$28,417
Housing	Median	-	-	-	-	-	-
	Average	-	-	-	-	-	-
Parsonage	Median	-	-	-	-	-	-
	Average	-	-	-	-	-	-
Total Compensation	**Median**	**$4,350**	**$11,500**	**$14,872**	**$14,760**	**$18,295**	**$27,250**
	Average	**$9,511**	**$12,893**	**$16,555**	**$15,182**	**$20,100**	**$28,417**
BENEFITS							
Health Insurance	Median	-	-	-	-	-	-
	Average	-	-	-	-	-	-
Life Insurance	Median	-	-	-	-	-	-
	Average	-	-	-	-	-	-
Disability Insurance	Median	-	-	-	-	-	-
	Average	-	-	-	-	-	-
Retirement	Median	-	-	$1,200	-	-	-
	Average	-	-	$1,760	-	-	-
Continuing Education	Median	-	-	-	-	-	-
	Average	-	-	-	-	-	-
Total Benefits	**Median**	-	**$1,590**	**$762**	-	-	-
	Average	-	**$2,527**	**$1,923**	-	-	-
TOTAL COMPENSATION PLUS BENEFITS	**Median**	**$4,200**	**$11,500**	**$14,872**	**$14,760**	**$18,295**	**$27,456**
	Average	**$6,965**	**$13,051**	**$17,105**	**$15,407**	**$20,972**	**$29,758**
Number of Respondents		43	119	73	26	18	21

- Not enough response to provide meaningful data.

* For detailed description and definitions of Data Distribution (Median and Average), see chapter 1, Explanation of Data Distribution.

Table 13-11: Annual Compensation of Part-Time Bookkeepers/Accountants by Church Setting

	Data Distribution*	CHURCH SETTING			
		Metro-politan city	Suburb of large city	Small town or rural city	Farming area
CHARACTERISTICS					
Average weekend worship attendance		524	525	367	262
Average church income		$878,352	$1,104,884	$554,631	$408,447
Average # of years employed		9	8	9	9
Average # of paid vacation days		14	12	10	11
% College graduate or higher		69%	58%	47%	50%
% Who receive auto reimbursement/allowance		16%	13%	5%	14%
% Ordained		2%	3%	3%	0%
% Supervise one or more people		18%	19%	13%	21%
Average % salary increase (for those who had an increase) this year		5.4%	3.7%	4.3%	-
HOURLY RATE					
Base Rate	Average	$19	$17	$15	$15
COMPENSATION					
Base Salary	Median	$13,578	$16,100	$10,499	$9,663
	Average	$17,428	$18,266	$11,784	$11,836
Housing	Median	-	-	-	-
	Average	-	-	-	-
Parsonage	Median	-	-	-	-
	Average	-	-	-	-
Total Compensation	**Median**	**$12,789**	**$16,100**	**$10,920**	**$11,526**
	Average	**$17,291**	**$18,453**	**$12,128**	**$12,691**
BENEFITS					
Health Insurance	Median	-	-	-	-
	Average	-	-	-	-
Life Insurance	Median	-	-	-	-
	Average	-	-	-	-
Disability Insurance	Median	-	-	-	-
	Average	-	-	-	-
Retirement	Median	-	$1,690	$2,000	-
	Average	-	$2,116	$1,957	-
Continuing Education	Median	-	-	-	-
	Average	-	-	-	-
Total Benefits	**Median**	**$912**	**$1,515**	**$2,000**	**-**
	Average	**$1,984**	**$2,350**	**$2,398**	**-**
TOTAL COMPENSATION PLUS BENEFITS	**Median**	**$12,789**	**$15,500**	**$11,248**	**$11,526**
	Average	**$17,742**	**$18,223**	**$12,411**	**$12,730**
Number of Respondents		44	110	135	14

- Not enough response to provide meaningful data.

* For detailed description and definitions of Data Distribution (Median and Average), see chapter 1, Explanation of Data Distribution.

Table 13-12: Annual Compensation of Part-Time Bookkeepers/Accountants by Region

	Data Distribution*	REGION								
		New England	Middle Atlantic	South Atlantic	E-N Central	E-S Central	W-N Central	W-S Central	Mountain	Pacific
CHARACTERISTICS										
Average weekend worship attendance	-		419	316	423	847	384	417	477	530
Average church income	-		$738,449	$587,546	$715,390	$1,158,637	$670,753	$1,201,826	$789,528	$895,490
Average # of years employed	-		7	10	9	9	10	9	6	7
Average # of paid vacation days	-		10	13	11	14	11	10	13	11
% College graduate or higher	-		60%	52%	58%	32%	50%	68%	82%	45%
% Who receive auto reimbursement/allowance	-		8%	14%	11%	5%	6%	7%	12%	12%
% Ordained	-		0%	3%	2%	6%	6%	0%	0%	4%
% Supervise one or more people	-		9%	16%	15%	21%	11%	29%	12%	16%
Average % salary increase (for those who had an increase) this year	-		3.6%	4.3%	3.0%	-	4.8%	5.6%	-	3.9%
HOURLY RATE										
Base Rate	Average	-	$14	$17	$15	$19	$15	$17	$16	$18
COMPENSATION										
Base Salary	Median	-	$14,500	$16,500	$11,876	$17,436	$9,600	$15,000	$12,000	$13,549
	Average	-	$17,338	$16,220	$13,081	$19,208	$10,359	$17,338	$13,065	$15,365
Housing	Median	-	-	-	-	-	-	-	-	-
	Average	-	-	-	-	-	-	-	-	-
Parsonage	Median	-	-	-	-	-	-	-	-	-
	Average	-	-	-	-	-	-	-	-	-
Total Compensation	**Median**	-	$12,962	$17,250	$11,876	$18,031	$10,140	$15,000	$12,000	$13,549
	Average	-	$17,925	$16,739	$13,081	$20,226	$10,752	$17,338	$13,065	$15,365
BENEFITS										
Health Insurance	Median	-	-	-	-	-	-	-	-	-
	Average	-	-	-	-	-	-	-	-	-
Life Insurance	Median	-	-	-	-	-	-	-	-	-
	Average	-	-	-	-	-	-	-	-	-
Disability Insurance	Median	-	-	-	-	-	-	-	-	-
	Average	-	-	-	-	-	-	-	-	-
Retirement	Median	-	-	$1,990	-	-	-	-	-	-
	Average	-	-	$2,276	-	-	-	-	-	-
Continuing Education	Median	-	-	$500	-	-	-	-	-	-
	Average	-	-	$481	-	-	-	-	-	-
Total Benefits	**Median**	-	-	$1,494	-	-	-	-	-	-
	Average	-	-	$2,094	-	-	-	-	-	-
TOTAL COMPENSATION PLUS BENEFITS	**Median**	-	$10,782	$17,250	$11,876	$18,345	$10,140	$15,200	$12,000	$13,549
	Average	-	$14,575	$17,099	$13,226	$20,534	$10,939	$18,407	$14,177	$15,670
Number of Respondents		7	25	66	55	19	36	28	17	51

- *Not enough response to provide meaningful data.*

* *For detailed description and definitions of Data Distribution (Median and Average), see chapter 1, Explanation of Data Distribution.*

Table 13-13: Annual Compensation of Part-Time Bookkeepers/Accountants by Education

	Data Distribution*	EDUCATION			
		Less than Bachelor	Bachelor	Master	Doctorate
CHARACTERISTICS					
Average weekend worship attendance		331	561	349	-
Average church income		$627,332	$948,175	$744,987	-
Average # of years employed		9	8	7	-
Average # of paid vacation days		12	11	17	-
% College graduate or higher		0%	100%	100%	-
% Who receive auto reimbursement/allowance		9%	11%	10%	-
% Ordained		1%	4%	0%	-
% Supervise one or more people		16%	16%	19%	-
Average % salary increase (for those who had an increase) this year		3.9%	4.5%	-	-
HOURLY RATE					
Base Rate	Average	$15	$17	$17	-
COMPENSATION					
Base Salary	Median	$12,286	$13,950	$10,140	-
	Average	$13,771	$16,055	$15,110	-
Housing	Median	-	-	-	-
	Average	-	-	-	-
Parsonage	Median	-	-	-	-
	Average	-	-	-	-
Total Compensation	**Median**	**$13,000**	**$14,000**	**$10,140**	-
	Average	**$14,343**	**$16,026**	**$15,110**	-
BENEFITS					
Health Insurance	Median	-	-	-	-
	Average	-	-	-	-
Life Insurance	Median	-	-	-	-
	Average	-	-	-	-
Disability Insurance	Median	-	-	-	-
	Average	-	-	-	-
Retirement	Median	$1,200	$1,400	-	-
	Average	$1,686	$1,419	-	-
Continuing Education	Median	-	-	-	-
	Average	-	-	-	-
Total Benefits	**Median**	**$880**	**$1,430**	-	-
	Average	**$1,744**	**$2,408**	-	-
TOTAL COMPENSATION PLUS BENEFITS	**Median**	**$12,686**	**$14,000**	**$10,140**	-
	Average	**$13,937**	**$16,460**	**$15,862**	-
Number of Respondents		138	143	21	0

- Not enough response to provide meaningful data.

* For detailed description and definitions of Data Distribution (Median and Average), see chapter 1, Explanation of Data Distribution.

Table 13-14: Annual Compensation of Part-Time Bookkeepers/Accountants by Years Employed

	Data Distribution*	YEARS EMPLOYED			
		Less than 6 years	6-10 years	11-15 years	Over 15 years
CHARACTERISTICS					
Average weekend worship attendance		505	423	406	397
Average church income		$849,887	$744,458	$671,804	$912,294
Average # of years employed		3	8	13	22
Average # of paid vacation days		9	13	14	15
% College graduate or higher		58%	59%	54%	40%
% Who receive auto reimbursement/allowance		8%	11%	15%	9%
% Ordained		2%	4%	5%	0%
% Supervise one or more people		20%	11%	18%	19%
Average % salary increase (for those who had an increase) this year		4.9%	4.0%	3.1%	3.4%
HOURLY RATE					
Base Rate	Average	$16	$17	$15	$16
COMPENSATION					
Base Salary	Median	$14,000	$11,543	$15,000	$12,888
	Average	$16,178	$13,819	$15,510	$15,041
Housing	Median	-	-	-	-
	Average	-	-	-	-
Parsonage	Median	-	-	-	-
	Average	-	-	-	-
Total Compensation	**Median**	**$14,000**	**$11,543**	**$15,500**	**$13,900**
	Average	**$16,554**	**$13,819**	**$16,017**	**$15,384**
BENEFITS					
Health Insurance	Median	$11,800	-	-	-
	Average	$14,656	-	-	-
Life Insurance	Median	-	-	-	-
	Average	-	-	-	-
Disability Insurance	Median	-	-	-	-
	Average	-	-	-	-
Retirement	Median	$1,145	-	-	-
	Average	$2,114	-	-	-
Continuing Education	Median	-	-	-	-
	Average	-	-	-	-
Total Benefits	**Median**	**$762**	**$1,230**	**$2,485**	**$2,325**
	Average	**$1,911**	**$1,807**	**$2,936**	**$2,772**
TOTAL COMPENSATION PLUS BENEFITS	**Median**	**$14,000**	**$11,543**	**$16,000**	**$13,900**
	Average	**$16,183**	**$14,045**	**$16,925**	**$15,900**
Number of Respondents		125	73	39	44

- Not enough response to provide meaningful data.

* For detailed description and definitions of Data Distribution (Median and Average), see chapter 1, Explanation of Data Distribution.

Table 13-15: Annual Compensation of Part-Time Bookkeepers/Accountants by Denomination

	Data Distribution*	DENOMINATION					
		Assemblies of God	Baptist	Independent/ Nondenom.	Lutheran	Methodist	Presby- terian
CHARACTERISTICS							
Average weekend worship attendance		319	508	500	277	380	322
Average church income		$602,785	$823,828	$800,442	$532,000	$749,765	$796,560
Average # of years employed		8	9	8	8	10	12
Average # of paid vacation days		8	11	13	13	12	16
% College graduate or higher		44%	52%	51%	67%	77%	52%
% Who receive auto reimbursement/allowance		3%	8%	17%	22%	14%	8%
% Ordained		6%	4%	2%	0%	5%	4%
% Supervise one or more people		11%	19%	12%	11%	24%	13%
Average % salary increase (for those who had an increase) this year		3.3%	5.2%	5.0%	-	4.7%	3.3%
HOURLY RATE							
Base Rate	Average	$16	$16	$16	-	$16	$15
COMPENSATION							
Base Salary	Median	$12,000	$12,200	$14,280	$11,500	$15,227	$15,091
	Average	$12,981	$14,478	$16,771	$15,787	$15,297	$16,491
Housing	Median	-	-	-	-	-	-
	Average	-	-	-	-	-	-
Parsonage	Median	-	-	-	-	-	-
	Average	-	-	-	-	-	-
Total Compensation	**Median**	**$12,100**	**$12,200**	**$14,560**	**$11,500**	**$15,227**	**$15,091**
	Average	**$13,410**	**$14,490**	**$17,492**	**$15,787**	**$15,297**	**$16,491**
BENEFITS							
Health Insurance	Median	-	-	-	-	-	-
	Average	-	-	-	-	-	-
Life Insurance	Median	-	-	-	-	-	-
	Average	-	-	-	-	-	-
Disability Insurance	Median	-	-	-	-	-	-
	Average	-	-	-	-	-	-
Retirement	Median	-	$1,145	-	-	-	-
	Average	-	$1,317	-	-	-	-
Continuing Education	Median	-	-	-	-	-	-
	Average	-	-	-	-	-	-
Total Benefits	**Median**	**-**	**$2,000**	**-**	**-**	**-**	**-**
	Average	**-**	**$2,622**	**-**	**-**	**-**	**-**
TOTAL COMPENSATION PLUS BENEFITS	**Median**	**$12,100**	**$12,200**	**$14,280**	**$11,500**	**$15,327**	**$15,091**
	Average	**$13,410**	**$15,171**	**$15,909**	**$16,007**	**$15,430**	**$17,421**
Number of Respondents		36	73	54	9	22	25

- Not enough response to provide meaningful data.

* For detailed description and definitions of Data Distribution (Median and Average), see chapter 1, Explanation of Data Distribution.

Table 13-16: Annual Compensation of Part-Time Bookkeepers/Accountants by Gender

	Data Distribution*	GENDER	
		Male	Female
CHARACTERISTICS			
Average weekend worship attendance		467	437
Average church income		$762,190	$798,970
Average # of years employed		9	8
Average # of paid vacation days		10	12
% College graduate or higher		67%	52%
% Who receive auto reimbursement/allowance		13%	9%
% Ordained		4%	2%
% Supervise one or more people		18%	16%
Average % salary increase (for those who had an increase) this year		3.3%	4.3%
HOURLY RATE			
Base Rate	Average	$16	$16
COMPENSATION			
Base Salary	Median	$10,185	$13,578
	Average	$13,063	$15,337
Housing	Median	-	-
	Average	-	-
Parsonage	Median	-	-
	Average	-	-
Total Compensation	**Median**	**$11,097**	**$14,010**
	Average	**$13,686**	**$15,531**
BENEFITS			
Health Insurance	Median	$13,000	$6,288
	Average	$18,000	$7,682
Life Insurance	Median	-	-
	Average	-	-
Disability Insurance	Median	-	$155
	Average	-	$721
Retirement	Median	-	$1,230
	Average	-	$1,739
Continuing Education	Median	-	$500
	Average	-	$504
Total Benefits	**Median**	**-**	**$1,200**
	Average	**-**	**$2,341**
TOTAL COMPENSATION PLUS BENEFITS	**Median**	**$10,185**	**$14,010**
	Average	**$12,017**	**$15,954**
Number of Respondents		52	251

- Not enough response to provide meaningful data.

* For detailed description and definitions of Data Distribution (Median and Average), see chapter 1, Explanation of Data Distribution.

Full-Time Bookkeeper/Accountant Worksheet

	Enter your church data below	The 2014–2015 Compensation Handbook for Church Staff		Enter *Compensation Handbook* data below			
				Highest 25%	Median	Lowest 25%	Average
Church Income	$	Table 13-1	page 223	$	$	$	$
Worship Attendance		Table 13-2	page 224	n/a	$	n/a	$
Church Setting (metro, suburb, small town, or farming area)		Table 13-3	page 225	n/a	$	n/a	$
Region		Table 13-4	page 226	n/a	$	n/a	$
Person's Education		Table 13-5	page 227	n/a	$	n/a	$
Years Employed		Table 13-6	page 228	n/a	$	n/a	$
Denomination (if applicable)		Table 13-7	page 229	n/a	$	n/a	$

Looking at the table and page number references indicated in the *2014–2015 Compensation Handbook for Church Staff* columns above, locate the appropriate range for your church. Refer to the instructions below for step-by-step help.

FILLING OUT THE WORKSHEET

1. Fill in the gray boxes under *Enter your church data* with your church demographic information as follows:

   ▶ **Income** (Total annual church budget in past year)
   ▶ **Worship attendance** (Number of people, including children, who attend all weekend services)
   ▶ **Church setting** (Metropolitan city, suburb of large city, small town or rural city, or farming area)

   ▶ **Region** (Locate your state's region in the appendix on page 346.)
   ▶ **Education** (Highest level of education: less than bachelor, bachelor, master, or doctorate)

2. Use Table 13-1 (page 223) in your *2014–2015 Compensation Handbook for Church Staff* to enter data pertinent to your church. In the heading (top row), locate your church **income** from the five available ranges. Follow that column to the bottom rows, and copy the *Highest 25%*, *Median*, *Lowest 25%*, and *Average* amounts onto your worksheet.

3. Use Table 13-2 (page 224) on your *2014–2015 Compensation Handbook for Church Staff* to enter data pertinent to your church. In the heading (top row), locate your church's

worship attendance from the six available ranges. Follow that column to the bottom rows, and copy the *Median* and *Average* amounts onto your worksheet.

4. Use Table 13-3 (page 225) on your *2014–2015 Compensation Handbook for Church Staff* to enter data pertinent to your church. In the heading (top row), choose the **church setting** that best describes your church. Follow that column to the bottom rows, and copy the *Median* and *Average* amounts onto your worksheet.

5. Use Table 13-4 (page 226) on your *2014–2015 Compensation Handbook for Church Staff* to enter data pertinent to your church. In the heading (top row), look for the **region** where your church is located. Follow that column to the bottom rows, and copy the *Median* and *Average* amounts onto your worksheet.

6. Use Table 13-5 (page 227) on your *2014–2015 Compensation Handbook for Church Staff* to enter data pertinent to your Bookkeeper/Accountant. In the heading (top row), look for **your Bookkeeper/Accountant's highest level of education**. Follow that column to the bottom rows, and copy the *Median* and *Average* amounts onto your worksheet.

7. Use Table 13-6 (page 228) on your *2014–2015 Compensation Handbook for Church Staff* to enter data pertinent to your Bookkeeper/Accountant. In the heading (top row), locate the **number of years your Bookkeeper/Accountant has been employed**. Follow that column to the bottom rows, and copy the *Median* and *Average* amounts onto your worksheet.

8. Use Table 13-7 (page 229) on your *2014–2015 Compensation Handbook for Church Staff* to enter data pertinent to your church. In the heading (top row), look for **your church's denominational affiliation**. Follow that column

to the bottom rows, and copy the *Median* and *Average* amounts onto your worksheet. If your church is not affiliated with a denomination, leave this section blank.

DETERMINING COMPENSATION

This tool will not provide you with a single compensation amount but rather with a range of values to help you determine the compensation appropriate to your situation.

1. Look at the values in the shaded *Median* column. Circle the **lowest** and the **highest** values. **This is the range of the median compensation plus benefits for churches similar to yours.**

2. For a variety of reasons, compensation plus benefits may be higher or lower than the range established in this table. Income and attendance are two significant factors affecting church compensation packages. If church income or attendance skews higher, you might want to consider moving toward or above the higher end of the range. Likewise, if church income or attendance skews lower, you may consider moving the package toward or below the lower end of the range.

3. Examine additional variables that might impact the compensation package you offer, such as years of service, education, and church setting.

4. Determine other circumstances unique to your situation, such as cost of living in your area, theological beliefs, pastoral performance, financial needs, the local economy, personal motivation, congregational goals, and others.

5. You now have a compensation package range based on the *2014–2015 Compensation Handbook*. Since each church and position are unique, your final compensation package will be based on additional factors unique to your situation.

Part-Time Bookkeeper/Accountant Worksheet

	Enter your church data below	The 2014–2015 Compensation Handbook for Church Staff		Enter *Compensation Handbook* data below			
				Highest 25%	Median	Lowest 25%	Average
Church Income	$	Table 13-9	page 231	$	$	$	$
Worship Attendance		Table 13-10	page 232	n/a	$	n/a	$
Church Setting (metro, suburb, small town, or farming area)		Table 13-11	page 233	n/a	$	n/a	$
Region		Table 13-12	page 234	n/a	$	n/a	$
Person's Education		Table 13-13	page 235	n/a	$	n/a	$
Years Employed		Table 13-14	page 236	n/a	$	n/a	$
Denomination (if applicable)		Table 13-15	page 237	n/a	$	n/a	$

Looking at the table and page number references indicated in the *2014–2015 Compensation Handbook for Church Staff* columns above, locate the appropriate range for your church. Refer to the instructions below for step-by-step help.

FILLING OUT THE WORKSHEET

1. Fill in the gray boxes under *Enter your church data* with your church demographic information as follows:

   ▶ **Income** (Total annual church budget in past year)
   ▶ **Worship attendance** (Number of people, including children, who attend all weekend services)
   ▶ **Church setting** (Metropolitan city, suburb of large city, small town or rural city, or farming area)

   ▶ **Region** (Locate your state's region in the appendix on page 346.)
   ▶ **Education** (Highest level of education: less than bachelor, bachelor, master, or doctorate)

2. Use Table 13-9 (page 231) in your *2014–2015 Compensation Handbook for Church Staff* to enter data pertinent to your church. In the heading (top row), locate your church **income** from the five available ranges. Follow that column to the bottom rows, and copy the *Highest 25%*, *Median*, *Lowest 25%*, and *Average* amounts onto your worksheet.

3. Use Table 13-10 (page 232) on your *2014–2015 Compensation Handbook for Church Staff* to enter data pertinent to your church. In the heading (top row), locate your church's

241

worship attendance from the six available ranges. Follow that column to the bottom rows, and copy the *Median* and *Average* amounts onto your worksheet.

4. Use Table 13-11 (page 233) on your *2014–2015 Compensation Handbook for Church Staff* to enter data pertinent to your church. In the heading (top row), choose the **church setting** that best describes your church. Follow that column to the bottom rows, and copy the *Median* and *Average* amounts onto your worksheet.

5. Use Table 13-12 (page 234) on your *2014–2015 Compensation Handbook for Church Staff* to enter data pertinent to your church. In the heading (top row), look for the **region** where your church is located. Follow that column to the bottom rows, and copy the *Median* and *Average* amounts onto your worksheet.

6. Use Table 13-13 (page 235) on your *2014–2015 Compensation Handbook for Church Staff* to enter data pertinent to your Bookkeeper/Accountant. In the heading (top row), look for **your Bookkeeper/Accountant's highest level of education**. Follow that column to the bottom rows, and copy the *Median* and *Average* amounts onto your worksheet.

7. Use Table 13-14 (page 236) on your *2014–2015 Compensation Handbook for Church Staff* to enter data pertinent to your Bookkeeper/Accountant. In the heading (top row), locate the **number of years your Bookkeeper/Accountant has been employed**. Follow that column to the bottom rows, and copy the *Median* and *Average* amounts onto your worksheet.

8. Use Table 13-15 (page 237) on your *2014–2015 Compensation Handbook for Church Staff* to enter data pertinent to your church. In the heading (top row), look for **your church's denominational affiliation**. Follow that column to the bottom rows, and copy the *Median* and *Average* amounts onto your worksheet. If your church is not affiliated with a denomination, leave this section blank.

DETERMINING COMPENSATION

This tool will not provide you with a single compensation amount but rather with a range of values to help you determine the compensation appropriate to your situation.

1. Look at the values in the shaded *Median* column. Circle the **lowest** and the **highest** values. **This is the range of the median compensation plus benefits for churches similar to yours.**

2. For a variety of reasons, compensation plus benefits may be higher or lower than the range established in this table. Income and attendance are two significant factors affecting church compensation packages. If church income or attendance skews higher, you might want to consider moving toward or above the higher end of the range. Likewise, if church income or attendance skews lower, you may consider moving the package toward or below the lower end of the range.

3. Examine additional variables that might impact the compensation package you offer, such as years of service, education, and church setting.

4. Determine other circumstances unique to your situation, such as cost of living in your area, theological beliefs, pastoral performance, financial needs, the local economy, personal motivation, congregational goals, and others.

5. You now have a compensation package range based on the *2014–2015 Compensation Handbook*. Since each church and position are unique, your final compensation package will be based on additional factors unique to your situation.

14

SECRETARIES/ ADMINISTRATIVE ASSISTANTS

Employment Profile

Secretaries/Administrative Assistants include paid personnel who provide clerical or administrative support. This category may include such positions as Administrative Assistant, Clerical Assistant, Executive Secretary, Lead Secretary, Office Assistant, Office Clerk, Office Manager, Publications Coordinator, Receptionist, Church Secretary, Secretary to any pastor or ministry, Secretary's Assistant, etc.

Nearly six in 10 reported Secretaries/Administrative Assistants are employed on a part-time basis.

Almost all, regardless of employment status, are females and are employed by the church rather than self-employed. More than half of the Secretaries/Administrative Assistants have more than a high school diploma.

The chart below provides a demographic profile of this sample.

	Full-Time	Part-Time
Number of respondents	**385**	**535**
Ordained	3%	3%
Average years employed	10	7
Male	3%	2%
Female	97%	98%
Self-employed (receives 1099)	2%	2%
Church employee (receives W-2)	98%	98%
High school diploma	45%	41%
Associate degree	20%	21%
Bachelor's degree	30%	33%
Master's degree	5%	5%
Doctoral degree	1%	0%

Total Compensation plus Benefits Package Analysis

The following analyses are based on data in the tables you will find later in this chapter. The tables show compensation plus benefits data for full-time and part-time Secretaries/Administrative Assistants and are presented according to church income, church attendance, church setting, region, education, years employed, denomination, and gender. In this way, the compensation plus benefits of Secretaries/Administrative Assistants can be analyzed and compared from a variety of useful perspectives.

The total compensation plus benefits amount includes the base salary; housing allowance and/or parsonage amount; health, life, and disability insurance payments; retirement contribution; and educational funds.

A worksheet at the end of this chapter is provided to help you apply the data to your church's situation.

Secretaries/Administrative Assistants receive fewer benefits for full-time work than pastoral staff members receive. Less than half of them receive health insurance and retirement benefits. While nearly all full-time Secretaries/Administrative Assistants receive paid vacation, they rarely receive housing or continuing education allowances. Only about two in 10 receive life or disability insurance or an auto allowance. Few benefits are provided for part-time Secretaries/Administrative Assistants apart from paid vacation. However, the majority do receive salary increases.

Compensation Plus Benefits	Full-Time	Part-Time
Base Salary	100%	100%
Housing	2%	1%
Parsonage	0%	0%
Health Insurance*	42%	4%
Life Insurance*	21%	1%
Disability Insurance*	16%	2%
Retirement	41%	6%
Continuing Education	8%	3%
Received salary increase	57%	50%
Received paid vacation	95%	58%
Received auto reimbursement/allowance	19%	11%

Only those reporting individual premiums for Health, Life, or Disability (not total insurance premiums) are included.

KEY POINTS

✳ More than half of full-time Secretaries/ Administrative Assistants who reported serve in churches with an income of over $750,000.

✳ For the most part, as church income and years employed increase, compensation and benefits for full-time Secretaries/Administrative Assistants also increase.

✳ About eight out of 10 full-time and part-time Secretaries/Administrative Assistants who reported serve in churches located in a suburb of a large city or in a small town or rural city. In both cases, those working in the suburbs are compensated at a higher rate than those in small-town churches.

Compensation & Benefits: National Averages for Full-Time Secretaries/Administrative Assistants	
2000	$21,965
2001	$23,316
2002	$24,132
2003	$24,875
2004	$25,007
2005	$26,624
2006	$29,551
2007	$30,840
2008	$30,835
2009	$30,727
2011	$32,408
2013	$33,404*

* The above trend is made available for your reference only. In addition to looking at this overall data, please refer to the detailed tables using your church's income, attendance, setting, region, and denomination as well as the person's education, gender, and years employed for guidance in compensating this position.

Table 14-1: Annual Compensation of Full-Time Secretaries/Administrative Assistants by Church Income

CHARACTERISTICS	Data Distribution*	$250K & Under	$251-$500K	$501-$750K	$751K-$1M	Over $1 Million
Average weekend worship attendance		318	251	335	572	1,039
Average church income		$181,895	$381,542	$624,071	$890,827	$2,081,552
Average # of years employed		11	9	11	12	10
Average # of paid vacation days		15	15	15	17	16
% College graduate or higher		32%	29%	31%	45%	36%
% Who receive auto reimbursement/allowance		19%	15%	13%	18%	23%
% Ordained		3%	5%	8%	5%	1%
% Supervise one or more people		16%	28%	36%	35%	23%
Average % salary increase (for those who had an increase) this year		2.9%	4.0%	3.3%	4.2%	3.7%
COMPENSATION						
Base Salary	Highest 25%	$25,932	$30,000	$34,047	$34,745	$36,663
	Median	$22,600	$27,000	$30,425	$30,000	$32,199
	Lowest 25%	$19,955	$23,500	$24,000	$26,040	$27,746
	Average	$22,409	$27,279	$29,096	$30,992	$32,677
Housing	Highest 25%	-	-	-	-	-
	Median	-	-	-	-	-
	Lowest 25%	-	-	-	-	-
	Average	-	-	-	-	-
Parsonage	Highest 25%	-	-	-	-	-
	Median	-	-	-	-	-
	Lowest 25%	-	-	-	-	-
	Average	-	-	-	-	-
Total Compensation	Highest 25%	$25,932	$30,659	$34,047	$34,745	$36,907
	Median	$22,600	$27,000	$30,425	$30,000	$32,199
	Lowest 25%	$19,955	$23,500	$24,000	$26,040	$27,746
	Average	$22,409	$27,522	$30,022	$30,992	$32,745
BENEFITS						
Health Insurance	Highest 25%	-	$6,980	$8,987	$8,000	$6,805
	Median	-	$5,130	$4,962	$6,000	$4,950
	Lowest 25%	-	$2,250	$3,181	$2,676	$3,296
	Average	-	$5,550	$6,803	$5,994	$5,595
Life Insurance	Highest 25%	-	-	$270	-	$259
	Median	-	-	$150	-	$168
	Lowest 25%	-	-	$72	-	$100
	Average	-	-	$232	-	$237
Disability Insurance	Highest 25%	-	-	-	-	$379
	Median	-	-	-	-	$264
	Lowest 25%	-	-	-	-	$165
	Average	-	-	-	-	$263
Retirement	Highest 25%	$2,070	$2,660	$2,498	$1,808	$3,063
	Median	$1,725	$1,111	$1,636	$1,500	$1,830
	Lowest 25%	$1,594	$886	$938	$979	$1,135
	Average	$2,373	$1,694	$2,020	$1,829	$2,310
Continuing Education	Highest 25%	-	-	-	-	$500
	Median	-	-	-	-	$400
	Lowest 25%	-	-	-	-	$300
	Average	-	-	-	-	$387
Total Benefits	Highest 25%	$5,251	$5,550	$10,000	$8,000	$8,412
	Median	$3,050	$2,300	$5,186	$5,043	$4,315
	Lowest 25%	$1,705	$966	$2,800	$1,302	$1,725
	Average	$3,555	$3,701	$6,428	$5,515	$5,535
TOTAL COMPENSATION PLUS BENEFITS	Highest 25%	$28,180	$33,000	$39,842	$41,749	$43,358
	Median	$23,000	$27,720	$32,000	$32,713	$36,100
	Lowest 25%	$20,800	$24,200	$25,613	$27,825	$30,408
	Average	$23,863	$29,348	$33,622	$34,424	$36,926
Number of Respondents		31	87	54	44	144

- Not enough response to provide meaningful data.

* For detailed description and definitions of Data Distribution (Highest 25%, Median, Lowest 25%, and Average), see chapter 1, Explanation of Data Distribution.

Table 14-2: Annual Compensation of Full-Time Secretaries/Administrative Assistants by Worship Attendance

	Data Distribution*	WORSHIP ATTENDANCE					
		100 or less	101-300	301-500	501-750	751-1,000	Over 1,000
CHARACTERISTICS							
Average weekend worship attendance		82	208	408	637	886	1,676
Average church income		$245,583	$459,755	$891,878	$1,166,638	$1,554,894	$2,807,853
Average # of years employed		13	10	11	9	9	10
Average # of paid vacation days		17	15	17	15	17	15
% College graduate or higher		19%	32%	41%	49%	25%	30%
% Who receive auto reimbursement/allowance		19%	19%	23%	11%	16%	23%
% Ordained		7%	3%	4%	4%	5%	2%
% Supervise one or more people		25%	27%	28%	35%	13%	30%
Average % salary increase (for those who had an increase) this year		3.3%	3.7%	3.3%	3.9%	4.2%	3.5%
COMPENSATION							
Base Salary	Median	$23,000	$27,394	$30,000	$31,084	$31,456	$30,302
	Average	$22,539	$28,241	$29,436	$32,501	$31,511	$32,021
Housing	Median	-	-	-	-	-	-
	Average	-	-	-	-	-	-
Parsonage	Median	-	-	-	-	-	-
	Average	-	-	-	-	-	-
Total Compensation	**Median**	**$23,000**	**$27,394**	**$30,000**	**$31,084**	**$31,456**	**$30,593**
	Average	**$22,539**	**$28,410**	**$29,816**	**$33,001**	**$31,511**	**$32,050**
BENEFITS							
Health Insurance	Median	-	$4,860	$7,125	$4,788	$5,929	$4,800
	Average	-	$5,110	$7,418	$5,207	$5,782	$5,389
Life Insurance	Median	-	$116	$150	$216	$250	$155
	Average	-	$226	$223	$259	$381	$224
Disability Insurance	Median	-	-	$323	$338	$325	$213
	Average	-	-	$316	$303	$308	$221
Retirement	Median	-	$1,700	$1,872	$1,500	$1,630	$1,598
	Average	-	$2,002	$2,496	$1,761	$2,044	$2,277
Continuing Education	Median	-	$300	$500	-	-	-
	Average	-	$469	$493	-	-	-
Total Benefits	**Median**	**-**	**$3,240**	**$6,208**	**$4,315**	**$6,934**	**$4,181**
	Average	**-**	**$4,152**	**$6,786**	**$4,554**	**$5,948**	**$5,349**
TOTAL COMPENSATION PLUS BENEFITS	**Median**	**$23,400**	**$28,650**	**$34,522**	**$34,422**	**$35,419**	**$33,141**
	Average	**$23,963**	**$30,528**	**$34,692**	**$35,233**	**$36,050**	**$34,722**
Number of Respondents		16	125	81	57	38	63

- Not enough response to provide meaningful data.

* For detailed description and definitions of Data Distribution (Median and Average), see chapter 1, Explanation of Data Distribution.

Table 14-3: Annual Compensation of Full-Time Secretaries/Administrative Assistants by Church Setting

CHARACTERISTICS	Data Distribution*	Metro-politan city	Suburb of large city	Small town or rural city	Farming area
Average weekend worship attendance		657	778	464	344
Average church income		$1,391,441	$1,448,654	$782,372	$581,065
Average # of years employed		11	11	10	11
Average # of paid vacation days		16	16	15	14
% College graduate or higher		35%	41%	32%	23%
% Who receive auto reimbursement/allowance		10%	26%	15%	15%
% Ordained		3%	3%	4%	0%
% Supervise one or more people		30%	35%	19%	23%
Average % salary increase (for those who had an increase) this year		3.5%	3.8%	3.4%	5.3%
COMPENSATION					
Base Salary	Median	$30,000	$31,860	$27,256	$25,100
	Average	$30,601	$32,537	$27,378	$25,878
Housing	Median	-	-	-	-
	Average	-	-	-	-
Parsonage	Median	-	-	-	-
	Average	-	-	-	-
Total Compensation	**Median**	**$30,000**	**$31,889**	**$27,256**	**$25,100**
	Average	**$30,638**	**$33,013**	**$27,432**	**$25,878**
BENEFITS					
Health Insurance	Median	$5,938	$5,286	$4,900	-
	Average	$5,578	$5,844	$5,951	-
Life Insurance	Median	$80	$155	$186	-
	Average	$194	$282	$219	-
Disability Insurance	Median	-	$281	$300	-
	Average	-	$294	$379	-
Retirement	Median	$1,284	$1,600	$1,700	-
	Average	$2,067	$2,183	$1,971	-
Continuing Education	Median	-	$500	$500	-
	Average	-	$495	$441	-
Total Benefits	**Median**	**$4,400**	**$3,944**	**$4,350**	**$3,322**
	Average	**$5,369**	**$5,170**	**$5,321**	**$3,626**
TOTAL COMPENSATION PLUS BENEFITS	**Median**	**$32,164**	**$34,635**	**$28,515**	**$27,143**
	Average	**$33,390**	**$35,697**	**$30,896**	**$28,339**
Number of Respondents		68	150	151	13

- Not enough response to provide meaningful data.

* For detailed description and definitions of Data Distribution (Median and Average), see chapter 1, Explanation of Data Distribution.

Table 14-4: Annual Compensation of Full-Time Secretaries/Administrative Assistants by Region

	Data Distribution*	REGION								
		New England	Middle Atlantic	South Atlantic	E-N Central	E-S Central	W-N Central	W-S Central	Mountain	Pacific
CHARACTERISTICS										
Average weekend worship attendance		356	722	613	535	588	583	610	753	748
Average church income		$649,799	$1,339,663	$1,355,085	$801,239	$1,045,050	$954,770	$1,061,301	$1,046,885	$1,716,223
Average # of years employed		13	13	11	10	10	9	10	8	10
Average # of paid vacation days		19	18	17	15	14	16	14	15	16
% College graduate or higher		55%	35%	36%	38%	25%	39%	26%	30%	46%
% Who receive auto reimbursement/allowance		45%	18%	25%	11%	11%	15%	22%	9%	27%
% Ordained		9%	3%	4%	5%	0%	0%	3%	4%	5%
% Supervise one or more people		45%	26%	22%	34%	20%	24%	26%	22%	38%
Average % salary increase (for those who had an increase) this year		3.1%	2.9%	3.6%	3.6%	5.2%	3.2%	3.5%	4.2%	4.0%
COMPENSATION										
Base Salary	Median	$35,000	$29,118	$31,500	$27,000	$28,750	$29,293	$27,690	$27,040	$30,659
	Average	$34,479	$29,539	$32,442	$27,888	$28,773	$30,505	$28,312	$26,740	$32,636
Housing	Median	-	-	-	-	-	-	-	-	-
	Average	-	-	-	-	-	-	-	-	-
Parsonage	Median	-	-	-	-	-	-	-	-	-
	Average	-	-	-	-	-	-	-	-	-
Total Compensation	**Median**	$37,152	$29,118	$31,500	$27,000	$28,750	$29,293	$27,690	$27,040	$31,000
	Average	$37,206	$29,539	$32,442	$28,206	$28,773	$30,505	$28,487	$26,740	$33,124
BENEFITS										
Health Insurance	Median	-	$4,514	$5,318	$4,177	$6,322	$6,242	$5,684	$4,000	$3,436
	Average	-	$6,024	$5,513	$6,937	$6,766	$5,465	$5,790	$4,400	$4,543
Life Insurance	Median	-	$204	$216	$222	-	$193	$149	-	$99
	Average	-	$294	$212	$332	-	$305	$317	-	$176
Disability Insurance	Median	-	-	$270	$360	-	$379	-	-	-
	Average	-	-	$262	$448	-	$310	-	-	-
Retirement	Median	-	$1,382	$1,683	$1,500	$2,400	$1,685	$1,725	-	$1,200
	Average	-	$1,626	$2,348	$2,006	$2,576	$2,030	$2,530	-	$1,303
Continuing Education	Median	-	-	$450	-	-	-	-	-	-
	Average	-	-	$458	-	-	-	-	-	-
Total Benefits	**Median**	-	$4,867	$4,450	$3,554	$5,794	$1,685	$4,164	$4,000	$2,991
	Average	-	$6,191	$4,850	$5,999	$6,121	$4,302	$4,838	$4,188	$4,251
TOTAL COMPENSATION PLUS BENEFITS	**Median**	$44,050	$34,685	$35,000	$27,785	$30,130	$31,820	$29,000	$29,095	$34,818
	Average	$39,122	$34,142	$35,855	$30,768	$32,621	$32,236	$30,922	$28,743	$36,604
Number of Respondents		11	39	73	66	37	33	61	23	42

- Not enough response to provide meaningful data.

* For detailed description and definitions of Data Distribution (Median and Average), see chapter 1, Explanation of Data Distribution.

Table 14-5: Annual Compensation of Full-Time Secretaries/Administrative Assistants by Education

	Data Distribution*	EDUCATION			
		Less than Bachelor	Bachelor	Master	Doctorate
CHARACTERISTICS					
Average weekend worship attendance		624	626	454	-
Average church income		$1,103,336	$1,242,973	$874,025	-
Average # of years employed		11	9	5	-
Average # of paid vacation days		16	16	13	-
% College graduate or higher		0%	100%	100%	-
% Who receive auto reimbursement/allowance		19%	18%	18%	-
% Ordained		0%	6%	24%	-
% Supervise one or more people		26%	29%	29%	-
Average % salary increase (for those who had an increase) this year		3.7%	3.4%	5.2%	-
COMPENSATION					
Base Salary	Median	$28,948	$29,025	$31,200	-
	Average	$29,446	$30,594	$31,779	-
Housing	Median	-	-	-	-
	Average	-	-	-	-
Parsonage	Median	-	-	-	-
	Average	-	-	-	-
Total Compensation	**Median**	**$28,948**	**$29,025**	**$31,200**	**-**
	Average	**$29,457**	**$31,230**	**$32,313**	**-**
BENEFITS					
Health Insurance	Median	$5,111	$5,100	-	-
	Average	$5,486	$6,462	-	-
Life Insurance	Median	$186	$150	-	-
	Average	$273	$212	-	-
Disability Insurance	Median	$340	$225	-	-
	Average	$357	$314	-	-
Retirement	Median	$1,500	$1,683	-	-
	Average	$2,041	$1,921	-	-
Continuing Education	Median	$450	$325	-	-
	Average	$443	$437	-	-
Total Benefits	**Median**	**$4,228**	**$3,760**	**$3,850**	**-**
	Average	**$4,987**	**$5,542**	**$4,733**	**-**
TOTAL COMPENSATION PLUS BENEFITS	**Median**	**$31,600**	**$31,728**	**$30,862**	**-**
	Average	**$32,269**	**$34,630**	**$33,723**	**-**
Number of Respondents		241	111	17	3

- Not enough response to provide meaningful data.

* For detailed description and definitions of Data Distribution (Median and Average), see chapter 1, Explanation of Data Distribution.

Table 14-6: Annual Compensation of Full-Time Secretaries/Administrative Assistants by Years Employed

	Data Distribution*	YEARS EMPLOYED			
		Less than 6 years	6-10 years	11-15 years	Over 15 years
CHARACTERISTICS					
Average weekend worship attendance		708	571	533	613
Average church income		$1,245,453	$1,078,073	$1,141,834	$1,150,486
Average # of years employed		3	8	13	23
Average # of paid vacation days		12	16	18	20
% College graduate or higher		41%	37%	34%	19%
% Who receive auto reimbursement/allowance		21%	18%	15%	21%
% Ordained		5%	2%	2%	5%
% Supervise one or more people		25%	17%	33%	38%
Average % salary increase (for those who had an increase) this year		3.8%	3.6%	3.4%	3.5%
COMPENSATION					
Base Salary	Median	$27,000	$28,000	$31,712	$32,240
	Average	$27,585	$28,580	$31,666	$33,618
Housing	Median	-	-	-	-
	Average	-	-	-	-
Parsonage	Median	-	-	-	-
	Average	-	-	-	-
Total Compensation	**Median**	**$27,000**	**$28,000**	**$31,860**	**$32,240**
	Average	**$27,655**	**$28,793**	**$31,994**	**$34,043**
BENEFITS					
Health Insurance	Median	$4,514	$4,515	$6,800	$5,006
	Average	$4,617	$6,213	$7,391	$5,134
Life Insurance	Median	$174	$180	$171	$144
	Average	$284	$277	$226	$186
Disability Insurance	Median	$255	$331	$305	-
	Average	$274	$469	$306	-
Retirement	Median	$1,466	$1,380	$1,600	$2,394
	Average	$1,792	$1,561	$2,249	$2,762
Continuing Education	Median	$500	-	-	$400
	Average	$406	-	-	$400
Total Benefits	**Median**	**$3,454**	**$3,676**	**$5,763**	**$4,350**
	Average	**$4,172**	**$5,174**	**$6,941**	**$5,392**
TOTAL COMPENSATION PLUS BENEFITS	**Median**	**$29,173**	**$30,076**	**$36,272**	**$36,086**
	Average	**$30,320**	**$31,674**	**$36,471**	**$36,945**
Number of Respondents		117	100	61	76

- Not enough response to provide meaningful data.

* For detailed description and definitions of Data Distribution (Median and Average), see chapter 1, Explanation of Data Distribution.

Table 14-7: Annual Compensation of Full-Time Secretaries/Administrative Assistants by Denomination

	Data Distribution*	DENOMINATION					
		Assemblies of God	Baptist	Independent/ Nondenom.	Lutheran	Methodist	Presby-terian
CHARACTERISTICS							
Average weekend worship attendance		609	596	829	404	557	594
Average church income		$914,429	$1,243,385	$1,384,290	$797,103	$1,014,306	$1,365,226
Average # of years employed		9	11	9	9	10	12
Average # of paid vacation days		14	16	15	14	16	17
% College graduate or higher		17%	36%	35%	29%	43%	21%
% Who receive auto reimbursement/allowance		4%	24%	12%	6%	7%	37%
% Ordained		8%	3%	4%	0%	3%	0%
% Supervise one or more people		25%	20%	29%	19%	31%	27%
Average % salary increase (for those who had an increase) this year		5.0%	3.3%	4.0%	3.1%	3.9%	2.7%
COMPENSATION							
Base Salary	Median	$28,000	$29,582	$30,000	$26,650	$27,720	$31,616
	Average	$27,788	$29,639	$30,140	$28,209	$28,686	$31,420
Housing	Median	-	-	-	-	-	-
	Average	-	-	-	-	-	-
Parsonage	Median	-	-	-	-	-	-
	Average	-	-	-	-	-	-
Total Compensation	**Median**	**$28,000**	**$29,582**	**$30,000**	**$26,650**	**$27,720**	**$31,616**
	Average	**$27,788**	**$29,639**	**$30,485**	**$28,209**	**$28,748**	**$31,420**
BENEFITS							
Health Insurance	Median	-	$5,840	$3,654	-	$6,635	$7,973
	Average	-	$6,467	$5,089	-	$7,085	$6,783
Life Insurance	Median	-	$161	$156	-	-	-
	Average	-	$320	$210	-	-	-
Disability Insurance	Median	-	$350	$210	-	-	-
	Average	-	$428	$225	-	-	-
Retirement	Median	-	$1,710	$1,106	$2,494	$1,109	$2,975
	Average	-	$2,079	$1,630	$2,397	$1,468	$2,949
Continuing Education	Median	-	$450	-	-	-	-
	Average	-	$435	-	-	-	-
Total Benefits	**Median**	**$2,328**	**$4,850**	**$3,537**	**$3,610**	**$4,788**	**$6,653**
	Average	**$2,944**	**$5,616**	**$4,458**	**$5,942**	**$5,241**	**$6,530**
TOTAL COMPENSATION PLUS BENEFITS	**Median**	**$28,000**	**$31,712**	**$32,100**	**$29,569**	**$30,130**	**$37,157**
	Average	**$28,812**	**$33,472**	**$33,507**	**$31,705**	**$32,543**	**$36,426**
Number of Respondents		24	110	84	17	29	30

- *Not enough response to provide meaningful data.*

* *For detailed description and definitions of Data Distribution (Median and Average), see chapter 1, Explanation of Data Distribution.*

Table 14-8: Annual Compensation of Full-Time Secretaries/Administrative Assistants by Gender

	Data Distribution*	GENDER	
		Male	Female
CHARACTERISTICS			
Average weekend worship attendance		664	616
Average church income		$1,011,520	$1,141,143
Average # of years employed		10	10
Average # of paid vacation days		15	16
% College graduate or higher		67%	34%
% Who receive auto reimbursement/allowance		45%	18%
% Ordained		50%	2%
% Supervise one or more people		50%	27%
Average % salary increase (for those who had an increase) this year		3.7%	3.7%
COMPENSATION			
Base Salary	Median	$31,593	$28,938
	Average	$33,657	$29,809
Housing	Median	-	-
	Average	-	-
Parsonage	Median	-	-
	Average	-	-
Total Compensation	**Median**	**$32,800**	**$28,938**
	Average	**$40,913**	**$29,811**
BENEFITS			
Health Insurance	Median	-	$4,900
	Average	-	$5,711
Life Insurance	Median	-	$177
	Average	-	$256
Disability Insurance	Median	-	$288
	Average	-	$335
Retirement	Median	-	$1,600
	Average	-	$2,070
Continuing Education	Median	-	$500
	Average	-	$457
Total Benefits	**Median**	**$7,656**	**$4,000**
	Average	**$7,480**	**$5,129**
TOTAL COMPENSATION PLUS BENEFITS	**Median**	**$34,737**	**$31,550**
	Average	**$39,426**	**$32,971**
Number of Respondents		12	370

- Not enough response to provide meaningful data.

* For detailed description and definitions of Data Distribution (Median and Average), see chapter 1, Explanation of Data Distribution.

Table 14-9: Annual Compensation of Part-Time Secretaries/Administrative Assistants by Church Income

	Data Distribution*	CHURCH INCOME				
		$250K & Under	$251-$500K	$501-$750K	$751K-$1M	Over 1 Million
CHARACTERISTICS						
Average weekend worship attendance		106	221	351	473	1,116
Average church income		$157,423	$359,679	$614,617	$890,822	$2,023,002
Average # of years employed		8	8	7	5	6
Average # of paid vacation days		10	12	14	11	13
% College graduate or higher		33%	37%	39%	40%	48%
% Who receive auto reimbursement/allowance		8%	8%	11%	10%	17%
% Ordained		2%	5%	1%	7%	2%
% Supervise one or more people		13%	17%	12%	10%	7%
Average % salary increase (for those who had an increase) this year		4.4%	3.7%	4.3%	4.3%	3.1%
HOURLY RATE						
Base Rate	Average	$12	$13	$13	$14	$14
COMPENSATION						
Base Salary	Median	$10,863	$14,664	$15,329	$16,151	$16,526
	Average	$12,817	$14,598	$15,034	$17,188	$16,965
Housing	Median	-	-	-	-	-
	Average	-	-	-	-	-
Parsonage	Median	-	-	-	-	-
	Average	-	-	-	-	-
Total Compensation	**Median**	**$10,800**	**$15,000**	**$15,329**	**$16,151**	**$16,526**
	Average	**$11,519**	**$14,859**	**$15,034**	**$17,188**	**$16,965**
BENEFITS						
Health Insurance	Median	$4,590	-	-	-	-
	Average	$5,911	-	-	-	-
Life Insurance	Median	-	-	-	-	-
	Average	-	-	-	-	-
Disability Insurance	Median	-	-	-	-	-
	Average	-	-	-	-	-
Retirement	Median	-	-	$627	-	$930
	Average	-	-	$846	-	$950
Continuing Education	Median	-	-	-	-	-
	Average	-	-	-	-	-
Total Benefits	**Median**	**$900**	**$1,500**	**$646**	**-**	**$1,403**
	Average	**$2,462**	**$3,612**	**$1,592**	**-**	**$3,934**
TOTAL COMPENSATION PLUS BENEFITS	**Median**	**$11,000**	**$15,134**	**$15,329**	**$16,427**	**$16,744**
	Average	**$11,850**	**$15,322**	**$15,271**	**$17,299**	**$17,537**
Number of Respondents		180	110	72	31	117

- Not enough response to provide meaningful data.

* For detailed description and definitions of Data Distribution (Median and Average), see chapter 1, Explanation of Data Distribution.

Table 14-10: Annual Compensation of Part-Time Secretaries/Administrative Assistants by Worship Attendance

	Data Distribution*	WORSHIP ATTENDANCE					
		100 or less	101-300	301-500	501-750	751-1,000	Over 1,000
CHARACTERISTICS							
Average weekend worship attendance		72	189	399	642	858	1,914
Average church income		$144,063	$368,238	$828,652	$1,046,079	$1,373,783	$3,104,670
Average # of years employed		9	8	7	6	8	4
Average # of paid vacation days		10	12	13	11	15	11
% College graduate or higher		35%	37%	41%	36%	35%	46%
% Who receive auto reimbursement/allowance		7%	9%	11%	9%	4%	30%
% Ordained		4%	3%	4%	0%	0%	2%
% Supervise one or more people		11%	16%	11%	5%	11%	2%
Average % salary increase (for those who had an increase) this year		4.8%	4.8%	3.0%	2.7%	6.0%	2.9%
HOURLY RATE							
Base Rate	Average	$11	$13	$13	$13	$13	$14
COMPENSATION							
Base Salary	Median	$9,950	$14,352	$14,813	$15,600	$16,250	$16,744
	Average	$12,279	$14,189	$15,654	$15,869	$16,721	$18,287
Housing	Median	-	-	-	-	-	-
	Average	-	-	-	-	-	-
Parsonage	Median	-	-	-	-	-	-
	Average	-	-	-	-	-	-
Total Compensation	**Median**	**$10,000**	**$14,458**	**$14,813**	**$15,600**	**$16,250**	**$16,744**
	Average	**$12,979**	**$14,474**	**$15,654**	**$15,869**	**$16,721**	**$18,287**
BENEFITS							
Health Insurance	Median	$4,590	-	-	-	-	-
	Average	$4,520	-	-	-	-	-
Life Insurance	Median	-	-	-	-	-	-
	Average	-	-	-	-	-	-
Disability Insurance	Median	-	-	-	-	-	-
	Average	-	-	-	-	-	-
Retirement	Median	-	$1,038	$554	-	-	-
	Average	-	$1,019	$821	-	-	-
Continuing Education	Median	-	$250	-	-	-	-
	Average	-	$298	-	-	-	-
Total Benefits	**Median**	**$1,800**	**$1,038**	**$554**	**-**	**-**	**-**
	Average	**$2,632**	**$2,760**	**$1,767**	**-**	**-**	**-**
TOTAL COMPENSATION PLUS BENEFITS	**Median**	**$10,000**	**$14,897**	**$15,402**	**$15,600**	**$18,600**	**$17,246**
	Average	**$10,912**	**$14,838**	**$15,875**	**$15,953**	**$18,012**	**$18,839**
Number of Respondents		128	199	81	44	27	49

- Not enough response to provide meaningful data.

* For detailed description and definitions of Data Distribution (Median and Average), see chapter 1, Explanation of Data Distribution.

Table 14-11: Annual Compensation of Part-Time Secretaries/Administrative Assistants by Church Setting

	Data Distribution*	CHURCH SETTING			
		Metro-politan city	Suburb of large city	Small town or rural city	Farming area
CHARACTERISTICS					
Average weekend worship attendance		553	601	284	174
Average church income		$994,405	$1,093,104	$455,435	$284,205
Average # of years employed		6	6	8	9
Average # of paid vacation days		11	12	11	11
% College graduate or higher		55%	45%	29%	38%
% Who receive auto reimbursement/allowance		5%	16%	8%	6%
% Ordained		8%	4%	1%	0%
% Supervise one or more people		11%	13%	10%	21%
Average % salary increase (for those who had an increase) this year		5.3%	3.8%	4.2%	3.4%
HOURLY RATE					
Base Rate	Average	$14	$14	$12	$12
COMPENSATION					
Base Salary	Median	$14,676	$15,925	$12,480	$10,648
	Average	$14,421	$16,693	$13,413	$11,172
Housing	Median	-	-	-	-
	Average	-	-	-	-
Parsonage	Median	-	-	-	-
	Average	-	-	-	-
Total Compensation	**Median**	**$15,283**	**$15,963**	**$12,480**	**$10,648**
	Average	**$15,407**	**$16,366**	**$12,895**	**$11,172**
BENEFITS					
Health Insurance	Median	-	$4,590	-	-
	Average	-	$7,038	-	-
Life Insurance	Median	-	-	-	-
	Average	-	-	-	-
Disability Insurance	Median	-	-	-	-
	Average	-	-	-	-
Retirement	Median	-	$700	$1,108	-
	Average	-	$859	$1,094	-
Continuing Education	Median	-	-	$300	-
	Average	-	-	$336	-
Total Benefits	**Median**	**$2,987**	**$1,048**	**$766**	**-**
	Average	**$3,377**	**$3,326**	**$2,324**	**-**
TOTAL COMPENSATION PLUS BENEFITS	**Median**	**$15,804**	**$16,276**	**$12,600**	**$10,648**
	Average	**$15,882**	**$16,903**	**$13,188**	**$11,224**
Number of Respondents		60	199	241	34

- Not enough response to provide meaningful data.

* For detailed description and definitions of Data Distribution (Median and Average), see chapter 1, Explanation of Data Distribution.

Table 14-12: Annual Compensation of Part-Time Secretaries/Administrative Assistants by Region

	Data Distribution*	REGION								
		New England	Middle Atlantic	South Atlantic	E-N Central	E-S Central	W-N Central	W-S Central	Mountain	Pacific
CHARACTERISTICS										
Average weekend worship attendance		273	450	239	387	291	294	775	504	632
Average church income		$583,647	$825,951	$509,783	$672,831	$519,089	$530,767	$1,071,424	$739,477	$1,135,381
Average # of years employed		8	8	7	8	9	7	7	5	7
Average # of paid vacation days		11	11	11	12	10	13	14	12	11
% College graduate or higher		27%	28%	46%	38%	36%	37%	50%	24%	44%
% Who receive auto reimbursement/allowance		0%	3%	12%	10%	3%	20%	3%	9%	22%
% Ordained		0%	3%	5%	2%	0%	5%	0%	2%	5%
% Supervise one or more people		17%	12%	5%	15%	7%	19%	15%	7%	13%
Average % salary increase (for those who had an increase) this year		-	5.2%	4.8%	3.8%	4.4%	3.3%	3.3%	5.4%	3.3%
HOURLY RATE										
Base Rate	Average	$13	$12	$13	$12	$11	$13	$13	$13	$14
COMPENSATION										
Base Salary	Median	$12,462	$10,348	$14,158	$13,478	$13,104	$17,463	$15,142	$14,246	$15,288
	Average	$13,276	$11,338	$15,416	$13,600	$13,234	$17,626	$18,077	$13,840	$16,374
Housing	Median	-	-	-	-	-	-	-	-	-
	Average	-	-	-	-	-	-	-	-	-
Parsonage	Median	-	-	-	-	-	-	-	-	-
	Average	-	-	-	-	-	-	-	-	-
Total Compensation	**Median**	**$12,462**	**$10,400**	**$14,227**	**$13,478**	**$13,104**	**$18,000**	**$15,000**	**$14,763**	**$15,441**
	Average	**$13,276**	**$11,685**	**$14,476**	**$13,600**	**$13,746**	**$18,219**	**$15,048**	**$14,182**	**$15,844**
BENEFITS										
Health Insurance	Median	-	-	-	-	-	-	-	-	-
	Average	-	-	-	-	-	-	-	-	-
Life Insurance	Median	-	-	-	-	-	-	-	-	-
	Average	-	-	-	-	-	-	-	-	-
Disability Insurance	Median	-	-	-	-	-	-	-	-	-
	Average	-	-	-	-	-	-	-	-	-
Retirement	Median	-	-	-	$1,003	-	-	-	-	-
	Average	-	-	-	$959	-	-	-	-	-
Continuing Education	Median	-	-	-	-	-	-	-	-	-
	Average	-	-	-	-	-	-	-	-	-
Total Benefits	**Median**	-	**$1,520**	**$550**	**$800**	-	**$1,150**	-	-	**$4,200**
	Average	-	**$4,650**	**$1,859**	**$941**	-	**$3,547**	-	-	**$3,294**
TOTAL COMPENSATION PLUS BENEFITS	**Median**	**$12,462**	**$10,400**	**$14,575**	**$13,500**	**$13,565**	**$19,000**	**$15,283**	**$14,763**	**$15,597**
	Average	**$13,724**	**$12,339**	**$14,804**	**$13,703**	**$14,020**	**$18,849**	**$15,465**	**$14,772**	**$16,321**
Number of Respondents		18	67	84	134	31	45	34	43	79

- Not enough response to provide meaningful data.

* For detailed description and definitions of Data Distribution (Median and Average), see chapter 1, Explanation of Data Distribution.

Table 14-13: Annual Compensation of Part-Time Secretaries/Administrative Assistants by Education

	Data Distribution*	EDUCATION			
		Less than Bachelor	Bachelor	Master	Doctorate
CHARACTERISTICS					
Average weekend worship attendance		394	491	368	-
Average church income		$643,632	$915,202	$594,569	-
Average # of years employed		8	6	6	-
Average # of paid vacation days		12	12	9	-
% College graduate or higher		0%	100%	100%	-
% Who receive auto reimbursement/allowance		8%	18%	4%	-
% Ordained		2%	4%	13%	-
% Supervise one or more people		10%	16%	16%	-
Average % salary increase (for those who had an increase) this year		4.6%	3.3%	3.1%	-
HOURLY RATE					
Base Rate	Average	$12	$13	$14	-
COMPENSATION					
Base Salary	Median	$13,500	$15,286	$14,587	-
	Average	$14,006	$15,747	$14,614	-
Housing	Median	-	-	-	-
	Average	-	-	-	-
Parsonage	Median	-	-	-	-
	Average	-	-	-	-
Total Compensation	**Median**	**$13,500**	**$15,288**	**$14,587**	**-**
	Average	**$13,778**	**$15,361**	**$14,614**	**-**
BENEFITS					
Health Insurance	Median	$4,200	-	-	-
	Average	$6,530	-	-	-
Life Insurance	Median	-	-	-	-
	Average	-	-	-	-
Disability Insurance	Median	$302	-	-	-
	Average	$291	-	-	-
Retirement	Median	$802	$952	-	-
	Average	$955	$993	-	-
Continuing Education	Median	$275	-	-	-
	Average	$328	-	-	-
Total Benefits	**Median**	**$1,050**	**$973**	**-**	**-**
	Average	**$3,045**	**$2,671**	**-**	**-**
TOTAL COMPENSATION PLUS BENEFITS	**Median**	**$13,521**	**$15,594**	**$14,587**	**-**
	Average	**$14,214**	**$15,693**	**$15,057**	**-**
Number of Respondents		319	171	25	0

- Not enough response to provide meaningful data.

* For detailed description and definitions of Data Distribution (Median and Average), see chapter 1, Explanation of Data Distribution.

Table 14-14: Annual Compensation of Part-Time Secretaries/Administrative Assistants by Years Employed

	Data Distribution*	YEARS EMPLOYED			
		Less than 6 years	6-10 years	11-15 years	Over 15 years
CHARACTERISTICS					
Average weekend worship attendance		514	416	255	319
Average church income		$882,975	$713,416	$507,942	$521,252
Average # of years employed		3	8	13	21
Average # of paid vacation days		10	13	12	15
% College graduate or higher		44%	34%	27%	27%
% Who receive auto reimbursement/allowance		12%	12%	11%	4%
% Ordained		4%	2%	0%	2%
% Supervise one or more people		10%	12%	13%	20%
Average % salary increase (for those who had an increase) this year		4.8%	2.7%	3.9%	3.5%
HOURLY RATE					
Base Rate	Average	$12	$13	$13	$13
COMPENSATION					
Base Salary	Median	$13,500	$15,000	$13,104	$14,000
	Average	$13,982	$16,391	$14,555	$13,935
Housing	Median	-	-	-	-
	Average	-	-	-	-
Parsonage	Median	-	-	-	-
	Average	-	-	-	-
Total Compensation	**Median**	**$13,500**	**$15,000**	**$14,500**	**$14,000**
	Average	**$13,840**	**$15,397**	**$15,108**	**$13,935**
BENEFITS					
Health Insurance	Median	-	$6,941	-	-
	Average	-	$8,064	-	-
Life Insurance	Median	-	-	-	-
	Average	-	-	-	-
Disability Insurance	Median	-	-	-	-
	Average	-	-	-	-
Retirement	Median	$750	$1,032	-	-
	Average	$967	$974	-	-
Continuing Education	Median	-	$275	-	-
	Average	-	$336	-	-
Total Benefits	**Median**	**$634**	**$1,048**	-	**$1,510**
	Average	**$2,145**	**$3,465**	-	**$3,985**
TOTAL COMPENSATION PLUS BENEFITS	**Median**	**$13,510**	**$15,109**	**$14,575**	**$14,000**
	Average	**$14,075**	**$16,214**	**$15,325**	**$14,495**
Number of Respondents		253	127	54	57

- *Not enough response to provide meaningful data.*

* *For detailed description and definitions of Data Distribution (Median and Average), see chapter 1, Explanation of Data Distribution.*

Table 14-15: Annual Compensation of Part-Time Secretaries/Administrative Assistants by Denomination

	Data Distribution*	DENOMINATION					
		Assemblies of God	Baptist	Independent/ Nondenom.	Lutheran	Methodist	Presby- terian
CHARACTERISTICS							
Average weekend worship attendance		383	389	517	197	537	256
Average church income		$656,840	$777,081	$860,600	$355,058	$731,818	$734,085
Average # of years employed		7	7	7	9	6	8
Average # of paid vacation days		14	11	11	11	12	13
% College graduate or higher		35%	37%	30%	23%	52%	66%
% Who receive auto reimbursement/allowance		9%	12%	7%	14%	5%	14%
% Ordained		10%	1%	2%	0%	2%	3%
% Supervise one or more people		23%	7%	12%	18%	12%	11%
Average % salary increase (for those who had an increase) this year		5.0%	4.6%	4.8%	-	2.9%	3.1%
HOURLY RATE							
Base Rate	Average	$12	$12	$13	$12	$13	$14
COMPENSATION							
Base Salary	Median	$10,296	$13,746	$13,500	$14,788	$15,283	$18,450
	Average	$12,668	$15,078	$14,590	$14,658	$15,887	$17,451
Housing	Median	-	-	-	-	-	-
	Average	-	-	-	-	-	-
Parsonage	Median	-	-	-	-	-	-
	Average	-	-	-	-	-	-
Total Compensation	**Median**	**$10,296**	**$13,565**	**$13,500**	**$14,788**	**$15,392**	**$18,450**
	Average	**$12,668**	**$13,753**	**$14,128**	**$14,658**	**$16,682**	**$17,451**
BENEFITS							
Health Insurance	Median	-	-	-	-	-	-
	Average	-	-	-	-	-	-
Life Insurance	Median	-	-	-	-	-	-
	Average	-	-	-	-	-	-
Disability Insurance	Median	-	-	-	-	-	-
	Average	-	-	-	-	-	-
Retirement	Median	-	-	-	-	-	-
	Average	-	-	-	-	-	-
Continuing Education	Median	-	-	-	-	-	-
	Average	-	-	-	-	-	-
Total Benefits	**Median**	-	**$1,046**	**$937**	-	**$689**	**$1,520**
	Average	-	**$3,045**	**$3,342**	-	**$1,090**	**$2,261**
TOTAL COMPENSATION PLUS BENEFITS	**Median**	**$10,296**	**$13,993**	**$14,000**	**$14,965**	**$15,392**	**$18,720**
	Average	**$12,730**	**$14,052**	**$14,582**	**$15,383**	**$16,933**	**$18,001**
Number of Respondents		33	146	107	22	43	37

- Not enough response to provide meaningful data.

* For detailed description and definitions of Data Distribution (Median and Average), see chapter 1, Explanation of Data Distribution.

Table 14-16: Annual Compensation of Part-Time Secretaries/Administrative Assistants by Gender

	Data Distribution*	GENDER	
		Male	Female
CHARACTERISTICS			
Average weekend worship attendance		347	430
Average church income		$713,909	$743,390
Average # of years employed		4	7
Average # of paid vacation days		11	12
% College graduate or higher		60%	38%
% Who receive auto reimbursement/allowance		18%	11%
% Ordained		9%	3%
% Supervise one or more people		18%	12%
Average % salary increase (for those who had an increase) this year		-	3.9%
HOURLY RATE			
Base Rate	Average	$13	$13
COMPENSATION			
Base Salary	Median	$12,400	$14,000
	Average	$11,923	$14,507
Housing	Median	-	-
	Average	-	-
Parsonage	Median	-	-
	Average	-	-
Total Compensation	**Median**	**$14,190**	**$14,000**
	Average	**$15,103**	**$14,363**
BENEFITS			
Health Insurance	Median	-	$5,500
	Average	-	$6,907
Life Insurance	Median	-	-
	Average	-	-
Disability Insurance	Median	-	$302
	Average	-	$286
Retirement	Median	-	$884
	Average	-	$940
Continuing Education	Median	-	$300
	Average	-	$352
Total Benefits	**Median**	**-**	**$973**
	Average	**-**	**$2,808**
TOTAL COMPENSATION PLUS BENEFITS	**Median**	**$14,190**	**$14,089**
	Average	**$15,103**	**$14,745**
Number of Respondents		11	519

- Not enough response to provide meaningful data.

* For detailed description and definitions of Data Distribution (Median and Average), see chapter 1, Explanation of Data Distribution.

Full-Time Secretary/Administrative Assistant Worksheet

	Enter your church data below	The 2014–2015 Compensation Handbook for Church Staff		Enter *Compensation Handbook* data below			
				Highest 25%	Median	Lowest 25%	Average
Church Income	$	Table 14-1	page 247	$	$	$	$
Worship Attendance		Table 14-2	page 248	n/a	$	n/a	$
Church Setting (metro, suburb, small town, or farming area)		Table 14-3	page 249	n/a	$	n/a	$
Region		Table 14-4	page 250	n/a	$	n/a	$
Person's Education		Table 14-5	page 251	n/a	$	n/a	$
Years Employed		Table 14-6	page 252	n/a	$	n/a	$
Denomination (if applicable)		Table 14-7	page 253	n/a	$	n/a	$

Looking at the table and page number references indicated in the *2014–2015 Compensation Handbook for Church Staff* columns above, locate the appropriate range for your church. Refer to the instructions below for step-by-step help.

FILLING OUT THE WORKSHEET

1. Fill in the gray boxes under *Enter your church data* with your church demographic information as follows:

   ▶ **Income** (Total annual church budget in past year)
   ▶ **Worship attendance** (Number of people, including children, who attend all weekend services)
   ▶ **Church setting** (Metropolitan city, suburb of large city, small town or rural city, or farming area)

   ▶ **Region** (Locate your state's region in the appendix on page 346.)
   ▶ **Education** (Highest level of education: less than bachelor, bachelor, master, or doctorate)

2. Use Table 14-1 (page 247) in your *2014–2015 Compensation Handbook for Church Staff* to enter data pertinent to your church. In the heading (top row), locate your church **income** from the five available ranges. Follow that column to the bottom rows, and copy the *Highest 25%*, *Median*, *Lowest 25%*, and *Average* amounts onto your worksheet.

3. Use Table 14-2 (page 248) on your *2014–2015 Compensation Handbook for Church Staff* to enter data pertinent to your church. In the heading (top row), locate your church's

worship attendance from the six available ranges. Follow that column to the bottom rows, and copy the *Median* and *Average* amounts onto your worksheet.

4. Use Table 14-3 (page 249) on your *2014–2015 Compensation Handbook for Church Staff* to enter data pertinent to your church. In the heading (top row), choose the **church setting** that best describes your church. Follow that column to the bottom rows, and copy the *Median* and *Average* amounts onto your worksheet.

5. Use Table 14-4 (page 250) on your *2014–2015 Compensation Handbook for Church Staff* to enter data pertinent to your church. In the heading (top row), look for the **region** where your church is located. Follow that column to the bottom rows, and copy the *Median* and *Average* amounts onto your worksheet.

6. Use Table 14-5 (page 251) on your *2014–2015 Compensation Handbook for Church Staff* to enter data pertinent to your Secretary/Administrative Assistant. In the heading (top row), look for **your Secretary/Administrative Assistant's highest level of education**. Follow that column to the bottom rows, and copy the *Median* and *Average* amounts onto your worksheet.

7. Use Table 14-6 (page 252) on your *2014–2015 Compensation Handbook for Church Staff* to enter data pertinent to your Secretary/Administrative Assistant. In the heading (top row), locate the **number of years your Secretary/Administrative Assistant has been employed**. Follow that column to the bottom rows, and copy the *Median* and *Average* amounts onto your worksheet.

8. Use Table 14-7 (page 253) on your *2014–2015 Compensation Handbook for Church Staff* to enter data pertinent to your church. In the

heading (top row), look for **your church's denominational affiliation**. Follow that column to the bottom rows, and copy the *Median* and *Average* amounts onto your worksheet. If your church is not affiliated with a denomination, leave this section blank.

DETERMINING COMPENSATION

This tool will not provide you with a single compensation amount but rather with a range of values to help you determine the compensation appropriate to your situation.

1. Look at the values in the shaded *Median* column. Circle the **lowest** and the **highest** values. **This is the range of the median compensation plus benefits for churches similar to yours.**

2. For a variety of reasons, compensation plus benefits may be higher or lower than the range established in this table. Income and attendance are two significant factors affecting church compensation packages. If church income or attendance skews higher, you might want to consider moving toward or above the higher end of the range. Likewise, if church income or attendance skews lower, you may consider moving the package toward or below the lower end of the range.

3. Examine additional variables that might impact the compensation package you offer, such as years of service, education, and church setting.

4. Determine other circumstances unique to your situation, such as cost of living in your area, theological beliefs, pastoral performance, financial needs, the local economy, personal motivation, congregational goals, and others.

5. You now have a compensation package range based on the *2014–2015 Compensation Handbook*. Since each church and position are unique, your final compensation package will be based on additional factors unique to your situation.

Part-Time Secretary/Administrative Assistant Worksheet

	Enter your church data below	The 2014–2015 Compensation Handbook for Church Staff		Enter *Compensation Handbook* data below			
				Highest 25%	Median	Lowest 25%	Average
Church Income	$	Table 14-9	page 255	$	$	$	$
Worship Attendance		Table 14-10	page 256	n/a	$	n/a	$
Church Setting (metro, suburb, small town, or farming area)		Table 14-11	page 257	n/a	$	n/a	$
Region		Table 14-12	page 258	n/a	$	n/a	$
Person's Education		Table 14-13	page 259	n/a	$	n/a	$
Years Employed		Table 14-14	page 260	n/a	$	n/a	$
Denomination (if applicable)		Table 14-15	page 261	n/a	$	n/a	$

Looking at the table and page number references indicated in the *2014–2015 Compensation Handbook for Church Staff* columns above, locate the appropriate range for your church. Refer to the instructions below for step-by-step help.

FILLING OUT THE WORKSHEET

1. Fill in the gray boxes under *Enter your church data* with your church demographic information as follows:

   ▶ **Income** (Total annual church budget in past year)
   ▶ **Worship attendance** (Number of people, including children, who attend all weekend services)
   ▶ **Church setting** (Metropolitan city, suburb of large city, small town or rural city, or farming area)

   ▶ **Region** (Locate your state's region in the appendix on page 346.)
   ▶ **Education** (Highest level of education: less than bachelor, bachelor, master, or doctorate)

2. Use Table 14-9 (page 255) in your *2014–2015 Compensation Handbook for Church Staff* to enter data pertinent to your church. In the heading (top row), locate your church **income** from the five available ranges. Follow that column to the bottom rows, and copy the *Highest 25%*, *Median*, *Lowest 25%*, and *Average* amounts onto your worksheet.

3. Use Table 14-10 (page 256) on your *2014–2015 Compensation Handbook for Church Staff* to enter data pertinent to your church. In the heading (top row), locate your church's

worship attendance from the six available ranges. Follow that column to the bottom rows, and copy the *Median* and *Average* amounts onto your worksheet.

4. Use Table 14-11 (page 257) on your *2014–2015 Compensation Handbook for Church Staff* to enter data pertinent to your church. In the heading (top row), choose the **church setting** that best describes your church. Follow that column to the bottom rows, and copy the *Median* and *Average* amounts onto your worksheet.

5. Use Table 14-12 (page 258) on your *2014–2015 Compensation Handbook for Church Staff* to enter data pertinent to your church. In the heading (top row), look for the **region** where your church is located. Follow that column to the bottom rows, and copy the *Median* and *Average* amounts onto your worksheet.

6. Use Table 14-13 (page 259) on your *2014–2015 Compensation Handbook for Church Staff* to enter data pertinent to your Secretary/Administrative Assistant. In the heading (top row), look for **your Secretary/Administrative Assistant's highest level of education**. Follow that column to the bottom rows, and copy the *Median* and *Average* amounts onto your worksheet.

7. Use Table 14-14 (page 260) on your *2014–2015 Compensation Handbook for Church Staff* to enter data pertinent to your Secretary/Administrative Assistant. In the heading (top row), locate the **number of years your Secretary/Administrative Assistant has been employed**. Follow that column to the bottom rows, and copy the *Median* and *Average* amounts onto your worksheet.

8. Use Table 14-15 (page 261) on your *2014–2015 Compensation Handbook for Church Staff* to enter data pertinent to your church. In the

heading (top row), look for **your church's denominational affiliation**. Follow that column to the bottom rows, and copy the *Median* and *Average* amounts onto your worksheet. If your church is not affiliated with a denomination, leave this section blank.

DETERMINING COMPENSATION

This tool will not provide you with a single compensation amount but rather with a range of values to help you determine the compensation appropriate to your situation.

1. Look at the values in the shaded *Median* column. Circle the **lowest** and the **highest** values. **This is the range of the median compensation plus benefits for churches similar to yours.**

2. For a variety of reasons, compensation plus benefits may be higher or lower than the range established in this table. Income and attendance are two significant factors affecting church compensation packages. If church income or attendance skews higher, you might want to consider moving toward or above the higher end of the range. Likewise, if church income or attendance skews lower, you may consider moving the package toward or below the lower end of the range.

3. Examine additional variables that might impact the compensation package you offer, such as years of service, education, and church setting.

4. Determine other circumstances unique to your situation, such as cost of living in your area, theological beliefs, pastoral performance, financial needs, the local economy, personal motivation, congregational goals, and others.

5. You now have a compensation package range based on the *2014–2015 Compensation Handbook*. Since each church and position are unique, your final compensation package will be based on additional factors unique to your situation.

15

CUSTODIANS

Employment Profile

Custodians include paid personnel who provide care and maintenance of facilities, buildings, grounds, and security. This category may include such positions as Building and Grounds Manager, Building Supervisor, Custodian, Facilities Manager, Groundskeeper, Housekeeper, Lawn Maintenance Assistant, Maid, Maintenance Assistant, Plant Manager, Property Manager, Security Manager or Assistant, Sexton, Traffic Coordinator, etc.

More than six in 10 Custodians in this survey serve part-time. Almost nine in 10 full-time Custodians are men, compared to 65% for part-time Custodians. The highest level of education for most full-time and part-time Custodians is a high school diploma. Almost all full-time and part-time Custodians are employed by the church rather than self-employed.

The chart below provides a demographic profile of this sample.

	Full-Time	Part-Time
Number of respondents	**188**	**314**
Ordained	3%	3%
Average years employed	9	6
Male	89%	65%
Female	11%	35%
Self-employed (receives 1099)	2%	3%
Church employee (receives W-2)	98%	97%
High school diploma	70%	73%
Associate degree	9%	10%
Bachelor's degree	20%	15%
Master's degree	23%	1%
Doctoral degree	0%	0%

Total Compensation plus Benefits Package Analysis

The following analyses are based on data in the tables you will find later in this chapter. The tables show compensation plus benefits data for full-time and part-time Custodians and are presented according to church income, church attendance, church setting, region, education, years employed, denomination, and gender. In this way, the Custodian's compensation plus benefits can be analyzed and compared from a variety of useful perspectives.

The total compensation plus benefits amount includes the base salary; housing allowance and/or parsonage amount; health, life, and disability insurance payments; retirement contribution; and educational funds.

A worksheet at the end of this chapter is provided to help you apply the data to your church's situation.

Custodians receive fewer benefits than people in pastoral positions, but their benefits are aligned with those for other nonpastoral positions. More than six in 10 full-time Custodians receive health insurance and salary increases. Paid vacation is part of nearly all full-time Custodians' compensation plus benefits packages. Churches provide part-time Custodians with few benefits compared to those of full-time employees. The percentage of full-time Custodians who received auto reimbursements nearly doubled to 25% since the previous study, conducted in 2011.

Compensation Plus Benefits	Full-Time	Part-Time
Base Salary	100%	100%
Housing	1%	0%
Parsonage	1%	0%
Health Insurance*	62%	3%
Life Insurance*	34%	2%
Disability Insurance*	26%	4%
Retirement	46%	4%
Continuing Education	4%	1%
Received salary increase	59%	41%
Received paid vacation	95%	34%
Received auto reimbursement/allowance	25%	7%

Only those reporting individual premiums for Health, Life, or Disability (not total insurance premiums) are included.

KEY POINTS

* Two-thirds of full-time Custodians reported in this sample serve in larger churches with income over $1,000,000.

* Four in 10 full-time Custodians are serving in churches set in a suburb of a large city.

* For the most part, as church income, worship attendance, and education level increase, compensation and benefits for full-time Custodians also increase.

* Full-time male Custodians earn 33% more than full-time female Custodians.

Compensation & Benefits: National Averages for Full-Time Custodians	
2000	$26,161
2001	$26,725
2002	$27,913
2003	$29,047
2004	$30,052
2005	$31,026
2006	$32,884
2007	$33,893
2008	$36,462
2009	$35,425
2011	$38,156
2013	$40,176*

* The above trend is made available for your reference only. In addition to looking at this overall data, please refer to the detailed tables using your church's income, attendance, setting, region, and denomination as well as the person's education, gender, and years employed for guidance in compensating this position.

Table 15-1: Annual Compensation of Full-Time Custodians by Church Income

CHARACTERISTICS	Data Distribution*	CHURCH INCOME				
		$250K & Under	$251-$500K	$501-$750K	$751K-$1M	Over $1 Million
Average weekend worship attendance		-	-	350	435	1,144
Average church income		-	-	$628,990	$884,499	$2,248,354
Average # of years employed		-	-	8	12	8
Average # of paid vacation days		-	-	14	16	16
% College graduate or higher		-	-	17%	17%	25%
% Who receive auto reimbursement/allowance		-	-	8%	22%	31%
% Ordained		-	-	0%	5%	3%
% Supervise one or more people		-	-	19%	55%	55%
Average % salary increase (for those who had an increase) this year		-	-	3.1%	2.1%	2.8%
COMPENSATION						
Base Salary	Highest 25%	-	-	$34,968	$39,750	$44,000
	Median	-	-	$28,440	$27,560	$35,510
	Lowest 25%	-	-	$22,338	$20,899	$28,993
	Average	-	-	$28,648	$30,337	$36,859
Housing	Highest 25%	-	-	-	-	-
	Median	-	-	-	-	-
	Lowest 25%	-	-	-	-	-
	Average	-	-	-	-	-
Parsonage	Highest 25%	-	-	-	-	-
	Median	-	-	-	-	-
	Lowest 25%	-	-	-	-	-
	Average	-	-	-	-	-
Total Compensation	**Highest 25%**	-	-	**$34,968**	**$39,750**	**$44,000**
	Median	-	-	**$28,440**	**$27,560**	**$35,510**
	Lowest 25%	-	-	**$22,338**	**$20,899**	**$28,993**
	Average	-	-	**$28,648**	**$30,337**	**$37,160**
BENEFITS						
Health Insurance	Highest 25%	-	-	$9,447	$12,509	$12,000
	Median	-	-	$8,153	$6,270	$6,536
	Lowest 25%	-	-	$3,326	$3,178	$4,474
	Average	-	-	$7,063	$7,409	$8,033
Life Insurance	Highest 25%	-	-	-	-	$300
	Median	-	-	-	-	$288
	Lowest 25%	-	-	-	-	$115
	Average	-	-	-	-	$241
Disability Insurance	Highest 25%	-	-	-	-	$360
	Median	-	-	-	-	$270
	Lowest 25%	-	-	-	-	$157
	Average	-	-	-	-	$279
Retirement	Highest 25%	-	-	-	$1,680	$3,127
	Median	-	-	-	$1,500	$2,131
	Lowest 25%	-	-	-	$1,260	$1,243
	Average	-	-	-	$1,723	$2,382
Continuing Education	Highest 25%	-	-	-	-	$1,350
	Median	-	-	-	-	$550
	Lowest 25%	-	-	-	-	$300
	Average	-	-	-	-	$823
Total Benefits	**Highest 25%**	-	-	**$8,697**	**$10,965**	**$12,123**
	Median	-	-	**$4,795**	**$5,389**	**$7,830**
	Lowest 25%	-	-	**$1,893**	**$1,715**	**$3,717**
	Average	-	-	**$5,930**	**$6,506**	**$8,499**
TOTAL COMPENSATION PLUS BENEFITS	**Highest 25%**	-	-	**$38,943**	**$41,680**	**$53,817**
	Median	-	-	**$31,968**	**$31,786**	**$41,560**
	Lowest 25%	-	-	**$22,748**	**$25,090**	**$32,860**
	Average	-	-	**$31,841**	**$34,863**	**$44,019**
Number of Respondents		5	7	26	23	120

- *Not enough response to provide meaningful data.*

* *For detailed description and definitions of Data Distribution (Highest 25%, Median, Lowest 25%, and Average), see chapter 1, Explanation of Data Distribution.*

Table 15-2: Annual Compensation of Full-Time Custodians by Worship Attendance

	Data Distribution*	WORSHIP ATTENDANCE					
		100 or less	101-300	301-500	501-750	751-1,000	Over 1,000
CHARACTERISTICS							
Average weekend worship attendance		-	249	409	643	896	1,973
Average church income		-	$878,983	$968,445	$1,437,240	$1,573,313	$3,291,810
Average # of years employed		-	10	8	10	7	9
Average # of paid vacation days		-	15	15	15	16	16
% College graduate or higher		-	26%	8%	25%	21%	30%
% Who receive auto reimbursement/allowance		-	21%	30%	22%	23%	33%
% Ordained		-	4%	3%	0%	3%	2%
% Supervise one or more people		-	33%	33%	52%	48%	63%
Average % salary increase (for those who had an increase) this year		-	2.7%	2.9%	2.9%	3.1%	2.7%
COMPENSATION							
Base Salary	Median	-	$28,040	$28,550	$35,662	$35,754	$36,394
	Average	-	$30,346	$29,379	$36,916	$35,421	$38,064
Housing	Median	-	-	-	-	-	-
	Average	-	-	-	-	-	-
Parsonage	Median	-	-	-	-	-	-
	Average	-	-	-	-	-	-
Total Compensation	**Median**	-	**$28,040**	**$28,550**	**$35,662**	**$37,724**	**$36,394**
	Average	-	**$30,346**	**$29,379**	**$36,916**	**$36,972**	**$38,064**
BENEFITS							
Health Insurance	Median	-	$6,531	$8,400	$8,040	$6,863	$5,916
	Average	-	$5,604	$8,715	$8,493	$8,808	$7,209
Life Insurance	Median	-	-	$251	-	$218	$156
	Average	-	-	$239	-	$280	$251
Disability Insurance	Median	-	-	-	-	$313	$220
	Average	-	-	-	-	$337	$249
Retirement	Median	-	$1,663	$2,448	$1,500	$1,998	$1,632
	Average	-	$2,151	$2,507	$2,015	$2,500	$1,996
Continuing Education	Median	-	-	-	-	-	-
	Average	-	-	-	-	-	-
Total Benefits	**Median**	-	**$2,606**	**$8,400**	**$8,510**	**$10,040**	**$7,100**
	Average	-	**$4,529**	**$8,954**	**$7,782**	**$10,364**	**$7,472**
TOTAL COMPENSATION PLUS BENEFITS	**Median**	-	**$30,016**	**$35,548**	**$38,943**	**$44,719**	**$39,774**
	Average	-	**$33,096**	**$35,393**	**$42,995**	**$43,696**	**$44,926**
Number of Respondents		3	28	40	32	31	49

- Not enough response to provide meaningful data.

* For detailed description and definitions of Data Distribution (Median and Average), see chapter 1, Explanation of Data Distribution.

Table 15-3: Annual Compensation of Full-Time Custodians by Church Setting

	Data Distribution*	CHURCH SETTING			
		Metro-politan city	Suburb of large city	Small town or rural city	Farming area
CHARACTERISTICS					
Average weekend worship attendance		946	1,085	723	-
Average church income		$1,942,868	$2,114,435	$1,169,236	-
Average # of years employed		10	9	8	-
Average # of paid vacation days		16	16	15	-
% College graduate or higher		26%	27%	11%	-
% Who receive auto reimbursement/allowance		17%	34%	21%	-
% Ordained		11%	1%	0%	-
% Supervise one or more people		57%	53%	32%	-
Average % salary increase (for those who had an increase) this year		2.4%	3.0%	3.1%	-
COMPENSATION					
Base Salary	Median	$38,000	$33,800	$28,290	-
	Average	$38,202	$35,788	$29,877	-
Housing	Median	-	-	-	-
	Average	-	-	-	-
Parsonage	Median	-	-	-	-
	Average	-	-	-	-
Total Compensation	**Median**	**$38,000**	**$33,930**	**$28,290**	**-**
	Average	**$38,202**	**$36,397**	**$29,877**	**-**
BENEFITS					
Health Insurance	Median	$6,635	$7,906	$6,414	-
	Average	$7,033	$8,396	$7,560	-
Life Insurance	Median	$212	$150	$222	-
	Average	$290	$222	$232	-
Disability Insurance	Median	-	$237	$318	-
	Average	-	$255	$340	-
Retirement	Median	$2,250	$1,687	$2,075	-
	Average	$2,702	$2,003	$2,259	-
Continuing Education	Median	-	-	-	-
	Average	-	-	-	-
Total Benefits	**Median**	**$6,410**	**$7,819**	**$6,431**	**-**
	Average	**$6,759**	**$8,358**	**$7,985**	**-**
TOTAL COMPENSATION PLUS BENEFITS	**Median**	**$40,000**	**$39,859**	**$33,600**	**-**
	Average	**$43,748**	**$42,271**	**$35,997**	**-**
Number of Respondents		39	79	67	3

- Not enough response to provide meaningful data.

* For detailed description and definitions of Data Distribution (Median and Average), see chapter 1, Explanation of Data Distribution.

Table 15-4: Annual Compensation of Full-Time Custodians by Region

	Data Distribution*	REGION								
		New England	Middle Atlantic	South Atlantic	E-N Central	E-S Central	W-N Central	W-S Central	Mountain	Pacific
CHARACTERISTICS										
Average weekend worship attendance	-	1,088	658	733	771	652	1,061	1,356	1,338	
Average church income	-	$2,486,993	$1,641,250	$1,232,602	$1,397,364	$1,407,567	$1,622,723	$1,336,686	$2,887,474
Average # of years employed	-	9	9	8	11	10	8	5	10
Average # of paid vacation days	-	14	17	15	16	17	14	15	15
% College graduate or higher	-	17%	30%	18%	6%	19%	13%	14%	45%
% Who receive auto reimbursement/allowance	-	13%	41%	21%	35%	32%	22%	0%	30%
% Ordained	-	4%	4%	3%	0%	5%	0%	0%	5%
% Supervise one or more people	-	38%	41%	42%	44%	60%	36%	57%	50%
Average % salary increase (for those who had an increase) this year	-	2.8%	3.7%	2.7%	3.7%	2.9%	2.6%	2.7%	2.2%
COMPENSATION										
Base Salary	Median	-	$31,579	$33,260	$30,015	$27,085	$39,000	$28,290	$34,400	$35,830
	Average	-	$36,200	$35,578	$32,106	$29,017	$37,709	$27,961	$33,253	$38,599
Housing	Median	-	-	-	-	-	-	-	-	-
	Average	-	-	-	-	-	-	-	-	-
Parsonage	Median	-	-	-	-	-	-	-	-	-
	Average	-	-	-	-	-	-	-	-	-
Total Compensation	**Median**	-	**$31,947**	**$33,260**	**$30,015**	**$27,085**	**$39,000**	**$28,290**	**$34,400**	**$35,830**
	Average	-	**$36,700**	**$36,823**	**$32,106**	**$29,017**	**$37,709**	**$27,961**	**$33,253**	**$38,599**
BENEFITS										
Health Insurance	Median	-	$6,816	$8,400	$7,334	$5,600	$10,000	$6,462	$6,444	$6,434
	Average	-	$8,212	$8,639	$8,289	$5,559	$9,297	$7,124	$6,892	$7,419
Life Insurance	Median	-	$163	$158	$143	-	$315	-	-	$132
	Average	-	$200	$189	$170	-	$384	-	-	$145
Disability Insurance	Median	-	-	$288	$209	-	-	-	-	$66
	Average	-	-	$335	$237	-	-	-	-	$145
Retirement	Median	-	$1,425	$3,000	$1,535	-	$2,190	-	-	-
	Average	-	$1,775	$3,187	$1,854	-	$2,380	-	-	-
Continuing Education	Median	-	-	-	-	-	-	-	-	-
	Average	-	-	-	-	-	-	-	-	-
Total Benefits	**Median**	-	**$6,477**	**$10,050**	**$7,117**	**$6,725**	**$4,955**	**$5,474**	**$7,858**	**$7,241**
	Average	-	**$8,234**	**$10,021**	**$7,735**	**$7,472**	**$7,359**	**$5,598**	**$6,995**	**$7,692**
TOTAL COMPENSATION PLUS BENEFITS	**Median**	-	**$38,334**	**$39,599**	**$34,000**	**$30,461**	**$41,040**	**$29,429**	**$38,371**	**$41,729**
	Average	-	**$44,249**	**$42,987**	**$37,966**	**$33,168**	**$43,730**	**$31,125**	**$38,249**	**$45,907**
Number of Respondents		5	24	29	33	18	22	23	14	20

- Not enough response to provide meaningful data.

* For detailed description and definitions of Data Distribution (Median and Average), see chapter 1, Explanation of Data Distribution.

Table 15-5: Annual Compensation of Full-Time Custodians by Education

	Data Distribution*	EDUCATION			
		Less than Bachelor	Bachelor	Master	Doctorate
CHARACTERISTICS					
Average weekend worship attendance		877	1,083	-	-
Average church income		$1,546,229	$2,165,987	-	-
Average # of years employed		9	8	-	-
Average # of paid vacation days		16	15	-	-
% College graduate or higher		0%	100%	-	-
% Who receive auto reimbursement/allowance		25%	29%	-	-
% Ordained		1%	6%	-	-
% Supervise one or more people		44%	58%	-	-
Average % salary increase (for those who had an increase) this year		2.9%	2.9%	-	-
COMPENSATION					
Base Salary	Median	$30,015	$40,000	-	-
	Average	$32,115	$40,087	-	-
Housing	Median	-	-	-	-
	Average	-	-	-	-
Parsonage	Median	-	-	-	-
	Average	-	-	-	-
Total Compensation	**Median**	**$30,122**	**$40,000**	**-**	**-**
	Average	**$32,199**	**$40,087**	**-**	**-**
BENEFITS					
Health Insurance	Median	$6,656	$6,656	-	-
	Average	$7,947	$6,750	-	-
Life Insurance	Median	$156	$137	-	-
	Average	$237	$228	-	-
Disability Insurance	Median	$299	$152	-	-
	Average	$288	$202	-	-
Retirement	Median	$1,860	$2,088	-	-
	Average	$2,160	$2,267	-	-
Continuing Education	Median	-	-	-	-
	Average	-	-	-	-
Total Benefits	**Median**	**$7,100**	**$6,869**	**-**	**-**
	Average	**$7,730**	**$7,332**	**-**	**-**
TOTAL COMPENSATION PLUS BENEFITS	**Median**	**$35,873**	**$43,239**	**-**	**-**
	Average	**$37,983**	**$46,197**	**-**	**-**
Number of Respondents		143	36	3	0

- Not enough response to provide meaningful data.

* For detailed description and definitions of Data Distribution (Median and Average), see chapter 1, Explanation of Data Distribution.

Table 15-6: Annual Compensation of Full-Time Custodians by Years Employed

	Data Distribution*	YEARS EMPLOYED			
		Less than 6 years	6-10 years	11-15 years	Over 15 years
CHARACTERISTICS					
Average weekend worship attendance		1,028	942	827	933
Average church income		$1,796,352	$1,805,754	$1,408,943	$1,985,851
Average # of years employed		3	8	13	22
Average # of paid vacation days		13	16	19	19
% College graduate or higher		26%	20%	9%	17%
% Who receive auto reimbursement/allowance		23%	27%	18%	33%
% Ordained		2%	0%	0%	8%
% Supervise one or more people		38%	49%	50%	83%
Average % salary increase (for those who had an increase) this year		3.4%	2.8%	2.1%	2.2%
COMPENSATION					
Base Salary	Median	$31,563	$34,284	$33,152	$40,000
	Average	$32,060	$35,222	$34,541	$41,777
Housing	Median	-	-	-	-
	Average	-	-	-	-
Parsonage	Median	-	-	-	-
	Average	-	-	-	-
Total Compensation	**Median**	**$31,563**	**$34,284**	**$36,203**	**$40,000**
	Average	**$32,060**	**$35,222**	**$35,086**	**$41,777**
BENEFITS					
Health Insurance	Median	$7,100	$6,444	$6,054	$11,859
	Average	$7,703	$6,823	$6,743	$9,943
Life Insurance	Median	$216	$141	-	$188
	Average	$281	$194	-	$222
Disability Insurance	Median	$220	$322	-	-
	Average	$238	$344	-	-
Retirement	Median	$1,500	$2,100	$1,832	$2,400
	Average	$1,911	$2,223	$2,078	$2,777
Continuing Education	Median	-	-	-	-
	Average	-	-	-	-
Total Benefits	**Median**	**$6,820**	**$7,100**	**$5,786**	**$11,601**
	Average	**$7,499**	**$7,241**	**$6,229**	**$10,070**
TOTAL COMPENSATION PLUS BENEFITS	**Median**	**$35,000**	**$39,293**	**$39,237**	**$48,126**
	Average	**$37,598**	**$41,070**	**$41,032**	**$49,749**
Number of Respondents		65	52	22	24

- Not enough response to provide meaningful data.

* For detailed description and definitions of Data Distribution (Median and Average), see chapter 1, Explanation of Data Distribution.

Table 15-7: Annual Compensation of Full-Time Custodians by Denomination

	Data Distribution*	DENOMINATION					
		Assemblies of God	Baptist	Independent/ Nondenom.	Lutheran	Methodist	Presby- terian
CHARACTERISTICS							
Average weekend worship attendance		709	813	1,354	-	1,424	457
Average church income		$1,125,444	$1,748,858	$2,186,034	-	$1,848,807	$1,627,852
Average # of years employed		8	8	9	-	8	11
Average # of paid vacation days		16	15	14	-	17	19
% College graduate or higher		13%	19%	17%	-	20%	20%
% Who receive auto reimbursement/allowance		14%	32%	17%	-	29%	45%
% Ordained		0%	3%	3%	-	0%	5%
% Supervise one or more people		60%	48%	53%	-	30%	55%
Average % salary increase (for those who had an increase) this year		2.4%	2.8%	3.5%	-	-	2.9%
COMPENSATION							
Base Salary	Median	$34,768	$30,784	$32,000	-	$32,441	$37,250
	Average	$33,975	$31,890	$34,990	-	$32,425	$39,100
Housing	Median	-	-	-	-	-	-
	Average	-	-	-	-	-	-
Parsonage	Median	-	-	-	-	-	-
	Average	-	-	-	-	-	-
Total Compensation	**Median**	**$34,768**	**$31,304**	**$32,000**	**-**	**$32,441**	**$37,250**
	Average	**$33,975**	**$32,679**	**$34,990**	**-**	**$32,425**	**$39,100**
BENEFITS							
Health Insurance	Median	$8,400	$6,988	$6,772	-	-	$8,400
	Average	$8,440	$8,619	$6,862	-	-	$8,209
Life Insurance	Median	-	$132	$219	-	-	$100
	Average	-	$235	$259	-	-	$177
Disability Insurance	Median	-	$222	$235	-	-	-
	Average	-	$273	$246	-	-	-
Retirement	Median	-	$2,145	$1,342	-	$1,632	$3,079
	Average	-	$2,378	$1,376	-	$2,299	$2,933
Continuing Education	Median	-	-	-	-	-	-
	Average	-	-	-	-	-	-
Total Benefits	**Median**	**$8,460**	**$8,697**	**$7,100**	**-**	**$3,574**	**$8,835**
	Average	**$8,639**	**$9,537**	**$6,807**	**-**	**$5,930**	**$8,515**
TOTAL COMPENSATION PLUS BENEFITS	**Median**	**$40,317**	**$35,819**	**$37,134**	**-**	**$37,851**	**$40,565**
	Average	**$40,887**	**$37,715**	**$40,473**	**-**	**$37,762**	**$47,197**
Number of Respondents		15	61	36	4	10	20

- Not enough response to provide meaningful data.

* For detailed description and definitions of Data Distribution (Median and Average), see chapter 1, Explanation of Data Distribution.

Table 15-8: Annual Compensation of Full-Time Custodians by Gender

	Data Distribution*	GENDER	
		Male	Female
CHARACTERISTICS			
Average weekend worship attendance		910	1,013
Average church income		$1,728,738	$1,559,523
Average # of years employed		9	9
Average # of paid vacation days		16	14
% College graduate or higher		24%	0%
% Who receive auto reimbursement/allowance		27%	10%
% Ordained		3%	0%
% Supervise one or more people		49%	26%
Average % salary increase (for those who had an increase) this year		2.8%	3.4%
COMPENSATION			
Base Salary	Median	$33,280	$26,983
	Average	$35,007	$27,266
Housing	Median	-	-
	Average	-	-
Parsonage	Median	-	-
	Average	-	-
Total Compensation	**Median**	**$33,500**	**$26,983**
	Average	**$35,295**	**$27,266**
BENEFITS			
Health Insurance	Median	$6,772	$6,772
	Average	$7,988	$6,121
Life Insurance	Median	$150	-
	Average	$226	-
Disability Insurance	Median	$288	-
	Average	$285	-
Retirement	Median	$1,950	-
	Average	$2,252	-
Continuing Education	Median	$550	-
	Average	$823	-
Total Benefits	**Median**	**$7,292**	**$6,057**
	Average	**$8,078**	**$5,940**
TOTAL COMPENSATION PLUS BENEFITS	**Median**	**$39,758**	**$30,311**
	Average	**$41,300**	**$30,944**
Number of Respondents		167	21

- Not enough response to provide meaningful data.

* For detailed description and definitions of Data Distribution (Median and Average), see chapter 1, Explanation of Data Distribution.

Table 15-9: Annual Compensation of Part-Time Custodians by Church Income

	Data Distribution*	$250K & Under	$251-$500K	$501-$750K	$751K-$1M	Over 1 Million
CHARACTERISTICS						
Average weekend worship attendance		135	252	327	476	865
Average church income		$142,376	$382,842	$628,698	$889,173	$1,819,658
Average # of years employed		7	6	6	6	5
Average # of paid vacation days		12	9	10	12	13
% College graduate or higher		13%	22%	12%	18%	18%
% Who receive auto reimbursement/allowance		5%	3%	7%	13%	12%
% Ordained		2%	1%	5%	8%	1%
% Supervise one or more people		8%	3%	11%	16%	9%
Average % salary increase (for those who had an increase) this year		4.2%	4.0%	3.8%	2.7%	2.6%
HOURLY RATE						
Base Rate	Average	$12	$14	$15	$13	$13
COMPENSATION						
Base Salary	Median	$5,200	$9,888	$13,715	$12,000	$13,780
	Average	$6,045	$9,958	$13,545	$13,344	$14,266
Housing	Median	-	-	-	-	-
	Average	-	-	-	-	-
Parsonage	Median	-	-	-	-	-
	Average	-	-	-	-	-
Total Compensation	**Median**	$5,200	$10,000	$13,715	$12,000	$13,780
	Average	$6,129	$10,091	$13,545	$13,344	$14,266
BENEFITS						
Health Insurance	Median	-	-	-	-	-
	Average	-	-	-	-	-
Life Insurance	Median	-	-	-	-	-
	Average	-	-	-	-	-
Disability Insurance	Median	-	-	-	-	-
	Average	-	-	-	-	-
Retirement	Median	-	-	-	-	-
	Average	-	-	-	-	-
Continuing Education	Median	-	-	-	-	-
	Average	-	-	-	-	-
Total Benefits	**Median**	-	-	-	-	$1,940
	Average	-	-	-	-	$4,581
TOTAL COMPENSATION PLUS BENEFITS	**Median**	$5,350	$10,000	$14,000	$12,000	$14,090
	Average	$6,211	$10,267	$13,805	$13,515	$15,097
Number of Respondents		66	75	44	40	78

- Not enough response to provide meaningful data.

* For detailed description and definitions of Data Distribution (Median and Average), see chapter 1, Explanation of Data Distribution.

Table 15-10: Annual Compensation of Part-Time Custodians by Worship Attendance

	Data Distribution*	WORSHIP ATTENDANCE					
		100 or less	101-300	301-500	501-750	751-1,000	Over 1,000
CHARACTERISTICS							
Average weekend worship attendance		68	207	398	620	866	1,663
Average church income		$135,517	$415,074	$794,398	$967,356	$1,518,080	$3,056,124
Average # of years employed		7	6	6	4	5	4
Average # of paid vacation days		14	9	13	10	16	9
% College graduate or higher		10%	21%	13%	13%	13%	27%
% Who receive auto reimbursement/allowance		0%	7%	14%	5%	4%	7%
% Ordained		3%	1%	4%	5%	4%	0%
% Supervise one or more people		7%	7%	8%	17%	17%	4%
Average % salary increase (for those who had an increase) this year		4.3%	4.4%	2.8%	2.4%	2.7%	3.1%
HOURLY RATE							
Base Rate	Average	$13	$13	$15	$13	$12	$12
COMPENSATION							
Base Salary	Median	$4,640	$9,547	$10,438	$14,327	$14,040	$13,470
	Average	$5,309	$10,220	$11,846	$14,456	$15,594	$14,409
Housing	Median	-	-	-	-	-	-
	Average	-	-	-	-	-	-
Parsonage	Median	-	-	-	-	-	-
	Average	-	-	-	-	-	-
Total Compensation	**Median**	**$4,640**	**$9,774**	**$10,438**	**$14,327**	**$14,040**	**$13,470**
	Average	**$5,309**	**$10,401**	**$11,846**	**$14,456**	**$15,594**	**$14,409**
BENEFITS							
Health Insurance	Median	-	-	-	-	-	-
	Average	-	-	-	-	-	-
Life Insurance	Median	-	-	-	-	-	-
	Average	-	-	-	-	-	-
Disability Insurance	Median	-	-	-	-	-	-
	Average	-	-	-	-	-	-
Retirement	Median	-	-	-	-	-	-
	Average	-	-	-	-	-	-
Continuing Education	Median	-	-	-	-	-	-
	Average	-	-	-	-	-	-
Total Benefits	**Median**	-	-	-	-	-	-
	Average	-	-	-	-	-	-
TOTAL COMPENSATION PLUS BENEFITS	**Median**	**$4,654**	**$9,917**	**$10,438**	**$14,327**	**$14,542**	**$13,544**
	Average	**$5,419**	**$10,547**	**$11,994**	**$14,815**	**$17,875**	**$14,550**
Number of Respondents		41	109	67	42	25	28

- Not enough response to provide meaningful data.

* For detailed description and definitions of Data Distribution (Median and Average), see chapter 1, Explanation of Data Distribution.

Table 15-11: Annual Compensation of Part-Time Custodians by Church Setting

	Data Distribution*	Metro-politan city	Suburb of large city	Small town or rural city	Farming area
CHARACTERISTICS					
Average weekend worship attendance		460	670	352	127
Average church income		$738,855	$1,285,632	$530,575	$223,662
Average # of years employed		5	5	6	6
Average # of paid vacation days		11	13	10	6
% College graduate or higher		21%	13%	16%	30%
% Who receive auto reimbursement/allowance		3%	14%	4%	9%
% Ordained		3%	2%	3%	9%
% Supervise one or more people		6%	12%	7%	9%
Average % salary increase (for those who had an increase) this year		5.2%	2.9%	3.1%	-
HOURLY RATE					
Base Rate	Average	$13	$14	$13	$12
COMPENSATION					
Base Salary	Median	$9,931	$12,800	$8,807	$6,500
	Average	$12,118	$13,888	$9,630	$8,356
Housing	Median	-	-	-	-
	Average	-	-	-	-
Parsonage	Median	-	-	-	-
	Average	-	-	-	-
Total Compensation	**Median**	**$9,931**	**$12,800**	**$8,824**	**$6,500**
	Average	**$12,118**	**$13,888**	**$9,688**	**$9,265**
BENEFITS					
Health Insurance	Median	-	-	-	-
	Average	-	-	-	-
Life Insurance	Median	-	-	-	-
	Average	-	-	-	-
Disability Insurance	Median	-	-	-	-
	Average	-	-	-	-
Retirement	Median	-	-	-	-
	Average	-	-	-	-
Continuing Education	Median	-	-	-	-
	Average	-	-	-	-
Total Benefits	**Median**	-	**$912**	-	-
	Average	-	**$2,386**	-	-
TOTAL COMPENSATION PLUS BENEFITS	**Median**	**$9,931**	**$12,948**	**$8,996**	**$6,500**
	Average	**$13,099**	**$14,078**	**$9,942**	**$9,469**
Number of Respondents		33	113	155	11

- Not enough response to provide meaningful data.

* For detailed description and definitions of Data Distribution (Median and Average), see chapter 1, Explanation of Data Distribution.

Table 15-12: Annual Compensation of Part-Time Custodians by Region

	Data Distribution*	New England	Middle Atlantic	South Atlantic	E-N Central	E-S Central	W-N Central	W-S Central	Mountain	Pacific
CHARACTERISTICS										
Average weekend worship attendance		254	812	330	413	335	362	590	411	439
Average church income		$587,529	$1,377,967	$755,912	$704,776	$565,784	$563,508	$1,204,178	$624,555	$618,197
Average # of years employed		6	5	8	7	6	5	5	4	5
Average # of paid vacation days		13	10	10	10	8	12	7	13	14
% College graduate or higher		30%	16%	21%	12%	30%	21%	9%	4%	25%
% Who receive auto reimbursement/allowance		0%	4%	12%	8%	20%	11%	0%	7%	8%
% Ordained		0%	0%	2%	4%	0%	7%	5%	0%	2%
% Supervise one or more people		0%	6%	0%	14%	11%	4%	4%	11%	17%
Average % salary increase (for those who had an increase) this year		-	2.8%	3.2%	3.4%	-	5.4%	3.5%	2.2%	3.2%
HOURLY RATE										
Base Rate	Average	$13	$12	$14	$14	-	$12	$13	$12	$14
COMPENSATION										
Base Salary	Median	$10,097	$8,210	$10,140	$10,437	$12,840	$8,218	$14,040	$7,500	$11,116
	Average	$12,016	$9,375	$12,271	$11,252	$14,310	$9,300	$14,688	$10,363	$12,414
Housing	Median	-	-	-	-	-	-	-	-	-
	Average	-	-	-	-	-	-	-	-	-
Parsonage	Median	-	-	-	-	-	-	-	-	-
	Average	-	-	-	-	-	-	-	-	-
Total Compensation	**Median**	$10,097	$8,210	$10,259	$10,438	$12,840	$8,218	$14,040	$7,500	$11,116
	Average	$12,016	$9,375	$12,548	$11,381	$14,310	$9,300	$14,688	$10,363	$12,414
BENEFITS										
Health Insurance	Median	-	-	-	-	-	-	-	-	-
	Average	-	-	-	-	-	-	-	-	-
Life Insurance	Median	-	-	-	-	-	-	-	-	-
	Average	-	-	-	-	-	-	-	-	-
Disability Insurance	Median	-	-	-	-	-	-	-	-	-
	Average	-	-	-	-	-	-	-	-	-
Retirement	Median	-	-	-	-	-	-	-	-	-
	Average	-	-	-	-	-	-	-	-	-
Continuing Education	Median	-	-	-	-	-	-	-	-	-
	Average	-	-	-	-	-	-	-	-	-
Total Benefits	**Median**	-	-	-	-	-	-	-	-	-
	Average	-	-	-	-	-	-	-	-	-
TOTAL COMPENSATION PLUS BENEFITS	**Median**	$10,240	$8,445	$10,259	$10,438	$12,840	$8,218	$14,542	$7,500	$11,400
	Average	$12,740	$9,727	$13,120	$11,422	$14,310	$9,611	$14,785	$10,462	$13,145
Number of Respondents		12	50	43	77	10	28	23	29	42

- Not enough response to provide meaningful data.

* For detailed description and definitions of Data Distribution (Median and Average), see chapter 1, Explanation of Data Distribution.

Table 15-13: Annual Compensation of Part-Time Custodians by Education

CHARACTERISTICS	Data Distribution*	EDUCATION			
		Less than Bachelor	Bachelor	Master	Doctorate
Average weekend worship attendance		456	556	-	-
Average church income		$760,540	$1,019,382	-	-
Average # of years employed		6	6	-	-
Average # of paid vacation days		11	10	-	-
% College graduate or higher		0%	100%	-	-
% Who receive auto reimbursement/allowance		7%	7%	-	-
% Ordained		1%	7%	-	-
% Supervise one or more people		8%	5%	-	-
Average % salary increase (for those who had an increase) this year		3.4%	3.2%	-	-
HOURLY RATE					
Base Rate	Average	$13	$13	-	-
COMPENSATION					
Base Salary	Median	$10,377	$9,933	-	-
	Average	$11,204	$12,105	-	-
Housing	Median	-	-	-	-
	Average	-	-	-	-
Parsonage	Median	-	-	-	-
	Average	-	-	-	-
Total Compensation	Median	$10,400	$9,939	-	-
	Average	$11,244	$12,367	-	-
BENEFITS					
Health Insurance	Median	-	-	-	-
	Average	-	-	-	-
Life Insurance	Median	-	-	-	-
	Average	-	-	-	-
Disability Insurance	Median	-	-	-	-
	Average	-	-	-	-
Retirement	Median	$827	-	-	-
	Average	$919	-	-	-
Continuing Education	Median	-	-	-	-
	Average	-	-	-	-
Total Benefits	Median	$912	-	-	-
	Average	$2,395	-	-	-
TOTAL COMPENSATION PLUS BENEFITS	Median	$10,400	$9,939	-	-
	Average	$11,496	$13,207	-	-
Number of Respondents		249	45	4	0

- Not enough response to provide meaningful data.

* For detailed description and definitions of Data Distribution (Median and Average), see chapter 1, Explanation of Data Distribution.

Table 15-14: Annual Compensation of Part-Time Custodians by Years Employed

	Data Distribution*	YEARS EMPLOYED			
		Less than 6 years	6-10 years	11-15 years	Over 15 years
CHARACTERISTICS					
Average weekend worship attendance		506	434	414	229
Average church income		$823,390	$713,084	$805,536	$407,073
Average # of years employed		3	8	13	24
Average # of paid vacation days		9	15	16	10
% College graduate or higher		16%	17%	5%	13%
% Who receive auto reimbursement/allowance		7%	11%	5%	0%
% Ordained		2%	3%	5%	0%
% Supervise one or more people		11%	8%	5%	7%
Average % salary increase (for those who had an increase) this year		3.3%	3.7%	3.4%	2.6%
HOURLY RATE					
Base Rate	Average	$13	$13	$14	$16
COMPENSATION					
Base Salary	Median	$9,718	$11,600	$10,900	$9,538
	Average	$10,810	$12,956	$11,051	$10,652
Housing	Median	-	-	-	-
	Average	-	-	-	-
Parsonage	Median	-	-	-	-
	Average	-	-	-	-
Total Compensation	**Median**	**$9,740**	**$11,800**	**$10,900**	**$9,538**
	Average	**$10,869**	**$13,152**	**$11,051**	**$10,652**
BENEFITS					
Health Insurance	Median	-	-	-	-
	Average	-	-	-	-
Life Insurance	Median	-	-	-	-
	Average	-	-	-	-
Disability Insurance	Median	-	-	-	-
	Average	-	-	-	-
Retirement	Median	-	-	-	-
	Average	-	-	-	-
Continuing Education	Median	-	-	-	-
	Average	-	-	-	-
Total Benefits	**Median**	-	**$6,418**	-	-
	Average	-	**$5,582**	-	-
TOTAL COMPENSATION PLUS BENEFITS	**Median**	**$9,945**	**$11,800**	**$10,900**	**$9,774**
	Average	**$11,071**	**$13,950**	**$11,161**	**$10,668**
Number of Respondents		170	64	21	15

- Not enough response to provide meaningful data.

* For detailed description and definitions of Data Distribution (Median and Average), see chapter 1, Explanation of Data Distribution.

Table 15-15: Annual Compensation of Part-Time Custodians by Denomination

	Data Distribution*	DENOMINATION					
		Assemblies of God	Baptist	Independent/ Nondenom.	Lutheran	Methodist	Presby- terian
CHARACTERISTICS							
Average weekend worship attendance		350	420	789	-	302	319
Average church income		$622,460	$779,087	$1,279,633	-	$613,207	$792,963
Average # of years employed		7	6	5	-	9	5
Average # of paid vacation days		15	11	7	-	12	9
% College graduate or higher		12%	13%	21%	-	33%	12%
% Who receive auto reimbursement/allowance		0%	5%	4%	-	8%	22%
% Ordained		3%	4%	3%	-	0%	8%
% Supervise one or more people		9%	12%	8%	-	8%	7%
Average % salary increase (for those who had an increase) this year		3.1%	3.0%	3.5%	-	-	3.7%
HOURLY RATE						-	
Base Rate	Average	$13	$13	$12	-	$13	$14
COMPENSATION							
Base Salary	Median	$8,819	$12,012	$9,322	-	$10,750	$9,000
	Average	$9,937	$11,930	$10,410	-	$11,714	$11,291
Housing	Median	-	-	-	-	-	-
	Average	-	-	-	-	-	-
Parsonage	Median	-	-	-	-	-	-
	Average	-	-	-	-	-	-
Total Compensation	**Median**	**$8,819**	**$12,012**	**$9,322**	-	**$11,500**	**$9,000**
	Average	**$9,937**	**$11,930**	**$10,577**	-	**$12,724**	**$11,291**
BENEFITS							
Health Insurance	Median	-	-	-	-	-	-
	Average	-	-	-	-	-	-
Life Insurance	Median	-	-	-	-	-	-
	Average	-	-	-	-	-	-
Disability Insurance	Median	-	-	-	-	-	-
	Average	-	-	-	-	-	-
Retirement	Median	-	-	-	-	-	-
	Average	-	-	-	-	-	-
Continuing Education	Median	-	-	-	-	-	-
	Average	-	-	-	-	-	-
Total Benefits	**Median**	-	-	-	-	-	-
	Average	-	-	-	-	-	-
TOTAL COMPENSATION PLUS BENEFITS	**Median**	**$9,526**	**$12,012**	**$9,322**	-	**$11,500**	**$9,000**
	Average	**$10,448**	**$11,944**	**$10,577**	-	**$12,742**	**$11,291**
Number of Respondents		35	79	60	6	12	27

- Not enough response to provide meaningful data.

* For detailed description and definitions of Data Distribution (Median and Average), see chapter 1, Explanation of Data Distribution.

Table 15-16: Annual Compensation of Part-Time Custodians by Gender

	Data Distribution*	GENDER	
		Male	Female
CHARACTERISTICS			
Average weekend worship attendance		497	391
Average church income		$922,237	$573,722
Average # of years employed		6	6
Average # of paid vacation days		11	10
% College graduate or higher		19%	11%
% Who receive auto reimbursement/allowance		10%	3%
% Ordained		3%	2%
% Supervise one or more people		13%	2%
Average % salary increase (for those who had an increase) this year		3.3%	3.4%
HOURLY RATE			
Base Rate	Average	$13	$13
COMPENSATION			
Base Salary	Median	$10,517	$8,050
	Average	$12,057	$9,849
Housing	Median	-	-
	Average	-	-
Parsonage	Median	-	-
	Average	-	-
Total Compensation	**Median**	**$10,647**	**$8,050**
	Average	**$12,164**	**$9,849**
BENEFITS			
Health Insurance	Median	-	-
	Average	-	-
Life Insurance	Median	-	-
	Average	-	-
Disability Insurance	Median	-	-
	Average	-	-
Retirement	Median	$959	-
	Average	$1,318	-
Continuing Education	Median	-	-
	Average	-	-
Total Benefits	**Median**	**$1,000**	**-**
	Average	**$3,300**	**-**
TOTAL COMPENSATION PLUS BENEFITS	**Median**	**$10,732**	**$8,147**
	Average	**$12,434**	**$10,142**
Number of Respondents		202	110

- Not enough response to provide meaningful data.

* For detailed description and definitions of Data Distribution (Median and Average), see chapter 1, Explanation of Data Distribution.

Full-Time Custodian Worksheet

	Enter your church data below	The 2014–2015 Compensation Handbook for Church Staff		Enter *Compensation Handbook* data below			
				Highest 25%	Median	Lowest 25%	Average
Church Income	$	Table 15-1	page 271	$	$	$	$
Worship Attendance		Table 15-2	page 272	n/a	$	n/a	$
Church Setting (metro, suburb, small town, or farming area)		Table 15-3	page 273	n/a	$	n/a	$
Region		Table 15-4	page 274	n/a	$	n/a	$
Person's Education		Table 15-5	page 275	n/a	$	n/a	$
Years Employed		Table 15-6	page 276	n/a	$	n/a	$
Denomination (if applicable)		Table 15-7	page 277	n/a	$	n/a	$

Looking at the table and page number references indicated in the *2014–2015 Compensation Handbook for Church Staff* columns above, locate the appropriate range for your church. Refer to the instructions below for step-by-step help.

FILLING OUT THE WORKSHEET

1. Fill in the gray boxes under *Enter your church data* with your church demographic information as follows:

   ▶ **Income** (Total annual church budget in past year)
   ▶ **Worship attendance** (Number of people, including children, who attend all weekend services)
   ▶ **Church setting** (Metropolitan city, suburb of large city, small town or rural city, or farming area)

   ▶ **Region** (Locate your state's region in the appendix on page 346.)
   ▶ **Education** (Highest level of education: less than bachelor, bachelor, master, or doctorate)

2. Use Table 15-1 (page 271) in your *2014–2015 Compensation Handbook for Church Staff* to enter data pertinent to your church. In the heading (top row), locate your church **income** from the five available ranges. Follow that column to the bottom rows, and copy the *Highest 25%*, *Median*, *Lowest 25%*, and *Average* amounts onto your worksheet.

3. Use Table 15-2 (page 272) on your *2014–2015 Compensation Handbook for Church Staff* to enter data pertinent to your church. In the heading (top row), locate your church's

worship attendance from the six available ranges. Follow that column to the bottom rows, and copy the *Median* and *Average* amounts onto your worksheet.

4. Use Table 15-3 (page 273) on your *2014–2015 Compensation Handbook for Church Staff* to enter data pertinent to your church. In the heading (top row), choose the **church setting** that best describes your church. Follow that column to the bottom rows, and copy the *Median* and *Average* amounts onto your worksheet.

5. Use Table 15-4 (page 274) on your *2014–2015 Compensation Handbook for Church Staff* to enter data pertinent to your church. In the heading (top row), look for the **region** where your church is located. Follow that column to the bottom rows, and copy the *Median* and *Average* amounts onto your worksheet.

6. Use Table 15-5 (page 275) on your *2014–2015 Compensation Handbook for Church Staff* to enter data pertinent to your Custodian. In the heading (top row), look for **your Custodian's highest level of education**. Follow that column to the bottom rows, and copy the *Median* and *Average* amounts onto your worksheet.

7. Use Table 15-6 (page 276) on your *2014–2015 Compensation Handbook for Church Staff* to enter data pertinent to your Custodian. In the heading (top row), locate the **number of years your Custodian has been employed**. Follow that column to the bottom rows, and copy the *Median* and *Average* amounts onto your worksheet.

8. Use Table 15-7 (page 277) on your *2014–2015 Compensation Handbook for Church Staff* to enter data pertinent to your church. In the heading (top row), look for **your church's denominational affiliation**. Follow that column to the bottom rows, and copy the *Median* and *Average* amounts onto your worksheet. If your church is not affiliated with a denomination, leave this section blank.

DETERMINING COMPENSATION

This tool will not provide you with a single compensation amount but rather with a range of values to help you determine the compensation appropriate to your situation.

1. Look at the values in the shaded *Median* column. Circle the **lowest** and the **highest** values. **This is the range of the median compensation plus benefits for churches similar to yours.**

2. For a variety of reasons, compensation plus benefits may be higher or lower than the range established in this table. Income and attendance are two significant factors affecting church compensation packages. If church income or attendance skews higher, you might want to consider moving toward or above the higher end of the range. Likewise, if church income or attendance skews lower, you may consider moving the package toward or below the lower end of the range.

3. Examine additional variables that might impact the compensation package you offer, such as years of service, education, and church setting.

4. Determine other circumstances unique to your situation, such as cost of living in your area, theological beliefs, pastoral performance, financial needs, the local economy, personal motivation, congregational goals, and others.

5. You now have a compensation package range based on the *2014–2015 Compensation Handbook*. Since each church and position are unique, your final compensation package will be based on additional factors unique to your situation.

Part-Time Custodian Worksheet

	Enter your church data below	The 2014–2015 Compensation Handbook for Church Staff		Enter *Compensation Handbook* data below			
				Highest 25%	Median	Lowest 25%	Average
Church Income	$	Table 15-9	page 279	$	$	$	$
Worship Attendance		Table 15-10	page 280	n/a	$	n/a	$
Church Setting (metro, suburb, small town, or farming area)		Table 15-11	page 281	n/a	$	n/a	$
Region		Table 15-12	page 282	n/a	$	n/a	$
Person's Education		Table 15-13	page 283	n/a	$	n/a	$
Years Employed		Table 15-14	page 284	n/a	$	n/a	$
Denomination (if applicable)		Table 15-15	page 285	n/a	$	n/a	$

Looking at the table and page number references indicated in the *2014–2015 Compensation Handbook for Church Staff* columns above, locate the appropriate range for your church. Refer to the instructions below for step-by-step help.

FILLING OUT THE WORKSHEET

1. Fill in the gray boxes under *Enter your church data* with your church demographic information as follows:

> **Income** (Total annual church budget in past year)
> **Worship attendance** (Number of people, including children, who attend all weekend services)
> **Church setting** (Metropolitan city, suburb of large city, small town or rural city, or farming area)

> **Region** (Locate your state's region in the appendix on page 346.)
> **Education** (Highest level of education: less than bachelor, bachelor, master, or doctorate)

2. Use Table 15-9 (page 279) in your *2014–2015 Compensation Handbook for Church Staff* to enter data pertinent to your church. In the heading (top row), locate your church **income** from the five available ranges. Follow that column to the bottom rows, and copy the *Highest 25%*, *Median*, *Lowest 25%*, and *Average* amounts onto your worksheet.

3. Use Table 15-10 (page 280) on your *2014–2015 Compensation Handbook for Church Staff* to enter data pertinent to your church. In the heading (top row), locate your church's

worship attendance from the six available ranges. Follow that column to the bottom rows, and copy the *Median* and *Average* amounts onto your worksheet.

4. Use Table 15-11 (page 281) on your *2014–2015 Compensation Handbook for Church Staff* to enter data pertinent to your church. In the heading (top row), choose the **church setting** that best describes your church. Follow that column to the bottom rows, and copy the *Median* and *Average* amounts onto your worksheet.

5. Use Table 15-12 (page 282) on your *2014–2015 Compensation Handbook for Church Staff* to enter data pertinent to your church. In the heading (top row), look for the **region** where your church is located. Follow that column to the bottom rows, and copy the *Median* and *Average* amounts onto your worksheet.

6. Use Table 15-13 (page 283) on your *2014–2015 Compensation Handbook for Church Staff* to enter data pertinent to your Custodian. In the heading (top row), look for **your Custodian's highest level of education**. Follow that column to the bottom rows, and copy the *Median* and *Average* amounts onto your worksheet.

7. Use Table 15-14 (page 284) on your *2014–2015 Compensation Handbook for Church Staff* to enter data pertinent to your Custodian. In the heading (top row), locate the **number of years your Custodian has been employed**. Follow that column to the bottom rows, and copy the *Median* and *Average* amounts onto your worksheet.

8. Use Table 15-15 (page 285) on your *2014–2015 Compensation Handbook for Church Staff* to enter data pertinent to your church. In the heading (top row), look for **your church's denominational affiliation**. Follow that column

to the bottom rows, and copy the *Median* and *Average* amounts onto your worksheet. If your church is not affiliated with a denomination, leave this section blank.

DETERMINING COMPENSATION

This tool will not provide you with a single compensation amount but rather with a range of values to help you determine the compensation appropriate to your situation.

1. Look at the values in the shaded *Median* column. Circle the **lowest** and the **highest** values. **This is the range of the median compensation plus benefits for churches similar to yours.**

2. For a variety of reasons, compensation plus benefits may be higher or lower than the range established in this table. Income and attendance are two significant factors affecting church compensation packages. If church income or attendance skews higher, you might want to consider moving toward or above the higher end of the range. Likewise, if church income or attendance skews lower, you may consider moving the package toward or below the lower end of the range.

3. Examine additional variables that might impact the compensation package you offer, such as years of service, education, and church setting.

4. Determine other circumstances unique to your situation, such as cost of living in your area, theological beliefs, pastoral performance, financial needs, the local economy, personal motivation, congregational goals, and others.

5. You now have a compensation package range based on the *2014–2015 Compensation Handbook*. Since each church and position are unique, your final compensation package will be based on additional factors unique to your situation.

16

PART-TIME MUSICIANS/ ACCOMPANISTS/ VOCALISTS

Employment Profile

Musicians/Accompanists/Vocalists include paid personnel who provide vocal or instrumental music or accompaniment. Titles under this category include such positions as Accompanist, Instrumentalist (of any kind), Organist, Pianist, Soloist, Vocalist, Worship Team Member, Praise Band Member, etc.

Six in 10 of these part-time musicians are female, and seven in 10 have a minimum of a bachelor's degree. They report long tenures, averaging 11 years. Nearly all are employed by the church rather than self-employed.

The chart below provides a demographic profile of this sample.

	Full-Time	Part-Time
Number of respondents	2	116
Ordained	-	5%
Average years employed	-	11
Male	-	39%
Female	-	61%
Self-employed (receives 1099)	-	5%
Church employee (receives W-2)	-	95%
High school diploma	-	24%
Associate degree	-	5%
Bachelor's degree	-	45%
Master's degree	-	20%
Doctoral degree	-	5%

Total Compensation plus Benefits Package Analysis

The following analyses are based on data in the tables you will find later in this chapter. The tables show compensation plus benefits data for Musicians/Accompanists/Vocalists who serve part-time and are presented according to church income, church attendance, church setting, region, education, years employed, denomination, and gender. In this way, the compensation plus benefits of Musicians/Accompanists/Vocalists can be analyzed and compared from a variety of useful perspectives.

The total compensation plus benefits amount includes the base salary; housing allowance and/or parsonage amount; health, life, and disability insurance payments; retirement contribution; and educational funds.

A worksheet at the end of this chapter is provided to help you apply the data to your church's situation.

Very few part-time church musicians receive fringe benefits such as retirement, health insurance, auto allowance, and funds for continuing education. However, more than one-third receive paid vacation and salary increases.

Compensation Plus Benefits	Full-Time	Part-Time
Base Salary	-	100%
Housing	-	0%
Parsonage	-	0%
Health Insurance*	-	1%
Life Insurance*	-	1%
Disability Insurance*	-	0%
Retirement	-	5%
Continuing Education	-	3%
Received salary increase	-	36%
Received paid vacation	-	36%
Received auto reimbursement/allowance	-	4%

Only those reporting individual premiums for Health, Life, or Disability (not total insurance premiums) are included.

KEY POINTS

✳ Nearly six in 10 part-time Musicians/ Accompanists/Vocalists serve in smaller churches with attendance of 300 or less.

✳ The hourly rate paid to Musicians/Accompanists/ Vocalists fluctuates across church income, education, and years employed. This means that it is not necessarily true, with this sample, that part-time church musicians earn more on an hourly basis if they have higher education or more years in their position.

NOTE: *There were not enough respondents to provide meaningful data to determine the average compensation and benefits packages for full-time Musicians/Accompanists/Vocalists.*

Table 16-1: Annual Compensation of Part-Time Musicians/Accompanists/Vocalists by Church Income

	Data Distribution*	\$250K & Under	\$251-\$500K	\$501-\$750K	\$751K-\$1M	Over 1 Million
CHARACTERISTICS						
Average weekend worship attendance		95	241	315	350	974
Average church income		\$140,391	\$367,796	\$619,918	\$841,101	\$1,953,704
Average # of years employed		13	8	12	6	14
Average # of paid vacation days		18	5	9	7	15
% College graduate or higher		58%	81%	79%	50%	82%
% Who receive auto reimbursement/allowance		3%	5%	0%	11%	5%
% Ordained		6%	10%	4%	0%	0%
% Supervise one or more people		6%	10%	0%	0%	0%
Average % salary increase (for those who had an increase) this year		3.6%	-	2.9%	-	2.3%
HOURLY RATE						
Base Rate	Average	\$23	\$23	\$23	\$13	\$21
COMPENSATION						
Base Salary	Median	\$4,680	\$7,800	\$9,000	\$8,491	\$13,970
	Average	\$6,331	\$8,148	\$9,270	\$11,723	\$16,124
Housing	Median	-	-	-	-	-
	Average	-	-	-	-	-
Parsonage	Median	-	-	-	-	-
	Average	-	-	-	-	-
Total Compensation	**Median**	\$4,740	\$7,800	\$9,012	\$8,491	\$13,970
	Average	\$6,527	\$8,148	\$9,594	\$11,723	\$16,124
BENEFITS						
Health Insurance	Median	-	-	-	-	-
	Average	-	-	-	-	-
Life Insurance	Median	-	-	-	-	-
	Average	-	-	-	-	-
Disability Insurance	Median	-	-	-	-	-
	Average	-	-	-	-	-
Retirement	Median	-	-	-	-	-
	Average	-	-	-	-	-
Continuing Education	Median	-	-	-	-	-
	Average	-	-	-	-	-
Total Benefits	**Median**	-	-	-	-	-
	Average	-	-	-	-	-
TOTAL COMPENSATION PLUS BENEFITS	**Median**	\$4,740	\$7,800	\$9,107	\$8,491	\$14,183
	Average	\$6,527	\$8,262	\$9,638	\$12,712	\$16,227
Number of Respondents		33	21	29	10	22

- Not enough response to provide meaningful data.

* For detailed description and definitions of Data Distribution (Median and Average), see chapter 1, Explanation of Data Distribution.

Table 16-2: Annual Compensation of Part-Time Musicians/Accompanists/Vocalists by Worship Attendance

	Data Distribution*	WORSHIP ATTENDANCE					
		100 or less	101-300	301-500	501-750	751-1,000	Over 1,000
CHARACTERISTICS							
Average weekend worship attendance		61	190	384	587	-	-
Average church income		$166,572	$435,507	$791,382	$1,019,610	-	-
Average # of years employed		11	12	8	13	-	-
Average # of paid vacation days		19	7	9	21	-	-
% College graduate or higher		71%	68%	65%	63%	-	-
% Who receive auto reimbursement/allowance		0%	5%	4%	0%	-	-
% Ordained		4%	8%	4%	0%	-	-
% Supervise one or more people		4%	5%	4%	0%	-	-
Average % salary increase (for those who had an increase) this year		-	2.7%	3.1%	-	-	-
HOURLY RATE							
Base Rate	Average	$24	$24	$18	-	-	-
COMPENSATION							
Base Salary	Median	$4,590	$8,190	$8,250	$11,556	-	-
	Average	$6,641	$9,160	$9,346	$13,397	-	-
Housing	Median	-	-	-	-	-	-
	Average	-	-	-	-	-	-
Parsonage	Median	-	-	-	-	-	-
	Average	-	-	-	-	-	-
Total Compensation	**Median**	$4,680	$8,190	$8,250	$12,400	-	-
	Average	$6,884	$9,160	$9,346	$14,864	-	-
BENEFITS							
Health Insurance	Median	-	-	-	-	-	-
	Average	-	-	-	-	-	-
Life Insurance	Median	-	-	-	-	-	-
	Average	-	-	-	-	-	-
Disability Insurance	Median	-	-	-	-	-	-
	Average	-	-	-	-	-	-
Retirement	Median	-	-	-	-	-	-
	Average	-	-	-	-	-	-
Continuing Education	Median	-	-	-	-	-	-
	Average	-	-	-	-	-	-
Total Benefits	**Median**	-	-	-	-	-	-
	Average	-	-	-	-	-	-
TOTAL COMPENSATION PLUS BENEFITS	**Median**	$4,680	$8,190	$8,250	$12,400	-	-
	Average	$6,884	$9,493	$9,386	$14,951	-	-
Number of Respondents		28	39	26	10	6	7

- Not enough response to provide meaningful data.

* For detailed description and definitions of Data Distribution (Median and Average), see chapter 1, Explanation of Data Distribution.

Table 16-3: Annual Compensation of Part-Time Musicians/Accompanists/Vocalists by Church Setting

	Data Distribution*	CHURCH SETTING			
		Metro-politan city	Suburb of large city	Small town or rural city	Farming area
CHARACTERISTICS					
Average weekend worship attendance		474	447	267	-
Average church income		$857,943	$938,040	$489,551	-
Average # of years employed		12	9	14	-
Average # of paid vacation days		10	10	14	-
% College graduate or higher		88%	71%	65%	-
% Who receive auto reimbursement/allowance		0%	5%	4%	-
% Ordained		6%	2%	6%	-
% Supervise one or more people		6%	2%	4%	-
Average % salary increase (for those who had an increase) this year		-	3.3%	2.9%	-
HOURLY RATE					
Base Rate	Average	$25	$20	$22	-
COMPENSATION					
Base Salary	Median	$10,900	$10,682	$6,240	-
	Average	$12,119	$12,262	$6,802	-
Housing	Median	-	-	-	-
	Average	-	-	-	-
Parsonage	Median	-	-	-	-
	Average	-	-	-	-
Total Compensation	**Median**	**$10,900**	**$11,000**	**$6,240**	**-**
	Average	**$12,119**	**$12,826**	**$6,802**	**-**
BENEFITS					
Health Insurance	Median	-	-	-	-
	Average	-	-	-	-
Life Insurance	Median	-	-	-	-
	Average	-	-	-	-
Disability Insurance	Median	-	-	-	-
	Average	-	-	-	-
Retirement	Median	-	-	-	-
	Average	-	-	-	-
Continuing Education	Median	-	-	-	-
	Average	-	-	-	-
Total Benefits	**Median**	**-**	**-**	**-**	**-**
	Average	**-**	**-**	**-**	**-**
TOTAL COMPENSATION PLUS BENEFITS	**Median**	**$11,160**	**$11,000**	**$6,240**	**-**
	Average	**$12,207**	**$13,087**	**$6,863**	**-**
Number of Respondents		18	45	49	3

- Not enough response to provide meaningful data.

* For detailed description and definitions of Data Distribution (Median and Average), see chapter 1, Explanation of Data Distribution.

Table 16-4: Annual Compensation of Part-Time Musicians/Accompanists/Vocalists by Region

	Data Distribution*	REGION								
		New England	Middle Atlantic	South Atlantic	E-N Central	E-S Central	W-N Central	W-S Central	Mountain	Pacific
CHARACTERISTICS										
Average weekend worship attendance		-	489	284	329	255	-	788	-	-
Average church income		-	$987,000	$693,653	$597,540	$478,553	-	$1,350,917	-	-
Average # of years employed		-	21	11	11	11	-	11	-	-
Average # of paid vacation days		-	37	8	11	5	-	13	-	-
% College graduate or higher		-	78%	71%	60%	75%	-	89%	-	-
% Who receive auto reimbursement/allowance		-	0%	3%	8%	0%	-	0%	-	-
% Ordained		-	0%	6%	0%	6%	-	0%	-	-
% Supervise one or more people		-	0%	0%	12%	0%	-	0%	-	-
Average % salary increase (for those who had an increase) this year		-	-	3.1%	4.5%	-	-	-	-	-
HOURLY RATE										
Base Rate	Average	-	$18	$24	$21	$19	-	$22	-	-
COMPENSATION										
Base Salary	Median	-	-	$7,957	$6,500	$6,905	-	$10,606	-	-
	Average	-	-	$10,380	$7,416	$6,401	-	$12,656	-	-
Housing	Median	-	-	-	-	-	-	-	-	-
	Average	-	-	-	-	-	-	-	-	-
Parsonage	Median	-	-	-	-	-	-	-	-	-
	Average	-	-	-	-	-	-	-	-	-
Total Compensation	**Median**	-	-	$8,074	$7,150	$6,905	-	$10,606	-	-
	Average	-	-	$10,699	$7,722	$6,401	-	$12,656	-	-
BENEFITS										
Health Insurance	Median	-	-	-	-	-	-	-	-	-
	Average	-	-	-	-	-	-	-	-	-
Life Insurance	Median	-	-	-	-	-	-	-	-	-
	Average	-	-	-	-	-	-	-	-	-
Disability Insurance	Median	-	-	-	-	-	-	-	-	-
	Average	-	-	-	-	-	-	-	-	-
Retirement	Median	-	-	-	-	-	-	-	-	-
	Average	-	-	-	-	-	-	-	-	-
Continuing Education	Median	-	-	-	-	-	-	-	-	-
	Average	-	-	-	-	-	-	-	-	-
Total Benefits	**Median**	-	-	-	-	-	-	-	-	-
	Average	-	-	-	-	-	-	-	-	-
TOTAL COMPENSATION PLUS BENEFITS	**Median**	-	-	$8,074	$7,150	$6,905	-	$10,856	-	-
	Average	-	-	$11,109	$7,751	$6,401	-	$12,699	-	-
Number of Respondents		3	9	33	25	16	7	12	4	7

- *Not enough response to provide meaningful data.*

* *For detailed description and definitions of Data Distribution (Median and Average), see chapter 1, Explanation of Data Distribution.*

Table 16-5: Annual Compensation of Part-Time Musicians/Accompanists/Vocalists by Education

	Data Distribution*	EDUCATION			
		Less than Bachelor	Bachelor	Master	Doctorate
CHARACTERISTICS					
Average weekend worship attendance		277	383	485	-
Average church income		$548,834	$761,051	$771,249	-
Average # of years employed		10	12	13	-
Average # of paid vacation days		11	13	10	-
% College graduate or higher		0%	100%	100%	-
% Who receive auto reimbursement/allowance		0%	8%	0%	-
% Ordained		0%	6%	10%	-
% Supervise one or more people		3%	2%	9%	-
Average % salary increase (for those who had an increase) this year		3.1%	3.2%	3.5%	-
HOURLY RATE					
Base Rate	Average	$23	$20	$25	-
COMPENSATION					
Base Salary	Median	$6,672	$7,453	$8,961	-
	Average	$8,022	$9,595	$12,536	-
Housing	Median	-	-	-	-
	Average	-	-	-	-
Parsonage	Median	-	-	-	-
	Average	-	-	-	-
Total Compensation	**Median**	$7,103	$7,500	$8,961	-
	Average	$8,278	$9,787	$12,536	-
BENEFITS					
Health Insurance	Median	-	-	-	-
	Average	-	-	-	-
Life Insurance	Median	-	-	-	-
	Average	-	-	-	-
Disability Insurance	Median	-	-	-	-
	Average	-	-	-	-
Retirement	Median	-	-	-	-
	Average	-	-	-	-
Continuing Education	Median	-	-	-	-
	Average	-	-	-	-
Total Benefits	**Median**	-	-	-	-
	Average	-	-	-	-
TOTAL COMPENSATION PLUS BENEFITS	**Median**	$7,103	$7,500	$9,306	-
	Average	$8,305	$10,035	$12,661	-
Number of Respondents		32	50	22	6

- Not enough response to provide meaningful data.

* For detailed description and definitions of Data Distribution (Median and Average), see chapter 1, Explanation of Data Distribution.

Table 16-6: Annual Compensation of Part-Time Musicians/Accompanists/Vocalists by Years Employed

	Data Distribution*	YEARS EMPLOYED			
		Less than 6 years	6-10 years	11-15 years	Over 15 years
CHARACTERISTICS					
Average weekend worship attendance		309	282	517	500
Average church income		$660,943	$585,897	$1,019,181	$836,493
Average # of years employed		3	8	14	26
Average # of paid vacation days		6	8	18	18
% College graduate or higher		67%	65%	83%	74%
% Who receive auto reimbursement/allowance		5%	5%	0%	4%
% Ordained		7%	0%	0%	8%
% Supervise one or more people		2%	5%	0%	4%
Average % salary increase (for those who had an increase) this year		3.5%	3.2%	-	3.4%
HOURLY RATE					
Base Rate	Average	$20	$19	$27	$23
COMPENSATION					
Base Salary	Median	$7,500	$6,000	$10,461	$8,850
	Average	$8,884	$7,604	$13,503	$10,414
Housing	Median	-	-	-	-
	Average	-	-	-	-
Parsonage	Median	-	-	-	-
	Average	-	-	-	-
Total Compensation	**Median**	**$7,650**	**$6,150**	**$10,461**	**$8,850**
	Average	**$9,084**	**$7,975**	**$13,503**	**$10,414**
BENEFITS					
Health Insurance	Median	-	-	-	-
	Average	-	-	-	-
Life Insurance	Median	-	-	-	-
	Average	-	-	-	-
Disability Insurance	Median	-	-	-	-
	Average	-	-	-	-
Retirement	Median	-	-	-	-
	Average	-	-	-	-
Continuing Education	Median	-	-	-	-
	Average	-	-	-	-
Total Benefits	**Median**	-	-	-	-
	Average	-	-	-	-
TOTAL COMPENSATION PLUS BENEFITS	**Median**	**$7,650**	**$6,150**	**$10,461**	**$8,850**
	Average	**$9,107**	**$8,050**	**$14,265**	**$10,483**
Number of Respondents		45	21	14	28

- Not enough response to provide meaningful data.

* For detailed description and definitions of Data Distribution (Median and Average), see chapter 1, Explanation of Data Distribution.

Table 16-7: Annual Compensation of Part-Time Musicians/Accompanists/Vocalists by Denomination

	Data Distribution*	DENOMINATION					
		Assemblies of God	Baptist	Independent/ Nondenom.	Lutheran	Methodist	Presby-terian
CHARACTERISTICS							
Average weekend worship attendance		-	329	497	-	538	224
Average church income		-	$739,353	$1,010,303	-	$913,356	$490,276
Average # of years employed		-	10	6	-	16	6
Average # of paid vacation days		-	8	9	-	26	10
% College graduate or higher		-	66%	86%	-	94%	50%
% Who receive auto reimbursement/allowance		-	0%	7%	-	6%	0%
% Ordained		-	5%	15%	-	0%	0%
% Supervise one or more people		-	5%	0%	-	0%	8%
Average % salary increase (for those who had an increase) this year		-	3.8%	3.8%	-	2.4%	2.0%
HOURLY RATE							
Base Rate	Average	-	$21	$24	-	$21	-
COMPENSATION							
Base Salary	Median	-	$7,750	$6,620	-	$12,000	$10,900
	Average	-	$7,995	$9,965	-	$14,014	$12,055
Housing	Median	-	-	-	-	-	-
	Average	-	-	-	-	-	-
Parsonage	Median	-	-	-	-	-	-
	Average	-	-	-	-	-	-
Total Compensation	**Median**	-	**$7,750**	**$7,150**	-	**$12,000**	**$10,900**
	Average	-	**$7,995**	**$10,717**	-	**$14,014**	**$12,055**
BENEFITS							
Health Insurance	Median	-	-	-	-	-	-
	Average	-	-	-	-	-	-
Life Insurance	Median	-	-	-	-	-	-
	Average	-	-	-	-	-	-
Disability Insurance	Median	-	-	-	-	-	-
	Average	-	-	-	-	-	-
Retirement	Median	-	-	-	-	-	-
	Average	-	-	-	-	-	-
Continuing Education	Median	-	-	-	-	-	-
	Average	-	-	-	-	-	-
Total Benefits	**Median**	-	-	-	-	-	-
	Average	-	-	-	-	-	-
TOTAL COMPENSATION PLUS BENEFITS	**Median**	-	**$7,750**	**$7,150**	-	**$12,000**	**$10,900**
	Average	-	**$8,012**	**$10,835**	-	**$14,095**	**$12,080**
Number of Respondents		1	42	14	3	19	12

- Not enough response to provide meaningful data.

* For detailed description and definitions of Data Distribution (Median and Average), see chapter 1, Explanation of Data Distribution.

Table 16-8: Annual Compensation of Part-Time Musicians/Accompanists/Vocalists by Gender

	Data Distribution*	GENDER	
		Male	Female
CHARACTERISTICS			
Average weekend worship attendance		437	328
Average church income		$794,979	$663,131
Average # of years employed		11	12
Average # of paid vacation days		10	13
% College graduate or higher		64%	75%
% Who receive auto reimbursement/allowance		2%	4%
% Ordained		9%	2%
% Supervise one or more people		7%	1%
Average % salary increase (for those who had an increase) this year		3.8%	3.0%
HOURLY RATE			
Base Rate	Average	$19	$23
COMPENSATION			
Base Salary	Median	$8,366	$7,700
	Average	$9,501	$9,639
Housing	Median	-	-
	Average	-	-
Parsonage	Median	-	-
	Average	-	-
Total Compensation	**Median**	**$8,500**	**$7,750**
	Average	**$9,718**	**$9,779**
BENEFITS			
Health Insurance	Median	-	-
	Average	-	-
Life Insurance	Median	-	-
	Average	-	-
Disability Insurance	Median	-	-
	Average	-	-
Retirement	Median	-	-
	Average	-	-
Continuing Education	Median	-	-
	Average	-	-
Total Benefits	**Median**	-	-
	Average	-	-
TOTAL COMPENSATION PLUS BENEFITS	**Median**	**$8,500**	**$7,750**
	Average	**$10,006**	**$9,829**
Number of Respondents		44	69

- Not enough response to provide meaningful data.

* For detailed description and definitions of Data Distribution (Median and Average), see chapter 1, Explanation of Data Distribution.

Part-Time Musician/Accompanist/Vocalist Worksheet

	Enter your church data below	The 2014–2015 Compensation Handbook for Church Staff		Enter *Compensation Handbook* data below			
				Highest 25%	Median	Lowest 25%	Average
Church Income	$	Table 16-1	page 295	$	$	$	$
Worship Attendance		Table 16-2	page 296	n/a	$	n/a	$
Church Setting (metro, suburb, small town, or farming area)		Table 16-3	page 297	n/a	$	n/a	$
Region		Table 16-4	page 298	n/a	$	n/a	$
Person's Education		Table 16-5	page 299	n/a	$	n/a	$
Years Employed		Table 16-6	page 300	n/a	$	n/a	$
Denomination (if applicable)		Table 16-7	page 301	n/a	$	n/a	$

Looking at the table and page number references indicated in the *2014–2015 Compensation Handbook for Church Staff* columns above, locate the appropriate range for your church. Refer to the instructions below for step-by-step help.

FILLING OUT THE WORKSHEET

1. Fill in the gray boxes under *Enter your church data* with your church demographic information as follows:

   ▶ **Income** (Total annual church budget in past year)
   ▶ **Worship attendance** (Number of people, including children, who attend all weekend services)
   ▶ **Church setting** (Metropolitan city, suburb of large city, small town or rural city, or farming area)

   ▶ **Region** (Locate your state's region in the appendix on page 346.)
   ▶ **Education** (Highest level of education: less than bachelor, bachelor, master, or doctorate)

2. Use Table 16-1 (page 295) in your *2014–2015 Compensation Handbook for Church Staff* to enter data pertinent to your church. In the heading (top row), locate your church **income** from the five available ranges. Follow that column to the bottom rows, and copy the *Highest 25%*, *Median*, *Lowest 25%*, and *Average* amounts onto your worksheet.

3. Use Table 16-2 (page 296) on your *2014–2015 Compensation Handbook for Church Staff* to enter data pertinent to your church. In the heading (top row), locate your church's

worship attendance from the six available ranges. Follow that column to the bottom rows, and copy the *Median* and *Average* amounts onto your worksheet.

4. Use Table 16-3 (page 297) on your *2014–2015 Compensation Handbook for Church Staff* to enter data pertinent to your church. In the heading (top row), choose the **church setting** that best describes your church. Follow that column to the bottom rows, and copy the *Median* and *Average* amounts onto your worksheet.

5. Use Table 16-4 (page 298) on your *2014–2015 Compensation Handbook for Church Staff* to enter data pertinent to your church. In the heading (top row), look for the **region** where your church is located. Follow that column to the bottom rows, and copy the *Median* and *Average* amounts onto your worksheet.

6. Use Table 16-5 (page 299) on your *2014–2015 Compensation Handbook for Church Staff* to enter data pertinent to your Musician/Accompanist/Vocalist. In the heading (top row), look for **your Musician/Accompanist/Vocalist's highest level of education**. Follow that column to the bottom rows, and copy the *Median* and *Average* amounts onto your worksheet.

7. Use Table 16-6 (page 300) on your *2014–2015 Compensation Handbook for Church Staff* to enter data pertinent to your Musician/Accompanist/Vocalist. In the heading (top row), locate the **number of years your Musician/Accompanist/Vocalist has been employed**. Follow that column to the bottom rows, and copy the *Median* and *Average* amounts onto your worksheet.

8. Use Table 16-7 (page 301) on your *2014–2015 Compensation Handbook for Church Staff* to enter data pertinent to your church. In the

heading (top row), look for **your church's denominational affiliation**. Follow that column to the bottom rows, and copy the *Median* and *Average* amounts onto your worksheet. If your church is not affiliated with a denomination, leave this section blank.

DETERMINING COMPENSATION

This tool will not provide you with a single compensation amount but rather with a range of values to help you determine the compensation appropriate to your situation.

1. Look at the values in the shaded *Median* column. Circle the **lowest** and the **highest** values. **This is the range of the median compensation plus benefits for churches similar to yours.**

2. For a variety of reasons, compensation plus benefits may be higher or lower than the range established in this table. Income and attendance are two significant factors affecting church compensation packages. If church income or attendance skews higher, you might want to consider moving toward or above the higher end of the range. Likewise, if church income or attendance skews lower, you may consider moving the package toward or below the lower end of the range.

3. Examine additional variables that might impact the compensation package you offer, such as years of service, education, and church setting.

4. Determine other circumstances unique to your situation, such as cost of living in your area, theological beliefs, pastoral performance, financial needs, the local economy, personal motivation, congregational goals, and others.

5. You now have a compensation package range based on the *2014–2015 Compensation Handbook*. Since each church and position are unique, your final compensation package will be based on additional factors unique to your situation.

17

PART-TIME CHILD-CARE PROVIDERS

Employment Profile

Child-Care Providers include paid personnel who provide regular or occasional child care and are on the church's payroll (not school staff). This may include positions such as Babysitter, Child-Care Assistant, Day-Care Staff, Nursery Attendant, Nursery Director, Nursery Helper, Nursery Worker, etc.

Nine in 10 of these part-time Child-Care Providers are female. The highest level of education for most of them is a high school diploma, and the average length of service is five years. Nearly all are employed by the church rather than self-employed.

The chart below provides a demographic profile of this sample.

	Full-Time	Part-Time
Number of respondents	**14**	**128**
Ordained	-	1%
Average years employed	-	5
Male	-	11%
Female	-	89%
Self-employed (receives 1099)	-	3%
Church employee (receives W-2)	-	97%
High school diploma	-	70%
Associate degree	-	9%
Bachelor's degree	-	20%
Master's degree	-	1%
Doctoral degree	-	0%

Total Compensation plus Benefits Package Analysis

The following analyses are based on data in the tables you will find later in this chapter. The tables show compensation plus benefits data for Child-Care Providers who serve part-time and are presented according to church income, church attendance, church setting, region, education, years employed, denomination, and gender. In this way, the Child-Care Provider's compensation plus benefits can be analyzed and compared from a variety of useful perspectives.

The total compensation plus benefits amount includes the base salary; housing allowance and/ or parsonage amount; health, life, and disability insurance payments; retirement contribution; and educational funds.

A worksheet at the end of this chapter is provided to help you apply the data to your church's situation.

Part-time Child-Care Providers receive few benefits compared to full-time employees. Their compensation plus benefits packages are comparable to those of part-time Custodians and Musicians, except that fewer Child-Care Providers receive paid vacation and salary increases.

Compensation Plus Benefits	Full-Time	Part-Time
Base Salary	-	100%
Housing	-	0%
Parsonage	-	0%
Health Insurance*	-	0%
Life Insurance*	-	0%
Disability Insurance*	-	1%
Retirement	-	4%
Continuing Education	-	0%
Received salary increase	-	22%
Received paid vacation	-	12%
Received auto reimbursement/allowance	-	4%

*Only those reporting individual premiums for Health, Life, or Disability (not total insurance premiums) are included.

KEY POINTS

* Four in 10 part-time Child-Care Providers serve in larger churches with income of over $1 million.

* The hourly rate paid to Child-Care Providers fluctuates across church income and worship attendance. This means that it is not necessarily true, with this sample, that part-time Child-Care Providers earn more on an hourly basis if they serve at larger churches.

NOTE: There were not enough respondents to provide meaningful data to determine the average compensation and benefits packages for full-time Child-Care Providers.

Table 17-1: Annual Compensation of Part-Time Child-Care Providers by Church Income

	Data Distribution*	CHURCH INCOME				
		$250K & Under	$251-$500K	$501-$750K	$751K-$1M	Over 1 Million
CHARACTERISTICS						
Average weekend worship attendance		168	247	261	480	2,362
Average church income		$129,466	$389,326	$595,027	$874,701	$2,793,211
Average # of years employed		4	5	8	3	5
Average # of paid vacation days		8	14	2	7	13
% College graduate or higher		17%	19%	53%	17%	15%
% Who receive auto reimbursement/allowance		0%	0%	0%	21%	2%
% Ordained		0%	0%	0%	0%	2%
% Supervise one or more people		25%	19%	17%	17%	19%
Average % salary increase (for those who had an increase) this year		-	-	-	-	2.4%
HOURLY RATE						
Base Rate	Average	$13	$10	$11	$13	$10
COMPENSATION						
Base Salary	Median	$1,604	$1,166	$3,324	$3,640	$1,872
	Average	$3,675	$2,432	$3,766	$6,462	$5,520
Housing	Median	-	-	-	-	-
	Average	-	-	-	-	-
Parsonage	Median	-	-	-	-	-
	Average	-	-	-	-	-
Total Compensation	**Median**	**$2,000**	**$1,166**	**$3,324**	**$3,640**	**$1,872**
	Average	**$4,006**	**$2,432**	**$3,766**	**$6,462**	**$5,520**
BENEFITS						
Health Insurance	Median	-	-	-	-	-
	Average	-	-	-	-	-
Life Insurance	Median	-	-	-	-	-
	Average	-	-	-	-	-
Disability Insurance	Median	-	-	-	-	-
	Average	-	-	-	-	-
Retirement	Median	-	-	-	-	-
	Average	-	-	-	-	-
Continuing Education	Median	-	-	-	-	-
	Average	-	-	-	-	-
Total Benefits	**Median**	-	-	-	-	-
	Average	-	-	-	-	-
TOTAL COMPENSATION PLUS BENEFITS	**Median**	**$2,000**	**$1,166**	**$3,324**	**$3,640**	**$1,872**
	Average	**$4,006**	**$2,432**	**$3,786**	**$6,462**	**$5,580**
Number of Respondents		12	28	18	19	51

- Not enough response to provide meaningful data.

* For detailed description and definitions of Data Distribution (Median and Average), see chapter 1, Explanation of Data Distribution.

Table 17-2: Annual Compensation of Part-Time Child-Care Providers by Worship Attendance

	Data Distribution*	WORSHIP ATTENDANCE					
		100 or less	101-300	301-500	501-750	751-1,000	Over 1,000
CHARACTERISTICS							
Average weekend worship attendance		64	206	374	611	-	3,130
Average church income		$255,712	$436,012	$624,593	$1,085,853	-	$3,430,000
Average # of years employed		4	7	3	5	-	5
Average # of paid vacation days		14	7	3	10	-	10
% College graduate or higher		33%	30%	30%	13%	-	6%
% Who receive auto reimbursement/allowance		0%	6%	8%	0%	-	3%
% Ordained		0%	0%	0%	0%	-	0%
% Supervise one or more people		22%	25%	16%	25%	-	9%
Average % salary increase (for those who had an increase) this year		-	-	-	2.8%	-	-
HOURLY RATE							
Base Rate	Average	$12	$11	$11	$15	-	$10
COMPENSATION							
Base Salary	Median	$2,000	$2,732	$1,333	$3,245	-	$1,872
	Average	$4,715	$3,944	$2,490	$5,445	-	$4,338
Housing	Median	-	-	-	-	-	-
	Average	-	-	-	-	-	-
Parsonage	Median	-	-	-	-	-	-
	Average	-	-	-	-	-	-
Total Compensation	**Median**	**$2,000**	**$2,732**	**$1,333**	**$3,245**	**-**	**$1,872**
	Average	**$4,715**	**$4,066**	**$2,490**	**$5,445**	**-**	**$4,338**
BENEFITS							
Health Insurance	Median	-	-	-	-	-	-
	Average	-	-	-	-	-	-
Life Insurance	Median	-	-	-	-	-	-
	Average	-	-	-	-	-	-
Disability Insurance	Median	-	-	-	-	-	-
	Average	-	-	-	-	-	-
Retirement	Median	-	-	-	-	-	-
	Average	-	-	-	-	-	-
Continuing Education	Median	-	-	-	-	-	-
	Average	-	-	-	-	-	-
Total Benefits	**Median**	-	-	-	-	-	-
	Average	-	-	-	-	-	-
TOTAL COMPENSATION PLUS BENEFITS	**Median**	**$2,000**	**$2,746**	**$1,333**	**$3,245**	**-**	**$1,872**
	Average	**$4,715**	**$4,077**	**$2,490**	**$5,445**	**-**	**$4,422**
Number of Respondents		9	33	25	17	5	35

- Not enough response to provide meaningful data.

* For detailed description and definitions of Data Distribution (Median and Average), see chapter 1, Explanation of Data Distribution.

Table 17-3: Annual Compensation of Part-Time Child-Care Providers by Church Setting

	Data Distribution*	Metro-politan city	Suburb of large city	Small town or rural city	Farming area
CHARACTERISTICS					
Average weekend worship attendance		2,430	504	442	-
Average church income		$2,618,946	$1,094,620	$674,553	-
Average # of years employed		5	5	6	-
Average # of paid vacation days		10	14	5	-
% College graduate or higher		15%	37%	20%	-
% Who receive auto reimbursement/allowance		7%	3%	2%	-
% Ordained		0%	4%	0%	-
% Supervise one or more people		14%	22%	22%	-
Average % salary increase (for those who had an increase) this year		-	3.7%	3.2%	-
HOURLY RATE					
Base Rate	Average	$9	$12	$12	-
COMPENSATION					
Base Salary	Median	$1,872	$4,763	$2,500	-
	Average	$3,272	$7,450	$4,188	-
Housing	Median	-	-	-	-
	Average	-	-	-	-
Parsonage	Median	-	-	-	-
	Average	-	-	-	-
Total Compensation	**Median**	**$1,872**	**$4,763**	**$2,500**	**-**
	Average	**$3,272**	**$7,450**	**$4,278**	**-**
BENEFITS					
Health Insurance	Median	-	-	-	-
	Average	-	-	-	-
Life Insurance	Median	-	-	-	-
	Average	-	-	-	-
Disability Insurance	Median	-	-	-	-
	Average	-	-	-	-
Retirement	Median	-	-	-	-
	Average	-	-	-	-
Continuing Education	Median	-	-	-	-
	Average	-	-	-	-
Total Benefits	**Median**	-	-	-	-
	Average	-	-	-	-
TOTAL COMPENSATION PLUS BENEFITS	**Median**	**$1,872**	**$4,763**	**$2,500**	**-**
	Average	**$3,295**	**$7,462**	**$4,291**	**-**
Number of Respondents		42	30	47	0

- Not enough response to provide meaningful data.

* For detailed description and definitions of Data Distribution (Median and Average), see chapter 1, Explanation of Data Distribution.

311

Table 17-4: Annual Compensation of Part-Time Child-Care Providers by Region

	Data Distribution*	New England	Middle Atlantic	South Atlantic	E-N Central	E-S Central	W-N Central	W-S Central	Mountain	Pacific
CHARACTERISTICS										
Average weekend worship attendance		-	-	380	525	541	319	2,691	357	287
Average church income		-	-	$963,672	$866,034	$930,731	$582,933	$2,843,747	$600,586	$437,453
Average # of years employed		-	-	5	3	14	2	5	5	6
Average # of paid vacation days		-	-	5	11	10	6	10	10	2
% College graduate or higher		-	-	33%	38%	25%	33%	8%	25%	15%
% Who receive auto reimbursement/allowance		-	-	0%	22%	0%	11%	0%	0%	0%
% Ordained		-	-	0%	11%	0%	0%	0%	0%	0%
% Supervise one or more people		-	-	7%	33%	13%	16%	13%	33%	23%
Average % salary increase (for those who had an increase) this year		-	-	-	-	-	3.4%	3.8%	2.0%	-
HOURLY RATE										
Base Rate	Average	-	-	$13	-	-	$10	$10	$10	$11
COMPENSATION										
Base Salary	Median	-	-	$3,500	$17,961	$2,500	$950	$1,872	$1,634	$2,732
	Average	-	-	$5,088	$13,220	$5,689	$2,741	$2,889	$3,522	$3,279
Housing	Median	-	-	-	-	-	-	-	-	-
	Average	-	-	-	-	-	-	-	-	-
Parsonage	Median	-	-	-	-	-	-	-	-	-
	Average	-	-	-	-	-	-	-	-	-
Total Compensation	**Median**	-	-	**$3,500**	**$17,961**	**$2,500**	**$950**	**$1,872**	**$1,634**	**$2,732**
	Average	-	-	**$5,088**	**$13,220**	**$5,689**	**$2,741**	**$2,889**	**$3,522**	**$3,528**
BENEFITS										
Health Insurance	Median	-	-	-	-	-	-	-	-	-
	Average	-	-	-	-	-	-	-	-	-
Life Insurance	Median	-	-	-	-	-	-	-	-	-
	Average	-	-	-	-	-	-	-	-	-
Disability Insurance	Median	-	-	-	-	-	-	-	-	-
	Average	-	-	-	-	-	-	-	-	-
Retirement	Median	-	-	-	-	-	-	-	-	-
	Average	-	-	-	-	-	-	-	-	-
Continuing Education	Median	-	-	-	-	-	-	-	-	-
	Average	-	-	-	-	-	-	-	-	-
Total Benefits	**Median**	-	-	-	-	-	-	-	-	-
	Average	-	-	-	-	-	-	-	-	-
TOTAL COMPENSATION PLUS BENEFITS	**Median**	-	-	**$3,500**	**$17,961**	**$2,500**	**$950**	**$1,872**	**$1,634**	**$2,732**
	Average	-	-	**$5,088**	**$13,220**	**$5,859**	**$2,760**	**$2,913**	**$3,522**	**$3,528**
Number of Respondents		0	6	15	9	10	19	39	16	14

- Not enough response to provide meaningful data.

* For detailed description and definitions of Data Distribution (Median and Average), see chapter 1, Explanation of Data Distribution.

Table 17-5: Annual Compensation of Part-Time Child-Care Providers by Education

	Data Distribution*	EDUCATION			
		Less than Bachelor	Bachelor	Master	Doctorate
CHARACTERISTICS					
Average weekend worship attendance		1,323	568	-	-
Average church income		$1,570,752	$904,884	-	-
Average # of years employed		6	3	-	-
Average # of paid vacation days		6	9	-	-
% College graduate or higher		0%	100%	-	-
% Who receive auto reimbursement/allowance		2%	8%	-	-
% Ordained		0%	4%	-	-
% Supervise one or more people		11%	40%	-	-
Average % salary increase (for those who had an increase) this year		2.8%	-	-	-
HOURLY RATE					
Base Rate	Average	$10	$13	-	-
COMPENSATION					
Base Salary	Median	$1,872	$4,030	-	-
	Average	$3,671	$6,839	-	-
Housing	Median	-	-	-	-
	Average	-	-	-	-
Parsonage	Median	-	-	-	-
	Average	-	-	-	-
Total Compensation	**Median**	$1,872	$4,030	-	-
	Average	$3,709	$6,839	-	-
BENEFITS					
Health Insurance	Median	-	-	-	-
	Average	-	-	-	-
Life Insurance	Median	-	-	-	-
	Average	-	-	-	-
Disability Insurance	Median	-	-	-	-
	Average	-	-	-	-
Retirement	Median	-	-	-	-
	Average	-	-	-	-
Continuing Education	Median	-	-	-	-
	Average	-	-	-	-
Total Benefits	**Median**	-	-	-	-
	Average	-	-	-	-
TOTAL COMPENSATION PLUS BENEFITS	**Median**	$1,872	$4,030	-	-
	Average	$3,715	$6,891	-	-
Number of Respondents		96	25	1	0

- Not enough response to provide meaningful data.

* For detailed description and definitions of Data Distribution (Median and Average), see chapter 1, Explanation of Data Distribution.

Table 17-6: Annual Compensation of Part-Time Child-Care Providers by Years Employed

	Data Distribution*	YEARS EMPLOYED			
		Less than 6 years	6-10 years	11-15 years	Over 15 years
CHARACTERISTICS					
Average weekend worship attendance		1,360	621	-	-
Average church income		$1,618,440	$854,908	-	-
Average # of years employed		3	8	-	-
Average # of paid vacation days		7	11	-	-
% College graduate or higher		26%	18%	-	-
% Who receive auto reimbursement/allowance		6%	0%	-	-
% Ordained		0%	5%	-	-
% Supervise one or more people		15%	41%	-	-
Average % salary increase (for those who had an increase) this year		3.4%	-	-	-
HOURLY RATE					
Base Rate	Average	$11	$12	-	-
COMPENSATION					
Base Salary	Median	$1,872	$2,777	-	-
	Average	$3,824	$5,779	-	-
Housing	Median	-	-	-	-
	Average	-	-	-	-
Parsonage	Median	-	-	-	-
	Average	-	-	-	-
Total Compensation	**Median**	**$1,872**	**$2,821**	-	-
	Average	**$3,824**	**$6,053**	-	-
BENEFITS					
Health Insurance	Median	-	-	-	-
	Average	-	-	-	-
Life Insurance	Median	-	-	-	-
	Average	-	-	-	-
Disability Insurance	Median	-	-	-	-
	Average	-	-	-	-
Retirement	Median	-	-	-	-
	Average	-	-	-	-
Continuing Education	Median	-	-	-	-
	Average	-	-	-	-
Total Benefits	**Median**	-	-	-	-
	Average	-	-	-	-
TOTAL COMPENSATION PLUS BENEFITS	**Median**	**$1,872**	**$2,821**	-	-
	Average	**$3,844**	**$6,058**	-	-
Number of Respondents		88	22	3	6

- Not enough response to provide meaningful data.

* For detailed description and definitions of Data Distribution (Median and Average), see chapter 1, Explanation of Data Distribution.

Table 17-7: Annual Compensation of Part-Time Child-Care Providers by Denomination

	Data Distribution*	DENOMINATION					
		Assemblies of God	Baptist	Independent/ Nondenom.	Lutheran	Methodist	Presby- terian
CHARACTERISTICS							
Average weekend worship attendance		258	371	559	-	2,714	573
Average church income		$512,977	$631,600	$992,893	-	$2,658,208	$1,277,345
Average # of years employed		7	8	4	-	4	5
Average # of paid vacation days		17	10	5	-	7	6
% College graduate or higher		38%	14%	8%	-	20%	25%
% Who receive auto reimbursement/allowance		0%	0%	14%	-	0%	8%
% Ordained		13%	0%	0%	-	0%	0%
% Supervise one or more people		57%	17%	8%	-	5%	50%
Average % salary increase (for those who had an increase) this year		-	3.5%	-	-	-	-
HOURLY RATE							
Base Rate	Average	-	$12	$11	-	$10	-
COMPENSATION							
Base Salary	Median	$2,732	$2,500	$2,711	-	$1,872	$3,700
	Average	$7,362	$4,244	$4,542	-	$3,329	$4,449
Housing	Median	-	-	-	-	-	-
	Average	-	-	-	-	-	-
Parsonage	Median	-	-	-	-	-	-
	Average	-	-	-	-	-	-
Total Compensation	**Median**	$2,732	$2,500	$2,711	-	$1,872	$3,837
	Average	$7,362	$4,244	$4,542	-	$3,329	$4,816
BENEFITS							
Health Insurance	Median	-	-	-	-	-	-
	Average	-	-	-	-	-	-
Life Insurance	Median	-	-	-	-	-	-
	Average	-	-	-	-	-	-
Disability Insurance	Median	-	-	-	-	-	-
	Average	-	-	-	-	-	-
Retirement	Median	-	-	-	-	-	-
	Average	-	-	-	-	-	-
Continuing Education	Median	-	-	-	-	-	-
	Average	-	-	-	-	-	-
Total Benefits	**Median**	-	-	-	-	-	-
	Average	-	-	-	-	-	-
TOTAL COMPENSATION PLUS BENEFITS	**Median**	$2,732	$2,500	$2,711	-	$1,872	$3,837
	Average	$7,362	$4,248	$4,640	-	$3,352	$4,816
Number of Respondents		8	29	16	2	41	13

- Not enough response to provide meaningful data.

* For detailed description and definitions of Data Distribution (Median and Average), see chapter 1, Explanation of Data Distribution.

Table 17-8: Annual Compensation of Part-Time Child-Care Providers by Gender

	Data Distribution*	GENDER	
		Male	Female
CHARACTERISTICS			
Average weekend worship attendance		3,046	888
Average church income		$3,187,534	$1,191,186
Average # of years employed		5	5
Average # of paid vacation days		-	8
% College graduate or higher		14%	22%
% Who receive auto reimbursement/allowance		7%	4%
% Ordained		0%	1%
% Supervise one or more people		0%	21%
Average % salary increase (for those who had an increase) this year		-	3.2%
HOURLY RATE			
Base Rate	Average	$9	$11
COMPENSATION			
Base Salary	Median	$1,872	$2,587
	Average	$1,952	$4,788
Housing	Median	-	-
	Average	-	-
Parsonage	Median	-	-
	Average	-	-
Total Compensation	**Median**	**$1,872**	**$2,600**
	Average	**$1,952**	**$4,831**
BENEFITS			
Health Insurance	Median	-	-
	Average	-	-
Life Insurance	Median	-	-
	Average	-	-
Disability Insurance	Median	-	-
	Average	-	-
Retirement	Median	-	-
	Average	-	-
Continuing Education	Median	-	-
	Average	-	-
Total Benefits	**Median**	-	-
	Average	-	-
TOTAL COMPENSATION PLUS BENEFITS	**Median**	**$1,872**	**$2,600**
	Average	**$1,952**	**$4,848**
Number of Respondents		14	112

- Not enough response to provide meaningful data.

* For detailed description and definitions of Data Distribution (Median and Average), see chapter 1, Explanation of Data Distribution.

Part-Time Child-Care Provider Worksheet

	Enter your church data below	The 2014–2015 Compensation Handbook for Church Staff		Enter *Compensation Handbook* data below			
				Highest 25%	Median	Lowest 25%	Average
Church Income	$	Table 17-1	page 309	$	$	$	$
Worship Attendance		Table 17-2	page 310	n/a	$	n/a	$
Church Setting (metro, suburb, small town, or farming area)		Table 17-3	page 311	n/a	$	n/a	$
Region		Table 17-4	page 312	n/a	$	n/a	$
Person's Education		Table 17-5	page 313	n/a	$	n/a	$
Years Employed		Table 17-6	page 314	n/a	$	n/a	$
Denomination (if applicable)		Table 17-7	page 315	n/a	$	n/a	$

Looking at the table and page number references indicated in the *2014–2015 Compensation Handbook for Church Staff* columns above, locate the appropriate range for your church. Refer to the instructions below for step-by-step help.

FILLING OUT THE WORKSHEET

1. Fill in the gray boxes under **Enter your church data** with your church demographic information as follows:

   ▶ **Income** (Total annual church budget in past year)
   ▶ **Worship attendance** (Number of people, including children, who attend all weekend services)
   ▶ **Church setting** (Metropolitan city, suburb of large city, small town or rural city, or farming area)

   ▶ **Region** (Locate your state's region in the appendix on page 346.)
   ▶ **Education** (Highest level of education: less than bachelor, bachelor, master, or doctorate)

2. Use Table 17-1 (page 309) in your *2014–2015 Compensation Handbook for Church Staff* to enter data pertinent to your church. In the heading (top row), locate your church **income** from the five available ranges. Follow that column to the bottom rows, and copy the *Highest 25%*, *Median*, *Lowest 25%*, and *Average* amounts onto your worksheet.

3. Use Table 17-2 (page 310) on your *2014–2015 Compensation Handbook for Church Staff* to enter data pertinent to your church. In the heading (top row), locate your church's

worship attendance from the six available ranges. Follow that column to the bottom rows, and copy the *Median* and *Average* amounts onto your worksheet.

4. Use Table 17-3 (page 311) on your *2014–2015 Compensation Handbook for Church Staff* to enter data pertinent to your church. In the heading (top row), choose the **church setting** that best describes your church. Follow that column to the bottom rows, and copy the *Median* and *Average* amounts onto your worksheet.

5. Use Table 17-4 (page 312) on your *2014–2015 Compensation Handbook for Church Staff* to enter data pertinent to your church. In the heading (top row), look for the **region** where your church is located. Follow that column to the bottom rows, and copy the *Median* and *Average* amounts onto your worksheet.

6. Use Table 17-5 (page 313) on your *2014–2015 Compensation Handbook for Church Staff* to enter data pertinent to your Child-Care Provider. In the heading (top row), look for **your Child-Care Provider's highest level of education**. Follow that column to the bottom rows, and copy the *Median* and *Average* amounts onto your worksheet.

7. Use Table 17-6 (page 314) on your *2014–2015 Compensation Handbook for Church Staff* to enter data pertinent to your Child-Care Provider. In the heading (top row), locate the **number of years your Child-Care Provider has been employed**. Follow that column to the bottom rows, and copy the *Median* and *Average* amounts onto your worksheet.

8. Use Table 17-7 (page 315) on your *2014–2015 Compensation Handbook for Church Staff* to enter data pertinent to your church. In the heading (top row), look for **your church's denominational affiliation**. Follow that column to the bottom rows, and copy the *Median* and *Average* amounts onto your worksheet. If your church is not affiliated with a denomination, leave this section blank.

DETERMINING COMPENSATION

This tool will not provide you with a single compensation amount but rather with a range of values to help you determine the compensation appropriate to your situation.

1. Look at the values in the shaded *Median* column. Circle the **lowest** and the **highest** values. **This is the range of the median compensation plus benefits for churches similar to yours.**

2. For a variety of reasons, compensation plus benefits may be higher or lower than the range established in this table. Income and attendance are two significant factors affecting church compensation packages. If church income or attendance skews higher, you might want to consider moving toward or above the higher end of the range. Likewise, if church income or attendance skews lower, you may consider moving the package toward or below the lower end of the range.

3. Examine additional variables that might impact the compensation package you offer, such as years of service, education, and church setting.

4. Determine other circumstances unique to your situation, such as cost of living in your area, theological beliefs, pastoral performance, financial needs, the local economy, personal motivation, congregational goals, and others.

5. You now have a compensation package range based on the *2014–2015 Compensation Handbook*. Since each church and position are unique, your final compensation package will be based on additional factors unique to your situation.

18

STATISTICAL ABSTRACT OF CHURCHES REPRESENTED IN DATA

In addition to the individual compensation surveys, respondents were also asked to complete a congregational profile. That information, as well as some detailed information about full-time Senior/Solo Pastors, is summarized here. The data are presented first according to worship attendance, with six size categories portrayed. Second, worship size and region are presented according to both church attendance and finances.

Key Findings

CHURCH PROFILE

On average, 48% of the churches' income/budget is devoted to salaries.

On average, churches have three full-time ordained staff and six full-time nonordained staff.

On average, churches have two part-time ordained staff and seven part-time nonordained staff.

SENIOR/SOLO PASTOR PROFILE

About 31% of churches provide additional salary to their Senior or Solo Pastor to assist with his or her Social Security payments. Of churches that do help, 78% pay half of the Social Security tax, while 22% pay all of it.

Seven in 10 churches reimburse the Senior or Solo Pastor's professional expenses. Those churches generally reimburse the pastor about 80% of his or her professional expenses per year.

One church in 10 (9%) counts reimbursements as income for the Senior or Solo Pastor's W-2 or 1099 form. Most (86%) Senior or Solo Pastors are treated as employees of the church, meaning they receive a W-2 rather than a 1099 form reporting their income at year's end.

More than six in 10 (62%) churches help their Senior or Solo Pastor with auto expenses.

About four in 10 (37%) churches experienced an increase in attendance over the past year.

An almost equal percentage of churches reported that their income exceeded expenses (39%) or met expenses (38%) in the past year. The percentage of those who reported that their finances exceeded expenses represents a 44% increase over those who reported the same in 2011.

Table 18-1: Church and Full-Time Senior/Solo Pastor Profiles by Worship Attendance

	All Churches Represented	WORSHIP ATTENDANCE					
		100 or less	101-300	301-500	501-750	751-1,000	Over 1,000
CHURCH PROFILE							
Average worship attendance	515	65	193	407	633	892	2,498
Average total church budget/income	$919,638	$137,402	$472,064	$857,367	$1,318,573	$1,626,592	$3,828,805
Average percentage compensation is of total church budget/income	48%	47%	48%	48%	50%	48%	46%
Average number of ordained staff							
Full-time	3	1	2	3	4	5	8
Part-time	2	1	2	2	2	2	3
Average number of non-ordained staff							
Full-time	6	2	2	3	5	7	16
Part-time	7	2	4	6	7	11	20
Number of Respondents	3,586	908	1,272	526	289	180	390
	All Full-Time Senior/Solo Pastors Represented	100 or less	101-300	301-500	501-750	751-1,000	Over 1,000
FULL-TIME SENIOR/ SOLO PASTOR PROFILE							
Percentage that contribute to Social Security payments of pastors	31%	28%	31%	39%	32%	31%	29%
Breakdown of church's contribution to pastor's Social Security payments							
Exempt	23%	18%	25%	27%	23%	27%	30%
Pays 0%	46%	54%	44%	34%	45%	41%	41%
Pays 50%	25%	21%	25%	32%	28%	27%	23%
Pays 100%	7%	8%	6%	7%	4%	4%	5%
Percentage of churches that reimburse the pastor for professional expenses	70%	65%	72%	71%	78%	69%	70%
Average percentage among those who get reimbursed	80%	73%	81%	88%	85%	80%	90%
Percentage of pastors receiving tax form							
1099	14%	22%	13%	7%	8%	9%	6%
W2	86%	78%	87%	93%	92%	91%	94%
Percentage of churches that reimburse pastors' expenses	90%	84%	89%	96%	92%	97%	96%
Percentage of churches that count reimbursements as income	9%	9%	9%	9%	9%	4%	8%
Percentage of churches that do not count reimbursements as income	81%	75%	80%	86%	83%	93%	88%
Percentage of churches that help the pastor with auto expenses	62%	58%	66%	62%	64%	61%	54%
Number of Respondents	1,743	550	684	216	111	70	98

321

Table 18-2: Worship Size by Church Attendance and Finances

Worship Size	Church Attendance over the Past Year		
	Decline	Stable	Increase
All Churches Represented (3,574)	18%	45%	37%
100 or less (904)	24%	49%	27%
101-300 (1,270)	19%	46%	35%
301-500 (526)	13%	47%	40%
501-750 (288)	14%	41%	45%
751-1,000 (180)	11%	41%	48%
Over 1,000 (388)	12%	37%	51%

Worship Size	Church Finances over the Past Year		
	Below expenses	Meets expenses	Exceeds expenses
All Churches Represented (3,570)	23%	38%	39%
100 or less (906)	33%	40%	28%
101-300 (1,268)	23%	40%	37%
301-500 (525)	17%	37%	46%
501-750 (288)	15%	36%	49%
751-1,000 (179)	15%	31%	54%
Over 1,000 (384)	15%	34%	51%

Table 18-3: Region by Church Attendance and Finances

Region	Church Attendance over the Past Year		
	Decline	Stable	Increase
All Churches Represented (3,574)	18%	45%	37%
New England (101)	18%	50%	33%
Middle Atlantic (371)	17%	46%	37%
South Atlantic (741)	16%	47%	37%
East-North Central (686)	20%	43%	37%
East-South Central (248)	14%	47%	40%
West-North Central (380)	15%	44%	40%
West-South Central (377)	20%	43%	37%
Mountain (208)	17%	47%	36%
Pacific (462)	19%	47%	34%

Region	Church Finances over the Past Year		
	Below expenses	Meets expenses	Exceeds expenses
All Churches Represented (3,563)	23%	38%	39%
New England (100)	27%	39%	34%
Middle Atlantic (371)	28%	34%	38%
South Atlantic (740)	24%	38%	38%
East-North Central (690)	24%	39%	37%
East-South Central (248)	17%	42%	42%
West-North Central (376)	19%	40%	41%
West-South Central (376)	21%	35%	44%
Mountain (209)	18%	33%	50%
Pacific (460)	23%	42%	35%

For breakdowns of regions by state, refer to the appendix.

Ministry Paid Staff Position Descriptions
Pastoral/Ministry Staff

Solo Pastor/Minister
This is the only ministry staff position. There are no other paid pastors or ministers in the church.

Senior Pastor/Minister
Lead pastor in a church where there are multiple paid ministry positions.

Executive/Administrative Pastor/Minister
Pastor who handles ministry staff supervision, management, and development.

Associate Pastor/Minister
Any paid pastor who assists the Senior Pastor in general or specific ministries other than those specifically listed in the survey. This may include such positions as Assimilation Pastor, Care Pastor, Church Life Pastor, Congregational Care Pastor, Connecting Pastor, Counseling Pastor, Disabilities Ministry Pastor (any), Ethnic Ministries Pastor (any), Evangelism Pastor, Family Life Pastor, Lay Pastor, Membership Pastor, Missions Pastor, Outreach Pastor, Pastoral Care Pastor, Pastoral Counselor, Prayer Pastor, Teaching/Preaching Pastor, Visitation Pastor, and so on.

Youth Pastor/Minister/Director
This includes paid pastors and directors to junior high, senior high, or college students. It may include such positions as Campus Pastor, College Minister, Junior High Pastor/Director, Senior High Pastor/Director, Youth Center Director, Youth Pastor/Minister/Director, and so on.

Adult Ministry Pastor/Minister/Director
Includes paid pastors and directors for adults, married couples, men, singles, seniors, women, young adults, and so on.

Children's/Preschool Pastor/Minister/Director
Church staff (not school staff) that includes paid pastors and directors for children from nursery through elementary school. This may include such positions as Early Childhood Pastor, Elementary School Pastor, Preschool Pastor/Director, Child-Care Director, Day-Care Director, and so on.

Christian Education Pastor/Minister/Director
Includes paid pastors and directors of broad educational ministries such as Bible studies, cell groups, Christian education, discipleship, equipping, small groups, spiritual formation, and so on.

Music/Choir/Worship Pastor/Minister/Director
This includes paid pastors and directors of band, bell/chimes choir, music ministry, orchestra, praise and worship team, vocal choir, and so on. It may include such positions as Music Pastor/Director, Worship Pastor/Director/Leader, and so on.

Media/Production/Arts Pastor/Minister/Director*
Includes paid pastors and directors who oversee drama, technical ministries, video, sound production, and so on. This may include positions such as Technical Director, Media Director, Drama Director, Production Director, Video Producer, Minister of Arts, and so on.

Not reported due to low response.

Ministry Paid Staff Position Descriptions

Support/Administrative Staff

Administrator

Includes paid staff (usually not ordained) who supervise the operational aspects of running the church, such as business or financial management. This may include such positions as Business Administrator, Business Manager, Chief Financial Officer, Chief Operating Officer, and so on.

Bookkeeper/Accountant

Includes paid personnel who assist with day-to-day financial matters in the church. This may include such positions as Accountant, Controller, Financial Administrative Assistant, Financial Secretary, Payroll Secretary, Treasurer, and so on.

Child-Care Provider

Includes paid personnel who provide regular or occasional child care and are on the church's payroll (not school staff). This may include such positions as Babysitter, Child-Care Assistant, Child-Care Provider, Day-Care Staff, Nursery Attendant, Nursery Director, Nursery Helper, Nursery Worker, and so on.

Custodian/Maintenance

Includes paid personnel who provide care and maintenance of physical facilities, buildings, grounds, and security. This may include such positions as Building and Grounds Manager, Building Supervisor, Custodian, Facilities Manager, Groundskeeper, Housekeeper, Lawn Maintenance Assistant, Maid, Maintenance Assistant, Plant Manager, Property Manager, Security Manager/Assistant, Sexton, Traffic Coordinator, and so on.

Musician/Accompanist/Vocalist

Includes paid personnel who provide vocal or instrumental music or accompaniment. This may include such positions as Accompanist, Instrumentalist (of any kind), Organist, Pianist, Soloist, Vocalist, and so on.

Secretary/Administrative Assistant

Includes paid personnel who provide clerical or administrative support. This may include such positions as Administrative Assistant, Clerical Assistant, Executive Secretary, Lead Secretary, Office Assistant, Office Clerk, Office Manager, Publications Secretary/Coordinator, Receptionist, Secretary (to any pastor or ministry), Secretary's Assistant, and so on.

Communications/Design Publications*

Includes paid personnel who provide design services, create publications, or otherwise oversee church communications. This may include such positions as Designer, Communications Coordinator, Publicist, Writer, Editor, and so on.

* Not reported due to low response.

TAX LAW & COMPENSATION PLANNING

Welcome to the special section on essentials in Tax Law and Compensation Planning. Compensation planning for clergy and other church staff members presents several unique tax issues that are not well understood by many church leaders and their advisers. This special section eliminates confusion and presents the key considerations to review when structuring compensation plans.

In adopting 2013 and 2014 compensation packages for your ministers and nonclergy staff members, review these possible components of the compensation package.

1. SALARY

The most basic component of church staff compensation is salary. There are two important considerations to keep in mind with respect to staff salaries: the amount of the salary and the use of salary reduction agreements. These two issues will be discussed separately.

A. Amount. Staff salaries ordinarily are set by the church board. Churches generally may pay any amount they wish, with one important exception. If a church pays unreasonably high compensation to a pastor or other employee, there are two possible consequences:

(1) Loss of tax-exempt status. In order for a church or any other charity to maintain its tax-exempt status, it must meet a number of conditions. One condition is that it cannot pay unreasonably high compensation to any person. There are two considerations to note. First, very few

charities have lost their exempt status for paying unreasonable compensation. The IRS has been reluctant to impose this remedy. Second, the law does not define what amount of compensation is unreasonable, and neither the IRS nor the courts have provided much clarification.

Example. A federal appeals court concluded that combined annual income of $115,680 paid by a religious organization to its founder and his wife was not excessive.

Example. A court ruled that maximum reasonable compensation for a prominent televangelist was $133,100 in 1984, $146,410 in 1985, $161,051 in 1986, and $177,156 in 1987. The court based its conclusions on a comparison of the salaries of other nonprofit officers in the state.

(2) Intermediate sanctions. The IRS can assess substantial excise taxes, called intermediate sanctions, against disqualified persons who are paid an excess benefit by a church or other charity. A disqualified person is any officer or director, or a relative of such a person. An excess benefit is compensation and fringe benefits in excess of what the IRS deems reasonable. Note that the IRS still can revoke the exempt status of a charity

that pays excessive compensation to an employee. However, it is more likely that excessive compensation will result in intermediate sanctions rather than loss of exempt status. To illustrate, why should a major private university lose its tax-exempt status because it pays excessive compensation to its head football coach?

The intermediate sanctions the IRS can impose include the following:

- **Tax on disqualified persons.** A disqualified person who benefits from an excess benefit transaction is subject to an excise tax equal to 25% of the amount of the excess benefit (the amount by which actual compensation exceeds the fair market value of services rendered). This tax is assessed against the disqualified person directly, not against his or her employer.

- **Additional tax on disqualified persons.** If a disqualified person fails to correct the excess benefit by the time the IRS assesses the 25% tax, then the IRS can assess an additional tax of up to 200% of the excess benefit. The law specifies that a disqualified person can correct the excess benefit transaction by "undoing the excess benefit to the extent possible, and taking any additional measures necessary to place the organization in a financial position not worse than that in which it would be if the disqualified person were dealing under the highest fiduciary standards."

- **Tax on organization managers.** If the IRS assesses the 25% tax against a disqualified person, it is permitted to impose an additional 10% tax (up to a maximum of $20,000) on any organization manager who participates in an excess benefit transaction knowing it is such a transaction, unless the manager's participation "is not willful and is due to reasonable cause." A manager is an officer, director, or trustee. IRS regulations clarify that the

managers collectively cannot be liable for more than $20,000 for any one transaction.

KEY POINT » *The intermediate sanctions law imposes an excise tax on members of a church's governing board who vote for a compensation package that the IRS determines to be excessive. This makes it essential for board members to carefully review the reasonableness of compensation packages.*

Charities, disqualified persons, and governing boards may rely on a presumption of reasonableness with respect to a compensation arrangement if it was approved by a board of directors (or committee of the board) that

(1) was composed entirely of individuals unrelated to and not subject to the control of the disqualified person involved in the arrangement;

(2) obtained and relied upon objective comparability information, such as (a) compensation paid by similar organizations, both taxable and tax-exempt, for comparable positions; (b) independent compensation surveys by nationally recognized independent firms; or (c) actual written offers from similar institutions competing for the services of the disqualified person; and

(3) adequately documented the basis for its decision.

The documentation should include the terms of the transaction and the date of its approval, the members of the board present during the debate and vote on the transaction, the comparability data obtained and relied upon, the actions of any members of the board having a conflict of interest, and the basis for the determination.

The IRS may refute the presumption of reasonableness only if it develops sufficient contrary evidence to rebut the comparability data relied upon by the board.

KEY POINT » *The law creates a presumption that a minister's compensation package is reasonable if* *approved by a church board that relied upon objective comparability information, including independent compensation surveys by nationally recognized independent firms. One of the more comprehensive compensation surveys for church employees is this text. This means that most ministers will be able to use this text to establish the presumption of reasonableness. But it also suggests that the IRS may rely on the data in this text in any attempt to impose intermediate sanctions against ministers.*

IRS regulations clarify that revenue-based pay arrangements in which an employee's compensation is based on a percentage of the employer's total revenues do not automatically result in an excess benefit transaction triggering intermediate sanctions. Rather, "all relevant facts and circumstances" must be considered.

▲ *Caution.* In a series of rulings published in 2004, the IRS assessed intermediate sanctions against a pastor as a result of excess benefits paid to him and members of his family by his church. The IRS concluded that taxable compensation and benefits a church pays to a disqualified person (any church officer or member of his or her family) that are not reported as taxable income to the recipient constitute automatic excess benefits that trigger intermediate sanctions regardless of the amount involved.

The IRS ruled that the following transactions resulted in excess benefits to the pastor because they were not reported as taxable income: (1) personal use of church property (vehicles, cell phones, credit cards, computers, etc.) by the pastor and members of his family; (2) reimbursements of personal expenses; and (3) nonaccountable reimbursements of business expenses (i.e., reimbursements of expenses that were not supported by adequate documentation of the business purpose of each expense). Since these taxable benefits were not reported as taxable income, they amounted to "automatic" excess benefits resulting in intermediate sanctions.

This is a stunning interpretation of the tax code and regulations that directly affects the compensation practices of every church and exposes some ministers and church board members to intermediate sanctions.

Recommendation | Churches that pay a minister (or any staff member) significantly more than the highest 25% for comparable positions should obtain a legal opinion from an experienced tax attorney confirming that the amount paid is not "unreasonable" and will not expose the employee or the board to intermediate sanctions.

Tax savings tip | Ministers and nonclergy employees should carefully review their Form W-2 or Form 1099 to be sure it does not report more income than was actually received. If an error was made, the church should issue a corrected tax form (Form W-2c for an employee, or a corrected Form 1099 for a self-employed worker).

B. Salary reduction agreements. Many churches have established salary reduction agreements to handle certain staff expenses. The objective is to reduce an employee's taxable income, since only the income remaining after the various reductions is reported on the employee's Form W-2 at the end of the year. It is important for church leaders to understand that they cannot reduce an employee's taxable income through salary reductions unless specifically allowed by law.

Here are three ways that taxable income can be reduced through salary reduction agreements:

(1) Tax-sheltered annuity contributions. Salary reduction agreements can be used to contribute to a tax-sheltered annuity (sometimes called a 403(b) annuity) if the salary reductions meet certain conditions.

(2) Cafeteria plans. Salary reduction agreements can be used to fund cafeteria plans (including flexible spending arrangements) if several conditions are met. A cafeteria plan is a written plan established by an employer that allows

employees to choose between cash and a menu of nontaxable benefits specified by law (including employer-provided medical insurance premiums, group term life insurance, and dependent care).

(3) Housing allowances. A church can designate a portion of a minister's salary as a housing allowance, and the amount so designated is not subject to income tax if certain conditions are met. Housing allowances are addressed below.

● Observation. Most other forms of salary reduction will not accomplish the goal of reducing a minister's taxable income. The income tax regulations prohibit the widespread practice of funding "accountable" reimbursement arrangements through salary reductions. This topic is addressed later in this chapter.

▶ Recommended Resources

For more information on salaries for church staff members, see chapter 4 in the
Church & Clergy Tax Guide
(available at **YourChurchResources.com**).

2. HOUSING ALLOWANCES

The most important tax benefit available to ministers who own or rent their home is the housing allowance. Ministers who own or rent their home do not pay federal income taxes on the amount of their compensation that their employing church designates in advance as a housing allowance to the extent that the allowance represents compensation for ministerial services, is used to pay housing expenses, and does not exceed the annual fair rental value of the home (furnished, plus utilities). Housing-related expenses include mortgage payments, rental payments, utilities, repairs, furnishings, insurance, property taxes, additions, and maintenance.

Unfortunately, many churches fail to designate a portion of a minister's compensation as a housing allowance. This deprives their minister of an important tax benefit that costs the church nothing.

Ministers who live in a church-owned parsonage that is provided rent free as compensation for ministerial services do not include the annual fair rental value of the parsonage as income in computing their federal income taxes. The annual fair rental value is not deducted from the minister's income. Rather, it is not reported as additional income anywhere on Form 1040 (as it generally would be by nonclergy workers). Further, ministers who live in a church-provided parsonage do not pay federal income taxes on the amount of their compensation that their employing church designates in advance as a parsonage allowance, to the extent that the allowance represents compensation for ministerial services and is used to pay parsonage-related expenses such as utilities, repairs, and furnishings.

Tax savings tip | Ministers who live in church parsonages and who incur any out-of-pocket expenses in maintaining the parsonage (such as utilities, property taxes, insurance, furnishings, or lawn care) should ask their employing church to designate a portion of their annual compensation in advance as a parsonage allowance. Such an allowance is not included on the minister's Form W-2 or Form 1099 at the end of the year and is nontaxable in computing federal income taxes to the extent the minister incurs housing expenses of at least that amount. This is a very important tax benefit for ministers living in church-provided parsonages. Many ministers and church boards are not aware of this benefit or are not taking advantage of it.

Note that the parsonage and housing allowance exclusions only apply in computing federal income taxes. Ministers cannot exclude them when computing their self-employment (Social Security) taxes.

Recommendation | Be sure the designation of a housing or parsonage allowance for the subsequent year is on the agenda of the church board for one of its final meetings of the current year. The designation should be an official action of the board or congregation, and it should be duly recorded in the minutes of the meeting. The IRS also recognizes designations included in employment contracts and budget line items—assuming in each case that the designation was duly adopted by the church board (or the congregation in a business meeting). Also, if the minister is a new hire, be sure the church designates a housing allowance prior to the date he or she begins working.

How much should a church board or congregation designate as a housing allowance? Many churches base the allowance on their minister's estimate of actual housing expenses for the new year. The church provides the minister with a form on which anticipated housing expenses for the new year are reported. For ministers who own their home, the form asks for projected expenses in the following categories: down payment, mortgage payments, property taxes, property insurance, utilities, furnishings and appliances, repairs and improvements, maintenance, and miscellaneous. Many churches designate an allowance in excess of the anticipated expenses itemized by the minister. Basing the allowance solely on a minister's actual expenses will penalize the minister if housing expenses in fact turn out to be higher than expected. In other words, the allowance should take into account unexpected housing costs and inaccurate projections of expenses.

Recommendation | Plan a mid-year review of the housing allowance to make sure the designated amount is sufficient to cover actual expenses. If a pastor's expenses will exceed the allowance, the church may amend the allowance. But any amendment will only operate prospectively.

● *Observation.* The compensation survey summarized in previous chapters reveals that housing allowances are claimed by several associate ministers, administrators, music directors, secretaries, and custodians. However, it is important to note that the housing allowance is available only if two conditions are met: (1) the recipient is a minister, and (2) the allowance is provided as compensation for services performed in the exercise of ministry. In many cases, these conditions will not be satisfied by administrators, music directors, secretaries, or custodians. See chapter 3 in Richard Hammar's *Church & Clergy Tax Guide* (available at **YourChurchResources.com**).

▶ Recommended Resources
For more detailed information about housing allowances, see chapter 6 in Richard Hammar's *Church & Clergy Tax Guide* (available at **YourChurchResources.com**).

3. EQUITY ALLOWANCES

Ministers who live in church-owned parsonages are denied one very important benefit of home ownership: the opportunity to accumulate equity in a home over the course of many years. Many ministers who have lived in parsonages during much of their active ministry often face retirement without housing. Their fellow ministers who purchased a home early in their ministry can often look forward to retirement with a home that is either substantially or completely debt free. To avoid the potential hardship often suffered by a minister who lives in a parsonage, some churches increase their minister's compensation by an amount that is sometimes referred to as an equity allowance. The idea is to provide the minister with the equivalent of equity in a home. This is an excellent idea that should be considered by any church having one or more ministers living in church-provided housing. Of course, for the concept to work properly, the equity allowance should not be accessible by the minister until retirement. Therefore, some churches choose to place the allowance directly in a minister's tax-sheltered retirement account.

Recommendation | Equity allowances should also be considered by a church whose minister rents a home.

▶ Recommended Resources
For more detailed information about equity allowances, see chapter 6, section A.7, in the *Church & Clergy Tax Guide* (available at **YourChurchResources.com**).

4. ACCOUNTABLE BUSINESS EXPENSE REIMBURSEMENT POLICY

An accountable plan is one that meets the following requirements: (1) only business expenses are reimbursed; (2) no reimbursement is allowed without an adequate accounting of expenses within a reasonable period of time (not more than 60 days after an expense is incurred); (3) any excess reimbursement or allowance must be returned to the employer within a reasonable period of time (not more than 120 days after an excess reimbursement is paid); and (4) an employer's reimbursements must come out of the employer's funds and not by reducing the employee's salary. Under an accountable plan, a church's reimbursements of an employee's business expenses are not reported as income to the employee, and the employee does not claim any deductions. This is the best way for churches to handle reimbursements of business expenses for the following reasons:

- Church staff report their business expenses to the church rather than to the IRS.

- Church staff who report their income taxes as employees, or who report as self-employed and who are reclassified as employees by the IRS in an audit, avoid the limitations on the deductibility of employee business expenses. These limitations include (1) the elimination of any deduction if the employee cannot itemize deductions on Schedule A (most taxpayers cannot) and (2) the deductibility of business expenses on Schedule A as an itemized expense only to the extent that these expenses exceed 2% of the employee's adjusted gross income.

- The so-called *Deason* allocation rule is avoided. Under this rule, ministers must reduce their business expense deduction by the percentage of their total compensation that consists of a tax-exempt housing allowance.

- The 50% limitation that applies to the deductibility of business meals and entertainment expenses is avoided. Unless these expenses are reimbursed by an employer under an accountable plan, only 50% of them are deductible by either employees or self-employed workers.

- Church staff who report their income taxes as self-employed avoid the risk of being reclassified as an employee by the IRS in an audit and assessed additional taxes.

○ *Observation.* The compensation data summarized in this text reveal that many churches provide automobile allowances to their ministers and to nonpastoral staff. In many cases, a church will simply provide a fixed dollar amount every month to an employee (for example, $300) and require no substantiation of business miles or a return of any excess reimbursements (those in excess of substantiated business miles). This is referred to as a nonaccountable reimbursement arrangement. What are the tax consequences of such an arrangement? The allowances must be added to the employee's Form W-2 at the end of the year, and the employee can claim a business deduction on Schedule A. If a worker is an employee with insufficient itemized deductions to use Schedule A, there is no deduction available for business expenses even though the full amount of the monthly allowances are added to taxable income. This is an unfortunate tax result that can be completely avoided through an accountable reimbursement arrangement. For a sample board resolution adopting an accountable business expense reimbursement arrangement, see chapter 7 of Richard Hammar's annual *Church & Clergy Tax Guide.*

Example. *A church pays its senior pastor an annual salary. In addition, it provides the pastor with a monthly car allowance of $400. This is an example of a nonaccountable reimbursement arrangement. Assume that the church treasurer reports none of these reimbursements as taxable income on the pastor's Form W-2 since she assumes that the pastor had at least $4,800 in expenses associated with the business use of his car and so there was no need to report the nonaccountable reimbursements as taxable income. This assumption not only is incorrect, but it also converts the nonaccountable reimbursements into an automatic excess benefit, exposing the pastor to intermediate sanctions as noted* *previously in this chapter. This assumes that the senior pastor is a disqualified person (i.e., an officer or director or a relative of an officer or director).*

The income tax regulations prohibit the funding of accountable reimbursement arrangements through salary reductions.

Example. Assume that a church pays Pastor Gary $700 each week and also agrees to reimburse his substantiated business expenses for each month out of the first weekly payroll check for the following month. Assume further that Pastor Gary substantiated $300 of business expenses for January. The church issued Pastor Gary his customary check of $700 for the first week of February but only accumulated $400 of this amount to his Form W-2 at the end of the year. This arrangement was once common and still is practiced by some churches. The income tax regulations do not prohibit the funding of business expense reimbursements out of salary reductions. Rather, a church's reimbursements under such arrangements cannot be accountable. This means that a church cannot reduce W-2 income by reducing an employee's salary to pay for business expense reimbursements. In this example, the full $700 paycheck must be accumulated to Pastor Gary's W-2. If it is not, the arrangement may constitute an automatic excess benefit transaction, exposing Pastor Gary to intermediate sanctions as explained previously in this chapter.

▶ Recommended Resources
For more detailed information about business expense reimbursement policies, see chapter 7, section E, in the *Church & Clergy Tax Guide* (available at **YourChurchResources.com**).

5. TRAVEL EXPENSES OF A SPOUSE
There is much confusion regarding the correct reporting of a church's reimbursement of the travel expenses of a spouse accompanying a minister or other staff member on a business trip. If the spouse's presence on the trip serves a legitimate business purpose, and if the spouse's travel expenses are reimbursed by the church under an accountable arrangement (described above), then the reimbursements represent a nontaxable fringe benefit. If these two requirements are not met, the reimbursements represent taxable income to the minister or staff member.

▲ *Caution.* If either of these conditions is not met, then a church's reimbursement of a nonemployee spouse's travel expenses will represent taxable income to the minister or other staff member. The same applies to children who accompany a minister or staff member on a business trip. Further, the IRS may assert that a church's failure to report the reimbursement of the spouse's expenses as taxable income to an employee meeting the definition of a disqualified person (see above) makes the reimbursement an automatic excess benefit, triggering intermediate sanctions as noted previously in this chapter.

Tax savings tip | If a church does not reimburse the travel expenses of a pastor's spouse who accompanies the pastor on a business trip, the spouse may be able to deduct travel expenses as a charitable contribution (assuming that the spouse's presence on the trip serves a legitimate charitable purpose). Some conditions apply.

▶ Recommended Resources
For more detailed information about travel expenses of a spouse, see chapter 7, section C.2, in Richard Hammar's *Church & Clergy Tax Guide* (available at **YourChurchResources.com**).

6. CHURCH-OWNED VEHICLES
Churches should consider the advantages of acquiring an automobile for employees' church-related travel. Here's why: if a church purchases a car and the church board adopts a resolution restricting use of the car to church-related activities, then the employee reports no income or deductions; better yet, there are no accountings, reimbursements, allowances, or recordkeeping requirements. This assumes that the car is in fact used exclusively for church-related purposes and that the conditions specified in the income tax regulations are satisfied.

Commuting is always considered to be personal use of a car, so this procedure would not be available if a church allowed an employee to commute to work in a church-owned vehicle. Fortunately, the income tax regulations permit certain church employees who use a church-owned vehicle exclusively for business purposes except for commuting to receive all of the benefits associated with business use of a church-owned vehicle if certain additional conditions are met.

Most churches that provide a staff member with a car do not consider either of these alternatives. Rather, they simply allow the employee to use the vehicle and impose no limitations on personal use. This arrangement results in taxable income to the staff member whether the staff member is a minister or a nonclergy employee.

❯ Recommended Resources

For more detailed information about church-owned vehicles, see chapter 4, section B.8, in the *Church & Clergy Tax Guide* (available at **YourChurchResources.com**).

7. SELF-EMPLOYMENT TAX

One provision in the tax code has caused more confusion for ministers and church treasurers than any other, and it is this: ministers are always treated as self-employed for Social Security purposes with regard to services they perform in the exercise of ministry. This is true even if they are employees for federal income tax reporting purposes. This is sometimes referred to as the dual tax status of ministers.

Social Security benefits are financed through two tax systems. Employers and employees each pay Social Security and Medicare (sometimes collectively referred to as FICA) taxes up to a specified amount. Self-employed persons pay the self-employment tax up to a specified amount. Note that self-employed workers are responsible for paying their entire Social Security tax liability, while employees pay only half (their employer pays the other half). (Watch for updates on the 2013 and 2014 FICA and self-employment tax amounts in Richard Hammar's annual *Church & Clergy Tax Guide*.)

KEY POINT » *Ministers always are treated as self-employed for Social Security purposes with respect to services performed in the exercise of ministry, so they do not pay Social Security and Medicare taxes. Rather, they pay the self-employment tax with respect to church compensation unless they have filed a timely application for exemption from Social Security taxes (and received a copy of their exemption application from the IRS marked "approved"). As a result, ministers must be familiar with the self-employment tax rules. So must nonclergy church employees who work for a church that filed a timely exemption from Social Security coverage (Form 8274), since they are considered self-employed in regard to Social Security.*

KEY POINT » *Many churches pay some or all of their pastor's self-employment taxes. After all, churches pay half of a nonminister employee's Social Security and Medicare taxes, so why shouldn't it do the same for its pastor? Research conducted by* Church Law & Tax Report *reveals that in 2011, about one-third (32%) of churches paid some or all of their senior pastor's self-employment taxes. Of those churches that did, 78% paid half of the self-employment tax, while 22% paid all of it. Any portion paid by the church is a taxable fringe benefit that must be reported as additional wages on the pastor's Form W-2 or Form 1099 and on Form 1040. It also should be reported as additional income by the pastor in computing self-employment taxes.*

KEY POINT » *Housing allowances and the fair rental value of parsonages are includable in self-employment earnings for Social Security purposes.*

▲ *Caution.* Many churches withhold the employees' share of Social Security and Medicare taxes from ministers' compensation and then pay the employer's share. In other words, they treat their minister as an employee with regard to Social Security. This is understandable, especially when the church treats the minister as an employee for purposes of federal income taxation. But it is always incorrect for a church to treat a minister as an employee for Social Security purposes with respect to services performed in the exercise of ministry.

Ministers may exempt themselves from self-employment taxes with respect to services performed in the exercise of ministry if several requirements are met. Among other things, the exemption application (IRS Form 4361) must be filed by the due date of a minister's federal tax return (Form 1040) for the second year in which he or she had net self-employment earnings of $400 or more, any part of which derived from the performance of ministerial duties. In most cases, this means the form is due by April 15 of the third year of ministry. Also, the minister must be opposed on the basis of religious convictions to accepting Social Security benefits.

As a self-employed person for Social Security, a minister computes self-employment taxes on Schedule SE of Form 1040.

▶ Recommended Resources

For more detailed information about the self-employment tax, see chapter 9 in Richard Hammar's *Church & Clergy Tax Guide* (available at **YourChurchResources.com**).

8. INSURANCE

Churches often provide ministers with life, health, or disability insurance coverage and pay all of the premiums for such coverage. In some cases, churches make the same benefits available to nonclergy staff members. The income tax regulations specify that the gross income of an employee does not include

> contributions which his employer makes to an accident or health plan for compensation (through insurance or otherwise) to the employee for personal injuries or sickness incurred by him, his spouse, or his dependents. . . . The employer may contribute to an accident or health plan by

paying the premium (or a portion of the premium) on a policy of accident or health insurance covering one or more of his employees, or by contributing to a separate trust or fund.

The exclusion of employer-paid health insurance premiums from the taxable income of employees is one of the main reasons ministers and other staff members often are better off reporting their income taxes as employees. This important benefit is not available to workers who report their income taxes as self-employed. A church wishing to make this benefit available to its ministers (or other employees) should adopt a plan in an appropriate board resolution. Plans that benefit only ministers are exempted from the nondiscrimination rules that apply to most of these kinds of plans.

⦿ *Observation.* The compensation survey data summarized in this text reveal that many churches provide ministers with health insurance. A smaller percentage of churches provide these benefits to nonclergy staff members. Such discrimination by church employers ordinarily does not violate federal law.

The cost of group term life insurance bought by an employer for its employees ordinarily is not taxable to the employees so long as the amount of coverage does not exceed $50,000 per employee. Generally, life insurance can qualify as group term life insurance only if it is available to at least 10 full-time employees. However, there are some exceptions to this rule. For example, the 10 full-time employee rule does not apply if (1) an employer provides the insurance to all full-time employees who provide satisfactory evidence of insurability, (2) insurance coverage is based on a uniform percentage of pay, and (3) evidence of insurability is limited to a medical questionnaire completed by the employee that does not require a physical examination.

Other kinds of insurance premiums paid by the church on behalf of a minister or nonclergy church employee ordinarily represent taxable income. For example, the cost of premiums on a whole life or universal life insurance policy paid by a church on the life of its minister (and naming the minister's spouse and children as beneficiaries) ordinarily must be reported as income to the minister.

> ❯ **Recommended Resources**

For more detailed information about insurance, see chapter 5 in the *Church & Clergy Tax Guide* (available at **YourChurchResources.com**).

9. RETIREMENT ACCOUNTS

Most ministers (and some nonclergy staff members) participate in some form of retirement plan. Such plans often are sponsored either by the local church or by a denomination or agency with which the church is affiliated. Church employees covered by certain kinds of plans can choose to have part of their pay set aside each year (through salary reductions) in the retirement fund rather than receiving it as income. Amounts set aside by the employing church under these plans may be excludable from gross income for tax purposes. These amounts are sometimes called elective deferrals because the employee elects to set aside the money, and tax on the money is deferred until it is taken out of the account. This option is available to ministers or nonclergy employees who are covered by tax-sheltered annuities (403(b) plans), simplified employee pensions (SEPs), and some other plans.

Payments made by an employing church to an employee's tax-sheltered annuity, SEP, and some other plans, and funded with church funds rather than through a reduction in an employee's compensation, may also be excluded from the employee's gross income for tax purposes under certain circumstances. There are limits on how much an employee can elect to contribute into such plans and on how much the employing church can contribute out of its own funds. Of course, ministers and nonclergy workers (whether employees or self-employed for income tax purposes) can also contribute to an IRA.

Recommendation | If a church has not established or contributed to a retirement plan for its staff members, it should consider doing so or at least ensuring that staff members are participating in an adequate alternative (particularly in the case of ministers who have exempted themselves from Social Security). Further, if staff members are participating in a retirement plan, then the end of the year is a good time to determine how contributions to the plan will be funded (e.g., through employee contributions, salary reductions, or church contributions) and in what amounts.

> ❯ **Recommended Resources**

For more detailed information about retirement accounts, see chapter 10 in Richard Hammar's *Church & Clergy Tax Guide* (available at **YourChurchResources.com**).

10. WORKS MADE FOR HIRE

It is common for church employees to compose music or write books or articles in their church office during office hours. What is often not understood is that such persons do not necessarily own the copyright to the works they create. While the one who creates a work generally is its author and the initial owner of the copyright of the work, section 201(b) of the Copyright Act specifies that "in the case of a work made for hire, the employer or other person for whom the work was prepared is considered the author . . . and, unless the parties have expressly agreed otherwise in a written instrument signed by them, owns all of the rights comprised in the copyright."

The copyright law defines work made for hire as "a work prepared by an employee within the scope of his or her employment." Two requirements must be met: (1) the person creating the work is an employee, and (2) the employee created the work within the scope of his or her employment.

Whether one is an employee will depend on the same factors used in determining whether one is an employee or self-employed for federal income tax reporting purposes (see chapter 2 of Richard Hammar's annual *Church & Clergy Tax Guide*). However, the courts have been liberal in finding employee status in this context, so it is possible that a court would conclude that a work is a work made for hire even though the author reports federal income taxes as a self-employed person.

The second requirement is that the work must have been created within the scope of employment. This requirement generally means that the work was created during regular working hours, on the employer's premises, using the employer's staff and equipment. This is often a difficult standard to apply. As a result, it is desirable for church employees to discuss this issue with the church leadership to avoid any potential misunderstandings.

Section 201(b), quoted above, allows an employer and employee to agree in a signed, written instrument that copyright ownership of works created by the employee within the scope of employment does not belong to the employer. This should be a matter for consideration by any church having a minister or other staff member who creates literary or musical works during office hours, on church premises, using church staff and church equipment (e.g., computers, printers, paper, library, secretaries, etc.). The services of an attorney will be needed to draft an appropriate instrument, assuming the church desires to divest itself of copyright ownership in a particular work made for hire. An attorney also will be able to explain the potential tax ramifications of such an instrument, which may include jeopardy to the church's tax-exempt status and the possible application of intermediate sanctions to the employee and members of the church board.

▶ Recommended Resources
For more detailed information about works made for hire, see Richard Hammar's *Church Guide to Copyright Law* (available at **YourChurchResources.com**).

11. QUALIFIED TUITION REDUCTIONS (QTR)
Many churches operate elementary or secondary schools and charge reduced tuition to certain school employees. For example, assume that a church operates an elementary school and charges annual tuition of $4,000 but only charges tuition of $500 for the children of school employees and charges no tuition at all for the child of Pastor Eric (the church's senior pastor and president of the school). Such tuition reductions are perfectly appropriate. Further, section 117(d) of the federal tax code specifies that they will not necessarily result in taxable income to the school employees. In other words, the church or school may not need to report the tuition reductions as taxable income.

However, section 117(d) also provides that highly compensated employees cannot exclude qualified tuition reductions from their income unless the same benefit is available on substantially similar terms to other employees. The term *highly compensated employee* is defined to include any employee who was paid compensation for the previous year in excess of a specified amount. For 2012, the amount was $115,000. The amounts for 2013 and 2014 were not available at the time of publication of this text.

If, in the example cited above, Pastor Eric is a highly compensated employee, the church would have to include $4,000 (the entire amount of the tuition reduction) in Pastor Eric's reportable income since he is a highly compensated employee and the benefit available to him is not available on substantially similar terms to other employees. However, this will not affect other school employees who are not highly compensated. They will be able to exclude tuition reductions from their income.

KEY POINT » *The IRS has ruled that tuition reductions are tax free only for school employees, so if a church operates a private school, only employees who perform duties on behalf of the school qualify for this benefit. If the school offers tuition reductions to church employees who perform no duties for the school, these reductions are a taxable fringe benefit.*

12. LOANS TO MINISTERS

Churches often make loans to ministers to enable a minister to pay for housing or some other major purchase. In some cases, the church charges no interest or charges a rate far below the prevailing market rate of interest. These loans can create problems for a number of reasons. Consider the following:

- Many state nonprofit corporation laws prohibit loans to officers and directors. No church should consider making any loan (even at a reasonable rate of interest) to a minister who is an officer or director of the church without first confirming that such loans are permissible under state law.

- No-interest or low-interest loans to ministers may be viewed as inurement of the church's income to a minister. As noted above, this can potentially jeopardize the church's tax-exempt status.

- For loans of $10,000 or more (or for loans of lower amounts where an intent to avoid taxes exists), a church must value the benefit to a minister of receiving a no-interest or low-interest loan and add this amount to the minister's reportable income. The point is this: even if loans to ministers are allowed under your state's nonprofit corporation law, the church must recognize that no-interest and low-interest loans of $10,000 or more will result in income to a minister that must be valued and reported on the minister's Form W-2 and Form 1040. Failure to do so could result in prohibited inurement of the church's income to a private individual, jeopardizing the church's tax-exempt status.

▶ *Observation.* Some ministers and nonclergy employees never fully repay a loan made to them by their church. The forgiveness of debt ordinarily represents taxable income to the debtor. As a result, if a church makes a loan to a minister or other staff member and the debt is later forgiven by the church, taxable income is generated in the amount of the forgiven debt.

13. VOLUNTARY WITHHOLDING

Ministers' compensation is exempt from income tax withholding whether a minister reports income taxes as an employee or as a self-employed person. While it is true that the tax code requires every employer, including churches and religious organizations, to withhold federal income taxes from employee wages, there are some exceptions to this rule. One exception is wages paid for "services performed by a duly ordained, commissioned, or licensed minister of a church in the exercise of his ministry." Therefore, a church need not withhold income taxes from the salary of a minister who is an employee for income tax reporting purposes. Further, since the withholding requirements only apply to the wages of employees, a church should not withhold taxes from the compensation of a minister (or any other worker, such as a part-time custodian) who reports his or her income taxes as a self-employed person.

The IRS maintains that a church and a minister-employee may agree voluntarily that federal income taxes be withheld from the minister's wages, but this is not required. Some ministers find voluntary withholding attractive since it eliminates the guesswork, quarterly reports, and penalties associated with the estimated tax procedure (which applies automatically if voluntary withholding is not elected). A minister-employee who elects to enter into a voluntary withholding arrangement with his or her church need only file a completed Form W-4 (Employee's Withholding Allowance Certificate) with the church. The filing of this form is deemed to be a request for voluntary withholding. Voluntary withholding arrangements can be terminated unilaterally by either a minister or the church, or by mutual consent. Alternatively, a minister can stipulate that the voluntary withholding arrangement will terminate on a specified date. In such a case, the minister must give the church a signed statement including (1) the date on which the voluntary withholding is to terminate, (2) the minister's name and address, and (3) a declaration that he or she wishes to enter into a voluntary withholding arrangement with his or her employer. This statement must be attached to a completed Form W-4. The voluntary withholding arrangement will terminate automatically on the date specified.

But what about a minister's self-employment taxes? Ministers who have not exempted themselves from Social Security coverage are required to pay the self-employment tax (Social Security tax for self-employed persons). Can a church withhold the self-employment tax from a minister-employee's wages? Yes. IRS Publication 517 (Social Security and Other Information for Members of the Clergy) states that "if you perform your services as an employee of the church (under the common law rules), you may be able to enter into a voluntary withholding agreement with your employer, the church, to cover any income and self-employment tax that may be due." A church whose minister has elected voluntary withholding (and who is not exempt from Social Security taxes) simply withholds an additional amount from each paycheck to cover the minister's estimated self-employment tax liability for the year. The additional amount withheld to cover self-employment taxes must be reported (on the minister's Form W-2 and the church's Forms 941) as additional income tax withheld and not as Social Security taxes (or FICA taxes). The minister should amend his or her Form W-4 by inserting on

line 6 the additional amount of tax to be withheld. The excess income tax withheld is a credit against tax that the minister claims on his or her federal income tax return, and it is, in effect, applied against the minister's self-employment tax liability. Further, it is considered to be a timely payment of the minister's self-employment tax obligation, so no penalties for late payment of the quarterly estimates will apply.

Recommendation | Churches should apprise ministers that they may enter into a voluntary withholding arrangement. For many ministers, such an arrangement will be preferable to the estimated tax procedure. This procedure requires ministers to estimate their income tax and self-employment tax liability for the year prior to April 15 and then to pay one-fourth of the total estimated tax liability on or by April 15, June 15, September 15, and the following January 15. These quarterly payments are accompanied by a payment voucher that is contained in IRS Form 1040-ES. Some ministers find the estimated tax procedure inconvenient and undesirable (it is often hard to budget for the quarterly payments).

▶ Recommended Resources

For more detailed information about voluntary withholding, see chapter 1, section D, in the *Church & Clergy Tax Guide* (available at **YourChurchResources.com**).

14. SPECIAL OCCASION GIFTS

It is common for ministers (and in some cases nonclergy employees) to receive special occasion gifts during the course of the year. Examples include Christmas, birthday, and anniversary gifts. Churches and church employees often do not understand how to report these payments for federal tax purposes. The general rule is this: if the gifts are funded through members' contributions to the church (i.e., the contributions are entered or recorded in the church's books as cash received and the members are given charitable contribution credit), then the distribution to the recipient should be reported as taxable compensation and included on his or her Form W-2 and Form 1040. The same rule applies to special occasion gifts made to a minister or nonclergy employee by the church out of the general fund. Members who contribute to special occasion offerings may be able to deduct their contributions if (1) the offering was authorized in advance by the church board; (2) the contributions are to the church and are entered or recorded in the church's books as cash received; and (3) they are able to itemize deductions on Schedule A (Form 1040). Churches should be prepared to report such gifts to a minister or nonclergy employee as taxable income on Form W-2. Of course, members are free to make personal gifts to ministers and nonclergy employees, such as a card at Christmas accompanied by a check or cash. Such payments may be tax-free gifts to the recipient (though they are not deductible by the donor). These same rules apply to other kinds of special occasion gifts as well.

It is common for churches to make generous retirement gifts to retiring ministers (and in some cases nonclergy employees). Do these gifts represent taxable income to the recipient? To the extent that the recipient is an employee (or would be classified as an employee by the IRS), there is little doubt that the gift would constitute taxable income since section 102(c) of the tax code specifies that "any amount transferred by or for an employer to or for the benefit of an employee" is not excludable from taxable income by the employee as a gift, other than certain employee achievement awards and insignificant holiday gifts. This conclusion is reinforced by the narrow definition of the term *gift*. The Supreme Court has noted that "a gift . . . proceeds from a detached and disinterested generosity . . . out of affection, respect, admiration, charity, or like impulses. . . . The most critical consideration . . . is the transferor's intention." *Commissioner v. Duberstein*, 363 U.S. 278, 285 (1960). The Court also observed that "it doubtless is the exceptional payment by an employer to an employee that amounts to a gift" and that the church's characterization of the distribution as a gift is "not determinative—there must be an objective inquiry as to whether what is called a gift amounts to it in reality."

KEY POINT » *Intermediate sanctions, discussed earlier in this chapter, may apply to a special occasion or retirement gift that results in unreasonable compensation to the recipient or that is not reported as taxable income regardless of the amount involved. Church leaders must be sure to consider this possibility when considering such a gift.*

❯ Recommended Resources
For more detailed information about special occasion gifts, see chapter 4, section B.2, in Richard Hammar's *Church & Clergy Tax Guide* (available at **YourChurchResources.com**).

15. BARGAIN SALES
Occasionally, a church will sell property to a staff member at a price that is below market value. To illustrate, some churches sell a parsonage to a retiring minister at a price well below the property's fair market value. Other churches may sell a car or other church-owned vehicle to a minister at a below-market price. The important consideration with such bargain sales is this—the bargain element (i.e., the difference between the sales price charged by the church and the property's market value) must be reported as income to the minister on Form W-2. Churches should consider the tax consequences of such sales before approving them.

❯ Recommended Resources
For more detailed information about bargain sales, see chapter 4, section B.4, in the *Church & Clergy Tax Guide* (available at **YourChurchResources.com**).

16. DIRECTOR IMMUNITY
Most states have adopted laws that provide uncompensated officers and directors of most charitable organizations (including churches) with limited immunity from legal liability. The federal Volunteer Protection Act provides similar protection as a matter of federal law. The immunity provided under state and federal law only applies to uncompensated officers and directors. What does this

have to do with compensation planning? Simply this: churches should consider adopting a resolution clarifying that a minister's annual compensation package is for ministerial duties rendered to the church and is not for any duties on the church board. Like any other church officer or director, the minister serves without compensation. Such a resolution might qualify the minister for protection under the legal immunity law. It is worth considering.

▶ Recommended Resources

For more detailed information about director immunity, see section 6-08 in Richard Hammar's *Pastor, Church & Law* (4th ed., 2008, Christianity Today International) (available at **YourChurchResources.com**).

17. DISCRETIONARY FUNDS

It is a fairly common practice for a church to set aside a sum of money in a discretionary fund and give the senior minister sole authority to distribute the money in the fund. In some cases, the minister has no instructions regarding permissible distributions. In other cases, the church establishes guidelines, but these often are oral and ambiguous. Many churches are unaware of the tax consequences of such arrangements. To the extent the minister has the authority to use any portion of the discretionary fund for his or her own personal use, the entire fund must be reported as taxable income to the minister in the year it is funded. This is true even if the minister does not personally benefit from the fund. The mere fact that the minister *could* personally benefit from the fund is enough for the fund to constitute taxable income. The basis for this result is the constructive receipt rule, which is explained in the income tax regulations as follows:

> Income although not actually reduced to a taxpayer's possession is constructively received by him in the taxable year during which it is credited to his account, set apart for him, or otherwise made available so that he may draw upon it at

any time, or so that he could have drawn upon it during the taxable year if notice of intention to withdraw had been given. However, income is not constructively received if the taxpayer's control of its receipt is subject to substantial limitations or restrictions.

For a discretionary fund to constitute taxable income to a minister, the minister must have the authority to draw upon it at any time for his or her own personal use. This means that the fund was established without any express prohibition against personal distributions. On the other hand, if a discretionary fund is set up by a board resolution that absolutely prohibits any distribution of the fund for the minister's personal use, then the constructive receipt rule is avoided. In the words of the regulation, "income is not constructively received if the taxpayer's control of its receipt is subject to substantial limitations or restrictions." In order to avoid the reporting of the entire discretionary fund as taxable income to the minister, the fund should be established by a board or congregational resolution that prohibits any use of the fund by the minister for personal purposes. Further, the resolution should specify that the fund may be distributed by the minister only for needs or projects that are consistent with the church's exempt purposes (as set forth in the church's governing documents). For accountability purposes, a member of the church board should review all distributions from the discretionary fund to be sure these requirements are met.

▶ Recommended Resources

For more detailed information about discretionary funds, see chapter 4, section B.13, in the *Church & Clergy Tax Guide* (available at **YourChurchResources.com**).

18. SEVERANCE PAY

Many churches have entered into severance pay arrangements with a pastor or other staff member. Such arrangements can apply when a pastor or staff member is dismissed, retires, or voluntarily resigns.

Church treasurers must determine whether severance pay is taxable so that it can be properly reported (on a Form W-2 and on the church's Forms 941). Also, taxes must be withheld from severance pay that is paid to nonminister employees (and ministers who have elected voluntary withholding). Failure to properly report severance pay can result in substantial penalties for both the church and the recipient.

In most cases, severance pay represents taxable income to the recipient. There is one exception that will apply in some cases. The tax code excludes from taxable income "the amount of any damages received (whether by suit or agreement and whether as lump sums or as periodic payments) on account of personal injuries or sickness." According to this provision, severance pay that is intended to settle personal injury claims may be nontaxable. The term "personal injuries" is defined broadly by the IRS and the courts and in some cases includes potential or threatened lawsuits based on discrimination and harassment.

KEY POINT » *The Tax Court has noted that "payments for terminating and canceling employment contracts are not payments for personal injuries."*

KEY POINT » *The tax code specifies that the term "personal injury" does not include emotional distress.*

Here are some factors to consider (based on actual cases) in deciding whether a severance payment made to a former employee represents taxable compensation or nontaxable damages in settlement of a personal injury claim:

- An amount paid to a former employee "to reward her for her past services and to make her severance as amicable as possible" is taxable compensation.

- An amount paid to a former employee under a severance agreement that contains no reference to a specific discrimination or other personal injury claim is taxable compensation.

- If an employer pays a former employee severance pay and reports the severance pay on a Form W-2, this is strong evidence that the amount represents taxable compensation.

- If an employer continues one or more employee benefits (such as health insurance) as part of a severance agreement, this suggests that any amount payable under the agreement represents taxable compensation.

- If an employer withholds taxes from amounts paid under a severance agreement, this "is a significant factor" in classifying the payments as taxable income. Of course, this factor will not be relevant in the case of ministers whose wages are not subject to withholding (unless they elect voluntary withholding).

- Referring to a payment as "severance pay" indicates that it is taxable compensation rather than nontaxable damages in settlement of a personal injury claim.

- Severance pay based on a former employee's salary (such as one year's salary) is more likely to be viewed as taxable compensation rather than nontaxable damages in settlement of a personal injury claim.

- To be nontaxable, severance pay must represent damages received in settlement of a personal injury claim. The IRS has noted that this language requires more than a settlement agreement in which a former employee waives any discrimination or other personal injury claims he or she may have against an employer. If the employee "never filed a lawsuit or any other type of claim against [the employer] . . . the payment cannot be characterized as damages for personal injuries" since "there is no indication that personal injuries actually exist."

KEY POINT » *Section 409A of the tax code imposes strict requirements on most nonqualified deferred compensation plans (NQDPs). IRS regulations define an NQDP to include any plan that provides for the deferral of compensation. This definition may be broad enough to include some severance agreements and many other kinds of church compensation arrangements. Any church or other organization that is considering a severance agreement with a current employee (or any other arrangement that defers compensation to a future year) should contact an attorney to have the arrangement reviewed to ensure compliance with both section 409A and the final regulations. Such a review will protect against the substantial penalties the IRS can assess for noncompliance. It also will help clarify whether a deferred compensation arrangement is a viable option in light of the limitations imposed by section 409A and the final regulations.*

▶ Recommended Resources

For more detailed information about severance pay, see chapter 4, section B.17, in Richard Hammar's *Church & Clergy Tax Guide* (available at **YourChurchResources.com**).

19. INCOME SPLITTING

Some ministers have attempted to "split" their church income with their spouse. This often is done to qualify the spouse for Social Security or other benefits or to avoid the Social Security annual earnings test (which reduces Social Security benefits to retired employees who are under full retirement age and who earn more than the amount prescribed by law). For income splitting arrangements to work, the courts have required proof that the spouse is in fact an employee of the church. This means that the spouse performs meaningful services on behalf of the church. The courts have

pointed to a number of factors indicating that a spouse is not an employee:

- The spouse did not receive a paycheck.

- The spouse was not employed elsewhere.

- The spouse's "compensation" was designed to provide a tax benefit (such as an IRA contribution) and lacked any economic reality.

- Neither the church nor the minister documented any of the services the spouse performed.

- Neither the church nor the minister could explain how the spouse's "salary" was determined.

- There was no employment contract between the church and the minister's spouse.

- No taxes were withheld from the spouse's "salary."

- The spouse's income was not reported on the church's employment tax returns (Forms 941).

- There was no evidence that wages were actually paid to the spouse, or that any employment contract existed, or that the spouse was treated as an employee.

The courts generally have been skeptical of attempts by taxpayers to shift income to a spouse. The message is clear: ministers should not attempt to obtain tax benefits by shifting income to a spouse unless there is economic reality to the arrangement.

▶ Recommended Resources

For more detailed information about income splitting, see chapter 4, section F, in the *Church & Clergy Tax Guide* (available at **YourChurchResources.com**).

COMPENSATION CHECKLIST FOR 2014–2015

ITEM	RECOMMENDATION
SALARY	■ Avoid unreasonable compensation. ■ Avoid use of salary reductions that are not recognized by federal tax law.
HOUSING ALLOWANCE	■ For ministers who own or rent their home, designate a portion of their compensation as a housing allowance prior to December 31 for the next year. ■ For ministers who live in a church-owned parsonage, designate a portion of their compensation as a parsonage allowance (if they will incur any housing expenses) prior to December 31 for the next year.
EQUITY ALLOWANCE	■ Consider contributing to a tax-sheltered investment (such as a retirement fund) for ministers who live in a church-owned parsonage, to compensate for their inability to accumulate equity in a home.
ACCOUNTABLE BUSINESS EXPENSE REIMBURSEMENT ARRANGEMENT	■ Adopt an accountable business expense reimbursement arrangement by reimbursing only those business expenses that are adequately substantiated and by requiring any excess reimbursements to be returned.
TRAVEL EXPENSES OF A SPOUSE	■ Reimburse a spouse's travel expenses incurred in accompanying a minister or nonclergy employee on a business trip only if the spouse's presence serves a legitimate business purpose and the expenses are duly substantiated. (If these requirements are not met, then the church's reimbursements represent taxable income to the minister or nonclergy employee.)
CHURCH-OWNED VEHICLES	■ Avoid allowing a minister or nonclergy employee unrestricted personal use of a church-owned car. (Such usage must be valued and reported as taxable income.) ■ Consider adopting a policy limiting use of the car to business purposes and requiring it to be kept on church property. (This avoids most record-keeping requirements and does not result in any income to the minister.) ■ An alternative is to limit use of the car to business purposes except for commuting to and from work (if the commuting is required for security reasons); each round trip commute represents $3 of reportable income.
SELF-EMPLOYMENT TAX PAID BY CHURCH	■ All ministers are self-employed for Social Security purposes with respect to their church work; this means they pay the self-employment tax rather than Social Security and Medicare (FICA) taxes. ■ Many churches pay a portion of a minister's self-employment tax (as they pay a portion of a nonminister employee's FICA taxes), but such payments represent taxable income. ■ Nonminister employees of churches that waived payment of FICA taxes by filing a timely Form 8274 are treated as self-employed for Social Security purposes. Churches may want to pay a portion of the self-employment taxes owed by these workers if they do so for ministers.
INSURANCE	■ Consider paying health insurance premiums for ministers and nonclergy employees (a tax-free fringe benefit for employees). ■ Consider paying premiums for up to $50,000 of group term life insurance (a tax-free fringe benefit for employees).

(continued on page 345)

COMPENSATION CHECKLIST FOR 2014–2015
(continued)

ITEM	RECOMMENDATION
RETIREMENT ACCOUNTS	■ Consider contributing toward a tax-sheltered retirement plan.
WORKS MADE FOR HIRE	■ Urge staff members not to write books and articles in the scope of their employment.
QUALIFIED TUITION REDUCTIONS	■ Consider tuition discounts for ministers and other church employees whose children attend church-operated schools or preschools (may be a tax-free fringe benefit).
LOANS TO MINISTERS	■ Avoid making any low- or no-interest loans to ministers. ■ Avoid making any loan to any officer or director, even at a reasonable rate of interest, unless permitted by state nonprofit corporation law.
VOLUNTARY WITHHOLDING	■ Ministers and nonclergy workers who report their income taxes as employees should consider entering into a voluntary withholding arrangement with the church (can avoid the quarterly estimated tax procedure); be sure to provide for the withholding of self-employment taxes too, but classify these extra withholdings as additional income taxes.
SPECIAL OCCASION GIFTS	■ Special occasion gifts to ministers and nonclergy employees that are processed through the church's books, and for which contribution credit is given to donors, are taxable income to the minister or nonclergy employee.
BARGAIN SALES	■ Any property sold to a minister or nonclergy employee at less than fair market value will result in taxable income (the amount by which the fair market value exceeds the sales price).
DIRECTOR IMMUNITY	■ Consider adopting a board resolution certifying that all church board members, including the senior minister, serve without compensation. (This may qualify the minister for the limited immunity the law provides to uncompensated directors of nonprofit organizations.)
DISCRETIONARY FUNDS	■ Avoid them unless (1) the minister cannot use the fund for his or her own personal use, (2) the fund may be distributed only for purposes consistent with the church's exempt purposes, and (3) a board member reviews all distributions to ensure compliance with these limits.
SEVERANCE PAY	■ Severance pay is perfectly appropriate, but be sure it is reported as additional taxable income unless it represents payment on account of personal injuries or sickness.
INCOME SPLITTING	■ Do not attempt to shift a portion of a minister's compensation to his or her spouse for tax savings purposes unless there is economic reality to the arrangement (the spouse performs services that otherwise would be compensated and receives a reasonable rate of compensation).

APPENDIX

Regions by State

PACIFIC
Alaska
California
Hawaii
Oregon
Washington

MOUNTAIN
Arizona
Colorado
Idaho
Montana
Nevada
New Mexico
Utah
Wyoming

WEST NORTH CENTRAL
Iowa
Kansas
Minnesota
Missouri
Nebraska
North Dakota
South Dakota

WEST SOUTH CENTRAL
Arkansas
Louisiana
Oklahoma
Texas

EAST NORTH CENTRAL
Illinois
Indiana
Michigan
Ohio
Wisconsin

EAST SOUTH CENTRAL
Alabama
Kentucky
Mississippi
Tennessee

MIDDLE ATLANTIC
New Jersey
New York
Pennsylvania
New England
Connecticut
Maine
Massachusetts
New Hampshire
Rhode Island
Vermont

SOUTH ATLANTIC
Delaware
District of Columbia
Florida
Georgia
Maryland
North Carolina
South Carolina
Virginia
West Virginia

10-Year Compensation Trend for Full-Time Church Staff

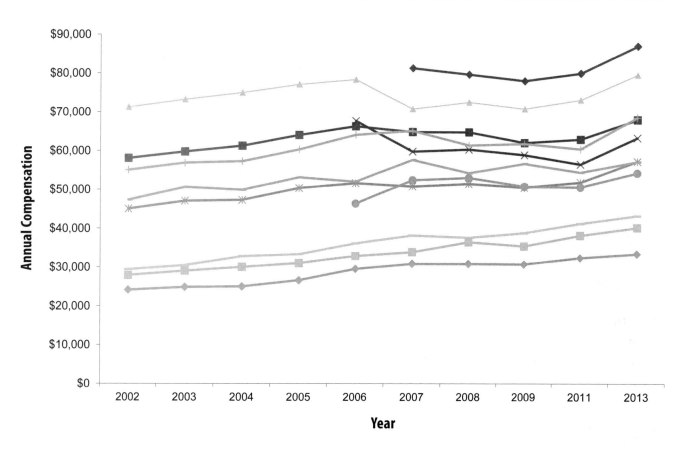

- Senior/Solo Pastor**
- Executive or Administrative Pastor
- Associate Pastor/Minister
- Adult Ministry/CE Pastor
- Youth Pastor/Minister/Director
- Children's Preschool Pastor
- Music Pastor/Minister/Director
- Administrator
- Bookkeeper/Accountant
- Secretary/Administrative Assistant
- Custodian/Maintenance

*Limited historical data: data collection started in 2006/2007 for Adult Ministry/Christian Education, Children's/Preschool Pastor/Director, or Executive/Administrative Pastor.

**Averages for Pastor include data for both Senior and Solo Pastors for comparison purposes.

The above trend is made available for your reference only. In addition to looking at this overall data, please refer to the detailed tables using your church's income, attendance, setting, region, and denominction as well as the person's education, gender, and years employed for guidance in compensating this position.